THOMAS MORE'S VOCATION

Frank Mitjans

THOMAS MORE'S VOCATION

THE CATHOLIC UNIVERSITY OF AMERICA PRESS
Washington, D.C.

The paper used in this publication meets the requirements of American
National Standards for Information Science—Permanence of Paper for
Printed Library Materials, ANSI z39.48–1992.

∞

Cataloging-in-Publication Data available at the Library of Congress
Hardcover ISBN 9780813236100
eBook ISBN 9780813236117

In memory of

Dominic Baker-Smith

with whom I discussed all the topics included in this

work and from whom I received a lot of advice

—

For my parents, brothers, and sisters

CONTENTS

ACKNOWLEDGMENTS

I should like to thank Andrew Hegarty, Director of the Thomas More Institute, London, and a historian, as well as Gerard Wegemer, Director of the Center for Thomas More Studies, University of Dallas, and a literary scholar, for encouragement and suggestions from the outset of this work. Jonathan Arnold, while at Worcester College, Oxford, and Timothy Graham went through the whole of different stages of the manuscript. Their comments and encouragement have been most helpful in completing the project, and I am most grateful to them. I am particularly grateful to Richard Rex, Professor of Reformation History, University of Cambridge, for going through one of the previous drafts of the manuscript pointing out mistakes and clarifying issues.

Marie-Claire Phélippeau, editor of *Moreana* (2007–16), made relevant suggestions to my essays published in that journal that included preliminary research for this book. Travis Curtright, the present editor, and John Guy have continued to provide encouragement and advice on more recent essays. Julian Reid, Archivist of Corpus Christi College, Oxford, Adam C. Green, Assistant Archivist at Trinity College, Cambridge, and Josephine Hutchings, Archivist of Lincoln's Inn, provided essential information for those essays that was lacking in earlier studies; for their assistance, I am much obliged. I am grateful also for the help received from Álvaro Sánchez-Ostiz, University of Navarre, and Jerónimo Leal, Professor of Patrology at the Università della Santa Croce, Rome.

I am very grateful especially to the late Dominic Baker-Smith (1937–2016) for his kindness and patience in discussing topics brought up here and for recommending further bibliography. I thank Trevor Lipscombe for his encouragement from the very moment I contacted the Catholic University of America Press; and I am indebted to all the team at the Press for their help, in particular to the copy-editor, Aldene Fredenburg, for standardizing citations and bibliography. The recommendations of the two anonymous reviewers have been very helpful, and I am grateful to them. I am particularly grateful to Peter Damian-Grint for his advice after having read one of the latest versions of the whole manuscript.

ABBREVIATIONS AND SYMBOLS

ASD	"Amsterdam Edition" of the works of Erasmus, *Opera Omnia Desiderii Erasmi Roterodami recognita et adnotatione critica instructa notisque illustrate* (Amsterdam, 1969–)
BL	British Library
Collectanea	Montagu Burrows, ed., *Collectanea* (Oxford: Oxford Historical Society, 1890). Part V, pp. 317–80, contains Linacre's Catalogue of books belonging to William Grocyn in 1520, together with his accounts as executor, followed by "A Memoir of William Grocyn" by the editor and a copy of the Will of Grocyn.
Companion	*The Cambridge Companion to Thomas More*, ed. George M. Logan (Cambridge: Cambridge University Press, 2011).
Correspondence	*The Correspondence of Sir Thomas More*, ed. Elizabeth Frances Rogers, (Princeton, N.J.: Princeton University Press, 1947).
Cresacre More	Cresacre More, *The Life of Sir Thomas More* (1627), ed. Joseph Hunter (London: William Pickering, 1828).
CU	Thomas More, *Utopia: Latin Text and English Translation*, ed. George M. Logan, Robert M. Adams, and Clarence H. Miller (Cambridge: Cambridge University Press, 1995).
CW	*The Complete Works of St. Thomas More*, 15 vols (New Haven and London: Yale University Press, 1963–97).
CWE	*The Collected Works of Erasmus*, 86 vols. (Toronto: University of Toronto Press); this project is still in progress. The correspondence of Erasmus from the year 1484 to August 1536 has appeared in volumes 1–21, published from 1974 to 2021. Apart from the correspondence, the *Antibarbari* and the *Enchiridion* are of special importance for this study: the texts of the *Antibarbari* and the Introductions are included in *CWE* 23; the indexes in *CWE* 24; and the *Enchiridion* in *CWE* 66.

EE	*Erasmi Epistolae*, in *Opus Epistolarum Des. Erasmi Roterodami*, ed. P. S. Allen, H. M. Allen, and H. W. Garrod (Oxford: Oxford University Press, Oxford, 1906–58).
EETS	Early English Text Society
Ep./Epp.	Letter from the *Epistolarum Erasmi*. The Latin text is included in *EE*; with the same number, the English translation is given in *CWE*. Line numbers follow after a dot in *EE* and a colon in *CWE*.
Harpsfield	Nicholas Harpsfield, *The Life and Death of Sir Thomas Moore, Knight*, ed. Elsie Vaughan Hitchcock (London: EETS, 1932; repr. 1963).
L'Univers	Germain Marc'hadour, *L'Univers de Thomas More* (Paris: Librairie Philosophique J. Vrin, 1963).
Moreana	Journal of Thomas More and Renaissance Studies published in Angers, France, 1963–2016, and by Edinburgh University Press from 2017 onward.
ODNB	*Oxford Dictionary of National Biography*
PG	J. P. Migne, ed., *Patrologiae Cursus Completus, Patrologiae Graecae* (Paris, 1857–86), followed by volume and column.
PL	J. P. Migne, ed., *Patrologiae Cursus Completus, Patrologiae Latinae* (Paris, 1844–90), followed by volume and column.
Ro: Ba:	Ro: Ba:, *The Life of Sir Thomas More* (1599), ed. Elsie Vaughan Hitchcock, P. E. Hallett, and A. W. Reed (London: EETS, 1950).
Roper	William Roper, *The Life of Sir Thomas Moore, Knighte*, ed. Elsie Vaughan Hitchcock (London: EETS, 1935).
SL	St. Thomas More, *Selected Letters*, ed. Elizabeth Frances Rogers (1961; repr. New Haven and London: Yale University Press, 1967); references are from the 1976 printing.
Stapleton	Thomas Stapleton, *The Life and Illustrious Martyrdom of Sir Thomas More*, trans. Philip E. Hallet, ed. E. E. Reynolds (London: Burns and Oates, 1966).
[ ]	A number in square brackets refers to the number of a letter as given in the *Correspondence*. Square brackets are also used for editorial comments.
< >	Angle brackets enclose places of origin or dates that are conjectural per *Correspondence*, *EE*, and *SL*.

THOMAS MORE'S VOCATION

Introduction

Thomas More was beheaded at Tower Hill, an open space outside the walls of the Tower of London, between the city walls and the northwestern corner of the Tower ditch; the scaffold was on the west side of Tower Hill. His body is buried in the crypt of the Anglican Church of St. Peter-in-Chains within the precinct of the Tower. There are many other people buried there in a common grave. Some belonged to the Tower garrison—it is their parish church—while others were imprisoned in the Tower and executed there or at Tower Hill; and yet Thomas More is the only one who has a funerary monument dedicated to him in the crypt. Beneath a bust there is an inscription that reads:

THOMAS MORE
Knight scholar writer statesman
Lord Chancellor of England 1529–32
Beheaded on Tower Hill, buried in this Chapel 1535
Canonised by Pope Pius XI 1935.

Thomas More's head is in the Roper family vault of the Anglican Church of St. Dunstan in Canterbury. The inscription on the flagstone reads:

Beneath this floor is the vault of the Roper family in
which is interred the head of Sir Thomas More of
illustrious memory sometime Lord Chancellor of
England who was beheaded on 6 July 1535
Ecclesia Anglicana Libera sit.

This last sentence is a quotation from the first clause of *Magna Carta*.

On February 12, 1496, More was admitted at Lincoln's Inn to study law, as recorded in the *Black Book*. In the Old Hall of the Inn, his is the only portrait in the stained-glass windows. His coat of arms is also there, among the many coats of arms of those members of the Inn who have been lord chancellors of England. More's coat of arms is also among those of prominent members displayed in the stained-glass windows in the New Great Hall, and the various painted portraits in the New Great Hall include—in a central position—a copy of his portrait in the Frick Collection of New York. A sixteenth-century miniature portrait is displayed in the Inn's meeting room. Clearly Thomas More is considered by its members to be a most illustrious former member of Lincoln's Inn. Nearby, within a niche in the wall at the corner of Carey Street and Serle Street, there stands a life-sized statue (1866), its inscription reading:

> SIR THOMAS MORE K/some time/
> Lord High Chancellor/of England/
> martyred July 6th 1535/the faithful
> servant both of God and the King

St. Lawrence Jewry, which was probably More's parish church and is now the church of the Lord Mayor and Corporation of London, has a stained-glass window (1957) at the right of the sanctuary depicting a life-sized figure of Thomas More with the titles of several of his books: *Utopia, A Dialogue Concerning Heresies, A Dialogue of Comfort against Tribulation,* and *A Treatise on the Passion.*

Opposite the church stands the Guildhall of the city of London, where Thomas More practiced as Under-Sheriff. In one of the six stained-glass windows of its medieval crypt (installed in 1971) there is another depiction of Thomas More; the other five windows depict the poet Geoffrey Chaucer, the printer William Caxton, the Great Fire of London, the diarist Samuel Pepys, and the architect Christopher Wren.

A statue of Thomas More appears on the façade of the city of London School; erected in 1883, it was the first of five to be placed there in honor of prominent Londoners or adopted Londoners—the others being Francis Bacon, William Shakespeare, John Milton, and Sir Isaac Newton. In St. Stephen's Hall, in the Palace of Westminster, there is a large mural of *More Defending the Liberties of the House of Commons.* Another mural, representing More and Erasmus visiting the young Prince Henry at Eltham Palace in 1499, is to be found just off the Central Lobby in the Palace of Westminster.

In Chelsea Old Church, latterly More's parish church, can be seen the epitaph that More himself wrote and had engraved for his tomb soon after he resigned as lord chancellor in 1532. Outside the church there is a life-sized statue unveiled in 1969. The inscriptions on the four sides of the base read:

SIR THOMAS MORE 1478–1535/
STATESMAN/SCHOLAR/SAINT

Not far from there, in Chelsea's Old Town Hall, there is a full-sized oil version of the portrait of Thomas More, his wife, his father, his son, his three daughters, his adopted daughters, and other members of his household; this is a contemporary copy of the "Family Portrait" (1593) by Rowland Lockey kept in Nostell Priory, near Wakefield, West Yorkshire, based on the sketch by Holbein (1527).[1] In the main reading room of the Old Town Hall, now the Chelsea branch of the Library of the Royal Borough of Kensington and Chelsea, there is a beautiful statuette of Thomas More by Ludwig Cauer (1866–1944), which was exhibited at the Royal Academy in 1895 and acquired for the library by public subscription in 1896. At the nearby Victoria and Albert Museum there is a miniature version of another painting by Lockey, "Thomas More, His Family, and Descendants" (1595–1600).

Thus in the streets of the present London, where he lived, worked, and died—the city of London, the Inns of Court, Westminster, Chelsea and the Tower—Thomas More is proclaimed SCHOLAR, WRITER, LAWYER, PARLIAMENTARIAN, STATESMAN, HUSBAND, FATHER, MARTYR, and SAINT. These monuments, erected in the nineteenth and twentieth centuries, are evidence that Thomas More's fame lives on. No less eloquent proof is the continuing stream of modern editions of his works and of books and essays about him. The early biographies by William Roper, Thomas Stapleton, and Cresacre More have been reprinted recently, as have his works. The year 2011 saw the publication of the *Cambridge Companion to Thomas More*, a collection of twelve essays by major scholars. A new translation of *Utopia* into English by Dominic Baker-Smith was published in 2012; the following year, the Catholic University of America Press published *The One Thomas More*, by Travis Curtright. In 2017 there appeared Joanne Paul's *Thomas More* and John Guy's *Thomas More: A Very Brief History*. Most recently, *The Essential Works of Thomas More*, an impressive 1,520-page volume, was published by Yale in 2020.

—

1. For a study of these paintings by Lockey, see Frank Mitjans, "Elizabethan Transformation of the Family Portrait," *Moreana*, no. 212 (December 2019): 133–59.

Apart from the roles carved in stone on monuments in the streets of London, Thomas More has also been acclaimed as—among other things—a poet,[2] a better theologian than John Colet, a better exegete than Erasmus, and a patron of the arts.[3] This work seeks to uncover the sources of these achievements and, above all, the early choices that mapped out his later life.

Most biographers' treating of More's youth cite the earliest of the many letters that have reached us through Thomas Stapleton's account. But this letter has a significance that seems to have been missed by biographers, owing to a mistranslation of the Latin original: this is why I have begun by venturing a new translation of the letter, following Cresacre More, More's grandson and a Londoner himself, who recognized the location mentioned in the letter and gave an accurate translation of it. Cresacre had the advantage of having access to the main previous biographies and of knowing the place where More lived—all of which increases our confidence in his account of some other aspects of More's youth. Nevertheless, the early accounts do not agree, and full reliance cannot be placed on any one of them: all must be weighed together with More's own writings.

Undoubtedly, Thomas More was influenced by his father and his family background. He had dealings with John Colet and other London humanists. He was in touch with the London Charterhouse. He studied Pico della Mirandola. He knew the works of Walter Hilton. He met and corresponded with Erasmus. All these relations are considered in the text, but we need to be cautious about asserting that he followed the advice of one or another or that he was influenced by one book or another. For John Guy, "One of Thomas More's defining characteristics is his refusal, except where religion is concerned, to accept unquestioningly the views of those in authority."[4] Guy makes the remark within the context of More's relations with his father, but that general statement undoubtedly also applies to his freedom of mind with regard to the views of Colet, Pico, and Erasmus.

My conclusion—if an introduction is really the place for a conclusion—is that More chose the active life of service to the city *and* the contemplative life of a Christian: that is, that he determined to seek holiness through engagement with the world, and that this decision gave unity of

---

2. See *The Yale Edition of The Complete Works of St. Thomas More* (New Haven and London: Yale University Press, 1963–97) (hereafter abbreviated as *CW*), vols. 1 and 3, and Mary Edith Willow, *An Analysis of the English Poems of St. Thomas More* (Nieuwkoop, The Netherlands: De Graaf, 1974).

3. See Susan Foister, *Holbein and England* (New Haven and London: Yale University Press, 2004), 11–.

4. John Guy, *A Daughter's Love: Thomas and Margaret More* (London: Fourth Estate, 2008), 79.

purpose to the rest of his life. Some well-known recent biographical studies share this view; others have misunderstood—it seems to me—this vital point. I will not pursue More's life beyond this "point of departure" of the choice made.[5] This book, in attempting to find out the purpose More gave to his life, aims to uncover some of the influences that shaped his early choices: the choices that gave direction to his life and were the source of that decision. The decision, in turn, is a mirror of More's spiritual outlook: it shows us his interior aspirations; it reveals who he wanted to be; it reveals that he was practicing a spiritual discipline for the purpose not of escaping the world, but of finding the right way to live in it.

An explanation needs to be given about the title of this book. My aim was only to investigate whether Thomas More's early life can give us a clue to his later thinking and developments. I was reluctant to use the word "vocation" because More himself did not use it, and because of the different meanings and nuances of the word: some scholars have written of More's vocation as a lawyer; others have presented More's vocation as a humanist and a political thinker.[6] Nevertheless, the late professor Dominic Baker-Smith, after reading the typescript twice, wrote the title in his precise pencil handwriting on the first page.

More knew Cicero's *De Officiis* well. Modern translators of that work often use the word "vocation" or equivalents in such phrases as "a man pursues a vocation of his own"—*institutum consequantur* (book I, no. 116)—and "deciding upon his calling in life"—*deligendo genere vitae* (book I, nos. 117, 120 and 121).[7] The question of More's calling or path in life is indeed the sense of the word "vocation" in the title.

—

Was it possible to succeed in all the different roles mentioned by those who have written about Thomas More—lawyer, scholar, statesman, husband...?

5. Nonetheless, because More wrote of that period in both of the epitaphs in Chelsea Old Church, a study of the two epitaphs has been included in the appendix, even though they actually cover much more of his later life.

6. Joanne Paul, *Thomas More*, Classic Thinkers (Cambridge: Polity Press, 2017).

7. Cicero, *De Officiis/On Duties*, trans. Walter Miller (1913; repr. Cambridge, Mass: Loeb Classical Library, Harvard University Press, 2005). There are six other recent translations of *De Officiis* into English: those of John Higginbotham (London: Faber and Faber, 1967); Harry G. Edinger (Indianapolis: Bobbs-Merrill, 1974); M. T. Griffin and E. M. Atkins (Cambridge: Cambridge University Press, 1991); P. G. Walsh (Oxford: Oxford University Press, 2000); and Benjamin Patrick Newton (Ithaca: Cornell University Press, 2016). Walsh translates the aforementioned phrases as "a path of their own" (book I, no. 116), "what pattern of life we wish to adopt" (book I, no. 117), and "choosing our manner of life" (book I, no. 120), while Newton has "what kind of life we wish to lead" (book I, no. 117), and "choosing on which path of life" (book I, no. 120).

It is clear that he was a successful lawyer, but that hardly explains why he was elected Lawyer of the Millennium by the Law Society of England. His *Utopia* and his Latin letters made him the most significant Christian humanist scholar in England of his time and the obvious choice for the defense of orthodoxy against Lutheranism; and yet the humanist project to invigorate the Church was derailed by the need to defend it in the face of the Reformers. As a statesman, his period as lord chancellor of England lasted little more than two and a half years. As a husband, it is a fact that his first wife died after only a few years of marriage. Was he successful in his life project? If to be a lawyer, scholar, statesman, and husband were his aims in life, he must be accounted a failure. But he is praised because his success did *not* rest on those objectives. As he put it in one of his last letters, it is "a case in which a man may lose his head and not be harmed"[8]: his goal was to be found beyond death. It is my contention that it was in his early life that he defined his goal—or rather, he *became aware* of it—and that he made the choices that pointed him toward that goal.

London, February 7, 2022

8. Letter to Alice Alington, August 1534, in *The Correspondence of Sir Thomas More*, ed. Elizabeth Frances Rogers (Princeton: Princeton University Press, 1947), Letter [206], line 590.

I

Ambulanti mihi dudum in foro

Introducing the Letter of October 23, 1502, 1503, or 1504

"*Ambulanti mihi dudum in foro, et inter aliena negotia ocianti obtulit se puer tuus.*" Thus starts a letter from Thomas More to John Colet dated October 23, 1502, 1503, or 1504,[1] when More was twenty-five or twenty-six. The letter, written in Latin, was published in *Tres Thomae* (Douai, 1588), a triple biography of Thomas the Apostle, Thomas of Canterbury, and Thomas More by Thomas Stapleton.

There are two earlier *Lives* of Thomas More. The first, written in 1557, was by William Roper, husband of Margaret, More's eldest daughter. Roper gave his manuscript to Nicholas Harpsfield, archdeacon of Canterbury, who worked it into a longer account—*The Life and Death of Sir Thomas Moore*—which he presented to Roper as a New Year's gift for 1559. Neither manuscript was published at the time, as Queen Mary had been succeeded by Queen Elizabeth in November 1558. Roper's *Life* was not printed until 1626 (in Saint-Omer), and no reliable text appeared until the critical edition was published in 1935 by the Early English Text Society.[2] Harpsfield's text circulated only in manuscript until the critical edition of 1932, also by EETS.[3]

Thomas Stapleton was born in England in 1535, educated at Winchester

1. *Correspondence*, Letter [3].

2. William Roper, *The Life of Sir Thomas Moore, Knighte*, ed. Elsie Vaughan Hitchcock (London: Oxford University Press for EETS, 1935), xxv–xxviii.

3. Nicholas Harpsfield, "Description of the Harpsfield Manuscripts," in *The Life and Death of Sir Thomas Moore, Knight, Sometymes Lord High Chancellor of England*, ed. Elsie Vaughan Hitchcock (London: Oxford University Press for EETS, 1932), xiii–xx.

College and New College, Oxford, and ordained to the priesthood in 1558, before the death of Queen Mary. He traveled to the Low Countries, studied theology at Louvain, and went on pilgrimage to Rome. He returned to England but left again in 1563 following his refusal to take the oath under the Act of Supremacy of 1559. The *Vita et Illustre Martyrium Thomae Mori, Angliae quondam Supremi Cancellarii*, the third part of the book *Tres Thomae*,[4] was based—as Stapleton writes in the Preface—on "the personal reminiscences of those who for many years lived either in the same house with" Thomas More "or otherwise on terms of intimacy, and afterwards … were fellow-exiles with me for the Faith, either here in Belgium[5] or in other parts of the world."[6] These fellow exiles included Margaret, *née* Giggs, adopted daughter of Thomas More, and her husband, John Clement; "John Harris with his wife Dorothy Coly—she is still living in Douai—of whom the one was Thomas More's private secretary, the other the maid of Margaret Roper, More's eldest daughter; also John Heywood,[7] for many years a close friend of More's; and lastly William Rastell, More's nephew by his sister Elizabeth."[8] Stapleton continued, "Nothing has helped me more than Harris's manuscript collections, including many of More's letters written in the martyr's own hand, all of which Mr. Harris's widow has handed over to me."[9] In the Introduction to his edition of Stapleton's *Life of Sir Thomas More*,[10] E. E. Reynolds asserts that Stapleton had a manuscript copy of William Roper's *Life* and perhaps also of Harpsfield's *Life*.[11] He is followed in this by Chambers, John Guy, and other scholars;[12] nevertheless, Staple-

4. In the preface to his *Life and Writings of Blessed Thomas More*, Bridgett wrote, "By far the best Life of More is that of Thomas Stapleton, published at Douai in 1588"; T. E. Bridgett, *Life and Writings of Blessed Thomas More* (London: Burns and Oates, 1891), ix.

5. "*Belgio*," in the Latin edition of Thomas Stapleton, *Vita Thomae Mori* (Douai 1588, ed. 1689); *Francofurti ad Moenum* (1689), reprinted in facsimile in 1964, 4. Neo-Latin "Belgium" included the current Belgium, the Netherlands, Luxemburg, and parts of Northern France and Western Germany: see Tom Deneire, "Neo-Latin: The Low Countries," in *Brill's Encyclopaedia of the Neo-Latin World: Micropaedia* (Leiden and Boston: Brill, 2014), 1,096–98.

6. Thomas Stapleton, *The Life and Illustrious Martyrdom of Sir Thomas More* (1588), trans. Philip E. Hallet (1588), ed. E. E. Reynolds (London: Burns and Oates, 1966), xvi.

7. His youngest son, Jasper, had a great admiration for Thomas More; see F. Mitjans, "*Non sum Oedipus sed Morus*: A Paper on the Portrait of Sir Thomas More and his Family," *Moreana*, nos. 168–70 (December 2006–June 2007): 56–58; and "Elizabethan Transformation of the Family Portrait," *Moreana*, no. 212 (December 2019): 141–45.

8. Stapleton, xvi–xvii.

9. Stapleton, xviii.

10. Stapleton, xii.

11. Later on, however, Reynolds wrote, "We cannot therefore deduce that Stapleton had a manuscript of Harpsfield to consult"; Stapleton, 65n6.

12. R. W. Chambers, *Thomas More* (1935; repr. London: Jonathan Cape, 1976), 39; John A. Guy, *Reputations: Thomas More* (London: Arnold, 2000), 10; William Sheils, "Polemic as Piety: Thomas

ton does not mention either Roper's or Harpsfield's *Life* in his Preface, in spite of his meticulous account of his sources.[13]

The early *Lives* written after Stapleton's—*The Life of Sir Thomas More* (1599) by an unidentified author known as Ro: Ba: and Cresacre More's *Life of Sir Thomas More* (1627)—had access to the previous biographies. Thus the early biographers provide us with essentially two sources: the account of William Roper, who wrote in England twenty years after his father-in-law's death, and the recollections of Catholics who left England after the accession of Elizabeth, bringing with them many of More's letters. For simplicity's sake, we might call them the *Roper tradition* and the *Stapleton tradition*.

It might be assumed that Roper's *Life* was based not only on his own recollections but also those of Margaret, his wife and Thomas More's eldest daughter, but she in fact died in 1542, fifteen years before her husband published his biography. It cannot, therefore, safely be asserted that the *Life* by Roper has Margaret's authority any more than that by Stapleton, who must also have received Margaret's recollections through her "fellow student," Margaret Giggs, her maid, Dorothy Coly, and Thomas More's secretary, John Harris.[14]

Until the publication of T. E. Bridgett's *Life and Writings of Blessed Thomas More* (1891), the only biography readily available was Cresacre More's *Life*, which logically enough was regarded as drawing on family tradition. But Bridgett thought Cresacre's biography a mere patchwork compilation from the earlier ones, writing, "This *Life of Sir Thomas* [by Cresacre More] is much esteemed and often quoted; but after collating it carefully with Stapleton, Roper, and Harpsfield, I find that it contains very little original matter. I have preferred, therefore, to quote directly from the sources from which Cresacre More drew."[15] This perception was accepted

---

Stapleton's *Tres Thomae* and Catholic Controversy in the 1580s," *Journal of Ecclesiastical History* 60, no. 1 (January 2009): 81.

13. Cf. Stapleton, *Vita Thomae Mori, Francofurti ad Moenum*, 1689, reprinted in facsimile in 1964, 3–4; also in the English edition by Reynolds (1966), xvi–xviii. Bridgett wrote, "It is certain [that Stapleton] had a copy of William Roper's notes"; see Bridgett, *Life and Writings*, x; while Bremond said, "It is commonly admitted that Stapleton may have consulted Roper's notes at leisure, though it is strange that a writer so careful always to mention his authorities, has forgotten to give references to the earliest and most authoritative of all. But for Father Bridgett's opinion, I should be tempted to raise a doubt on the subject"; Bremond, *The Blessed Thomas More* (London: R. and T. Washbourne, 1920), ix–x.

14. For Margaret Roper's determination to publish her father's works and life, see John A. Guy, *A Daughter's Love: Thomas and Margaret More* (London: Fourth Estate 2008), 266–68.

15. Bridgett, *Life and Writings*, xi.

by the scholarly consensus and continues to dominate, so that Elizabeth Frances Rogers does not even mention Cresacre's work in the bibliography of her edition of the *Selected Letters of St. Thomas More* (1961), although she includes Roper, Harpsfield, Stapleton, and Ro: Ba: among the sixteenth-century biographies. This omission is unfortunate, because she relies on the standard translation of the first letter we have from Thomas More to Colet.[16]

The opening phrase of the letter, quoted earlier, is translated by Bridgett: "I was walking up and down the law courts when your servant met me." Philip Hallett's translation of the *Vita Thomae Mori*[17] similarly gives the sentence as, "As I was walking in the law-courts the other day, occupied with business of various kinds, I met your servant"; and this translation is taken up by Chambers.[18] Rogers takes the translation from Hallett,[19] introducing certain changes,[20] so that the version given in the *Selected Letters* reads, "As I was walking in the law courts the other day, unbusy where everybody else was busy, I met your servant."[21]

This letter will be examined again in detail elsewhere in this book, but let us now seek to elucidate this first sentence. Bridgett, Hallett, Chambers, and Rogers all translate "*in foro*" as "in the law courts," which is understandable because Thomas More himself used the word *forum* in this sense in the epitaph he wrote in 1532 for his tomb (see Appendix). Reynolds likewise translates it as "law-courts," adding "Westminster Hall" between square brackets.[22] The content of the letter, however, suggests that this is a mistranslation.

16. Rogers does, however, refer to Cresacre More's biography in her edition of *Correspondence*, 249n101, and corresponding bibliography.

17. Hallett's translation, made in 1928, is given in Stapleton, 10.

18. Chambers, *Thomas More* (1935/1976), 88.

19. St. Thomas More, *Selected Letters*, ed. Elizabeth Frances Rogers (1961; rev. ed. New Haven and London: Yale University Press, 1967, repr. 1976), ix.

20. *SL*, xvi.

21. *SL*, 4.

22. E. E. Reynolds, *Thomas More and Erasmus* (London: Burns and Oates, 1965), 37. The reference of Reynolds to Westminster Hall points to the use of *forum* by More in *Richard III* (c. 1513–1518): "V*enit in forum, non illud Londinense, sed maius atque augustius, quod est in palatio apud occidentale coenobium vbi ab omni parte regni promiscue aguntur causae*" (*CW* 15, 482, lines 25–27), translated in 483–95 by "he arrived at the forum, not the one situated in London but a larger and grander one located in the palace right next to Westminster Abbey, where all types of cases are argued from every part of the realm. There he took the seat called the King's Bench because the judgements of that court have the same force as if they came straight from the king's mouth"; and previously, "*in forum venit locum et elegantem et maximae turbae capacem: tum conuocato in curiam populo Dux*" (*CW* 15, 454, line 17), though in p. 454 *forum* does not seem to be the law-courts either but the large civic space in front of the hall [the Guildhall], and thus, it is left as "forum" in the English translation in *CW* 15, 455.

The common translation of *forum* is "marketplace," and so Cresacre More translates it, "As I was lately walking in Cheapside, and busying myself about other men's causes, I met by chance your servant."[23] "Cheapside" is the name of the main street in the present-day city of London, running from St. Paul's to Mansion House, and it was the chief marketplace of medieval London; the name means just that: "marketplace" (*ceap* or *chepe* was the Old English word for "market"). Members of assorted craft guilds lived and worked in specific areas nearby: the bakers in BREAD STREET, the fishmongers in FRIDAY STREET, while IRONMONGERS LANE, POULTRY LANE, WOOD STREET, and so on, are self-explanatory. Thomas More himself was born at MILK STREET, just off Cheapside. In line 23 of the same letter *forum* appears again—"*forenses strepitus*," "the din of the marketplace"—and the description follows in lines 24–25: "Wherever you turn your eyes, what else will you see but confectioners, fishmongers, butchers, cooks, poulterers, fishermen, fowlers." Chaucer mentions Cheapside in *The Cook's Tale*, and from then on it appears again and again in accounts of London. More himself speaks of "two young ... apprentices in Cheapside"[24] who were the instigators of the Evil May Day riot; and his *Dialogue* of 1529 was printed at the printing press of his brother-in-law John Rastell at St. Paul's Gate, next to Cheapside.[25] More uses *forum* to mean "marketplace" in two Latin poems[26] and in *Utopia*[27]—indeed, the market in Utopia resembles that described in the letter, as it provides "all sorts of vegetables, fruit and bread, fish, meat and poultry."[28]

Thomas More often paraphrased Classical authors in his Latin texts, and in several places of his *History of Richard III* he follows the style and turn of phrase of Livy. Surely, is there not at least an echo in More's "*Ambulanti mihi dudum in foro ... ocianti*" of Livy's "*in foro ... otiose inambulavit*" (*Ab Urbe Condita*, Liber XXIII, §7.10)[29]—"he walked at leisure through the marketplace"? And all through the letter, More writes of the *urbs* when speaking of the city of London.

23. Cresacre More, *The Life of Sir Thomas More* (1627), ed. the Rev. Joseph Hunter (London, 1828), 30. He is the first author to provide an English translation of the letter.

24. *CW* 9:19.

25. *CW* 8, 1142.

26. Cf. *CW* 3, part II, Poems no. 91, 150, and no. 95, 156. The first one is undated; the second is dated late in 1512 or early in 1513.

27. Cf. *CW* 4, 136:27, and 140:21, translated by "market" in *CW* 4, and "market" and "marketplace" in *Utopia*, ed. George M. Logan and Robert M. Adams (Cambridge: Cambridge University Press, 1989), 56 and 58.

28. Cf. *CW* 4, 138:9, and translation in the edition of Cambridge University Press, 57.

29. The text from Livy reads: *in foro cum filio clientibusque otiose inambulavit.*

A possible translation might thus be, "As I was walking recently in Cheapside, the marketplace, at leisure among the business stalls of others, your servant made his presence felt"—that is, among the stalls of the confectioners, fishmongers, butchers, cooks, poulterers, fishermen, and fowlers he mentions later on (Bridgett omits "*inter aliena negotia ocianti*"; Hallet omits "*ocianti*"; Rogers's translation misses only "the marketplace").

Alexandre Martin's French translation of Stapleton's work (1849, prior to Bridgett's and Hallett's English translations) gives *foro* as "la place publique"; the phrase reads, "Me promenant hier sur la place publique, au milieu d'une foule importune, j'ai rencontré votre domestique."[30] And indeed, "la place publique" conveys the meaning of "civic center" very similar to the Roman forum, where other public business was done, as well as buying and selling. But the specific meaning of "marketplace" is corroborated by Erasmus,[31] who compared More to a Pythagorean philosopher "who strolled unthinking through the market-place watching the crowds of people buying and selling": "*qui vacuus animo per mercatum obambulans contemplatur tumultus vendentium atque ementium.*"[32] More writes "*foro,*" while Erasmus uses "*mercatum,*" but that is not surprising, for More was paraphrasing Livy, while Erasmus was comparing his friend with the Greek philosopher. The relevance of taking the *forum* as the marketplace or public space, rather than restricted to the law courts, is the link with the Roman classical authors such as Cicero, Tacitus, and Sallust;[33] but more important is the link with St. John Chrysostom, as we will consider in chapter 3.

The sixteenth-century humanists, while using classical Latin, were also aware of other layers of meaning. If More was conversant with Livy, he was certainly more familiar with the Latin Vulgate New Testament.[34] His "*in foro ... ocianti*" not only echoes Livy's "*in foro ... otiose,*" but also has clear resonances with the account of the householder in the Parable of the Vine-

30. Stapleton, *Histoire de Thomas More*, translated from the Latin into French by M. Alexandre Martin (Paris: L. Maison, 1849), 27. Martin gives the text in Latin as well as a footnote. In the introduction he mentions the biography by Cresacre More.

31. On this point I am indebted to a private communication from Robert M. Keane, author of "Thomas More as a Young Lawyer," *Moreana*, no. 160 (December 2004).

32. The letter from Erasmus to Ulrich von Hutten, 1519, is considered by some the first biography we have of Thomas More, and it was known by Stapleton (cf. Stapleton, 5) and Cresacre More (cf. Cresacre More, 95). The text is found in *EE*, 4, Ep. 999:126–30; and the translation in *CWE* 7, Ep. 999:133–34.

33. See for instance, Cicero, *De Officiis* I.53 and 145, II.27, and III.75; Tacitus, *Annales* II; and Sallust, *Bellum Catilinae*.

34. See Germain Marc'hadour, *The Bible in the Works of St. Thomas More*, 5 vols. (Nieuwkoop: De Graaf, 1969–71). The Latin text used here is that of the Sixto-Clementine Vulgate of 1592, in the edition of *Novum Testamentum* (Rome, 1964).

yard, who "*Vidit alios stantes in foro otiosos*"—saw others standing idle in the marketplace (Mt 20:3), and called them to work in his vineyard. More refers to this passage from St. Matthew's Gospel in his letter to Bugenhagen, *Cur paterfamilias denario diurno otiosorum hominum operas conducit in vineam?*—"Why does the owner of the estate hire idle men to work in the vineyard for one denarius a day?"[35] Was Thomas More simply walking at leisure through the marketplace? Or—bearing in mind that he was writing to his spiritual director—did he in fact mean that he was feeling idle and unengaged, in a sense not unlike those standing around in the marketplace waiting to be called by the Lord? In these lines from the letter to Bugenhagen, More sounds personally committed: "Even when we have done everything, we are still unprofitable servants and have not done anything other than what we ought to do. And yet he hires our labours at a high salary."[36]

More's "*Ambulanti mihi*" may also hint at other Gospel passages: ***Ambulans autem Iesus*** *iuxta mare Galilaeae, vidit duos fratres, Simonem, qui vocatur Petrus, et Andream, fratrem eius, mittentes rete in mare; erant enim piscatores. Et ait illis: Venite post me, et faciam vos fieri piscatores hominum*: "As he walked by the Sea of Galilee, he saw two brothers, Simon who is called Peter and Andrew his brother, casting a net into the sea; for they were fishermen. And he said to them, 'Follow me, and I will make you fishers of men'" (Mt 4:18–19). *Et respiciens **Iesum ambulantem**, dicit: Ecce agnus Dei. Et audierunt eum duo discipuli loquentem et secuti sunt Iesum*: "[John the Baptist] looked at Jesus as he walked, and said, 'Behold, the Lamb of God!' The two disciples heard him say this and they followed Jesus" (Jn 1:36–37). The passage from Matthew is referred to by More in *The Four Last Things*: "Whereas saint Peter & other holy apostles, at the first call left theyre nets, which was in effect al y^t they had, & followed him";[37] and that from John's Gospel in *A Treatise upon the Passion*.[38]

Who was this young man whom we—twenty-first-century inquirers, following Cresacre More and others after him—visualize walking through Cheapside? What were the dilemmas and choices he was contemplating in those days in the early 1500s? To answer these questions, we must examine the whole of this key letter more closely. But first, it will be helpful to summarize what we know of More's earlier life.

<hr>

35. *Correspondence*, Ep. 143:684; *CW* 7, 54:4.
36. *CW* 7, 53:35–38.
37. *CW* 1, 172:1–3.
38. *CW* 13, 62:21–23.

Thomas Morvs vrbe londinensi familia
non celebri sed honesta natus

THOMAS MORVS VRBE LONDINENSI FAMILIA
NON CELEBRI SED HONESTA NATVS
IN LITERIS VTCVNQ VERSATVS:
QVVM ET CAVSAS ALIQVOT ANNOS
IVVENIS ECISSET IN FORO ET IN VRBE SVA
PRO SHIREVO IVS DIXISSET

Thomas More was born in the city of London,
of an honourable though not illustrious family, and was
always engaged in letters in one way or another.
After spending several years of his youth pleading in
the law courts and administering justice on
behalf of the sheriff in his city …

—[first words of his epitaph at Chelsea Old Church, dated 1532][39]

Thomas More was born in the city of London on February 7, 1478,[40] at Milk Street,[41] off Cheapside. His father, Sir John More, was a lawyer who was to reach the position of justice of the king's bench; he died in 1530, aged seventy-nine. Thomas was very respectful of his father throughout his life. He placed Sir John next to himself in the Family Portrait at Chelsea, as we can see from the sketch by Holbein. A surprisingly large part of his own epitaph is likewise devoted to his father:

John More was a knight and chosen by the Prince as member of that body of judges known as the King's Bench; he was an affable man, charming, irreproachable, gentle, merciful, fair, and upright; though venerable in age, he was vigorous for a man of his years; after he had lived to see the day when his son became Chancellor of England, he deemed his sojourn upon earth complete and gladly departed for heaven. The son, all through his father's lifetime, had been compared with him, and was commonly known as the young More, and so he considered himself to be.

In *The Life of Sir Thomas More*, Roper wrote that while Sir John lay on his deathbed, Thomas went to visit him often and comforted him with kind words, "but also at his departure out of the world with tears taking

---

39. See Appendix.

40. See the two articles by F. Mitjans, "The Date of Birth of Thomas More," and "Reviewing and Correcting the Article on the Date of Birth of Thomas More," published in *Moreana*, respectively in vol. 47, nos. 181–82 (December 2010): 109–28, and in vol. 49, nos. 189–90 (December 2012): 251–61.

41. Cresacre More, 14. Neither Roper nor Stapleton gives More's birthplace.

him about the neck, most lovingly embraced him, commending him into the merciful hands of Almighty God."[42]

John and his wife, Agnes, née Graunger, had six children, but only three of them survived childhood: Thomas and two sisters. The eldest, Joan, born in 1475, married Richard Staverton; his younger sister, Elizabeth, born in 1482, married John Rastell. Thomas's mother, Agnes, died in 1499,[43] when he was 21; this year was especially important for him, as will be seen. The family was well connected and had a comfortable position. Sir John was a member of the Mercers' Guild, the senior guild among the livery companies of the Corporation of the City of London. Soon after starting his professional life, Thomas became lawyer to the same guild, and he rented a house from the guild when he married and set up his new family home.

Sir John was well acquainted with John Morton, bishop of Ely (1479–86), whose London townhouse was Ely Palace, just outside the boundaries of the city; Thomas may have gone with his father to Ely Palace, for he kept childhood memories of fresh strawberries from the large garden there.[44] In 1486 Morton became archbishop of Canterbury; he was appointed lord chancellor of England in 1487 and was created a cardinal in 1493. As archbishop of Canterbury, he resided in Lambeth Palace while in the London area. Thomas More started his schooling at St. Anthony's,[45] the only school in the city where Latin was taught, but he then entered Morton's household at Lambeth. Later Morton sent him to continue his education at Oxford. Thus, Thomas was fluent in Latin from an early age, and most of his early writing was in this language. At the age of sixteen he started studying law at New Inn[46] outside the city of London, and when he became eighteen he followed in his father's footsteps by entering Lincoln's Inn, of which his father was a member.

—

The Roman *Londinium* was a walled city that extended from St. Paul's Cathedral to Tower Hill; the Tower of London was built outside the old city's east wall. Edward the Confessor had moved the royal court to Westminster in about 1060, thus separating the commercial center of the capital from

---

42. Roper, 44.

43. Marc'hadour, "The Death-Year of Thomas More's Mother," *Moreana* 2, no. 63 (December 1979): 13–16; and Guy, *Daughter's Love*, 77–79.

44. *CW* 2, *History of Richard III*, 217. The story was taken up by Shakespeare in his play *Richard III*.

45. Cf. John Stow, *Survey of London* (1598), ed. William J. Thoms (London: Chatto and Windus, London, 1876), 28; Roper, 5; Harpsfield, 10; Cresacre More, 15.

46. Stow, *Survey of London*, 167; Roper, 5; and Harpsfield, 12.

the seat of royal power and justice. In More's time the king held his court at Westminster, Greenwich, Windsor, or elsewhere.

By the end of the fifteenth century the city of London had outgrown the Roman walls, and its boundaries were similar to the present ones, reaching Temple Bar and Holborn Bar on the west. The commercial activity of the city was concentrated around Cheapside, just east of St. Paul's and south of the Guildhall. There were 114 parish churches within the city.[47] St. Lawrence Jewry, next to the Guildhall and a few minutes' walk from his home, was probably John More's parish church, and in his will he bequeathed his body to be buried at St. Lawrence's, in a tomb made for him "in the chapel of our Lady."[48] Cresacre More confirms that John More was buried there,[49] though St. Mary Magdalen's in Milk Street was closest to his home.[50] The young Thomas, on his way to school, would go most days past the Chapel of St. Thomas of Acon, on the corner of Cheapside and Ironmongers Lane. St. Thomas of Canterbury had been born there on December 21, 1118 (then the liturgical feast of St. Thomas the Apostle). Probably the young More was baptized Thomas after his maternal grandfather, Sir Thomas Graunger;[51] in any case, St. Thomas of Canterbury was the local saint, and Thomas More admired him greatly. In his last letter from the Tower of London before his execution, written on July 5, 1535, he said that he wished to die on the following day, the eve of St. Thomas,[52] "and therefore tomorrow long I to go to God, it were a day very fitting and convenient for me."[53]

So Thomas More had from his father his profession as a lawyer, his connections with the Mercers' Guild and Lincoln's Inn, and those with Cardinal Morton. All these facilitated his acquaintance with scholars and humanists. Sir John dated his son's birth "on the Friday next after the Feast of the Purification of the Blessed Virgin Mary"—an example of the Christian atmosphere and traditions in which More grew up.

47. Stow, *Survey of London*, 183.

48. The text of the will of Sir John More is available from the National Archives, Public Record Office, Catalogue reference: PROB 11/23, London; a translation is given by Margaret Hastings, "The Ancestry of Sir Thomas More," Appendix B, *Guildhall Miscellany* 2, no. 2 (July 1961): 47–62.

49. Cresacre More, 53.

50. After the fire of London in 1666 the parish of St. Mary Magdalen was combined with that of St. Lawrence Jewry.

51. See *Memoranda*, written by John More, in MS. Cambridge, Trinity College, O.2.21; the text is reproduced in Mitjans, "The Date of Birth of Thomas More," *Moreana*, nos. 181–82 (December 2010): 111.

52. His feast was celebrated on December 29, for he died on that day in 1170, but his translation on July 7, for on that day in 1220 his relics were moved to a newly built shrine in the chapel of the Holy Trinity in Canterbury Cathedral. His translation is no longer celebrated.

53. *Correspondence,* [218], lines 19–20.

Early Classical Education up to 1494

As we have seen, Thomas More's early education was largely in Latin. Latin had continued to be the language of learning and education after the collapse of the Roman empire of the West, largely because it was the language of the Church; throughout the Middle Ages it was the international language of secular and ecclesiastical administration and diplomacy as well as philosophy and theology, law, medicine, and the sciences.[54] The post-Classical Latin of the fourth or fifth centuries was already quite different from that of the Classical period, and in spite of reforms[55] had continued to develop over the centuries, among other things accumulating both barbarisms (in Northern Europe, largely words from Germanic languages)[56] and neologisms (technical terms for use in the Church, the law and government, and university studies). In the fifteenth century there was a movement to return to Classical Latin, originating in Italy and extending through the rest of Europe.

An important landmark in the history of Classical education in England is the foundation of two establishments by the fourteenth-century bishop of Winchester, William of Wykeham: the *Collegium Sanctae Mariae prope Winton* (Winchester College) in 1378, and the *Collegium Beatae Marie Wynton in Oxon* (New College, University of Oxford) in 1379. In the foundation deed of Winchester College he wrote that

grammar is the foundation, gate, and source of all the other liberal arts, without which such arts cannot be known, nor can anyone arrive at practising them. Moreover, by the knowledge of letters justice is cultivated and the prosperity of the human condition is increased.[57]

Humfrey, Duke of Gloucester (1390–1447), who held the tutelage of Henry VI (1421–1471) while the king was a minor, is often considered to be the first English patron of Italian humanism and a link to "the arrival in England of the new priorities associated with the subtle cultural stimulus that we now call northern humanism."[58] The duke fostered friendship with Italian collectors, employed prominent humanists as his secretaries, com-

---

54. Nicholas Orme, *English Schools in the Middle Ages* (London: Methuen, 1973), 87.

55. The most important was the Carolingian reform of the eighth century.

56. Word imports into Vulgar Latin (particularly from Celtic languages) were frequent even in the Classical period.

57. Orme (1973), *English Schools*, 88.

58. James McConica, "Thomas More as Humanist," in *Cambridge Companion to Thomas More*, ed. George M. Logan (Cambridge and New York: Cambridge University Press, 2011), 22.

missioned literary works, and collected a large library of classical texts,[59] some of which he bequeathed to the University of Oxford.[60]

Another patron was Henry VI himself. He had received a Classical education, and on ending his minority in 1437 he showed himself keen to establish educational foundations; he seems to have acceded enthusiastically to a petition from the city of London to make endowments for free grammar schools and to create a college at Cambridge to train schoolmasters,[61] so that, Nicholas Orme writes, "for a short period in the 1440s we can talk of an educational movement based on the king and the court in favour of grammar schools."[62] Fruit of the king's passion for education was the foundation in 1441 not only of Eton College near Windsor and King's College, at the University of Cambridge,[63] but also, in the same year, of St. Anthony's grammar school in London.[64]

The first master of St. Anthony's grammar school was John Carpenter, a fellow of Oriel College, Oxford, and provost of the college from 1428 to 1435. As clerk and chaplain to Henry VI, he accompanied the king to France in May 1430, and in 1433 the king appointed him master of the school attached to St. Anthony's Hospital. There, in 1441, he set up St. Anthony's as the first free grammar school in London, and the king provided for grants to be made to pupils from the school for five presentations to Eton and five Oxford scholarships.[65] Carpenter was consecrated bishop of Worcester in 1444, but he kept up his links with Oriel and St. Anthony's. He bequeathed property to Oriel and leased estates to St. Anthony's for the maintenance of scholars from the school to study at Oriel;[66] according to Carpenter's ordinances, they were to stay at St. Mary's Hall, a dependency of the college.[67]

All this information reveals the connection between St. Anthony's

59. Article on Humfrey, Duke of Gloucester in *Oxford Dictionary of National Biography* (*ODNB*), accessed online on June 30, 2021.

60. A first installment of 129 manuscripts arrived there in 1439, and a second of 134 in 1444. The oldest part of the Bodleian Library is still called Duke Humfrey's Library.

61. Nicholas Orme, *Education and Society in Medieval and Renaissance England* (London and Ronceverte: Hambledon Press, 1989), 13.

62. Orme, *Education and Society* (1989), 14.

63. Named "The King's College of Our Lady of Eton beside Windsor" and "King's College of Our Lady and St. Nicholas at Cambridge."

64. "The credit of this foundation is due to Henry VI"; cf. Arthur F. Leach, *The Schools of Medieval England* (London: Methuen, 1969), 252–66.

65. *British History Online* accessed on June 19, 2021, and John Stow's *Survey of London* (1598).

66. Article on John Carpenter in *ODNB*, accessed online on June 17, 2021

67. "The ordinances have disappeared, but the accounts of St. Anthony's and Oriel College show that scholars were duly taken from St. Anthony's School": Leach, *Schools of Medieval England*, 261.

grammar school, Oriel College Oxford, and St. Mary's Hall, and agrees with the recollection of Miles Windsor (who was at St. Mary's Hall in Queen Mary's time) that Thomas More lived there as an exhibitioner of John Morton's; the funds of Morton's Oxford scholarships were administered by the warden of Canterbury College.[68]

The reputation of St. Anthony's shortly before More's time can be seen in a letter of 1472 to the archbishop of Canterbury from William Selling, newly elected prior of Christ Church, Canterbury, who tells the archbishop that he had provided a schoolmaster for the grammar school in that city: a man who "hath lately taught grammar at Winchester and S. Anthony's in London."[69] Leach suggests that this reference to the master of St. Anthony's as having been also a master at Winchester shows that St. Anthony's School already had a high reputation. The excellence of St. Anthony's was noted seventy years later when Stow, in his *Survey of London*, wrote that the pupils of St. Anthony's were the best scholars at a competition in the 1530s attended by pupils from other London schools such as St. Paul's, Westminster School, and St. Thomas's Acon.

There are no extant records of the curriculum of St. Anthony's for the period More was there. The buildings of St. Anthony's were burned down by the fire of London in 1666 and were not rebuilt, and it seems that the school itself ceased to exist from then on. Nevertheless, we have no reason to think that it would have been very different from that followed at other grammar schools of the period: Winchester College, Eton College, or St. Paul's. The list of authors read in the grammar schools in the late fifteenth century included the standard authors of the Classical period (most of them familiar to schoolboys from at least the twelfth century): Cicero, Terence, Plautus, Virgil, Horace, Ovid, and Seneca, as well as the great historians—Livy, Sallust, Tacitus, and Lucian. Thomas More makes use of all these authors in *Utopia*, whether citing them by name, as a source (Tacitus's *Germania*),[70]

---

68. Cresacre states that Morton placed More in Canterbury College (Cresacre More, 18), but Anthony à Wood quotes Miles Windsor's notes that More stayed in St. Mary's Hall (*Athenae Oxoniensis*, 1691–92, vol. 1, col. 32, ed. P. Bliss 2 vols. (Oxford, 1815–20), cited by Jeremy Catto, *Oriel College: A History* (Oxford: Oxford University Press, 2013), 60–70. Catto notes that Morton's exhibitioners at Oxford were housed in one of the colleges or halls of the university, so More could have been a Morton scholar and a member of the Hall of St. Mary the Virgin. All the sources agree that More was a Morton scholar. Catto favors Windsor's testimony, and suggests that Cresacre's error is due to the fact that the warden of Canterbury College administered the funds of Morton's exhibitions. See also Catto, "The Triumph of the Hall in Fifteenth-Century Oxford," in *Lordship and Learning: Studies in Memory of Trevor Aston*, ed. Ralph Evans (Woodbridge: Boydell Press, 2004), 222.

69. Leach, *Schools of Medieval England*, 262.

70. *CW* 4, clxii.

or in quotation (for instance, "*Caelo tegitur qui non habet urnam*" comes from Lucan's *De bello civili*),[71] or imitating their style (Virgil, Horace, and Ovid). All of them must have been available to him between 1486 and 1494, whether at St. Anthony's School in London, in the household of John Morton in Lambeth, or at St. Mary's Hall in Oxford.

St. Mary's Hall was where most of the younger pupils of Oriel College were educated. Oxford masters were adjusting to changing values, in the first place to the more classical and elegant Latinity taught at the new endowed schools such as Winchester, Eton, Magdalen College School, and St. Anthony's. But the Oxford colleges and academic halls also took pride in imparting to their alumni a broader education than the limited training that the traditional faculties had provided until then. Emphasis was laid on inculcating a Ciceronian sense of public responsibility. In the *Statuta aularia*, a code drawn up about 1490 for undergraduates in academic halls, university education was no longer restricted to those aiming for a doctorate in the traditional subjects of theology, laws, or medicine, but offered to students who might seek a more general and humanistic education in which residence at Oxford was only part of a path that might also include a season at the Inns of Court, as was the case of Thomas More, or a period of study of Greek or humanistic letters in Italy.[72]

Legal Training; London Lawyer

In the period between Thomas More's return from Oxford at the age of sixteen and his wedding, shortly before he turned twenty-seven, we can see various important facets to his life, including his training in the law and later practice and teaching of it; his dedication to letters; his study of the scriptures and Church Fathers; the practice of his Christian life; and his relations with friends. At times biographers have seen contradictions between these different facets; but there is nothing surprising in a young man having varied interests, activities, and influences. Though all aspects of his life are in fact related, consideration will be given to the areas mentioned. We will start with his law training and move on to his study of the Christian faith, and then—in the following chapters—his desires for sanctity and finally his involvement in literary matters; nevertheless, it is important to bear in mind that all these facets are present throughout this period of his *formative years*.

71. Lucan, *De bello civili* 7.818–19. However, More could have encountered the phrase in St. Augustine, *De civitate Dei* 1.12, rather than during his school or Oxford days.

72. Catto, *Oriel College: A History*, 60.

Thomas More's outlook throughout his life was shaped, in part, by his legal training. After two years in Oxford University he returned to London and enrolled at New Inn, one of the Inns of Chancery: these were essentially preparatory schools for those aspiring to join one of the Inns of Court. It was not uncommon in this period to leave Oxford or Cambridge without pursuing a university degree: in fact, this was often the route followed by those preparing for public life via a legal career in one of the Inns.[73] Fifty years later this was still the case; a figure like Sir Francis Walsingham (c. 1532–90), principal secretary to Elizabeth I, attended King's College Cambridge without gaining a degree, and then moved to Gray's Inn in London. Oxford and Cambridge and the Inns of Court were the natural path for those not in the nobility who aspired to play a leading role in the society of the time. Roper, himself a member of the same Inn of Court as More, Lincoln's Inn, shows no surprise when recounting that Cardinal Morton placed More in Oxford, but that when he was "sufficiently instructed, he was then for the study of the laws of the Realm put to an Inn of Chancellery called New Inn," and "from thence was admitted to Lincoln's Inn … continuing there his study until he was made and accompted a worthy utter barrister."[74] Thomas More's name appears in the register of Lincoln's Inn on February 12, 1496, soon after he reached eighteen years of age.[75]

More seems to have acquired considerable prestige during his training at Lincoln's Inn. Once a barrister he taught law at Furnival's Inn, an Inn of Chancery that depended on Lincoln's Inn; later he gave lectures at Lincoln's Inn as *Autumn Reader* (1511), and on All Saints' Day 1514 he was nominated Lenten Reader for 1515, the highest honor that an Inn of Court could confer on a barrister.[76] He was elected one of the Inn's four governors and treasurer for 1511–12, although he declined to serve as treasurer. In 1514 he was admitted to the Society of Advocates, which at a later time came to be known as Doctors' Commons. At the date of his election, Cuthbert Tunstall, John Colet, and William Grocyn were members of the Society.[77]

---

73. Joanne Paul, *Thomas More*, Classic Thinkers (Cambridge: Polity Press), 17.

74. Roper, 5:15–23.

75. The entry reads, "Thomas More admissus est in Societatem xij Februarii anno supradicto et pardonatur ei quatuor vacationes ad instanciam Johannis More patris sui." The commentary provided by Lincoln's Inn indicates that the "vacationes" were periods of intense study. More's time at New Inn would have enabled him to progress quickly though the established stages of legal training, although the dispensation was requested by John More, who was a Bencher (senior member) of the Inn.

76. Guy, *The Public Career of Sir Thomas More* (New Haven: Yale University Press, 1980), 5; Germain Marc'hadour, *L'Univers de Thomas More*, Librairie Philosophique (Paris: J. Vrin, 1963), 207.

77. Richard O'Sullivan, "St. Thomas More and Lincoln's Inn," in *Essential Articles for the Study of Thomas More*, ed. Richard S. Sylvester and Germain Marc'hadour (Hamden, Conn.: Archon, 1977), 165.

More's involvement in public life began early, for in 1504, soon after becoming a barrister, he served in Parliament as a burgess, representing the London merchants that his family knew so well.[78] In 1509 he was appointed Justice of the Peace for Middlesex, the county that included London (although the city was an independent corporation). In 1510 he was appointed undersheriff of the city of London: in this capacity he provided legal advice to senior officers of the corporation, and presided over the sheriff's court. The undersheriff was in fact a key post, which placed More at the heart of the city's life and at the same time gave him a vivid sense of the social problems played out before the courts.[79] When in 1516 he completed *Utopia*, he signed himself as "Citizen and Undersheriff of the Famous City of London"—*clarissimi disertissimique viri Thomae Mori inclytae civitatis Londinensis civis et Vicecomitis.* It was as a representative of the city's interests that he was first drawn into the king's service; as a royal servant he subsequently became a member of the Court of Star Chamber (1516); king's councillor and master of requests (1518); undertreasurer of the realm (1521; he was knighted the same year); high steward of the University of Oxford (1524) and of the University of Cambridge (1525); and chancellor of the Duchy of Lancaster (1525). Finally, at the fall of Cardinal Wolsey, he was chosen to be lord chancellor on October 29, 1529.

But here the focus is not More's later achievements as a lawyer and royal servant, but the legal training that he acquired early on and its influence in fields other than his legal career. A key feature of such training in the Inns of Court was the practice of moots, mock trials arranged to examine hypothetical cases as academic exercises: this mock-judicial examination of cases appears throughout More's writings. The first published instance of this is the response to *The Declamation pro tyrannicida* that More added to his *Translations of Lucian* (1506). This work will be considered later, but here it is worth noticing that in the 1517 edition More emphasised his professional qualification as a lawyer by stating that he was the undersheriff of London.[80]

As undersheriff of the city of London, More went together with Cuthbert Tunstall in 1515 on a commission to negotiate with the representatives of Prince Charles of Habsburg, Duke of Burgundy. Tunstall was a church-

---

78. Gerard B. Wegemer, *Thomas More: A Profile of Courage* (Princeton, N.J.: Scepter Press, 1996), 17.

79. Dominic Baker-Smith, *Stanford Encyclopaedia of Philosophy*, 2014, entry on Thomas More, accessed online on May 12, 2021.

80. *CW* 3.I, lix: *Thoma Moro Britanno vicecomite et ciue Londinensi interprete.*

man (he was later bishop of London) and the political leader of the embassy; More was included as a voice for city interests, since the matters related to English trade.[81] This and subsequent embassies were occasions for More to get acquainted with European humanists such as Peter Giles, Frans van Cranevelt, and Guillaume Budé—all of them, like him, married laymen and highly educated lawyer-humanists.

Peter Giles (1486–1533) was a magistrate and the chief secretary of Antwerp (his father had been the assistant treasurer of the city), and he had been trained in Latin and Greek, as well as in Roman and canon law. Erasmus had met Giles around 1505; having traveled to England in early May 1515, on May 7 he wrote to Giles introducing Tunstall and More:

Two of the best scholars in the whole of England, Cuthbert Tunstall, the chancellor of the archbishop of Canterbury, and Thomas More, to whom I dedicated my *Moria*, both great friends of mine, are in Bruges. If anything should emerge in which you can do them a service, your civility will prove to have been very well invested.[82]

The English delegation arrived in Bruges on May 17, 1515, and discussions between the Englishmen and the representatives of Prince Charles continued until July, when the Flemish negotiators were recalled in order to consult with the prince in Brussels. This gave More the opportunity to travel to Antwerp and meet Giles. Later he was to write to Erasmus, "In all my travels I had no greater good fortune than the society of Peter Giles."[83] The two of them had a similar background as lawyers in the service of their cities, and the description of the cities of Utopia and their government occupies a large part of the "Discourse on Utopia," the main section of book 2 of *Utopia*.[84] It is not, perhaps, too fanciful to imagine that this description may have arisen from conversations between them[85] while More was staying in Giles's house, as Marc'hadour suggests.[86] Back in Bruges More would then have put down the description of Utopia in writing, adding the fictional setting: his house in Antwerp, Giles's visit there and his introduction of Raphael Hythloday to More, and More's invitation to Hythloday to talk as they sat on a bench in his garden.[87] Back in London, More wrote the rest

81. Thomas More, *Utopia*, trans., ed., with an introduction by Dominic Baker-Smith (London: Penguin, 2012), xiv.

82. *CWE*, Letter 332.

83. *CWE* Letter 388:158.

84. CW 4, 110–236.

85. *CW* 4, xxxi–xxxii.

86. *L'Univers*, 221.

87. *CW* 4, 47–51 and 109.

of book 1 and completed the whole work, including a preface addressed to Peter Giles.

Frans van Cranevelt (1485–1564) became a *Doctor utriusque juris* (of canon and civil law) in 1510, and from 1515 followed a legal career in government, first as a legal adviser to the magistrate of the city of Bruges and later as a member of the Burgundian Great Council at Mechlin, where he lived until his death. He became the focal point of humanism at the court of Burgundy.[88] There are thirteen extant letters from More to Cranevelt: they are delightful letters that show the friendship between the two humanists. More had met Cranevelt while on diplomatic mission (although he did not meet either him or Budé during that first visit to the Netherlands), but the letters remain strictly informal, omitting any reference to More's official business, and do not add any further insights into More's legal training.

Guillaume Budé (1467/8–1540) had also studied law and worked as one of the royal secretaries of the French king Francis I. His friendship and correspondence with More are dealt with in more detail in chapter 7; but it may be of interest here to mention a long letter he wrote to Thomas Lupset on July 31, 1517, which was included in the second edition of *Utopia*, as his praise of *Utopia* concentrates on what it has to say about the law. Budé writes:

I might almost say we are bound to admit that the aim of legal training and the profession of the civil law, is to make each man act with ingrained and calculated malice towards the neighbour to whom he is linked by ties of citizenship and sometimes of blood. He is always grabbing something, taking it away, extorting it, suing for it, squeezing it out, breaking it loose, gouging it away, twisting it off, snatching it, snitching it, filching it, pinching it, pilfering it, pouncing on it—partly with the tacit complicity of laws, partly with their direct sanction, he carries off what he wants and makes it his own.[89]

Budé saw in More's hints in *Utopia* a refutation of the opinion that

only men skilled in the ways—or perhaps just the wiles—of the law, only those who set snares for unwary citizens, artist of the legal phrase or fraud, contrivers of complicated contracts, fosters of litigation, exponents of a perverse, confused and unjust justice—only such men as these are to be thought the high priests of justice and equity. They only are qualified to say peremptorily what is just and good.[90]

88. Hubertus Schulte Herbrüggen, "More to Cranevelt, New Baudouin Letters," *Supplementa Humanistica Lovaniensia* XI (Leuven: Leuven University Press, 1997); introduction, 31.

89. *CU* 8:19–26.

90. *CU* 8:29–34.

In book 2 of *Utopia*, Raphael Hythloday explains to More and Peter Giles what he found in the imaginary island, including much of legal interest. The society in the Isle of Utopia is by no means an ideal society: there are disputes between private parties;[91] there are idle people;[92] there are offenses such as clandestine premarital intercourse;[93] husbands chastise their wives, and parents their children; the gravest crimes are punished by slavery or even death; seduction and attempted seduction are penalized;[94] to mock a person for being deformed or crippled is reproachable; and running for office is condemned. So the citizens of Utopia share in the human condition of being attracted by evil as well as good. Nevertheless, the legal system, according to Hythloday, is praiseworthy in many ways: magistrates are held in honor and called "Fathers," and that indeed is the way they behave;[95] there are very few laws and so they are well known to all.

—

So far More's legal mind has been considered up to the time of publishing *Utopia*. In 1518 he entered the service of Henry VIII; in that same year Martin Luther's theses began to circulate, in Germany and more widely in Europe, and soon Lutheran books started arriving in England. In 1528 Cuthbert Tunstall, by then bishop of London, asked More to defend orthodoxy through his writings, and More wrote *A Dialogue of Sir Thomas More, Knight* (1529) in which he criticized the ideas of Luther and Tyndale.

In his *Dialogue*, More went back to the use of moots that he had practiced at Lincoln's Inn. The setting is similar to that of the dialogue-form of *Utopia*. There the conversation between Raphael Hythloday, Peter Giles, and More took place in the garden of Peter Giles's house; the *Dialogue* of 1529 takes place in More's house in Chelsea, where he receives a fictional young messenger who has heard of, and seems influenced by, the Lutheran ideas that were circulating. More takes up the objections that he thinks are being raised by the Lutheran and, as in a moot, gives arguments against them. His interlocutor accepts some of More's answers but returns for further questions or clarifications. The *Dialogue* is the most successful of More's polemical works precisely because it is not written as a direct riposte to an opponent but as dialogue that enacts the process of persuasion.[96] The full title is

91. *CU* 123.
92. *CU* 127.
93. *CU* 188.
94. *CU* 193.
95. *CU* 195.
96. Baker-Smith, "Thomas More," in *Stanford Encyclopaedia of Philosophy*, accessed online on

A Dialogue of Sir Thomas More, Knight, one of the Council of our sovereign lord the King, and Chancellor of his Duchy of Lancaster. Wherein be treated diverse matters, as of the veneration and worship of images and relics, praying to saints, and going on pilgrimage, with many other things touching the pestilent sect of Luther and Tyndale, by the one begun in Saxony, and by the other labored to be brought into England.

Therefore, it is not surprising that Tyndale replied by his *Answer* to More's *Dialogue*, and More wrote his lengthy *Confutation of Tyndale's Answer*.[97] It was no longer a matter of making use of the practice of moots or dealing with hypothetical cases; rather More, in his capacity of lord chancellor of England, as he introduced himself in the title of the *Confutation and* emphasized in the Preface to the Reader, undertook the task of replying to each statement put forward by Tyndale.

Now—seeing the King's gracious purpose in this point—I reckon that, being his unworthy Chancellor, it appertains, as I said, unto my part and duty to follow the example of his noble Grace.[98]

In this More uses the professional skills and thoroughness he had acquired as a lawyer,[99] trying to convey accurately the meaning of Tyndale's arguments, as he explained in *The Apology of Sir Thomas More, Knight* (1533) after his resignation as Chancellor. There he explained that in his polemical works he tried never "to misrehearse [misrepresent] any man's argument," but always to "rehearse their reason to the best that they can make it themselves."[100] This required More to quote much of Tyndale's text directly and made the *Confutation* extraordinarily long; as More remarks, not without a touch of humor, "It is a shorter thing and sooner done to write heresies than to answer them."[101]

More's legal mind is also apparent in *De Tristitia*, his last work, written in the Tower when he was deprived of most of his usual sources and had to limit himself to John Gerson's *Monotessaron* (which he explicitly says he is following in writing of Christ's agony) and the *Catena aurea* of St. Thomas Aquinas. The *Catena* is a compilation of commentaries on each passage of the four Gospels from the Fathers of the Church and some other ancient Christian writers. At times More found conflicting opinions in the *Catena*,

---

May 12, 2021; see also Eamon Duffy, "Thomas More and Heresy," in *Reformation Divided* (London: Bloomsbury, 2017), 74.

    97. The *Confutation* occupies 1,034 pages in *CW* 8.

    98. *CW* 8, 28:17–20.

    99. Duffy, *Reformation Divided*, 81.

    100. *CW* 9, 6:26–28.

    101. *CW* 9, 8:15.

and he seems to be in dialogue with various authors, listening to their arguments before then, having made up his mind, presenting his own conclusions.

Of course, More's caution and prudence in dealing with Henry VIII's attempt to get his marriage with Queen Catherine annulled, and later in More's own defense, were those of a skillful lawyer, but a crucial point in considering More as a lawyer is his adherence to the truth. On the morning of Monday April 13, 1534, More refused to swear the Act of Succession, because to have done so would have been to assert that the king's marriage to Catherine was invalid, and More knew that it was valid. "Thus, taking the oath would be, for him, asserting publicly, and with God as his witness before men, a deliberate falsehood, intended to deceive others about the state of his own belief—in short, it would be to lie."[102] It would be wrong to see the final and fatal developments of More's life as based on his study of rhetoric, the practice of moots, and the knowledge of the laws of the realm that he acquired in Lincoln's Inn. John Finnis puts it as follows:

In refusing the Oath, More was (I believe) relying on two conscientious judgements: (a) that the marriage to Catherine was valid and in conformity with divine law, and (b) that to declare on oath that something is *not* the case when one actually judges that it *is* the case is to lie, which is always against divine law.[103]

At the same time that Thomas More was studying and beginning to practice law, he developed an interest in the Fathers of the Church and Church history. Of course, this cannot be dissociated from his pursuit of piety: Erasmus, in his letter to von Hutten, brings these two aspects together, writing that More "devoted himself actively to reading the works of the orthodox Fathers. On St. Augustine's *City of God* he gave public lectures before large audiences while still a young man [c. 1501]; priests and old men were not ashamed to seek instruction in holy things from a young man and a layman, or sorry they had done so. And all the time he applied his whole mind to the pursuit of piety."[104]

All through his life More showed deep knowledge of sacred scripture and of the Fathers of the Church. In some of the works written while he was in the Tower of London, he cites scripture and the Fathers by heart. Especially interesting is the dedicatory letter of 1506 to Thomas Ruthall that prefaces his translations of Lucian's *Dialogues*, where he says, "My choice …

---

102. John Finnis, "Faith, Morals, and Thomas More," in *Collected Essays: Volume V, Religion and Public Reasons* (Oxford: Oxford University Press, 2011), 163–78. John Finnis is a professor of law and political and legal philosophy in the University of Oxford and at the University of Notre Dame.

103. Finnis, "Faith, Morals, and Thomas More," 170.

104. Erasmus (1519), in *CWE* 7, Ep. 999:168–73.

is endorsed by the estimable approval of St. John Chrysostom, a man of the most acute judgment, of all learned men perhaps the most Christian and (at least in my opinion) of all Christians the most learned."[105] To express such an opinion at the age of twenty-eight implies a considerable prior study of the matter. In the same letter More refers to St. Augustine several times; and he has definite views on particular issues of doctrine, shown in such statements as, "We ought to place unquestioning trust in the stories commended to us by divinely inspired scripture, but testing the others carefully and deliberately by the teaching of Christ."[106]

The Text of the Letter of October 23

Thomas Stapleton introduces the letter of October 23, saying, "I add a copy of the letter because up to now it has not been printed, and it is an eloquent testimony to More's piety as a young man."[107] A revised translation of the letter follows, one that takes into account prior versions.

A commentary on the letter is given in the footnotes. In summary, More writes that while walking through the marketplace and meeting a servant of John Colet, he was disappointed to learn that Colet was not returning to London, because he was a great help to More's spiritual life. Without Colet, More finds himself at a loss and without support in his struggle to grow in virtue, for in the city and in the marketplace his soul has to endure the dangers of the world's attractions. More understands the advantages Colet finds in the country as opposed to the city, but asks him to return, not only for More's own sake but because London requires the service of such a spiritual physician.

In the letter there are references and allusions to, or echoes of, Plato, Terence, Cicero, Virgil, Ovid, Seneca, and Boethius, as well as St. John Chrysostom and St. Ambrose. The description of one's spiritual advisor as the physician of the soul[108] comes from St. John Chrysostom's *Homilies on the Gospel of St. Matthew*,[109] which will be considered in chapter 3; it is also mentioned in the *Regula Pastoralis* of St. Gregory the Great.[110] It is, of course, something of a commonplace in spiritual writing.

---

105. *CW* 3, part I, *Translations of Lucian*, 3, lines 28–31.
106. *CW* 3, part I, *Translations of Lucian*, 7, lines 17–20.
107. Stapleton, 10.
108. See letter, lines 41–59.
109. Homily 29 §3 on Matthew 9:1–2.
110. St. Gregory the Great, *Regulae Pastoralis Liber*, part I, chapter 1.

	THOMAS MORUS IOANNI COLETO SUO S.D.[111]	Thomas More greets his own dear John Colet.
1 [112]	Ambulanti mihi dudum in foro, et inter aliena negotia ocianti obtulit se puer tuus.	As I was recently walking in Cheapside,[113] the market-place, at leisure among the business stalls of others, your servant made his presence felt.
2–3	Quem quum primum intuerer, vehementer sum gauisus; tum quod hic ipse mihi semper charus extitit, tum praecipue quod arbitrabar eum non sine te venisse.	At first I was delighted to see him, both because he has always been dear to me, and especially because I thought he would not have come without you.
4–6	At vbi ab illo didici te non modo non rediisse, sed nec adhuc diu rediturum, dici non potest ex quanta laetitia in quantam moestitiam reiectus sum.	But when I heard from him not only that you had not returned, but that you would not return for a long time, I cannot tell you from what rejoicing I was cast into what dejection.
7–10	Quid enim mihi potest esse molestius quam suauissima consuetudine tua priuari? cuius prudentissimo consilio frui, cuius iucundissimo conuictu recreari, cuius grauissimis concionibus excitari, cuius exemplo et vita promoueri; in cuius denique vultu ipso ac nutu solebam conquiescere.	For what could be more grievous to me than to be deprived of your most pleasant companionship, whose prudent advice I enjoyed, by whose most delightful company I was refreshed, by whose powerful sermons I was stirred, by whose example and life I was guided, and, finally, in whose very countenance and nod I was accustomed to find pleasure?
11–12	Itaque vt his praesidiis vallatus aliquando me sensi roborari; ita eisdem destitutus languere mihi ferme videor ac solui.	And while protected by these defences I felt myself strengthened; now that I am deprived of them I almost seem to languish and grow feeble.
13–17	Et qui tua nuper vestigia sequutus iam pene ex ipsis orci faucibus emerseram, nunc rursum tanquam Euridice (contraria tamen lege; Euridice quidem quod illam respexit Orpheus, ego vero quia tu me non respicis) in obscuras retro caligines nescio qua vi ac necessitate relabor.	By following your footsteps I had recently escaped almost from the very gates of hell, and now, driven by some force and necessity, I am falling back again into gruesome darkness. I am like Eurydice, except that she was lost because Orpheus looked back at her, but I am sinking because you do not look back at me.[114]

111. Salutem dicit.

112. The numbers correspond to the line numbers of the Latin text given in the *Correspondence* (1947), Letter [3].

113. The name of Cheapside was introduced here by Cresacre More, as explained at the beginning of this chapter.

114. The story of Orpheus and Eurydice was well known at the time of More, mainly through

18–20	Nam in vrbe quid est quod quenquam ad bene viuendum moueat, ac non potius suopte ingenio nitentem in arduum virtutis callem euadere, mille machinamentis reuocet, illecebris mille resorbeat?	For in the city what is there to move one to live well? But rather, when a man is straining in his own power to climb the steep path of virtue,[115] it turns him back by a thousand devices and sucks him back by a thousand enticements.
21	Quocunque te conferas, quid aliud quam hinc fictus amor et blande adulatorurm mellita venena circumsonant;	Wherever you turn, on one side nothing but feigned love and the honeyed poisons of smooth flatterers resound;
22–23	hinc odia saeua et querulae lites ac forenses strepitus obmurmurant?	on the other, fierce hatreds and complaints, quarrels and the din of the market place[116] murmur against you.
24–25	Quocunque tuleris oculos, quid aliud videas quam cupedinarios, cetarios, lanios, coquos, fartores, piscatores, aucupes, qui materiam ventri ministrant,[117] ac mundo et principi eius diabolo?	Wherever you turn your eyes, what else will you see but confectioners, fishmongers, butchers, cooks, poulterers, fishermen, fowlers, who supply the materials for the belly and for the world and the world's lord, the devil?

the works of Ovid, *Metamorphoses*, 10, 1–85, and Virgil, *Georgics* 4, 453–56. It was also depicted in paintings from antiquity, and soon after this letter it was painted by Titian (*c.* 1508). In More's allusion there is a reproach which may be related to Plato's reference to Orpheus in the *Symposium*, 179d. For the reference to Orpheus and Eurydice in Boethius's *De Consolatione Philosophiae,* see chapter 2. Boethius often mentions Seneca, and Seneca narrates the tale of Orpheus and Eurydice in *Hercules Furens,* 570–95. Thomas More mentioned Orpheus and Eurydice later on in his Latin poem on how to choose a wife (*CW* 3, II, Poem no. 143:158); there he assumes that Orpheus would never have devoted such great effort to recovering Eurydice if she had been an uncultivated woman.

115. Álvaro de Silva (*La Correspondencia de Tomás Moro, 1499–1534* [Madrid: Rialp, 1998]) translates these words into Spanish as "el camino empinado de la santidad," "the steep path to holiness," which seems an accurate translation within More's Christian context.

116. Elizabeth Rogers translates "forenses strepitus" as "the din of the forum" (*SL*, Letter 2).

117. Cicero, *De Officiis* I, XLII, 150: *Minimeque artes eae probandae, que ministrae sunt voluptatum: cetárii, lanií, coqui, fartóres, piscatóres, ut ait Terentius.* Terence, *Eunuchus*, II-II, 25–26: *cupediarii omnes, cetarii, lanii, coqui, fartores, piscatores.* Here More follows both Cicero and Terence; his list of trades includes "cupedinarios," who are included in Terence's list but not in Cicero's, and he finds these trades in the market place as mentioned by Terence, *Eunuchus*, II-II, 24. But the last words of More's sentence—*qui materiam ventri ministrant*—echo Cicero, who writes that all those trades cater to sensual pleasures, although More goes further in saying that they supply material for gluttony and the world and the devil.

Cicero had mentioned Terence previously in Book I.IX, 30: *"Quamquam Terentianus ille Chremes 'humani nihil a se alienum putat.'"* This citation is taken up by More in one of his last works: "Certainly if that saying of the comic poet is so highly approved, 'Since I am a man, I consider nothing human to be foreign to me—*Homo quum sim, humani nihil a me alienum puto*—how could it be anything but disgraceful for Christians to snore while other Christians are in danger?" (*De Tristitia Christi*, in *CW* 14, 339:1–2). Here again More's citation is taken from Terence's text.

The references to the *De Officiis* in this letter seem especially relevant because in book I,

26–27	Tecta quin etiam ipsa nescio quo modo bonam partem lucis eripiunt, nec coelum libere sinunt intueri.	Indeed, even houses block out from us I know not how large a measure of the light, and do not permit us freely to see the heavens.
28	Aërem itaque non ὁρίζωνος[118] ille circulus, sed domorum culmen determinat.	And it is not the round horizon, but rather the lofty roofs, that define the sky.
29–31	Quo aequior tibi sum si minime te adhuc ruris paeniteat; quippe vbi simplicem turbam vides, et vrbicae fraudis expertem:	I really cannot blame you if you are not yet tired of the country[119] where you live among simple people, unversed in the deceits of the city;
31–32	vbi quoquo versus oculos intendas, blanda telluris facies iuuat, aëris grata reficit temperies, ipse te coeli delectat aspectus.	wherever you cast your eyes, the smiling face of the earth greets you, the sweet fresh air invigorates you, the very sight of the heavens charms you.
33–34	Nihil ibi vides nisi benigna naturae munera et sancta quaedam innocentiae vestigia.	There you see nothing but the generous gifts of nature and some holy traces of innocence.
35	Nolo tamen his oblectationibus adeo capiaris, quin quum primum possis ad nos reuoles.	But yet I do not wish you to be so captivated by these delights as to be unwilling to fly back to us as soon as possible.
36–40	Nam si tibi displicent vrbis incommoda, at Stephani rus (cuius etiam non minus debes esse sollicitus) haud minora tibi commoda suppeditabit, quam quod nunc incolis: vnde etiam in vrbem (vbi magna tibi merendi materia est) potes interdum tanquam in hospitium diuertere.	For if the inconveniences of the city so displease you, your country parish of Stepney (of which you should have no less care) will afford you hardly fewer advantages than where you now dwell, whence you can sometimes turn aside, as to an inn, to the city (where you have great opportunity of acquiring merit).

nos. 115–51, Cicero is dealing with one's "vocation and mode of life" or "calling in life" (translation by Walter Miller in Loeb, no. 30, from *institutum*—XXXII, no. 116, *morum institutorumque*—no. 120, *autem genere vitae*—no. 121).

118. More uses the Greek word because it was not recognised in Classical Latin: Cicero used "finiens orbis," and Seneca "finiens circulus" (see "finio," I.B., in Lewis and Short, *Latin Dictionary* [Oxford: Clarendon Press, 1962]).

119. The contraposition between the country, a place of study and contemplation, and the busy-ness of the city is a common theme from Antiquity and was taken up in the Renaissance; see, e.g., Erasmus's letter to Budé of 1521 (*EE* Ep. 1233:185–87). Cicero touches on the theme in *De Officiis*, book I.VI, 19: "To be drawn by study away from active life is contrary to moral duty. For the whole glory of virtue is in activity; activity, however, may often be interrupted, and many opportunities for returning to study are opened." In this letter More similarly tells Colet that he cannot keep away from his task of ministering in London in order to be able to study in the country, as he is needed in the city—but he will have opportunities for study in then-rural Stepney.

41–42	Nam ruri quum sint homines ipsi per se aut fere innocui, aut certe non adeo magnis sceleribus irretiti, cuiusque medici manus vtilis esse potest.	For in the country, where men are of themselves either almost innocent, or at least not ensnared in great sins, the services of any physician can be useful.
43–44	At in vrbe tum propter ingentem magnitudinem, tum ob inueteratam morborum consuetudinem medicus omnis frustra nisi peritissimus accesserit.	But in the city because of the great numbers that congregate there, and because of their long-standing habits of disease, any physician will have come in vain unless he be the most skillful.
45	Veniunt certe in D. Pauli suggestum aliquando qui sanitatem pollicentur.	Certainly, there come from time to time into the pulpit at St Paul's preachers who promise health;
46–47	Sed quum speciose perorasse videntur, adeo vita cum verbis litigat, vt irritent potius quam mitigent.	but, although they seem to have spoken very eloquently, their life is in such sharp contrast to their words that they irritate rather than soothe.
48–49	Non enim persuadere possent hominibus, vt quum ipsi sunt omnium aegrotissimi, idonei credantur quibus alienarum aegritudinum cura merito committatur.	For they cannot bring men to believe that though they are themselves obviously in direst need of the physician's help, they are yet fit to be entrusted with the cure of other men's ailments.[120]
50–51	Itaque morbos suos quum ab his tractari sentiunt quos exulceratos vident, indignantur illicet atque recalcitrant.	And thus when men see that their diseases are being prescribed for by physicians who are themselves covered with ulcers, they immediately become indignant and obstinate.
52–54	At si (vt naturarum indagatores affirmant) is demum medicus ad sanitatem appositus est, in quo aegrotus maximam habet spem; quis dubitet quin te vno ad curandam vniuersam vrbem nemo possit esse salubrior?	But if (as observers of human nature assert), he is the best physician in whom the patient has the greatest confidence, who can doubt that you are the one who can do most for the cure of all in the city?
55–59	A quo quam aequo animo vulnera sua tractari patiantur, quantum confidant, quantum pareant, et tute antehac satis expertus es, et nunc apud omnes tui desiderium atque incredibilis quaedam expectatio declarat.	Their readiness to allow you to treat their wounds, their trust, their obedience you have yourself proved in the past, and now the universal desire and anticipation of you proclaim it all again.

120. St Gregory the Great writes that "he is a poor and unskilled physician who aims at healing others but is ignorant of his own ailment"; *Regula Pastoralis*, part III, ch. 24.

60–63	Venias ergo tandem, mi Colete, vel Stephani tui gratia qui haud secus diuturnam tui gemit absentiam quam infantuli matris; vel patriae tuae causa cuius haud minor tibi cura esse debet quam parentum.	Come then, my dear Colet, for Stepney's sake, which mourns your long absence as children their mother's; or for the sake of your native place which should be no less dear to you than are your parents.
63–64	Postremo (quanquam hoc minimum sit reducendi tui momentum) mei te respectus commoueat, qui me tibi totum dedidi, et in aduentum tuum sollicitus pendeo.	Finally (though this will be but a weak reason for your return), let your regard for me, who am entirely devoted to you and hang anxiously upon your coming, move you.
65–68	Interea cum Grocino, Linacro, et Lilio nostro tempus transigam, altero (vt tu scis) solo (dum tu abes) vitae meae magistro; altero studiorum praeceptore; tertio charissimo rerum mearum socio.	Meanwhile, I shall pass my time with Grocyn, Linacre, and our dear friend Lily: the first (as you know) the sole guide of my life while you are away; the second my master in learning; the third the dearest partner of my endeavours.
69	Vale: et nos, vt facis, ama. Londini 10. Calend. Nouembres.	Farewell, and continue to love us as you do. London, 23 October

Date of the Letter

The year of the letter is not given in Stapleton's *Tres Thomae*, but it is certainly relevant to ascertain it, if possible, in the context of Thomas More's early choices. Stapleton seems to assume that when More wrote the letter, Colet was dean of St. Paul's Cathedral.[121] On the other hand, Cresacre More, who gives an English translation of the letter in his account, takes it for granted that the letter was written before More got married. However, the marriage took place in January 1505 at the latest, and Colet was appointed dean of St. Paul's in 1505; thus, the proposed chronology does not fit.

Samuel Knight[122] tried to determine the date Colet became dean of St. Paul by reference to the inscription on Colet's monument in the cathedral. The monument was destroyed in the Fire of London in 1666, but in

121. Stapleton, 10.

122. Samuel Knight, *The Life of Dr J. Colet, Dean of St Paul's and founder of S. Paul's School* (Oxford: Clarendon Press, 1823), 227.

1656 the Mercers' Company commissioned a plaque with a line engraving of the monument, "lest the building of St. Paul were to collapse." William Dugdale's *History of St. Paul's Cathedral with Figures of Tombs and Monuments* (1658)[123] includes the plaque on page 64, together with (on the facing page, page 65) a transcription of the various texts inscribed on the monument. The text on the tomb in the lower part of the monument reads:

> HIC SITUS EST D. Jo. Coletus, … : vixit An. 53,
> administravit xvi. obiit anno 1519.

Based on this inscription, Knight argued that Colet was made dean of St. Paul's in 1503, sixteen years before 1519, and that More's letter to Colet was written on October 23, 1504. Allen and Rogers accepted this explanation,[124] but it is problematic. J. H. Lupton recorded an equivalent version of the inscription (*administravit 16. obviit anno 1519*) in his *Life of John Colet*, but added in a footnote that in Payne Fisher's account "the last two lines differ considerably: *Ecclesiam vigil multos annos administravit Et decessit Anno Dom. MDXVIII*."[125] But this is incorrect: the phrase is not to be found in Fisher's *The Tombs, Monuments, &c., visible in S. Paul's Cathedral Previous to its Destruction by Fire*.[126] Instead, on page 74 Fisher reproduces exactly the same Latin text as that given in Dugdale's *History*: *vixit An. 53, administravit xvi. obiit anno 1519*. It is his English translation (on the facing page, page 75) that gives the vaguer turn of phrase: "He many Years together vigilantly Administered, and Governed The Affairs of this Church, And Dyed in the Year of Grace, 1519." Perhaps Fisher was aware that the Latin chronology was incorrect; in any case, it is clear that the chronology proposed by Knight, based on Dugdale, is not trustworthy.

In the volume of the *Fasti Ecclesiae Anglicanae* dedicated to St. Paul's Cathedral, it is stated that the dean of St. Paul's was Robert Sherborne from 1499 to 1505, and John Colet from 1505 to 1519. However, a footnote to the entry in the *Fasti* states that "there is some evidence to suggest that Colet succeeded in early 1504 … but Robert Sherborne [was] still dean on 27 January 1504 (Lamb., Reg. Warham 1 f. 6)." Pope Julius II appointed

---

123. William Dugdale, *The History of St. Pauls Cathedral, … with figures of Tombs, and Monuments* (London: T. Warren, 1658). A copy of the line engraving is kept in the National Portrait Gallery, NPG D24287, where it is suggested that it may have been done by Wenceslaus Hollar.

124. *EE* vol. I, Ep.181, page 404, note to line 18; *Correspondence*, page 5, introduction to Letter [3].

125. J. H. Lupton, *Life of John Colet* (London, 1887), 238fn1.

126. Payne Fisher, *Tombs, Monuments, &c, Visible in S. Paul's Cathedral Previous to Its Destruction by Fire, A.D. 1666* (1668), rev., ed. George Blacker Morgan, (1885), 73–76.

Sherborne bishop of St. David's on January 5, 1505, to succeed John Morgan, who had died between April 24 and May 19, 1504. Erasmus wrote to Colet in December 1504, congratulating him on obtaining his doctor's degree on being appointed dean of St. Paul's.[127] It is probable that possible replacements for first the bishopric of St. David's and then the deanship of St. Paul's would have been considered following John Morgan's death in early 1504. In any event, More's letter to Colet does not assume that Colet was already dean of St. Paul's; he mentions the preachers to be found at St. Paul's pulpit from time to time, but that does not imply any present or future relationship of Colet with the deanship, particularly as the reference is probably to the Cathedral's open-air pulpit of Paul's Cross, which was often used by "guest" preachers. In fact, Grocyn preached at St. Paul's in 1501.

Like Grocyn, Linacre, and Lily, Colet spent some years in Europe. The date of his return to England is unknown but was probably sometime in 1495 or 1496. At this point he went to Oxford, where he is said to have settled in Magdalen College; it is assumed he remained there until 1504 or 1505. It would seem, however, that during this period Colet spent enough time in London or Stepney to become an intimate of More's; we know, for instance, that More was with Colet in Stepney on January 26, 1503. Colet was in Oxford when Erasmus met him in October 1499, but it does not seem likely that More would refer to a college in Oxford as staying in the countryside—"*rus … quod nunc incolis*" (Letter, lines 29 and 39); although, curiously, Magdalen College was outside the old city walls. Lupton suggests that perhaps Colet was at Dennington, Suffolk, the rectory he held from August 6, 1485, until his death.[128]

In the letter of October 23, More also mentions Lily, who seems to have returned from a trip to Rhodes and Italy by 1495; Grocyn, who was rector of the parish St. Lawrence Jewry from 1496; and Linacre, who had spent twelve years in Italy but returned to England in mid-1499.[129] It seems that Linacre went back to Magdalen College, Oxford, and was present for Prince Arthur's visit to Oxford in 1501, prior to his marriage to Princess Catherine of Aragon. After Arthur's visit, Linacre was summoned to the court to become tutor to the prince.[130] Arthur and Catherine were mar-

---

127. *CWE* 2, letter 181:20–21.

128. Lupton, *Life of John Colet*, 145fn2.

129. Grocyn wrote to his friend Aldus Manutius on August 27, 1499, telling him that "Thomas Linacre recently returned to Britain safe and sound"; Aldus Manutius, *The Greek Classics*, ed. N.G. Wilson (Cambridge, Mass.: Harvard University Press, 2016), 285.

130. John Noble Johnson, *The Life of Thomas Linacre: Doctor in Medicine* (London, 1835), 161–62.

ried on November 14, 1501, and in December they settled in Ludlow Castle, the seat of the Council of Wales and the Marches; he and she were prince and princess of Wales. It would seem, therefore, that the letter of More mentioning Linacre as his "studiorum praeceptore" must be dated after Linacre's involvement with the prince: that is, after Arthur's death on April 2, 1502. A further precision is given by the reference to Stepney in the last paragraph of the letter: Colet held that living (one of the richest in England at the time) from 1499 until he resigned it on September 21, 1505. All this indicates that the letter may be dated on any October 23 from 1502 to 1504.

The date of the letter is relevant, because there is a significance in the time that elapsed between writing the letter—in which More seems unsettled because of Colet's absence—and January 1505, when he went to Netherhall in Essex and married Jane Colt. Did he write it just three months before his marriage? Or two years earlier?[131] What were the dilemmas faced and choices taken by More at the time?

London Needs You!

As mentioned, Erasmus speaks of Colet, Grocyn, Linacre, and More together in his letter of December 5, <1499>,[132] and More refers to Grocyn and Linacre in his letter to Colet of October 23, <1502–4>; this seems to suggest that More kept in close contact with Grocyn and Linacre during this period. In fact, the three of them had already quite a lot in common. William Grocyn had studied at Oxford. He then studied Greek in Italy from 1488 to 1490, and on his return to England he taught Greek in Oxford until he moved to London in 1496 to become the Rector of St. Lawrence Jewry. Thomas Linacre was also educated in Oxford; it was

131. There is no record of the date of marriage of Thomas More. It is ascertained that Margaret, his eldest daughter, was born between late August and the beginning of October 1505. From this, it is assumed that More was married in January 1505 at the latest. Marc'hadour, in *L'Univers*, 133, suggests that he was married in November 1504 or January 1505. Before the Council of Trent it was forbidden to give the solemn nuptial blessing from Advent until the end of Christmastide, which went from December 1, 1504, to January 13, 1505, the week after the Epiphany, and from Septuagint to the end of Easter week—that is, from January 19, 1505, to March 30. More precisely, therefore, that would mean that More was possibly married in November 1504 or from January 14 to 18. It should be borne in mind, however, that the prohibition refers only to the solemn blessing, not to the marriage ceremony itself, and that a dispensation from the prohibition was easily obtained; therefore, there is simply not enough information so far to ascertain the date of More's marriage, other than to say that it took place at the latest in January 1505.

132. *CWE* 1, Ep.118. Angle brackets enclose places of origin or dates that are conjectural, per *Correspondence*, *EE*, and *SL*.

there that he began his acquaintance with Grocyn, although the latter
was more than a dozen years his senior. Linacre then studied Greek and
medicine in Italy—both he and Grocyn studied Greek with the Florentine
humanist and poet Angelo Polliziano (1454–94) at the court of Lorenzo
de Medici. Afterward Linacre spent some time in Rome, but his medical
studies also took him to Ferrara and Padua; and he even spent several years
in Venice in order to assist in the publication of the Greek Aristotle. He
returned to England in 1499.

The fact that More, in his letter of October 23, addresses Colet as his
spiritual adviser has led many authors to assume that Colet had great influence on More; but it is worth revisiting the evidence carefully. Colet
studied at Cambridge University[133] and took his BA in 1485 and his MA
in 1488. Richard Rex considers that his commitment to preaching, education, and Church reform was a feature shared by other contemporaries of
his at Cambridge,[134] such as William Melton (BA 1476, MA 1480) and
John Fisher (BA 1488, MA 1491).[135] Melton was the eldest of the three,
eight or nine years older than Colet, but there is some evidence of their
personal and academic relationship:[136] Colet wrote a commendation at the
end of a sermon by Melton published around 1510, and he is mentioned
in Melton's will. Melton's library included a large number of patristic and
early Christian writers: Origen, Eusebius, Athanasius, Chrysostom, Hesychius, Pseudo-Dionysius, John Damascene, Cyprian, Jerome, Ambrose,
Augustine, Gregory, Cassiodorus, and Bede; he also possessed two Greek
grammars and several books by Valla and Pico de la Mirandola. This is an
interesting background, considering Colet's possible influence on More.

Like Grocyn and Linacre, Colet traveled to Italy, returning in 1496; he
was ordained to the priesthood on March 25, 1498, and settled at Oxford,
until he took up his appointment as dean of St. Paul's. It seems that Colet
acquired an interest in neo-Platonism during his stay in Italy. Armed with
his new philosophy, he returned to Oxford and began writing in earnest;

133. Cf. W. R. Godfrey, "John Colet of Cambridge," *Archiv für Reformations-geschichte* 65 (1975):
6–17; J. B. Gleason, *John Colet*, Berkeley and Los Angeles: University of California Press, 1989, 39–42;
Richard Rex, *The Theology of John Fisher* (Cambridge: Cambridge University Press, 1991), 22 and
n. 56; Jonathan Arnold, *Dean Colet of St. Paul's: Humanism and Reform in Early Tudor England*,
London and New York: I. B. Tauris, 2007, 20.

134. Rex, *Theology of John Fisher*, 22–29.

135. Melton's date of birth is not known, but the dates of his, Colet's, and Fisher's BA and MA
help to place their chronology.

136. Rex, *Theology of John Fisher*, 24.

he developed his own theological ideas while he was teaching at Oxford. According to Jonathan Arnold,[137] Colet's key field of interest was the theological study of the Church, which he studied above all in the writings of St. Paul, Pseudo-Dionysius, Plato, the neo-Platonists, and St. Augustine. (Grocyn lectured also on Pseudo-Dionysius, and More on St. Augustine.) Arnold argues that Colet was devoted to the service of the Church: this can be seen in the accounts of his life, as well as in his tracts and correspondence. It would be no surprise if he succeeded in transmitting this zeal for Christ and for his Church to More, his spiritual disciple.

In the first place it is clear from More's letter of October 23, <1502–4> that he had been captivated by John Colet:

> For what could be more grievous to me than to be deprived of your most pleasant companionship, whose prudent advice I enjoyed, by whose most delightful company I was refreshed, by whose powerful sermons I was stirred, by whose example and life I was guided, and finally, in whose very countenance and nod I was accustomed to find pleasure? And while protected by these defences I felt myself strengthened; now that I am deprived of them I seem to languish and grow feeble.[138]

Colet's influence on More was not exerted simply through sporadic advice but through his companionship, his example, and his whole life. Later in the letter More asks Colet to return to the city or to his parish of Stepney, and it is reasonable to assume that the two of them met on a number of occasions. As More also brings in the names of Grocyn, Linacre, and Lily in a casual way, he seems to suggest that there may have been meetings of the five of them. While their humanistic studies would have been an obvious topic of conversation, we should also bear in mind that living a Christian life and communicating one's Christian zeal to others were particular concerns of Colet, as can be seen from the topics of his sermons both at St. Paul's and at his church in Stepney. This was what More had learned from Colet. But now, it seems, Colet was holding back from pastoral work and staying in quieter and more serene surroundings.[139] Hence More tells Colet that he is needed in the city of London: it is a call to the active life of preaching the gospel where he is required, to fly back to London as soon

---

137. Jonathan Arnold, *Dean John Colet of St. Paul's: Humanism and Reform in Early Tudor England* (London, 2007), 23.

138. *Correspondence* [3], October 23, <1502–4>, lines 7–10.

139. Lupton suggests that Colet could have been staying at Dennington in Suffolk, a rectory Colet held till his death; cf. J. H. Lupton, *A Life of John Colet* (London, 1887), 145n2.

as possible: "Who can doubt that you are the one who can do most for the cure of all in the city?"

More appeals also to Colet's recent experience: "[The London citizens'] readiness to allow you to treat their wounds, their trust, their obedience you have yourself proved in the past, and now the universal desire and anticipation of you proclaim it all again."[140] These lines suggest that crowds had gathered for Colet's London sermons, and so More was able to say that his return was eagerly anticipated.

At a first glance it might seem that More was afraid of the city, but a more careful reading of the letter shows that this is not so. He is not considering leaving the city himself: he is describing its dangers precisely in order to show Colet how much he is needed in London:

For in the country, where men are of themselves either almost innocent, or at least not ensnared in great sins, the services of any physician can be useful. But in the city because of the great numbers that congregate there, and because of their long-standing habits of vice, any physician will have come in vain unless he be the most skilful.[141]

Anticipating that Colet would find some excuse for being away from his post at St. Paul's, More tells him:

For if the inconveniences of the City so displease you, your country parish of Stepney (of which you should have no less care) will afford you hardly less advantages than where you now dwell, whence you can sometimes turn aside, as to an inn, to the City.[142]

More ends the letter:

Meanwhile, I shall pass my time with Grocyn, Linacre, and our dear friend Lily, the first as you know the sole guide of my life (in your absence), the second my master in learning, the third the dearest partner of my endeavours.[143]

William Lily (1468? –1522) appears in the letter as a friend and companion of More's. After taking his degree at Oxford, he went on pilgrimage to Jerusalem; on his way back he stayed for some time on Rhodes learning Greek. On his return in about 1495 he settled in London, but he is not mentioned in Erasmus's letter of December 1499, although Erasmus

---

140. *Correspondence* [3], October 23, <1502–4>, lines 55–59.
141. *Correspondence* [3], October 23, <1502–4>, lines 41–44.
142. *Correspondence* [3], October 23, <1502–4>, lines 36–40.
143. *Correspondence* [3], October 23, <1502–4>, lines 65–68.

praises him in several later letters;[144] possibly Grocyn (his godfather)[145] introduced him to More only after Erasmus's visit.

One result of More's and Lily's working together on their Greek was their *Progymnasmata* ("warming-up exercises"), in which they each provided a different Latin translation of the same Greek poems: they were later published by More among his Latin poems. They are headed, "Exercises by the Friendly Rivals Thomas More and William Lily," and conclude, "End of the Preparatory Exercises written in friendly collaboration by Thomas More and William Lily."[146] But the focus of the letter is not so much More's Greek studies as his desire to practice a Christian life with the support of his friends' company, and in particular with the help of personal spiritual guidance either from Colet or—in his absence—from his own parish priest, Grocyn.

Grocyn appears in an earlier letter of More's, dated <c. November 1501>, as "*praeceptor meus*"; in the letter of <1502–4>, Linacre is referred more specifically as "*studiorum praeceptore.*" More may have been receiving spiritual guidance from Grocyn for a long time before taking Colet as his spiritual director; and he may have continued going to Grocyn for advice until January 1505, when he married and moved to the parish of St. Stephen's Walbrook. It is clear, nonetheless, that when More wrote his October 23 letter to Colet he was especially devoted to him, even though he did not share some of Colet's ideas—for instance, on marriage, neo-Platonism, Pseudo-Dionysius, Pico, and the Kabbalah. More seems to have benefited from receiving spiritual guidance from Grocyn, who may have introduced him to St. John Chrysostom's Homilies on the Gospel of St. Matthew.

The letter of More dated <c. November 1501> mentioned earlier was addressed to the Latinist and teacher John Holt. Holt studied at Oxford before becoming a fellow of Magdalen College (1490–95) and then usher —deputy head—at Magdalen College School (1494–96); in 1495 or 1496 he was made master to the boys in the household of Cardinal Morton at Lambeth. At that time More was probably already studying at Lincoln's Inn, although he might have still been at New Inn; he and Holt may have met in Oxford, but most probably in London: in either case they would have been introduced (whether directly or indirectly) by Morton. It may

144. See *CWE*, Epp. 277:16, 341:21.
145. See the will of William Grocyn in *Collectanea*, 379.
146. *CW* 3, part II, 78–95.

be that More, back from Oxford, continued his Latin studies under him. When Holt later published for his pupils at Lambeth the first Latin grammar in English, *Lac Puerorum* (before 1500), Thomas, as a grateful former pupil, composed a pair of Latin epigrams to introduce and close that little book.[147] After the cardinal's death in 1500, Holt became master of the Cathedral School at Chichester; and after Prince Arthur's death he was appointed Latin tutor to Prince Henry.[148]

Holt must have written to More asking for material for his Latin classes; in the same letter, it seems, he inquired how More was doing. More sent Holt the material he asked for, thus showing the truth of Erasmus's assessment: "No one could take more trouble in furthering the business of his friends." More begins his letter:

I have sent you everything you wanted, except the additions I have made to the comedy about Solomon; those I could not send you at the moment, as I did not have them with me. I shall arrange for you to get them next week, along with any other of my materials you wish.[149]

Then, in reply to Holt's inquiries, he goes on to give an account of himself. It is worth analyzing that account carefully.

	In the present tense
line 9	*As for myself, thanks be to God, I am feeling quite well; and—something few people can say for themselves—I am living my life just as I desire;*[150]
	Subjunctive
line 10	*so please God, may my desires be good.*
	Preterite
line 11	*You ask how I am doing in my studies. Wonderfully, of course; things could not be better. I have shelved my Latin books, to take up the study of Greek; however, while dropping the one, I have not as yet completely caught up with the other. But enough on that point.*

147. Poems nos. 273 and 274, in *CW* 3, part II, 294–97.

148. N. Orme, "John Holt (d.1504), The Tudor Schoolmaster and Grammarian," *Library* (1996): 283–305, and *Medieval Schools from Roman Britain to Renaissance England* (New Haven and London: Yale University Press, 2006), 289.

149. *Correspondence* [2]. Unless otherwise stated, the translation of the letters from Thomas More comes from *SL*.

150. In the original—*ita vivimus ut volumus*—is the definition of *libertas* given by Cicero in *De Officiis* 1.20.70: *cuius proprium est sic vivere ut velis*. Thomas More used it also in the mouth of Raphael in *Utopia*: *Atqui nunc sic vivo ut volo*—"As it is, I now live as I please": *CW* 4, 56:1.

So what we read here is that Thomas More, who has finished his studies at Lincoln's Inn and is lecturing in law at Furnivall's Inn, is *feeling well* as he works hard to advance in his humanistic studies. Around that same year, 1501, he was giving public lectures on St. Augustine's *City of God*, and he was starting to study Greek. The reference to his studies comes at the end of the paragraph, and this should alert us to the fact that More's comment, "I am living my life just as I desire," does not necessarily refer simply to his studies, but should be taken together with the comment that immediately follows, "so please God, may my desires be good." That is, he hopes that this period of study may not be divorced from his desires to follow God's will. "Living my life just as I desire" denotes a unity of purpose that in principle incorporated whatever horizons were opened to him by Colet or Grocyn.

However, the joy that transpires in More's letter of 1501 is not apparent in the one of October 23, <1502–4>: here, instead of living his life just as he desires, More wanders around the marketplace, disengaged, in *foro otioso* (Mt 20:3), awaiting *Iesum ambulantem* (Jn 1:36), Christ passing by, wondering what God wants from him. And the generosity he shows by his promptness in sending Latin materials to his former teacher is replaced by a hankering after having Colet back—for More's own sake. Nevertheless, even in that situation he realizes that it is a weak argument and that the one really powerful argument is the good of souls: "London needs you!" he tells Colet.

2

Qum exaltatus fuero a terra,
omnia traham ad meipsum

Introducing Erasmus and Colet in 1499

In the summer of 1499, Thomas More, aged twenty-one and still training at
Lincoln's Inn, visited a friend of his, William Blount, Lord Mountjoy, who
was staying at the house of Mountjoy's father-in-law, Sir William Say, near
Greenwich, and there he met Erasmus. Mountjoy had married Elizabeth
Say in 1497; the following year he had been in Paris, where he had engaged
Erasmus as his tutor. There is no evidence that More had met Erasmus before. Erasmus describes the encounter with More in a long letter to a friend
of his, Johann von Botzeheim, in which he gives an account of his literary
work. The reference to his encounter with More is given by Erasmus simply
to explain how he had come to write some verses for Prince Henry:[1]

This was three days' work; but work it really was, for it was some years since
I had either read or written anything in verse. It was extracted from me partly
by embarrassment, partly by irritation. I had been carried off by Thomas More,
who had come to pay me a visit on an estate of Mountjoy's where I was then
staying, to take a walk by way of diversion as far as the nearest town [Eltham];
for that was where all the royal children were being brought up, except only Arthur, who at that time was the eldest. When we reached the court, there was a
solemn gathering not only of that household but of Mountjoy's as well. In the
middle stood Henry, who was then nine years old and already looked somehow
like a natural king.... More and his friend Arnold greeted the boy Henry, under
whose rule England now flourishes, and gave him something he had written. I

The quotation and spelling are as they appear in Erasmus's *Antibarbari* (c. 1495).
1. *CWE* 9, Ep. 1341A:174–95, to Johann von Botzeheim, from Basel, January 30, 1523.

was expecting nothing of the kind and, having nothing to produce, I promised that someday I would prove my devotion to him somehow. At the time I was slightly indignant with More for not having warned me, all the more so as during dinner the boy sent me a note, calling on me to write something. I went home, and even in despite of the Muses, from whom I had lived apart so long, I finished a poem within three days. Thus I got the better of my annoyance and cured my embarrassment.

More made a great impression upon Erasmus, who tried to befriend him. But it seems that More, however, did not correspond at that time, for he did not bother to reply to Erasmus's letters. By the end of the summer Erasmus had moved to Oxford, where he stayed at the then St. Mary's College, and from there he wrote to More on 28 October:[2]

I can hardly find any expressions strong enough to do justice to the execrations I have poured on the head of this messenger, whose carelessness or dishonesty I blame for the fact that I have been cheated of the letters from my dear More to which I was so greatly looking forward. For I must not, and would not, suppose that you have been remiss in the duty of writing; though I have reproached you about this in previous letters with just a shade of indignation. Nor am I afraid that my plain-speaking may have upset you, for you are quite well aware of my Spartan habit of sparring until I draw blood. But, joking apart, dearest Thomas, I ask you to cure, adding a bit of interest, the sick mood that I have caught from yearning too long for yourself and your letters.... I think, you see, that it makes no difference to you in what strain I write to you, since you are an easy-going fellow; and I have come to believe that you have, besides, a considerable affection for me. Farewell, dearest More.

I would suggest that it was not that More was lazy or overburdened by his studies at Lincoln's Inn: he was simply not impressed by Erasmus. More, Arnold, and Mountjoy were three young friends at ease in the royal palace at Eltham; but Erasmus, already thirty-three and the tutor of his friend, would have seemed an old man, frivolous in his manner and clearly unfamiliar with courtly expectations—he, the famous scholar, had been embarrassingly unaware of the fact that he ought to have had some literary trifle ready for his meeting with Prince Henry. That frivolous streak in Erasmus's character is emphasized by the annotator of the volume of the *Collected Works of Erasmus* in introducing the letter that in the summer of 1499 Erasmus wrote to a flippant humanist poet-friend whom he had left behind in Paris:[3]

---

2. *CWE* 1, Ep. 114:1–12 and 18–20.

3. Cf. introductory note by Wallace K. Ferguson to the letter from Erasmus to Fausto Andrelini, Ep. 103, *CWE* 1, page 192.

We have made some progress in England. The Erasmus you once knew has now become a sportsman, not the worst possible rider, a fairly skilful courtier.... To mention only one attraction out of many; there are girls here with divine features, gentle and kind; you may well prefer them to your Muses. And, moreover, there is a custom which cannot be sufficiently praised. Wherever you go, you are received with kisses from everybody; when you leave you are dismissed with kisses. You go back, and your kisses are returned to you. People arrive: kisses; they depart: kisses; wherever people foregather, there are lots of kisses; in fact, whatever way you turn, everything is full of kisses. Oh, Faustus, if you had once tasted how soft, how fragrant those kisses are, you would wish to exile yourself, not, as Solon did, for ten years, but all your life, in England.[4]

However, by the end of Michaelmas term the situation seems to have changed, for More had evidently responded to Erasmus's overtures. On December 5 Erasmus wrote a letter to an old pupil of his, Robert Fisher, who was studying in Italy; he was a relative of John Fisher, the future bishop of Rochester and himself a correspondent of Erasmus.

Yes, you will say, but how do I like our England? If you have any confidence in me, Robert, I ask you to believe me, that nothing in my life has ever pleased me so much. I have found the climate both pleasant and healthy. And I have met with so much kindness and so much learning, not hackneyed and trivial, but deep, exact, ancient, Latin and Greek, that I am not hankering so much after Italy, except just for the sake of seeing it. When I hear my Colet, I seem to be listening to Plato himself. In Grocyn, who does not wonder at that perfect compass of all knowledge? What is more acute, more profound, more keen than the judgement of Linacre? What did nature ever create milder, sweeter or happier than the genius of Thomas More? But why should I run through the whole list? It is marvelous how widespread and how abundant is the harvest of ancient learning which is flourishing in this country. All the more reason for your returning to it quickly. From London, in haste.[5]

The letter was written from London, for in October Erasmus received an invitation from John Colet, who had heard of him during his—Colet's—time in Paris.[6] Colet was interested in engaging Erasmus in some serious work on theology,[7] and that December Erasmus stayed with Colet at his parents' house in Stepney, one and a half miles east of London (a 30 minutes' walk). Either Erasmus invited More to join them or Colet brought

4. *CWE* 1, Ep. 103.
5. *CWE* 1, Ep. 118.
6. *CWE* 1, Ep. 106.
7. The admiration between Colet and Erasmus was mutual. For instance, in Ep. 106 from Colet to Erasmus and in Ep. 107 from Erasmus to Colet, both of October 1499, it can be seen that they praised each other, though their approach to theology did not coincide.

More along; both scenarios are possible. It is likely that the families of Colet and More knew each other, for both Colet's and More's father were mercers; Colet had probably attended St. Anthony's school, as had More, though years apart.[8] Another possible link would be William Grocyn (1446?–1519), who was parish priest at St. Lawrence Jewry (1496–1517), where More was a parishioner. What is clear is that from that December— if not before—More had accepted Erasmus's friendship. Twenty years later, Erasmus would write:

Friendships he seems born and designed for; no one is more openhearted in making friends or more tenacious in keeping them, nor has he any fear of that plethora of friendships against which Hesiod warns us.... Though somewhat negligent in his own affairs, no one could take more trouble in furthering the business of his friends. In a word, whoever desires a perfect example of true friendship, will seek it nowhere to better purpose than in More.[9]

Apart from the many references in the letters and other works of Erasmus, his friendship for Thomas More becomes obvious also in *De Copia*, a work in which Erasmus gives advice on learning Latin, or "The Foundations of the Abundant Style." Here Erasmus takes the topic of his friendship with More to provide examples of how to express the same idea in different words; although it is very repetitive (Erasmus finishes by noting that he has "put one basic sentence ... into about two hundred different forms"), even a short passage gives some flavor of Erasmus's insistence:

I shall myself depart from the living before More departs from my memory. The memory of More will not steal from our breast before this soul steals from us. Only then will Erasmus prove able to forget his beloved More, when he ceases to be mindful of himself. More is hidden deep within my heart, and nothing can cast him out from thence, save only Death. I shall be outside this self before More ceases to be within this breast. Erasmus will no longer exist when he is heedless of More. As long as my portion of life shall remain in these limbs, More will never be absent from the thoughts of Erasmus. While any drop of blood retains its warmth in this feeble frame, the memory of More will never grow cold in my heart. More will never pass from Erasmus's thought, while Erasmus lives. While Erasmus lives, More's memory will never fade away. The memory of my beloved More shall breathe within me until I breathe my last. More is inscribed in my heart in letters that no injurious time can ever erode. I shall be cast out of

---

8. Evidence for Colet attending St. Anthony's School comes from a conjecture by Anthony à Wood in his *Athenae* of 1691, and repeated in Samuel Knight's biography of Colet; but in the *ODNB* accessed on July 15, 2021, it is said that he could have attended the school of St. Anthony's in Threadneedle Street or the hospital school of St. Thomas of Acon. J. B. Gleason discusses this in his biography of Colet (1989).

9. *CWE* 7, Ep. 999 (1519): 98–114.

myself before the name of More is driven from my heart's shrine. As long as I shall be earth-propped, to use a Homeric word, I shall continually preserve the memory of More. As long as it shall be my lot to be numbered among the eaters of bread, to speak in Homeric fashion, never shall the face of More fade from my breast. My beloved More is so closely embraced in my soul that he cannot escape while I live. More's memory will never perish within me, unless I perish myself.

Indeed, More is present even when his name is omitted: "Could I ever, while alive, forget so delightful a companion? I will forget my own name before I forget so rare a friend."[10]

This list of variations on the theme shows also that in his writings Erasmus is always the grammarian and rhetorician, and perhaps we should not always take him at face value—or, rather, just accept that it is always a hazardous affair to take any Renaissance humanist at face value. The first edition of *De Copia* published by Erasmus (with More's encouragement) was dedicated to the pupils of St. Paul's, the school founded by Colet, and it is prefaced by a letter to Colet (April 29, 1512). It makes sense, therefore, for Erasmus to mention the name of their common friend.

Antibarbari

But how is it that after meeting in 1499, Thomas More and Erasmus became such good friends? What impact did Erasmus have on More? The next time Erasmus came to London, he stayed at More's house, and they worked together. How did that come about?

The answer may be found in their conversations at the time. When he met More in 1499, Erasmus "was occupied with" his *Antibarbari*.[11] This was among the first of his works; the first draft may date from c. 1488. *Antibarbari* is a defense of the study of the classics, in the form of a dialogue between Erasmus and four friends:[12] they meet and talk, and their conversation develops into a debate on the grounds for the resistance they have met to the introduction of classical studies. The setting is not dissimilar to that used later by More in *Utopia* or in the *Dialogue* of 1529; the immediate circumstances provide the *dramatis personae* and the setting, which is

---

10. *CWE* 24, 354–64.

11. James McConica, *Erasmus* (Oxford: Oxford University Press, 1991), 31.

12. For the general placing of the *Antibarbari* I am indebted to the Introductory Note by Margaret Mann Phillips in *CWE* 23:1–15 and to the Introduction in ASD I–1 by Kazimierz Kumaniecki. For its importance within the teaching of Erasmus, see James McConica, *Erasmus* (1991), in particular chapter 1, "The Making of the Grammarian," chapter 2, "The Educational Mission," and chapter 3, "Adorning the Temple of the Lord."

realistic and recreates the garden of a country house in the Low Countries. Erasmus puts his own ideas into a long speech by Jacob Batt, the young town clerk of Bergen. The Platonic inspiration is expressly stated.[13]

Erasmus gives an account of the composition of *Antibarbari* in the dedicatory letter to his friend Johann Witz that prefaces the first printed edition of 1520.[14] There he explains that he set to work on it when he had not yet reached his twentieth year; that he later refashioned the text as a dialogue; that he arranged it in four books, but completed only the first two—the third book was left unfinished, and the fourth was only a mass of material for future use.

In introducing her translation for the *Collected Works of Erasmus*, Margaret Mann Phillips suggests that the book must have been an "obsessive thought with Erasmus. If he did indeed begin it before he was twenty, he went on tinkering with it for a long time."[15] The work started as a simple speech put into the mouth of Erasmus's childhood friend Cornelis Gerard, but he then changed it into dialogue form in two books during his stay at a country house near Bergen[16] in the spring of 1494 or 1495.[17] Erasmus left Bergen for Paris, probably in September 1495, and soon after his arrival submitted *Antibarbari* as it was then to the historian Robert Gaguin, then the doyen of Paris humanists; the manuscript, which is extant, may be dated somewhere between the spring of 1494 and October 1495. In 1499 Erasmus went to England, and it was probably then that he showed the manuscript of the two finished books to John Colet, who was favorably impressed.[18] Mann Phillips, indeed, suggests that *Antibarbari* was his scholarly "passport," which he showed to the intellectual leaders of the circles he frequented in France and England. And here we reach the present point of interest in the story: it seems very likely that Erasmus would have mentioned the *Antibarbari*, or at least its theme, when he met More in the summer of 1499 on his way to Eltham with Mountjoy, or at the latest in December of that year in a company that included Colet. On his return from England Erasmus continued working on his *Antibarbari*; he wrote to Batt on April 12 of the following year that he intended to devote all his efforts to finishing it off.[19] Interestingly, in the same letter he mentions

13. *CWE* 23, 3.
14. Ep. 1110, in *CWE* 7 and *CWE* 23.
15. *CWE* 23, 3.
16. Ep. 371.
17. ASD I–1,7–10.
18. ASD I–1, 10, and Ep. 1110:32–36, in *CWE* 7, 305, and *CWE* 23, 16.
19. Ep. 124:68 and corresponding footnote in *CWE* 1.

More,[20] a circumstance that indicates that their meeting in London was still fresh in Erasmus's mind. From another letter to Batt it seems that Erasmus continued to be engaged on *Antibarbari* in September 1500.[21] Batt, the main speaker in *Antibarbari*, died in 1502; but fifteen years later, More wrote that he had developed a strong liking for him from the way Erasmus spoke about him. From that letter it is also clear that *Antibarbari* had been a common topic of conversation between Erasmus and More.[22]

Before considering what Erasmus told Thomas More about his *Antibarbari* in 1499, we should note that Erasmus kept revising it and that—as he explains in the dedicatory letter—when he was about to leave Italy he deposited books I and II with the English priest and humanist Richard Pace, but, not by Pace's fault, both were lost.[23] Erasmus does not say when he left the books with Pace, but it seems it was in December 1508 when Erasmus was passing through Ferrara.[24] In 1517 he was considering rewriting *Antibarbari*, but had not yet recovered the manuscript from Pace.[25] Later he found that manuscript copies of book I were circulating in Louvain, and after revising it he sent it to the publisher Johann Froben, who printed it in May 1520.[26] The title of the first edition—*Antibarborum Liber Primus, Autore D. Erasmo Roterodamo*—shows that Erasmus intended to publish more, and in the prefatory letter he writes that book II will join book I if he can secure a text. "The rest of the work shall be added out of my own head, unless the persons who are keeping my own drafts secret prefer to behave like honourable men."[27]

The manuscript of 1494–95 was much enlarged in the 1520 edition. Mann Phillips asserts that it can be seen that the attacks on the religious orders were largely added at this stage,[28] as well as many more references to the Fathers.[29] Therefore, in order to grasp what Erasmus must have conveyed to Thomas More in 1499, we need to look at the 1494/5 manuscript rather than the printed edition of 1520.

—

20. Ep. 124:27.

21. Ep. 129:52 and corresponding footnote in *CWE* 1.

22. Ep. 706:43–45.

23. *CWE* 23, 17, Ep. 1110:41.

24. Cf. Epp. 30:17n, 211:53n, and 216A:21n.

25. Cf. *EE*, vol. III, footnote to Ep. 706.32.

26. Ep. 1110.

27. Ep. 1110:59–61.

28. *CWE* 23, 5.

29. The same changes can be seen in a comparison between the 1518 edition of Erasmus's *Enchiridion* and his first version of 1503.

If Erasmus was obsessed with his *Antibarbari*, the central phrase that summarizes it is the quotation from the Gospel of St. John (Jn 12:32) that—in his own spelling—he places in Batt's long speech[30] and comments:

"*Qum, inquiens, exaltatus fuero a terra, omnia traham ad me ipsum*—When I am lifted up from the earth,"[31] he [Christ] says, "I will draw all unto me." Here it seems that he most aptly uses the word *traho*, "I draw," so that one may understand that all things, whether hostile or heathen or in any other way far removed from him, must be drawn, even if they do not follow, even against their will, to the service of Christ.[32]

Erasmus's meaning is that Christ draws all the knowledge of the pagans to himself: the wisdom of Socrates, Plato, Aristotle, Cicero, Virgil, and all the classics. Through the mouth of Batt, Erasmus continues:

What of the great universal harmony, which in the eyes of St. Augustine meant that not even bad things were created without intention? … Not to speak of the transfer of empires, what was the purpose of "founding the Roman nation with such vast effort," and through such great disasters and blood-stained victories subjugating the entire world to the City which held sway? Was it not according to the divine plan, so that when the Christian religion was born, it might spread abroad the more easily into different parts of the world, diffused as it were from one head into the separate members? And again, what was his intention in allowing almost the whole earth to be entangled with such lunatic, scandalous religions? What, so that when One arose, it would overturn all the others with the utmost glory. Nothing fine is ever done without struggle.

It was Greece, devoted to study, that discovered the arts; then Latium.… Everything in the pagan world that was valiantly done, brilliantly said, ingeniously thought, diligently transmitted, had been prepared by Christ for his society.[33]

Later on Erasmus refers to the "spoils of the Egyptians," the gold and silver jewelry and clothes the Hebrews took from the Egyptians when they left Egypt under the leadership of Moses (Ex 12:35–36). Erasmus argues

---

30. *CWE* 23, 41–61.

31. The modern translation given in *CWE* 23 has "I, if I be lifted up from the earth," but this translates the Vulgate rather than Erasmus's Latin text: see *Antibarbarum liber primus*, in Albert Hyma, *The Youth of Erasmus* (Ann Arbor: University of Michigan Press, 1930), 283, 10–11, and in *Opera Omnia Desiderii Erasmi Roterodami* (Amsterdam: 1969–), I-1, 82. The text differs from that given by Erasmus in his *Novum Instrumentum* (1516): "*Et ego si exaltatus fuero a terra, omnes traham ad meipsum.*" The Sixto-Clementine Vulgate (1592) gives *omnia*, but the New Vulgate (1979), following the Greek text more literally, gives *omnes*.

32. *CWE* 23, 59:22.

33. *CWE* 23, 59. Hyma, *Youth of Erasmus* (1930), Appendix B, 239–31, gives the Latin texts of the first known manuscript and of the printed edition and shows that for these lines, there is no relevant difference between them. The same is shown in ASD I-1, 82–83, where the manuscript is dated between the spring of 1494 and October 1495 (cf. 7–10).

that, following St. Augustine's interpretation of this passage from the book of Exodus, Christians should leave behind the vices and superstitions of the heathen but, "if there is among them any gold of wisdom, any silver of good speech," Christians should make use of them; and by the clothes of the Egyptians St. Augustine understood—as he wrote in *De doctrina Christiana*, citing earlier Christian authors such as Cyprian, Lactantius, Victorinus, Optatus, and Hilary—all human disciplines.[34] Erasmus's aim was to emphasize the importance of studying secular literature, specifically the classics, and he backs this up in his book with the testimony of Augustine and Jerome, as well as Cyprian, Lactantius, Severus, Ambrose, and even Bede, Bernard, Aquinas, and Scotus.[35]

We know that, shortly after meeting Erasmus, More finished his studies at Lincoln's Inn and started the practice and teaching of law; but what we also know is that from around this time, he devoted what time he had available to studying the classics, the Fathers of the Church and other early Christian writers. Was this due in part to his meeting? The impromptu verses he offered to Prince Henry at Eltham when he first met Erasmus are evidence enough that More was already keen on literary pursuits, and he had received a classical education at St. Anthony's and in Oxford; but it seems that, though More's enthusiasm for the classics anteceded his encounter with Erasmus, once he was introduced to Erasmus's classical project he took it to heart. In fact, Erasmus even thought of making More one of the speakers in *Antibarbari*,[36] and More was keen to accept a role in it as he wrote to Erasmus in 1517.[37] The extent to which More shared his friend's enthusiasm for the classics and the Fathers can be seen clearly in his letter introducing his translations of Lucian, which he undertook together with Erasmus.

St. Augustine was the author most used by Erasmus to support his ar-

---

34. *CWE* 23, 97:5–98:22, and *De doctrina Christiana* 2.40.60 and 61.

35. Erasmus was clearly conversant with Augustine and Jerome by 1494/5 and did not increase the number of quotations from their works in the printed edition of 1520. But he did add references to the Greek Fathers Basil and Chrysostom (ASD I–1, 78), where he had previously named only Augustine; he similarly adds the names of Basil, Origen, and Chrysostom on another page (Hyma, *Youth of Erasmus* [1930], 289), and those of the Latin Fathers Hilary and Gregory on yet another (ASD, I–1, 22–23).

36. See Craig R. Thompson, "Introduction," to *CWE* 23, xxvi, note. In the same Introduction, xxiv, Thompson claims that More was "the man who for many years knew and understood him [Erasmus] best," and that he considered him a Christian scholar because of his use of the language that he acquired through the knowledge of the classics. See also ASD I–1, 12, where the date of the correspondence on this matter is given as November 5, 1517 (*EE*, Ep. 706).

37. Ep. 706:45–50.

gument. Erasmus points out that for Augustine, the liberal arts were like so many sparks glittering forth from the eternal light and that, led by them, we may approach the source of light itself.[38] The vision put across by Erasmus through Batt's speech comes mainly from St. Jerome and St. Augustine,[39] "both weighty," he says.[40] In particular, he cites *De doctrina Christiana* where St. Augustine writes that a Christian should do his best to learn human knowledge, including the wisdom and histories of antiquity. It is, however, in *De civitate Dei* where St. Augustine shows most clearly his wide learning in Greek and Roman authors, and More undertook a careful study of that book and lectured on it, as Erasmus reported later on.

Erasmus's enthusiasm is somehow encapsulated in the quotation from the Gospel of St. John that summarized his argument: "*Qum exaltatus fuero a terra, omnia traham ad meipsum.*" Erasmus gave a particular, though limited, meaning to it: Christ on the cross draws everything to his service, even the heathen world and—for Erasmus's own purpose—knowledge of the classics. There was a certain novelty in Erasmus's interpretation, although it was in fact based on St. Augustine.[41] With regard to Erasmus's reading within the tradition of the Church, we can say the following:

1. For the *omnia/omnes* of John 12:32, some older Greek manuscripts give the form παντα (*omnia*) and others the form παντας (*omnes*); both manuscript traditions seem equally reliable.

2. The Greek Fathers who comment on the text use παντας, while the Latin Fathers use *omnia*, and this reading was adopted in the Latin Vulgate in the fourth century.

3. The text has been commented on by many Fathers, both Greek and Latin. Among the Greeks, in addition to Origen, Cyril, Gregory Nazianzen, Didymus the Blind, Basil, and John Chrysostom (all mentioned in *Antibarbari*) we can number Ignatius of Antioch, Irenaeus, Hippolytus, Clement of Alexandria, and Athanasius. Among Latin authors, we can add to *Antibarbari*'s Lactantius, Hilary, Ambrose, Augustine, Jerome, Gregory

---

38. *Antibarbari, CWE* 23, 109:18–29.

39. *CWE* 23, 93:6–98:25.

40. *CWE* 23, 94:23.

41. For John 12:32 in the context of biblical exegesis and history of theology, see José Luís González Gullón, *La Fecundidad de la Cruz: Una reflexión sobre la exaltación y la atracción de Cristo en los textos joánicos y la literatura cristiana antigua* (Rome: Pontificia Università della Santa Croce, 2003), and Jorge Federico Herrera Gabler, *La exaltación y atracción de Cristo en la cruz: Análisis de la tradición exegética y teológica desde la patrística hasta nuestros días* (Pamplona: Ediciones Universidad de Navarra, 2010). I am grateful to Professor Antonio Aranda for pointing out these two works to me.

the Great, Bede, Bernard, Thomas Aquinas, and Duns Scotus names such as Tertullian and Bonaventure.

4. For all of these, the object of the attraction is men, whether the word used is παντας (*omnes*) or *omnia*: that is, *omnia* has an anthropological meaning. For some writers, it has also a cosmological meaning (the whole of creation), but this is secondary to the anthropological meaning. In fact, from reading the various commentaries it seems that *omnia* conveys a more universal meaning, because it implies all the faculties or capacities of man, and all kinds of men, from everywhere, whether Jews or Gentiles (Jesus is speaking in response to a request from some Greeks: Jn 12:20).

The commentaries of St. John Chrysostom and St. Augustine on this passage are included in the *Catena Aurea*,[42] which was used by More in later writings. Both authors are of capital importance for an understanding of More: we have already seen his opinion of Chrysostom,[43] and he made Augustine the object of special study. Augustine, commenting on *omnia*, points out that it refers to the whole creature: "the creature in its personal integrity, that is, to spirit, and soul, and body; or all that which makes us the intelligent, living, visible, and tangible beings we are," and he adds that the *omnia* indicates not just completeness but extension, as well:

If by "all things" it is men that are to be understood, we can speak of all things that are foreordained to salvation: of all which [Jesus Christ] declared, when previously speaking of his sheep, that not one of them would be lost. And of all classes of men, both of every language and every age, and all grades of rank, and all diversities of talents, and *all the professions of lawful and useful arts*,[44] and all else that can be named in accordance with the innumerable differences by which men, save in sin alone, are mutually separated, from the highest to the low, and from the king to the beggar, "all," he says, "will I draw after me"; that he may be their head, and they his members.[45]

Chrysostom, writing in Greek (*Homilies on the Gospel of St. John*, homily 67:3), refers simply to all people, specifying in his commentary, "even the Gentiles."[46]

It is unclear whether More knew Augustine's and Chrysostom's com-

---

42. St. Thomas Aquinas, *Expositio Continua super Quatuor Evangelistas simul ac Catena Aurea* (Avignon, 1851), 4:120–21.

43. *Correspondence* [5], 21–25.

44. My emphasis.

45. St. Augustine, *In Ioannis Evangelium*, homily 52:11.

46. St. John Chrysostom, *Homilies on the Gospel of St. John*, homily 67:3, translation from *Fathers of the Church* 41 (Washington, D.C.: The Catholic University of America Press, 1960), 233.

mentaries on John 12:32 at all; there is no evidence that he was exposed to Chrysostom's commentary on St. John, although he was certainly introduced in 1499 to his commentary on St. Matthew. But we do know that around this time More started studying the works of St. Augustine in earnest; and we have seen that Augustine's commentary on *omnia* speaks both of "all things" and "all men."

This point is more than a simple question of semantics. Christ on the cross, "drawing" all men to himself, is a topic evident in many of More's later devotional works: it appears in his *Treatise upon the Passion*,[47] *Treatise on the Blessed Body*,[48] and *A Godly Meditation*.[49] It even appears—in inchoate form—in one of his first English poems: the last verses of his "Twelve Properties of a Lover" (1505) reads,

> Who is so good and so lovely also as he
> Who had already done so much for you?
> As he that first made you: and on the rode [the cross]
> Afterwards redeemed you with his precious blood.[50]

At the same time, St. Augustine also notes that the *omnia* that is to be directed to Christ includes "all the professions of lawful and useful arts." How far would More have understood these words as directed to him and calling for personal commitment?

What Kind of Humanism?

Erasmus, in his *Antibarbari*, was attempting to foster what he calls variously *good letters, literature, the learning of antiquity, the republic of letters*;[51] for him, these letters and learning were embodied in the works of Plato and Aristotle; the Latin prose writers Cicero, Quintilian, Pliny, Aulus Gellius, and Livy; and the Latin poets Horace, Virgil, and Ovid.[52]

But we must not forget that for Erasmus, his classical renewal was in the first place a Christian renewal. His argument was that these *good letters* were valued by the Fathers of the Church for understanding and explaining Christianity. James McConica writes that the central texts of the humanism of the European Renaissance were the classical writings of Greece and

47. *CW* 13, 11–146.
48. *CW* 13, 195:29.
49. *CW* 13, 226:29.
50. *CW* 1, 120:8–11.
51. *CWE* 23, 25–43.
52. *CWE* 23, 24–36.

Rome but also—especially in northern Europe—the foundational texts of Christian Antiquity: the scriptures and the Church Fathers.[53] This, he argues, was a Christian humanism.[54] Erasmus expresses it clearly in *Antibarbari*, saying, "None of the liberal disciplines is Christian, because they neither treat of Christ nor were invented by Christians; but they all concern Christ."[55]

It has been suggested that from the time of his encounter with Erasmus, More committed himself to this same enterprise, learning classical Latin and Greek and immersing himself in the study of both the Church Fathers and the classical authors. Whether More's determination in this direction dates from then or earlier—specifically, from 1492, when he might have learned Greek from William Grocyn at Oxford or from 1496 when Grocyn was appointed rector of the parish church of the Mores, St. Lawrence Jewry—it is clear in any event that at least from the end of 1499 it is possible to speak of a shared project that included Erasmus, Colet, Grocyn, Linacre, and More, as seen in Erasmus's aforementioned letter to Robert Fisher of December 5 of that year.[56]

Although Erasmus's first draft of *Antibarbari* preceded his first visit to England, it was only after meeting Colet, Grocyn, Linacre, and More that he made up his mind to study Greek. From then on it can be said that Erasmus had a sense of mission regarding Greek;[57] his correspondence with Jacob Batt manifests this resolve. In his first letter after his return from England, dated March 1500, Erasmus acknowledges his poor grasp of Greek—but also his lack of money to purchase books or to employ the services of a tutor.[58] By April 12, he declares that he has nevertheless turned all his attention to Greek.[59] In September, he encourages Batt to study the language as a shared effort, for friendship's sake;[60] in December he tells him that he has now begun to study Greek, but that he needs to get hold of Greek books and to pay for the services of a Greek tutor.[61] In a letter to Antoon van Bergen dated March 1501, Erasmus expands on his plans, explaining that

53. *Companion*, 22.

54. *Companion*, 27.

55. *CWE* 23, 90:10–12. The reference is cited also by Mann Phillips in her Introduction to *Antibarbari*, *CWE* 23, 9, in which she, like McConica, argues that Erasmus was fostering a Christian humanism.

56. Ep. 118:24–29.

57. Simon Goldhill, *Who Needs Greek?* (Cambridge: Cambridge University Press, 2002), 14–59.

58. Ep. 123.

59. Ep. 124.

60. Ep. 129.

61. Ep. 138.

he has decided to spend several months learning from a Greek tutor;[62] in the same letter he regrets not having studied it earlier[63] and argues that it is necessary for the accurate understanding of the scriptures and therefore for a sound theology.[64] He also states his resolve to follow the example of St. Jerome, who mastered Greek and Latin and was the only scholar in the Universal Church who had a perfect command of all learning both sacred and secular (an idea he takes from Augustine)[65]—St. Jerome, of course, mastered Hebrew, as well.

The translation of Lucian's dialogues from Greek into Latin that the two did together (some by More and others by Erasmus) in More's house in 1506 was part of this common endeavor of learning Greek. In choosing the works of Lucian to translate, they may have been following advice from Linacre, mentioned by More as his "master in learning" in his letter of October 23, for Linacre also encouraged John Claymond, president of Magdalen College (1507–16), to learn Greek and added, "Your toil will become light and amusing, and your progress sure, if only you will read a little Lucian every day."[66] But it is also possible that it was Linacre who was influenced by More; in any case, they seem to have been of the same mind on the usefulness of Lucian.

By 1516 Erasmus's project had produced what More praised as his *magnum opus*, a bilingual *Novum Testamentum*; this consisted of Erasmus's edition of the Greek text, together with a new translation of his own into Latin. This achievement, together with a reference to his mentor St. Jerome, is celebrated in the diptych of Erasmus and Peter Giles,[67] painted by Quentin Metsys[68] and sent by the two sitters as a present to More, their mutual friend.[69] Erasmus is seen writing the opening words of his *Paraphrase of*

---

62. Ep. 149:76.

63. Ep. 149:14–15.

64. Ep. 149:24–48.

65. Ep. 149:72.

66. Letter of Thomas Linacre to John Claymond, president of Corpus Christi College, Oxford, reproduced by P. S. Allen, *Erasmus: Lectures and Wayfaring Sketches* (Oxford: Clarendon Press, 1934), 153.

67. He is often called also by his Latin name, Petrus Aegidius, or the Dutch version, Pieter Gillis. Here the familiar anglicized form is used.

68. The diptych is mentioned in the correspondence between Thomas More, Erasmus, and Peter Giles in 1517; cf. *CWE*, letter from More to Erasmus of July 16 (Ep. 601); Erasmus to More, September 8 (Ep. 654); Giles to Erasmus, September 27 (Ep. 681); More to Erasmus, October 7 (Ep. 683); More to Giles, October 7 (Ep. 684); Erasmus to Giles, <Louvain, c. October 1517> (Ep. 687); More to Erasmus, October 25 (Ep. 688); and More to Erasmus, November 5 (Ep. 706).

69. The two panels of this diptych are described in J. B. Trapp and H. S. Herbrüggen, *The King's Good Servant: Sir Thomas More* (London: National Portrait Gallery 1977), Catalogue item no. 54 and

St. Paul's Epistle to the Romans, the work on which he was engaged in May 1517. On his left there is a bookcase containing four of his works. On the top shelf is his *Novum Testamentum*: the first edition (1516) is sometimes known as the *Novum Instrumentum*, following the first lines of its introduction, but the subsequent editions (1519, 1522, 1527, and 1535) are entitled *Novum Testamentum*, which is also the title used by More in his letter to Erasmus of February 17, 1516: *Gaudeo Hieronymum ac Nouum Testamentum tam bene procedere*[70]—"I am glad Jerome and the New Testament are coming along so well." So it is not surprising that the title *Novum Testamentum* is used in the painting. The book on the bottom shelf is Erasmus's edition of Jerome's *Letters*, also published in 1516 and keenly anticipated by More. On top of Jerome is the volume of translations from Lucian produced jointly by More and Erasmus in 1506: in the painting this book is identified in Greek, ΛΟΥΚΙΑΝΟΣ. The fourth volume is *Moriae Encomium*, which was dedicated to More.[71] St. Jerome appears in the preface of *Moriae Encomium*, which, alongside the edition of Jerome's letters and the translations from Lucian, was also part of the project that led to Erasmus's *Novum Testamentum*.

The same bookcase appears to continue behind the portrait of Peter Giles; there are several books on its shelves, too, among them works by Seneca, Plutarch, Quintus Curtius Rufus, and Suetonius, all of which were edited by Erasmus and published at some stage before the date of the painting or in the same year.[72] Erasmus's *Education of a Christian Prince* (1516) is also there, along with others that cannot be identified, implying that it is not meant to be an exhaustive list. Peter Giles, holding in his left hand a let-

---

plate II; Lorne Campbell, Margaret Mann Phillips, Hubertus Schulte Herbrüggen, and J. B. Trapp, "Quentin Matsys, Desiderius Erasmus, Pieter Gillis and Thomas More," *Burlington Magazine* 120, no. 908 (1978): 716–25; Lisa Jardine, *Erasmus Man of Letters: The Construction of Charisma in Print* (Princeton, N.J.: Princeton University Press, 1993; Goldhill, *Who Needs Greek?* (2002), 17–59; Susan Foister, *Holbein and England* (New Haven and London: Yale University Press, 2004), 95–96; Jennifer Scott in *Catalogue of the Exhibition, The Northern Renaissance* (London: Royal Collection Publications, 2013), item 6, page 41; F. Mitjans, "Thomas More on Seneca," *Moreana* (June 2007): 44–47, and F. Mitjans, "Review of the Exhibition *The Northern Renaissance*," *Moreana* (June 2013): 320–21.

70. Ep. 388:162.

71. *Moriae Encomium* was written in More's house in 1509. The dedicatory letter addressed to More is dated June 9 without specifying the year. The first edition was published in Paris without a date and reprinted in Strasburg in August 1511, hence the dedicatory letter is dated June 9, <1511>; see *EE* 222, introduction, and *CWE* 222, introduction. Froben's edition of July 1522 added the impossible year-date of 1508 at the end of the letter.

72. Erasmus was one of the editors of Seneca's *Tragedies*, published in Paris in 1514. His edition of Plutarch's *Opuscula* first came out in 1512 (Campbell et al., "Quentin Matsys," 719). The dedicatory epistle of his *Quintus Curtius* is dated November 4, 1517 (Ep. 704) and that of his *Suetonius* June 5, 1517 (Ep. 586).

ter, which More describes as a letter from More to Giles[73] (the painter has managed to imitate More's handwriting),[74] looks at the viewer—that is, at More and, with him, all of us—and with his right forefinger points out to us the long-awaited edition of *Antibarbari*,[75] signaling Erasmus's programmatic work, the one that—by advising study of the classics—culminated in his *Novum Testamentum*. In order to emphasize the point, the *Education of a Christian Prince* and the *Antibarbari* are given their titles in Greek, the former in Roman cursive characters—*Archontopaideia*—and the latter in Greek capitals.[76]

Undoubtedly, Erasmus and Giles were involved in the 1516 and 1517 editions of *Utopia*, and it might even be argued that the letter in Giles's hand could have been More's second letter to Giles, which appeared in the 1517 edition of *Utopia*. But it is equally clear that *Antibarbari* was in their minds at the time. On May 10, 1517, Beatus Rhenanus writes to Erasmus saying that his paraphrase on St. Paul's Letters, besides *Antibarbari* and other works, was eagerly awaited;[77] and in a letter of November 5, 1517, More tells Erasmus that he is delighted that the paraphrase on the Letter to the Romans is in the press[78] and surprised that Pace has not returned the manuscript of *Antibarbari*.[79] He adds:

73. Ep. 684:17 and 55. Trapp and Herbrüggen, *King's Good Servant* (1977), Catalogue item no. 54 *in fine*, and Campbell et al., "Quentin Matsys," corroborate that the letter in Giles's hand is supposed to be from More to Giles. Scott, *Catalogue of the Exhibition* (2013), item 6, and Foister, *Holbein and England* (2004), 110, accept that the letter in Giles's hand is supposed to be from More and that the book he is pointing to is *Antibarbari*.

74. More, in his letter to Giles dated October 6–7, 1517, acknowledges that Metsys had imitated his handwriting very well (Ep. 684:19 and 53–60).

75. Metsys's diptych was painted in 1517, but the first edition of the *Antibarbari* was not printed until 1520.

76. The study of Campbell et al., "Quentin Matsys," deals with the questions of the letter and the book in great detail. It confirms that the portrait of Giles in the Earl of Radnor's collection at Longford Castle in Wiltshire is the original by Metsys sent to More (717), while the version in the Museum of Fine Arts, Antwerp, is probably a copy by a Netherlandish artist of a lost copy (724). The Antwerp version shows Giles holding a rolled-up piece of paper instead of More's letter, and the titles of *Antibarbari* and several other books do not appear; instead of the title *Antibarbari* on the cover of the book, it bears along its fore-edge the letters CIS (or RIS) ERAS: R., which may refer to the *Querela Pacis* of *Erasmus Roterodami*. It has been suggested that the book indicated by Giles is a copy of *Utopia*; cf. Lisa Jardine's *Erasmus, Man of Letters* (1993), 34–41. She refers to the study by Campbell et al., and in particular to the arguments for the book signaled by Peter Giles to be that of the *Antibarbari* or the *Querela Pacis*, and she finds the case for the *Antibarbari* the more likely (34–35). But then she adds, "In the diptych, however, it seems to me irresistible to identify this book as More's *Utopia*" (38). She has no pictorial source for this suggestion.

77. Ep. 581:24–25.

78. Ep. 706:28.

79. Ep. 706:38.

I will write to him about it to some effect; for there is nothing I would rather achieve, for the cause of good letters or my own sake, perceiving that you intend to set up a monument to our friendship in that work.[80]

More goes on to discuss his part in the projected revision of *Antibarbari*, protesting that he does not want to take over Batt's role, as he has developed a great fondness for him on account of the way in which Erasmus had spoken about him. More leaves it to Erasmus to determine how to bring him in while keeping Batt: "I am almost as keen to see his memory flourish as my own. Only you must consider how you will couple me with him." Then, jokingly, he continues:

Mind you: I am my own closest neighbor.[81] I insist on a part second only to yours, and no mistake. I am too fond of talking, as you know, to submit to a walking-on part, especially in a comedy from which I promise myself immortality.[82]

More finishes the letter referring to the verses he had sent Erasmus to thank him for the picture, thus bringing together the two works indicated in the picture, the paraphrase on the Letter to the Romans and the revision of *Antibarbari*.

—

Although the *Antibarbari* gave Erasmus a direction for his personal endeavors, it is also true that the ideas it contained were not wholly original. Particular mention must be made of Alexander Hegius (1433–98),[83] author of a poem entitled *On the Utility of the Greek Language*[84] and rector of the school at Deventer, where Erasmus was his pupil and learned the rudiments of Latin and Greek.[85] Hegius's opinions can be seen in a literary dialogue, where he writes in disgust that "the current grammars are barbarous." "Grammar is a fine art, but not that which at present is being studied at great expense by the boys, since they compel them to learn barbarous Latin. The Church Fathers like Augustine, Jerome, Gregory, Ambrose, and Cyprian wrote correct Latin, for their models were the best writers among the ancients, such as Cicero, Sallust, Livy, and Virgil." And he gives his solution: "Let those grammars be cast away, and let those teachers take

---

80. Ep. 706:38–41.
81. Terence, *Andria* 635.
82. Ep. 706:49–50.
83. See Hyma, *Youth of Erasmus* (1930), *passim*, from 36 onward.
84. Hyma, *Youth of Erasmus*, 110.
85. Hyma, *Youth of Erasmus*, 111.

their leave who adhere to the barbarous and corrupt vocabularies."[86] All these are ideas and authors included in Erasmus's *Antibarbari*.

To see the impact of *Antibarbari* on More from 1499 onward, we can return to Erasmus's reference to the "spoils of the Egyptians." This topos was first commented upon by Philo of Alexandria in reference to the right of the Jews to make use of pagan culture, but it was then taken up by early Church Fathers such as St. Irenaeus, Clement of Alexandria, and Tertullian, as well as St. Hilary, St. Gregory Nazianzen, and St. Gregory of Nyssa. Origen, following Philo, specifically suggests using Greek philosophy for the benefit of the Christian faith in the same way that geometry and astronomy are used for the interpretation of sacred scripture, and St. Jerome and St. Augustine similarly refer to the spoils of the Egyptians in the sense later used by Erasmus in *Antibarbari*.[87]

Among the works that Erasmus quotes from directly in *Antibarbari* is St. Augustine's *De doctrina Christiana*, a short work dealing mainly with the interpretation of sacred scripture; it is a work that More will make extensive use of in later writings.

St. Augustine knew a number of Latin translations of the scriptures (the so-called *Vetus Latina* was by no means a monolithic text), and in *De doctrina Christiana* he advises his reader to compare the different translations in order to grasp the true sense of the text.[88] More refers to this advice in his letter to Dorp of October 21, 1515, in which he defends Erasmus's freedom to produce a new translation. In the same treatise St. Augustine recommends the study of Greek on account of the differences between translations,[89] although he admits that he himself did not know much Greek. This recommendation in *De doctrina Christiana* seems to have been a major influence on More's taking up Greek after his encounter with Erasmus. Although More may have studied Greek previously under Grocyn, from his letter to Holt it would seem that he did not have much interest in it before 1501.[90] From then on, however, the recommendation appears in many of More's writings: in his letter to Dorp he suggests that Christians should eagerly embrace Greek,[91] and he reiterates this in his letter to the

---

86. Hegius, *Dialogi*, Deventer, 1503, fol. O^4 verso, cited by Hyma, *Youth of Erasmus*, 108.

87. For a comprehensive study of the subject, see Georges Folliet, "La 'Spoliatio Aegyptiorum': Les interprétations de cette image chez les Pères et autres écrivains ecclésiastiques," *Traditio*, 57 (2002): 1–48.

88. Letter to Dorp, *CW* 15, 82:19–21.

89. *De doctrina Christiana* 2.13.16.

90. *Correspondence*, Letter [2], line 12.

91. Letter to Dorp, *CW* 15, 98:4–104:12.

University of Oxford (March 29, 1518, or 1519).[92] He writes that no one can master theology without

either Hebrew or Greek or Latin, unless, of course [he] has convinced himself that there are enough books on that subject written in English, or unless he thinks that all theology falls within the confines of those problems which they dispute about so assiduously, for I grant that one needs little Latin to learn those.

In this letter he makes use of the "spoils of the Egyptians" topos when referring to the knowledge of philosophy and liberal arts needed for the proper study of theology.[93] In his *Letter to a Monk*, also of 1519, More again cites from *De doctrina Christiana*, pointing out that St. Augustine and St. Jerome held opposite opinions on specific interpretations of scripture;[94] and once more he repeats St. Augustine's advice to turn to the Greek text of scriptures wherever there is doubt about the meaning of the Latin text.[95]

More also uses ideas from *De doctrina Christiana* to defend the Church in the *Dialogue* of 1529, in his dispute with the Messenger over the Lutheran opinions he has heard: he tells the Messenger how to interpret scripture and emphasizes the Church's authority over scripture because we have received it from her;[96] and he argues in defense of the liberal arts against the opinions reported by the Messenger.[97]

Ideas from *De doctrina Christiana* appear elsewhere, too. In *A Confutation of Tyndale's Answer* (1532–33) More proposes the exegetical principle that clear passages of scripture should illuminate obscure ones,[98] a principle that St. Augustine invokes repeatedly in *De doctrina Christiana*.[99] In the *Dialogue of Comfort against Tribulation* More makes use of St. Augustine's distinction between *uti* (to use) and *frui* (to delight in)[100] found in *De doctrina Christiana*.[101] In *De tristitia*,[102] More picks up another idea from *De*

92. *CW* 15, 143:13–144:33.

93. *CW* 15, 138:25–140:1.

94. *CW* 15, 212:22–214:1, and *De doctrina Christiana* 2.15.22.

95. *CW* 15, 254:13–15.

96. Also in the *Treatise on the Passion*, *CW* 13, 113:5–8 and 150:7–10, citing St. Augustine, *Contra epistolam Manichaei* V.

97. *CW* 6, 132:10–22. In the same chapter More again uses the topos of the spoils of the Egyptians, although in this case he quotes not from *De doctrina Christiana* but from St. Jerome's Epistle 70 to argue that the Hebrews deservedly despoil the Egyptians when "Christ's learned men take from pagan writers the riches and learning and wisdom that God gave unto them."

98. *CW* 8, 157:14–15, 425:21–23, and 668:18.

99. *De doctrina Christiana* 2.12.17 and 3.26.37, among others.

100. *CW* 12, 223:14–26.

101. *De doctrina Christiana* 1.4.4.

102. In F. Mitjans, "*De tristitia tedio pavore et oratione christi ante captionem eius*: The Last work

doctrina Christiana concerning the hidden meaning of certain place-names that appear in scripture, considering that

God had veiled under these place-names some mysterious meanings which attentive men, with the help of the Holy Spirit, would try to uncover.[103]

Later on in *De tristitia* More uses the example of the snake sloughing its skin, given by Augustine in *De doctrina Christiana*. St. Augustine wrote:

The statement that the serpent gets rid of its old skin by squeezing itself through a narrow hole, and thus acquires new strength—how appropriately it fits with the direction to imitate the wisdom of the serpent, and to put off the old man, as the Apostle says, that we may put on the new; and to put it off, too, by coming through a narrow place, according to the saying of our Lord, "Enter in at the strait gate!"[104]

More's text reads:

If we patiently endure the loss of the body for the love of God, then, just as the snake sloughs off its old skin—called, I think, its "senecta"—[*quemadmodum anguis pellem ueterem quem opinor senectam uocant*] by rubbing it against thorns and thistles, and leaving it behind in the thick hedges comes forth young and shining, so too those of us who follow Christ's advice and become wise as serpents will leave behind on earth our old bodies, rubbed off like a snake's old skin among the thorns of tribulation suffered for the love of God, and will quickly be carried up to heaven, shining and young and never more to feel the effects of old age.[105]

By drawing attention to the Latin name used to designate the shed skin of the snake—*senecta*—More underlines the idea of getting rid of old age—that is, the "old man"—*senectus* (in Cicero, *De senectute* 8, 26 and throughout, and Tacitus, *Annales* 4, 17).

—

If Thomas More all through his literary production—in defense of Erasmus, in addressing the scholars of the University of Oxford, in his controversial works and even at the very end of his life—repeatedly cites *De doctrina Christiana*, showing that he knew it at least from the time of his discussions about *Antibarbari* with Erasmus, it is worth having a more detailed look at this text of St. Augustine's. The main theme of *De doctrina*

---

of St. Thomas More," *Annales Theologici* (June 2021), the use of the first two words, *De tristitia*, as abbreviated title, is favored.

103. *CW* 14, 13:7–15:1.
104. *De doctrina Christiana* 2.16.24.
105. *CW* 14, 615–17.

Christiana is the interpretation of sacred scripture: how to deal with obscure passages and with variant Latin translations, and, in particular, the usefulness of the liberal arts in scriptural interpretation. But there are other points that also need emphasizing. At the end of book 1, St. Augustine states that the fulfillment and end of scripture are the love of God and of our neighbor:[106] that is, St. Augustine's interest is not just a scholarly or exegetical but one of fostering Christian life. He continues:

Whoever, then, thinks that he understands the Holy Scriptures, or any part of them, but puts such an interpretation upon them as does not tend to build up this twofold love of God and our neighbour, does not yet understand them as he ought.[107]

In this respect what he says in the very first chapter is illuminating:

A possession which is not diminished by being shared by others, if it is possessed and not shared, is not yet possessed as it ought to be possessed.[108]

The implication is obvious: we need to pass on Christian doctrine to others.

—

As we have spoken of More's determination to master Greek, it is worth considering the Greek texts he mentions in *Utopia* (1516). Raphael Hythloday, the narrator, explains that the Utopians received from him "most of Plato's works and many of Aristotle's,"[109] and that "they are very fond of Plutarch's writings, and delighted with the witty persiflage of Lucian."[110]

Praise of Plato is not unqualified. Raphael took with him only a selection of his works: there are allusions in *Utopia* to *The Statesman*, *Philebus*, *Gorgias*, *The Republic*, *The Laws*, and *Epistle VII*.[111] *Gorgias*, for instance, gives us Socrates in discussion with the Sophists and getting them to agree that it is better to suffer harm than to do evil, an idea that points irresistibly to More's own situation at the end of his life, and that he characterizes with typical wit as "a case in which a man may lose his head and have no harm," as he put it in conversation with his daughter Meg;[112] but the same idea is found in *De doctrina Christiana* in not dissimilar terms: "It is better

106. *De doctrina Christiana* 1.35.39.
107. *De doctrina Christiana* 1.36.40.
108. *De doctrina Christiana* 1.1.1.
109. *CW* 4, 181:34.
110. *CW* 4, 183:2.
111. *Utopia, Latin Text and English Translation*, ed. George M. Logan, Robert M. Adam, and Clarence H. Miller (Cambridge: Cambridge University Press, 1995), 288.
112. Reported in the Letter from Margaret Roper to Alice Alington, August 1534, *Correspondence* [206], line 590.

to suffer than to commit injustice,"[113] and is indeed a *locus communis* of Christian thought.

In the *Gorgias*, those listening to Socrates ask him to summarize his argument. But instead of doing so he replies with a legend,[114] which recounts that at first the gods judged men before death, when they were still clothed in all their regalia, and as a result mistakes were made. In order to avoid such mistakes Zeus established that to ascertain whether a person had lived a virtuous life or not, everyone must be judged when already dead and stripped naked of all appearances. Then the virtuous would be led to the Isles of the Blessed; "the ones whose errors are curable"[115] would undergo purification; and tyrants and those who "commit the most grievous and impious" crimes would undergo eternal punishment in Hades.[116] The message of this Socratic dialogue is plainly congruent with the Christian vision of the afterlife, and More refers to the philosophers and writers of ancient times in his *The Last Things* (c. 1522) and *The Supplication of Souls* (1529),[117] writing explicitly in the latter work that the pagans believed in purgatory.

But other Platonic dialogues are less consistent with the Christian teaching that More had received. In describing the number of citizens in each city of Utopia, More writes that the Utopians "cannot of course regulate the number of minor children in a family,"[118] directly contradicting the statement in Plato's *Laws* that "if too many children are being born, there are measures to check propagation."[119]

There was also much in *The Republic* to which More objected, and there is a sharp point to his declaration in *Utopia* that the commonwealth described by Raphael was a rival to Plato's *Republic*.[120] He took particular issue with Plato's proposal to abolish marriage and the family, which appears both in *The Republic* and in *Timaeus*; the latter work starts with Socrates reminding Timaeus and Critias what had been decided in the previous discussion, that, in the ideal city, "they should all have spouses and children in common and that schemes should be devised to prevent

---

113. *De doctrina Christiana* 1.36.40.

114. Plato, *Gorgias* 524 b, 526 d.

115. *Gorgias* 525 b.

116. *Gorgias* 525 d.

117. See More, *The Last Things*, CW 1, 139:1–11, and *The Supplication of Souls*, book II, CW 7, 172:25–173:31.

118. Logan, Adam, and Miller, *Utopia* (Cambridge), 135.

119. Plato, *Laws* 740 d.

120. *CW* 4, 20.

anyone of them from recognizing his or her own particular child."[121] Aristotle (who is also cited by More)[122] argued against Plato that the sharing of wives and abolition of the family would destroy natural affection, a sentiment clearly shared by More, for society in Utopia is based almost entirely on the family. But here again the question of sources is unclear, for St. Augustine also states, in *De civitate Dei*, that the family ought to be the beginning of the city, or the cell of it.[123]

If the Utopians—together with More—were delighted with Lucian,[124] it was perhaps in part because he had laughed at all the Greek philosophers. There is more to this than is conveyed by the commentary in the *Complete Works*, in which the editor seems to suggest that Lucian simply added a humorous tone to *Utopia*.[125] By sharing in Lucian's laughter at Plato, Pythagoras, and others, More establishes a detachment and independence from their conclusions; by laughing at them through Lucian, he frees himself from the contradictions of the pre-Aristotelian philosophers.

An example might help to elucidate this. Marsilio Ficino, the Italian humanist who died in 1499 (the year of More's first encounter with Erasmus), was full of praise for Plato, and even saw him—via the so-called *prisca theologia*—as a forerunner of Christian revelation. More, on the other hand, puts himself in a position from which he can criticize Plato; and it may not be a coincidence that More, when translating the *Life of Pico* into English, removes the two mentions of Ficino that appear in the Latin original.[126]

Then there is the Utopians' fondness for Plutarch. Reading Plutarch's *Lives* will have given More an early—and influential—lesson in tyranny through the parallel lives of Alexander the Great and Caesar. More also shows his knowledge of Plutarch's *Moralia* in many of his Latin poems.[127]

"Among the poets," Raphael continues, "they have Aristophanes, Homer, and Euripides, together with Sophocles in the small Aldine edition. Of the historians they possess Thucydides and Herodotus, as well as Hero-

---

121. Plato 18d. More had access to the Greek manuscripts of Grocyn; one of them, dating from the late fifteenth century (the present Oxford, Corpus Christi College, MS 96) contains *The Republic*, *Timaeus*, *The Laws*, and *Epinomis*.

122. In *Utopia* there are references to Aristotle's *Nicomachean Ethics* and *Politics*.

123. St. Augustine, *The City of God*, book 19, ch. 16; see Baker-Smith, "Reading *Utopia*," in *Companion*, 150.

124. There are references in *Utopia* to *Phalaris*, *A True Story*, *Menippus*, *The Wisdom of Nigrimus*, *Demonax*, *Philosophies for Sale*, and *Alexander*.

125. *CW* 4, clxi–clxii.

126. *CW* 1, 223, 255, 314, and 328.

127. *CW* 3, part II, Latin poems nos. 8, 53, 78, 117, 120, 127, 214, and 240.

dian." The Aldine edition of Sophocles was printed in 1502,[128] and there is no evidence that More had access to any of these works before then;[129] certainly none of them have left their imprint on *Utopia*. The obvious Greek influences are Plato and Aristotle, together with Plutarch and Lucian.

Utopia features Latin influences, too, of course: Terence, Cicero, Seneca, Sallust, and Tacitus. These standard classical authors can also be identified in other works of More's; they all appear in his *History of Richard III*, together with Plautus, Virgil, and Ovid.[130] Of these, Terence, Cicero, Virgil, and Ovid also feature in Erasmus's *Antibarbari*. Many, if not all, would have been part of the curriculum at St. Anthony's school and at Oxford; More got to know others later on. But we can see that More's literary attractions grew from early childhood. Stapleton pointed out that "More studied with avidity all the historical works he could find."[131] In fact, Sir John More wrote the memorandum of his son Thomas's birth on the last pages of a manuscript containing Geoffrey of Monmouth's pseudo-historical *Historia Regum Britanniae*.[132] That More was well acquainted with this text seems to be suggested by the beginning of book II of *Utopia*: *Utopiensium insula … millia passuum ducenta porrigitur*.… The phrase echoes the description of England—taken from Bede—at the very beginning of Geoffrey's work (on the second page of Sir John More's manuscript): *Britannia insularum optima, in occidentali Oceano inter Galliam est et Hiberniam sita: Octingenta millia in longum: Ducenta vero in latum continens*[133]—"Britain, the best of islands, is situated in the Western Ocean, between France and Ireland, eight hundred miles long and two hundred miles wide." The same manuscript contains two extracts (on ff. 2–4 and 134–38) of the *Secreta Secretorum*, supposedly a letter from Aristotle to Alexander the Great; it has been suggested that the *Secreta Secretorum* influenced the account of *Utopia*.[134] One of Hippocrates's treatises, the *Secreta Hippocratis*, also features in the manuscript, and the treatises of Hippocrates were also taken to

---

128. Cf. Logan, Adam, and Miller, *Utopia* (Cambridge (1995), 183n82.

129. See chapter 9.

130. George M. Logan, "More on Tyranny: *The History of King Richard the Third*," in *Companion*, 179.

131. Stapleton, *Histoire de Thomas More*, 14, quoted in *Companion*, 169.

132. MS. O.2.21 contains six texts or extracts: (1) the poem *Cur mundus militat sub uana gloria*, f. 1v; (2) extracts of the *Secreta Secretorum*, ff. 2–4, 134–38; (3) the complete *Galfridi Monumetensis Historia Britonum*, ff. 5–117v; (4) *Visio beati Pauli de penis inferni*, ff. 117v–118; (5) *Quo tendit anima*, f. 119; (6) tract attributed to Walter de Bibbesworth, ff. 120–33v; (7) *Secreta Hippocratis*, ff. 138v–39.

133. MS. O.2.21, part II, f. 5v: for a description of this MS, see Appendix.

134. Edward Surtz, "Sources, Parallels, and Influences," *CW* 4, cxxxvii.

Utopia;[135] but this is hardly surprising, as his works account for a significant proportion of all surviving Classical Greek literature. Of course, the *Historia Regum Britanniae*, the *Secreta Secretorum*, and the *Secreta Hippocratis* were well known at the time; nevertheless, it is noteworthy that the three texts appear together in the very manuscript in which Sir John More recorded the births of his children. *Utopia*, it would seem, draws not only from classical authors but from childhood memories, too.

—

Returning to the circumstances of the translation of the dialogues of Lucian: More married Joanna Colt in January 1505; soon after, in March 1505 Erasmus visited England for the second time and stayed in More's house until May or June 1506. The two of them had been learning Greek since their meeting in 1499. There is written evidence of Erasmus's efforts in this direction from the letter of March 1500 cited earlier, and of More's from the letter to Holt of November 1501. The first edition of Lucian's works had been printed at Florence in 1496 and would have become available thereafter to More. There is, however, a more precise pointer for ascertaining that More knew Lucian by 1501 when he lectured on the *City of God* of St. Augustine. Years later, Juan Luis Vives included part of a translation of Lucian's *Menippus* by More in his commentaries to the *City of God*. That comment may well have been made by More in his lectures and brought up in his conversation with Vives.[136] Be that as it may, when Erasmus arrived back in England, at More's "suggestion" and "as a recreation"[137] the two of them translated a number of Lucian's dialogues from the Greek into Latin, and Erasmus got them published together in one volume in November 1506. This was to be the first edition of the book and, in addition to the four by More, included the translations of eighteen short dialogues and ten longer ones by Erasmus. Each of them undertook his own translation of the *Declamatio pro tyrannicida* and a response to it. The four translations provided by More, in addition to *Tyrannicida*, were *Cynicus*, *Menippus*, and *Philopseudes*. More's contribution to the shared edition was introduced by a dedicatory letter addressed to Thomas Ruthall, the royal secretary, in which More wrote that Lucian ranked among the foremost authors in combining delight with instruction: "Refraining from the arrogant pronouncements of the philosophers as well as from the wanton wiles of the

---

135. *CW* 4, 182:7.
136. See chapter 10.
137. *CWE* 2, Letter 191:6 and 35, from Erasmus to Richard Whitford, May 1, 1506.

poets, he everywhere reprimands and censures, with very honest and at the same time very entertaining wit, our human frailties."[138] More went on to praise the three dialogues that he had chosen,[139] to describe them briefly, and to point out that they were the first fruits of his Greek studies.

In the *Cynicus*, which reads like a short Socratic dialogue between *Lycinus* and *Cynicus*, Lucian presents a contrast or paradox in the use of material goods. The Cynic argues that the virtue of temperance leads him to choose only what he needs; that those who place their ambition in riches choose to have worries and troubles rather than to live a carefree live. His approach to gold, silver, expensive houses, and elaborate dresses is that which More ascribed later to the Utopians. The Cynic advises making a feast of what is in his reach, to be content with having what is needed, avoiding superfluous things, such as gold and silver. Those who lack self-control are led where their appetites choose. The message of the Cynic is echoed in *Utopia* and in More's treatment of the vice of covetousness and the virtue of temperance in his *Treatise on the Last Things* (1522), and, more specifically, in *A Dialogue of Comfort against Tribulation*.[140]

In *Menippus sive Necromantia* (*Menippus or the Descent into Hades*), the two interlocutors are Menippus himself, who is identified as the Cynic, and a friend called Philonides. The dialogue starts when Menippus returns from visiting Hades, and he tells his friend what he had learned there. In brief, after death each man is examined carefully and sent away to the Place of the Wicked to be punished in proportion to his crimes, most hardly those who were swollen with pride of wealth and place; all of them stood there naked, and they were being punished all together, kings, slaves, poor, rich, and beggars. In particular, Menippus witnesses the passing of a new decree by which the bodies of the rich will be punished like those of other malefactors, while "their souls be sent back up into life and enter into donkeys until they shall have passed two hundred and fifty thousand years in that condition, transmigrating from donkey to donkey."[141]

There are many passages from *Menippus* that have their parallels or echoes in future writings of More. For instance, Menippus was disappointed as seeing "wise" men practicing the opposite of that which they preached, "although—he said—I consoled myself somewhat with the thought that if I was still foolish and went about in ignorance of the truth,

---

138. *CW* 3, part I, 3:5–11.
139. *CW* 3.I, 3:14.
140. *CW* 12, 210:6–12: book 3, chapter 8.
141. *CW* 3.I, 178.

at all events I had the company of many wise men, widely renowned for intelligence." This idea is present in More's dialogue on conscience in the Tower: his daughter Margaret advised him to follow the example of the many "wise" men that had given the oath to the Act of Succession, while he argued against ignoring his conscience for "company's sake."

In that dialogue Lucian used the idea of human life as a long pageant.[142] Baker-Smith had this to say about it:

This is the same device that More exploits in Richard III, using the performance of a mystery play to represent political life which, as he sardonically notes, is usually acted out on scaffolds.[143]

It can be argued that life as a play was a commonplace, but the point to bear in mind is that the dialogue was chosen by More. The concluding advice to *Menippus*, after having considered the case of the philosophers and of famous people, was, as translated by More:

Optima est, inquit, idiotarum privatorumque vita, ac prudentissima.[144]

Which Gerald Malsbary puts into English as follows: "The life of private and ordinary citizens is the best life and the most prudent one. So leaving off this empty consideration of lofty matters, give up seeking for origins and ends; … spend your life as cheerfully as you can, and smiling."[145]

The last of the three dialogues is *Philopseudes*, of which More, in his letter to Ruthall writes:

Surely the dialogue will teach us this lesson: that we should put no trust in magic and that we should eschew superstition, which obtrudes everywhere under the guise of religion.

In his introductory letter More wrote that in *Menippus* Lucian rebukes the fruitless contentions of the philosophers. Therefore, it is fitting to focus a bit more on what Lucian has to say about the philosophers. Two of his *Dialogues* are especially relevant: the *Sale of Creeds* or *Philosophies for Sale* and its sequel, *The Dead Come to Life* or *The Fisherman*.

In *Philosophies for Sale* Lucian portrays Zeus, helped by Hermes, putting up for sale in a slave market various philosophers such as Pythagoras,

---

142. *CW* 3.I, 176.

143. Dominic Baker-Smith, *More's Utopia* (Toronto: University of Toronto Press, 2000), 53.

144. *CW* 3.I, 41:34–35.

145. *The Essential Works of Thomas More*, ed. Gerard B. Wegemer and Stephen W. Smith (New Haven and London: Yale University Press, 2020), 33.

Diogenes, Democritus, Socrates, and representative figures of Epicurean-ism, Stoicism, and Skepticism. Thus Socrates, when interrogated by a pro-spective buyer, claims to have built his own city and composed his own laws and constitution,[146] as described in the *Republic*; Lucian laughs at the morals portrayed there. When asked where the Ideas are, Socrates replies "*Nowhere.*"[147] This, of course, is a reference to the text in the *Republic* that hints at the name, *Utopia*, made up by More for his critique of Plato's work. It reads:

You mean that he'll be willing to take part in the politics of the city we were founding and describing, the one that exits in theory, for I think it exists no-where on earth.[148]

In *The Fisherman*, the philosophers come back from Hades to stone Lucian for outraging them as well as Philosophy herself. Lucian manages to convince them that he should be judged by a proper jury and suggests that Philosophy be the president of the jury, along with her companions, Virtue, Temperance, Justice, and Truth, and Truth's maidservants—namely, Freedom, Frankness, Exposure, and Demonstration. Diogenes volunteers to be the prosecutor, as he has been the worst treated of all (he was sold for an insulting three pence, or two obols).[149] Lucian invites the philosophers to join the jury. Of course, once he makes his defense he is acquitted; he demonstrates that he has not been criticizing Philosophy or the philoso-phers themselves but the swarm of their followers—Platonists, Pythagore-ans, Stoics, Peripatetics, Epicureans, and Cynics—who, instead of impart-ing true philosophy, are in pursuit only of gold and glory.

Such is the author More praised in his dedicatory letter to Ruthall, and so it seems likely that he could identify with Erasmus's words in *Antibar-bari*: "Augustine 'despised' heathen culture ... but only after becoming a prince of learning in this field. Jerome's 'contempt' for the writings of Ci-cero and Plato did not debar him from an excellent mastery of them, and he used them continuously."[150] More's attitude might be summarized in

146. Lucian, *The Works of Lucian of Samosata*, trans. H. W. Fowler and F. G. Fowler (Oxford: Clarendon Press, 1905), 1:255; and *The Works of Lucian*, trans. A. H. Harmon, Loeb Classics (London: William Heinemann, 1919), 2:481.

147. Written οὐδαμοῦ in *The Works of Lucian*, 2:482; reprinted with the same pagination in 1960 (L054).

148. Plato, *Republic* 592a–b.

149. In *Works of Lucian of Samosata*, 1:276; *Works of Lucian*, 3:37.

150. In the 1520 edition of *Antibarbari*, Erasmus inserted here references to Basil and John Chrysostom: *CWE* 23, 55:7–9. However, these references are missing from the manuscript of 1494–95: see Hyma, *Youth of Erasmus* (1930), 279. St. Basil also wrote a treatise *For the Young on How They*

words from the letter he wrote to Peter Giles, which was included only in the second edition of *Utopia*:

Did anyone of all the philosophers who have offered a pattern of a society, a ruler, or a private household set down everything so well that nothing ought to be changed? Actually, if it weren't for the great respect I retain for certain highly distinguished names, I could easily produce from each of them a number of notions which I can hardly doubt would be universally condemned as absurd.[151]

The Case of Boethius: *The Consolation of Philosophy*

The editors of *Utopia* in the Yale Edition of More's complete works suggest that Renaissance scholars aimed at the mastery of all knowledge, pagan and Christian, whether in Latin, Greek, or Hebrew, from sacred scriptures and Homer down to Boethius.[152]

Indeed, Boethius (c. 480–524), the man whom the humanist scholar Lorenzo Valla (1407–57) is said to have called "the last of the Romans and the first of the Scholastics,"[153] was a key figure in both the pagan and the Christian traditions; he and St. Augustine were the two most influential scholars in the Christian West from their own times until the synthesis of St. Thomas Aquinas in the thirteenth century.[154] Boethius's *Consolation of Philosophy*, written when he was in prison awaiting execution, was commonly part of the curriculum of Rhetoric in the first year of the *Trivium*. In England it was well known from the time of King Alfred, who had himself translated it into Old English in the year 899; Chaucer's version in English prose was one of the first books to be printed in England by Caxton—precisely in 1478, the year Thomas More was born.

There were many early editions of the *Consolation*, such as those of Verona in 1471, Nuremberg in 1473, Basel in 1474, and Venice in 1492; these editions often included a prologue (supposed to be by St. Thomas Aqui-

---

Might Derive Profit from Hellenic Literature (A.D. 364); but More and Erasmus only discovered him later. More quotes Basil in defense of studying Greek in his *Letter to the University of Oxford*, and frequently elsewhere; indeed, among the Greek Church Fathers cited by More he is second only to John Chrysostom.

151. Logan, Adam, and Miller, *Utopia* (Cambridge (1995), 267. One might speculate that this could be the very letter held in Giles's hand in his portrait of 1517.

152. *CW* 4, 436.

153. The expression is often attributed to Valla but is nowhere to be found in his work.

154. Boethius is quoted extensively in Aquinas's *Summa Theologiae*. See Christopher J. F. Martin, *An Introduction to Medieval Philosophy* (Edinburgh: Edinburgh University Press, 1996); Alasdair MacIntyre, *God, Philosophy, Universities: A Selective History of the Catholic Philosophical Tradition* (Lanham, Md.: Rowman and Littlefield, 2009), 33–41.

nas) in which the *Consolation* was praised with references from Seneca and Aristotle, and its prose was asserted to be as good as Cicero's and its verse as good as Virgil's.[155] The same prologue was included in the edition that contained a commentary by Jean Gerson (Cologne, 1488).[156] The works of Boethius—specifically *The Consolation of Philosophy*—were in Grocyn's library, which was available to More; and Linacre may have brought a copy of the Venice edition on his return to England in July 1499, or at least the news of that new edition, together with a copy of the *Life of Pico*.

That More was familiar with Boethius's *Consolation* is thus obvious. A further link, however, has been made by scholars between More and Boethius, as well as Seneca, noting that the books of Boethius's *Consolation* and Seneca's tragedy *Oedipus* are depicted in the version of the portrait of the *Family of Thomas More* painted by Rowland Lockey c. 1593. The *Consolation of Philosophy* continued to be very popular throughout the sixteenth century. A bilingual Latin-English edition translated by George Colville and dedicated to Queen Mary was printed in London in 1556[157] and reprinted in 1561; another edition of the *Consolation* was produced in England in 1563, the same year that Alexander Neville translated the tragedy of *Oedipus*,[158] when the English Seneca was in fashion. And in 1593, just after her sixtieth birthday, Queen Elizabeth made another translation into English of the *Consolation*.[159] The prayer books that figure on Holbein's sketch of the *Family of Thomas More* (1527) had been forbidden,[160] and so whoever suggested the composition of the *Family Portrait* of 1593 substituted the proscribed books for others acceptable to the court of Elizabeth; nevertheless the new books, while politically correct, can be seen as a coded reference to More's fate under Henry VIII.[161]

155. This is the case of the editions of 1480, 1487, 1497, 1498, and 1499.

156. In this case the prologue was not attributed to St. Thomas. For Jean Gerson's influence on Thomas More, see chapters 6 and 12.

157. Cf. Boethius's *Consolation of Philosophy*, trans. George Colville (1556), ed. Ernest Belfort Bax (London, 1897).

158. Seneca, *Oedipus*, trans. Alexander Neville (London: T. Colwell, 1563), British Library C. 3. a. 9. Neville's translation was republished in one volume in 1581 together with other translations of Seneca by Jasper Heywood. Mitjans, "*Non sum Oedipus sed Morus*, 12–67, suggests that the inclusion of the text of Seneca in the *Family Portrait* might be attributed to Jasper Heywood. He is mentioned in More's biography by Cresacre More.

159. *The Consolation of Queen Elizabeth I: The Queen's Translation of Boethius' De Consolatione Philosophiae*, Introduction by Quan Manh (Phoenix: Arizona Center for Medieval and Renaissance Studies, Arizona State University, 2009). The translation is dated October 10–November 8, 1593.

160. Eamon Duffy, *Marking the Hours: English People and Their Prayers, 1240–1570* (New Haven and London: Yale University Press, 2006), 58.

161. Mitjans, "Elizabethan Transformation of the Family Portrait of Thomas More," *Moreana* 56, no. 212 (December 2019): 133–59.

In the first paragraph of his letter to Colet of October 23, <1502–4>, More refers to the story of Orpheus and Eurydice recorded in book III, song XII of the *Consolation*.[162] The *Consolation* starts with a reflection on the plight of the author:

> I used to write cheerful poems, happy and life-affirming,
> but my eyes are wet with tears[163]

These verses compare (albeit hyperbolically) with the feelings More describes in his letter of October 23, deprived of Colet's company and in the city instead of the leisure of the country; they certainly contrast with the happier mood seen in More's letter to Holt of 1501 or in Erasmus's letter of 1499. It may, then, be instructive to consider what More had found in his reading of the five books of the *Consolation*.

The topics of Death and Fame mentioned in book I, and of Eternity that is described in the last prose of book V, all appear in More's *Pageant Verses* (the full list is: Childhood, Manhood, Venus, Age, Death, Fame, and Eternity). Of course, they were common topics at the time; Fate and the Wheel of Fortune appear all through the *Consolation*, and they are echoed in More's verses introducing the *Book of Fortune.*

In the *Consolation* Lady Philosophy criticizes the ruffians who have done violence to her elegant dress:[164] the squabbling mobs of Stoics and Epicureans who fought to claim Socrates's legacy, each side trying to carry Lady Philosophy off, tearing the lovely mantle she had woven with her own hands so that each of them could wear at least shreds of her raiment, which they pretended quite absurdly to be the entire garment.[165] Boethius here echoes the criticism of Lucian mentioned earlier.

Utopia clearly draws on the *Consolation*, as for instance in the statement that without money there would be no need of lawsuits,[166] or the well-known definition of happiness given by Boethius.[167] More uses Boethius in a number of other works, such as the *Fortune Verses*,[168] his *Letter*

---

162. *Consolation*, trans. David R. Slavitt (Cambridge, Mass.: Harvard University Press, 2008), 103–5.

163. *Consolation*, bk I, song I:1–2, trans. Slavitt, 1.

164. *Consolation*, bk I, ch. I, 3.

165. *Consolation*, bk I, ch. III, 8.

166. *Consolation*, bk III, ch. III, 67.

167. *Statum bonorum omnium congregatione perfectum* (*De Consolatione*, Liber III, prosa II, 3), translated by Slavitt as "that state that is perfect and that includes within it everything a man could want"; *Consolation*, bk III, ch. II, 61.

168. *CW* 1, 33:67–70.

to *Dorp*,[169] and *De tristitia*.[170] In his *Confutation of Tyndale's Answer*,[171] More's argument in favor of free will is similarly taken from the *Consolation*. Some authors have suggested that the idea of the world as a prison that More uses in the *Dialogue of Comfort against Tribulation* is taken from the *Consolation*, although it is admittedly a *locus communis*. In his conversation with Margaret as recorded in the letter to his stepdaughter Alice Alington <August 1534>[172] and in his letter to his children on March 23, <1521>, More exhorts them to keep that beautiful and holy song[173] of Boethius sounding in their ears, "teaching you to raise your mind to heaven, lest the soul look downwards to the earth, after the manner of the brutes, while the body is raised aloft."[174] The reference is to the *Consolation*, book V, poem V. The same image may also be reflected in More's *Twelve Properties of a Lover*, Sixth Property: "Still he whose body's riveted to earth/Can yet his mind raise heavenward to Him."

The reading of the *Consolation*, however, would above all have brought to young More's mind the case of Boethius himself. In book I, prose I, Boethius sees embroidered on the dress of Lady Philosophy the Greek letters Π (for *praxis*) and Θ (for *theoria*), meaning action and contemplation, the two activities of the philosopher. Soon afterward, Boethius complains to Lady Philosophy about her advice to accept Plato's teaching that government would be well run if there were philosopher-kings and her inference from Plato's writings that philosophers should take part in politics in order to prevent the state from falling into the hands of the stupid and the wicked. Boethius goes on, telling Lady Philosophy:

And I listened to you and went into public life, figuring that I could apply in the real world those ideas that we had been discussing there in the library. God knows—as you do, too—that that was all I had in mind, to apply myself to the betterment of the government. And what happened?[175]

So, at the beginning of his adult life, Thomas More must have been aware of the case of Boethius, a married Christian layman, philosopher, and theologian, who went into public life only to find himself imprisoned and executed by the tyrant whom he had served. Boethius recalls the case

169. *CW* 15, 561:68.
170. *CW* 15, 259:6 and 459:4.
171. *CW* 8, 243:31–37, 938:30–939:16.
172. *Correspondence* [206], line 203.
173. *Carmen*, in the *Correspondence* [101], line 21. *De Consolatione* starts with the word *Carmina*.
174. *SL*, 146.
175. *Consolation*, bk I, ch. IV, 11.

of Seneca, Nero's teacher and adviser, whom Nero later sentenced to death. Some scholars have seen this association of Seneca and Boethius as pointing forward to More's fate; but without needing to peer into the future, it is plausible to assume that in reading the *Consolation*, More would have been made acquainted with the difficulties that scholars faced when entering political life. Lady Philosophy states in the *Consolation* that a number of philosophers died only as a result of their dedication to her and of their indifference to and contempt for the beliefs and pursuits of wicked men that her teaching had instilled in them; she then goes on to propose practical examples from history:

But even if you never heard Anaxagoras' banishment from Athens, or Socrates drinking the hemlock, or the torture of Zeno, all of which happened abroad, surely you would know about such Romans as Canius, and Seneca, and Soranus, whose stories are neither so old nor from so far away.[176]

The situation was not alien to More's time and place; historians consider that the risk of tyranny that More points out in his writings might well be a reflection on the latter years of Henry VII.[177] So we can see the dilemma that might present itself to young More on reading the *Consolation*, once his enthusiasm for the classics had been awakened: whether to engage in public life, or not?

In his letter to Colet dated October 23, More recalled the story of Orpheus and Eurydice. It was a familiar tale, but it is worth noting that Boethius gives it a Christian reading (lacking, of course, in the versions received from Virgil and Ovid); it is also worth noting that October 23 was the anniversary of Boethius's execution, though More may not have been aware of the coincidence of dates.

The story of Orpheus occupies lines 3–25 of the poem that ends book III of the *Consolation*. In chapter I of that book, Lady Philosophy states that everyone has a longing for happiness; men seek to satisfy this innate desire with wealth, honor, power, fame, and pleasure (chapter II); but all these give limited happiness (III, IV, V, VI, VII), and they lead in the wrong direction, and even to wickedness (VIII). Men should seek perfect happiness (IX), the true happiness that is to be found only in the supreme goodness that is God (X–XII). Once Boethius has agreed with this conclusion, Philosophy breaks into song:

---

176. *Consolation*, bk I, ch. III, 8.
177. Richard Rex, *The Tudors* (Stroud, Gloucestershire: Tempus, 2005), 28.

Felix qui potuit boni fontem visere lucidum;
felix qui potuit gravis terrae solvere vincula.

"Happy is he who is able to see the shining fountain of goodness/and happy, too, is he who can free himself from the chains that bind him to heavy earth."

Then the tale of Orpheus follows, and Philosophy tells Boethius:

Vos haec fabula respicit …

This tale refers to you, as you make your ascent leading your mind to the light, for if, in a moment of weakness you should look back on the darkness, the excellence you have achieved you will lose, looking back, looking down.

The poem takes forward the argument given in book III. Once that argument is accepted—that is, once man has found the fountain of goodness that, according to the argument of the *Consolation*, is God—man has reached happiness. This happiness also implies (v. 2) freeing oneself from the chains that bind him to heavy earth.

The "ascent leading … to the light" of which Philosophy speaks at the end of the poem is an ascetical ascent, one for which More needs the help of Colet's guidance. In Colet's absence, More claims that he is in need:

I am falling back again into darkness.… I am sinking because you do not look back at me.[178]

In the *Consolation*, finally, More would also have found a praise of marriage and friendship that reflects his own later experience:

Love, too, holds peoples joined
by sacred bond of treaty,
and weaves the holy knot
of marriage's pure love.
Love promulgates the laws
friendship's faithful bond.
O happy race of men,
if Love who rules the sky
could rule your hearts as well![179]

---

178. Letter, October 23, <1502–4>, lines 13–17.

179. *Consolation*, Bk II, Poem VIII, trans., introduction Victor Watts, rev. ed. (London: Penguin Classics, 1999), 45–46. The translation in Slavitt, 58, reads, "Love binds people too,/in matrimony's sacred bonds/where chaste lovers are met,/and friends cement their trust and friendship./How happy is mankind,/if the love that orders the stars above/rules, too, in your hearts!" Watts's translation seems more accurate. Henry Chadwick paraphrases thus in *Boethius: The Consolations of Music, Logic, Theology, and Philosophy* (Oxford: Clarendon Press, 1981), 232: "How happy men would be if only the love by which the stars are ruled could reign in their hearts."

3

Introducing St. John Chrysostom in 1499

In chapter 1 the change undergone by Thomas More between writing his letters of <November 1501> and of October 23<1502–4> was mentioned. We need to return to the events of 1499, when he was twenty-one. Undoubtedly More's meeting with Erasmus was a landmark; at least it is well documented: it marked the beginning of their friendship and of their shared humanistic project. There were, however, three other relevant events in the life of More that year. The first was the death of his mother; it seems that he took it well and remained cheerful, for Erasmus wrote in his letter of December 5, 1499, "Did Nature ever create anything kinder, sweeter, or more harmonious than the character of Thomas More?"[1] And Jacob Batt, reporting on what Erasmus had told him during the two days they stayed together after Erasmus returned from England, said that Erasmus spoke of the "sweetness of More."[2] The other two events that relate to More's humanistic interests were Grocyn's acquisition of a new Greek manuscript of the *Homilies on the Gospel of St. Matthew* by St. John Chrysostom, completed by the scribe on September 25 that year,[3] and the return of Thomas Linacre from Italy.

William Roper wrote that Cardinal Morton "placed [More] at Oxford; where when he was both in the greake and latine tongue sufficiently instructed, he was then" moved to New Inn in London.[4] Harpsfield, who

1. *CWE* 1, Ep. 118:28.
2. *CWE* 1, Ep. 120:32.
3. Oxford, Corpus Christi College, MS. 23, which gives the date and Grocyn's name; see N. G. Wilson, *A Descriptive Catalogue of the Greek Manuscripts of Corpus Christi College, Oxford* (Cambridge: D. S. Brewer, 2011), 5–6 and plate 4.
4. Roper, 5:16–17.

based his biography of More on Roper's account but who was more circumspect, wrote that More was sent to the University of Oxford "where, for the short time of his abode (being not fully two years) and for his age, he wonderfully profited in the knowledge of the latin and greeke tonges."[5] Stapleton corroborated by saying that More was sent to Oxford "for the study of philosophy and Greek."[6] Cresacre More, who considered carefully the previous biographies, omits, however, any reference to More having learned Greek at Oxford. Works as recent as John Guy's *A Daughter's Love* (2008) still maintain that More met Grocyn in Oxford,[7] but there is no firm evidence of such possibility.

It seems more likely that Grocyn got to know the young Thomas after 1496, when he became the rector of St. Lawrence Jewry, just a few yards from More's family house at Milk Street. More was then studying at Lincoln's Inn. Grocyn had built up an extensive humanistic library, which included Latin and Greek manuscripts and recent printed editions.[8] Thomas Linacre was a disciple of Grocyn, and at his return from Italy he brought a number of Greek and Latin books and manuscripts—among others, the works of Galen and the *Meteorologica* of Aristotle, which More studied while learning Greek "under the tutelage of Linacre."[9] He may have brought also a copy of the 1498 edition of the Latin *Life of Pico* and the *Works of Lucian*.

Grocyn may well have introduced Linacre to More and to Colet. These four, together with Erasmus, formed a circle of friends seeking to master the Greek and Latin authors with great enthusiasm, thinking that this new knowledge would change their society for the better. Authors such as John Guy and André Prévost describe their zeal and efforts superbly;[10] what I would like to focus on here is the influence on the young lawyer of these

---

5. Harpsfield, 12:13–16.

6. Stapleton, 2.

7. See Guy, *Daughter's Love* (2008), 80.

8. See "The Catalogue of Books Belonging to William Grocyn: Taken after His Death by His Executor, Thomas Linacre, in 1520," published in Burrows, *Collectanea*, 319–24. The catalogue includes 103 printed books and seventeen manuscripts; there is a further list of fifty-four Greek books owned by Grocyn in P. S. Allen and H. W. Garrod, *Merton Muniments* (Oxford: Oxford Historical Society, 1928), 86:47, chart XXVI: most of them are manuscripts copied in the late fifteenth or early sixteenth centuries, although a few are printed books. Of the Greek manuscripts, twenty-four found their way to Corpus Christi College, Oxford; see Wilson, *Descriptive Catalogue*, ix–x, and throughout. Only two of these are mentioned in the Catalogue of 1520.

9. Letter to Dorp, *CW* 15, 103:13.

10. See Guy, "Speaking in Tongues," in *Daughter's Love* (2008), 81–82; André Prévost, *Thomas More et la Crise de la Pensée Européenne* (Tours: Maison Mame, 1969), 109–11.

two books, Chrysostom's *Homilies on the Gospel of St. Matthew* and the *Life of Pico*.

As I mentioned before, Erasmus was thinking of Colet, Grocyn, Linacre, and More when he exclaimed enthusiastically in his letter of December 5, 1499, "What an extensive and rich crop of ancient learning is springing up here in England,"[11] "truly classical, in both Latin and Greek."[12] In this context, the arrival, by August 27, 1499, of Linacre who, together with Grocyn, was going to be More's Greek teacher, and Grocyn's acquisition of the new manuscript on September 25 of the same year, were to be of great help to More's Latin and Greek studies and his knowledge of the Fathers of the Church.

It is to be noticed that More's keenness for Latin poetry preceded, of course, his encounter with Erasmus, for Erasmus describes More's poem addressed to young prince Henry at Elham on the day Erasmus first met More. It is also to be noticed that More's studies must have progressed gradually. We know first of his lectures on *De civitate Dei* around 1501; it was probably after he had delivered those lectures that he wrote to John Holt in November 1501 saying that he had "shelved [his] Latin books, to take up the study of Greek." Then, as he tells Holt, Grocyn was his teacher. By <1502–4> he is practicing Greek with Lily, and Linacre is their teacher. The letter to Holt, however, does not mean that he ceased his practice of Latin, for in 1505 he translated the *Life of Pico* from Latin to English, and all his life he continued to write in Latin; it does not mean either that he was not attracted to learn Greek from early on—from his contact with Grocyn, with Linacre, and from his shared project with Erasmus.

"Of All Christians (in My Opinion) the Most Learned"

In the dedicatory letter of 1506 introducing his translations of Lucian, More mentions only two Fathers of the Church, St. Augustine and St. John Chrysostom. As we have seen, although he had previously lectured on St. Augustine's *City of God*, he states that in his opinion (*ut ego certe puto*) Chrysostom was the most learned of the Fathers.[13] With these words of praise, More seems to be saying that Chrysostom was in a certain sense his mentor; so it is worth considering how much and what More had absorbed

---

11. *CWE* 1, Ep. 118:30.
12. *CWE* 1, Ep. 118:23.
13. *CW* 3, part I: *Translations of Lucian*, 3:30–31.

from the great Father by that time. In later works More frequently quotes Chrysostom. The question here is, however, how much he knew when he expressed his opinion.

There is a passage in St. John Chrysostom's *Homilies on St. Matthew's Gospel* that is clearly echoed in a text written by More. In Homily 1, which is an introductory homily to the rest, we read that Christians practiced their faith not only in the cities or in the midst of the marketplace but also on the summits of mountains: the standard Latin translation is *"non in urbibus tantum, nec in medio foro; sed et in montium verticibus."*[14]

The reference to *urbibus* and *foro* should alert the reader to a possible link with More's letter to Colet of October 23, <1502–4>, where the physical setting is also defined by *urbs* and *forum*. This leads us to inquire whether More knew that homily, either in the original Greek or in its Latin translation (it is worth investigating both possibilities), before he wrote his letter to Colet.

Many Fathers of the Church were known in England throughout the Middle Ages,[15] and some of the Greek Fathers were accessible in Latin translations made in the patristic period or, increasingly, from the twelfth century onward.[16] In the fifteenth century, however, there was a new interest in accessing the texts of the Greek Fathers, both in their original language and in Latin translations, which was met both by new manuscripts and by the new technology of print.[17] The British Library, for instance, holds a splendid Italian manuscript of eighty-eight homilies of St. John Chrysostom on the Gospel of St. Matthew, translated into Latin by the Greek humanist George of Trebizond around 1448.[18] But he gives a different translation for the phrase from that quoted earlier: *"et non in urbibus/*

---

14. St. John Chrysostom, *Homiliae in Matthaeum*, Homilia I, 5, in *Patrologiae Cursus Completus, Patrologiae Graecae*, Tomus LVII (Paris: J. P. Migne, 1860), col. 20, para. 5.

15. See, for instance, Irena Backus, ed., *The Reception of the Church Fathers in the West*, 2 vols. (Leiden, New York, and Cologne: E. J. Brill, 1997).

16. Knowledge of Greek in the West was quite rare up to the twelfth century but became increasingly common thereafter, and many Greek texts were translated. The works of St. John Chrysostom were preserved particularly in a monastic context; Jean Leclercq, OSB, *The Love of Learning and the Desire for God: A Study of Monastic Culture* (New York: Fordham University Press, 1974), 114–16.

17. See, for instance, Montague Rhodes James, "Greek Manuscripts in England before the Renaissance," in *Library*, new series, no. 4 (March 1927): 337–53; J. R. Liddell, "The Library of Corpus Christi College, Oxford, in the Sixteenth Century," *Library*, 4th series, no. 18 (1958): 385–416; and N. R. Ker, "The Provision of Books," in *The History of the University of Oxford*, vol. 2, *The Collegiate University*, ed. James McConica (Oxford: Clarendon Press, 1984–92), 441–519.

18. London, BL, MS Egerton 875: *Chrysostom: Homiliae in Evangelium S. Matthaei, Latine per Georgium Trapezuntium*. There is another copy of the same translation in the Vatican Library, Vat. Lat. 385.

solum atq; plateis, sed in his quoq; verticibus montium,"[19] so he can hardly have been the source for the terms *urbe/foro* used by More in his letter to Colet.[20] The two extant contemporary printed Latin editions—one published in Strasburg in 1466 and the other in Cologne in 1487[21]—both use George of Trebizond's translation; neither of them includes the introductory homily.

The edition of St. John Chrysostom published in Migne's *Patrologia Graeca*[22] cites as its first source the Greek text MSS. 23 and 24 of Corpus Christi College, Oxford, which were copied at Reading Abbey by a certain Joannes Serbopoulos. The two manuscripts include the complete ninety homilies on the Gospel of St. Matthew; the first was copied in 1499 and contains Grocyn's name in Latin, *W. Grocini*, seemingly as its owner; the second was finished in 1500.[23]

Little is known about Serbopoulos except that he was a refugee from Constantinople who took up residence in England in 1484 or earlier,[24] possibly first at Oxford, then certainly at Reading; he was not a member of the community at Reading Abbey, but only a lodger. He seems to have lived at the abbey from at least 1489 to 1500 and supported himself by copying books for scholars and perhaps also teaching at Oxford; we may have as many as ten surviving manuscripts that he copied during the period.[25] Several manuscripts copied by Serbopoulos were commissioned or acquired by Grocyn.[26] Probably the news of the new manuscript com-

19. BL, Egerton 875, 4, ll. 15–16.

20. Another book by George of Trebizond, *Rethorica* (Venice 1470, Milan 1479), is among the books of Grocyn catalogued by Linacre in 1520 (*Collectanea*, 322, title 5), but we have no reason for thinking More knew of George of Trebizond's translation of Chrysostom.

21. Johannes Chrysostomus, *Homiliae super Mattheum* (Strasburgh: Johann Mentelin, 1466), starts with Homily XXVI (which corresponds to Mt 8:5); the edition published by Johann Koelhoff the Elder, Cologne, 1487, starts with Homily I (Mt 1:1).

22. PG 57, Praefatio, ii, sect. II: Primum nobis exhibuit bibliotheca college Corporis Christi Oxonii, a Serbopulo quodam, homine Graeco, anno MCCCCXCIX satis negligenter imperite scriptum, Redingae in Anglia, XLV tantum priores Homilias continentem.

23. Wilson, *Descriptive Catalogue* (2011), MSS 23 and 24 and plates 4–6. Also H. O. Coxe, *Catalogus Codicum MSS. qui in Collegiis Aulisque Oxoniensibus Hodie Adservantur* (Oxford, 1852), vol. 2 (Pars II), under the section for Corpus Christi College, 5–6; and in Liddell, "Library of Corpus Christi College, Oxford, in the Sixteenth Century," 385–416.

24. He was recipient of a royal grant from the Exchequer in 1455/6. For more on his career, see Jonathan Harris, *Greek Emigres in the West 1400–1520* (Camberley: Porphyrogenitus, 1995), 147–48; Jac Dean Perrin Jr., "Family 13 in Saint John's Gospel" (Ph.D. thesis, University of Birmingham, 2012), 70–74.

25. Alan Coates, in *English Medieval Books: The Reading Abbey Collection from Foundation to Dispersal* (Oxford: Clarendon Press, 1999), 110, writes "at least seven," but Montague Rhodes James, "Greek Manuscripts in England before the Renaissance," 352, lists ten.

26. Coates, *English Medieval Books*, 108–12.

pleted on September 25, 1499, and acquired by Grocyn reached Colet and Erasmus, who met that year at Oxford, and therefore also More, who met them later in the year in London. On December 5, Erasmus wrote to Robert Fisher exulting over the Latin and Greek scholarship that he found in England. He was astonished at Grocyn's accomplishments.[27]

The Greek text in the manuscript that Grocyn acquired in September 1499 reads: καὶ οὐκ ἐν ταῖς πόλεσι μόνον, οὐδὲ ἐν μέσαις ταῖς ἀγοραῖς, ἀλλὰ καὶ ἐν ταῖς κορυφαῖς τῶν ὀρῶν:[28] "not only in the cities [*polesi*], nor in the middle of the marketplaces [*agorais*]."

The linking of the 1499 Greek manuscript with Grocyn sheds new light on his possible importance for More. His influence features in More's first two extant Latin letters: Grocyn is mentioned as his instructor in Greek already in the letter of 1501,[29] and by then Grocyn would have had plenty of opportunity to show his new Greek manuscript to More. In any case, it would have been surprising if More had still not seen the manuscript when he used the terms *urbs/forum* in his letter to Colet of October 23, <1502–4>,[30] and when he praised Chrysostom in 1506.[31]

Polis and *Agora* in St. John Chrysostom's Homilies

In his introductory homily to St. Matthew's Gospel, St. John Chrysostom explains that the teaching of Christ can be understood by everyone—by a laborer, a servant, a widow, a child, or even by one who seems exceedingly slow in understanding; and that it is not only easily learned, but has also been practiced by all kinds of people "in the cities and marketplaces, as well as on the summits of mountains." This turn of phrase seems to convey the idea that the fullness of Christian life—holiness—can be attained by everyone, everywhere. The fact that all Christians are called to holiness was commonly understood among the first Christians and the general teaching of the Fathers of the Church, and in particular St. John Chrysostom and St. Augustine, the two Fathers mentioned by More in his dedicatory letter of 1506.

In his notes to the text of the homily, however, Migne suggests that the

27. *CWE* 1, Ep. 118:23–26.
28. St. John Chrysostom, *Homiliae in Matthaeum*, Homilia I, 5, in *Patrologiae Cursus Completus*, Patrologiae Graecae 57 (Paris: J. P. Migne, 1860), col. 20.
29. *Correspondence* [2:12–14].
30. *Correspondence* [3].
31. *Correspondence* [5].

"summits of mountains" refers to monks,[32] who retired to the mountains in search of a life of solitude to devote themselves exclusively to seeking holiness. This is certainly a commonplace of Chrysostom; Erasmus, writing to Cranevelt, quotes a text from Chrysostom[33] describing those who have adopted the monastic life: "Shunning the market-place and cities and all the turmoil, they have chosen a life in the hills that has nothing in common with the present and does not suffer the lot of common men."[34] Thus, Erasmus and most of his contemporaries would probably have considered that the "summit of mountains" referred to those who have chosen the *contemptus mundi*. And in fact, in his homilies on the Gospel of St. Matthew, Chrysostom often refers to the monks as those who have gone to live "on the summit of the mountains," "have taken up their dwelling on the mountains," "have occupied the mountains" (Homilies 7, 13, 20, 43, 55, 61, 68, and 79). Chrysostom is thinking particularly of the monks on the mountains around Antioch, among whom he himself had spent a number of years (c. 374–81) before being ordained. The homilies on St. Matthew's Gospel, however, are clearly addressed to the ordinary citizens of Antioch, who have chosen to practice their faith in the cities and in the marketplaces. He tells them, for instance, that they have to practice decency and chastity, that these are not virtues just for those who "occupy the mountains," for

assuredly Christ made his laws common to all. So, when he says, "if anyone look on a woman to lust after her," he speaks not to the solitary, but to him also that has a wife; since in fact that mount [where Jesus preached the Sermon on the Mount] was at that time filled with all kinds of persons of that description. (Homily 7, Mt 2:4–5)

Chrysostom preached, "I do not say, do not marry. I do not say, forsake cities, and withdraw yourself from public affairs; but being engaged in them, show virtue." Indeed, he considered that those living an ordinary life had a greater need to seek holiness:

Yes, and such as are busy amid cities, I would like to have more approved than such as have occupied the mountains. Why is [this] so? Because great is the profit thence arising. "For no man lights a candle, and sets it under the bushel."[35]

---

32. "*De monachis in monte degentibus loquitur.*"

33. In *CWE* 8 it is said that the quotation comes from a series of sermons (*Ad populum Antiochenum*, nos. 22–80) no longer attributed to Chrysostom. In Erasmus's edition of Chrysostom in Latin (Basel: Froben, 1530) they are found in vol. IV, 569, 571, and 573 (Sermons 55 and 56); but in vol. V of the Froben edition of 1547, they are identified as not belonging to Chrysostom. The quotation, however, is also found in the certainly authentic Homily 68 on the Gospel of St. Matthew.

34. *CWE* 8, 130, Ep. 1173, Louvain, December 18, 1520.

35. Mt 5:15, cf. Mk 4:21, Lk 8:16, 11:33.

Therefore I wish that all the candles were set upon the candlestick, that the light might wax great. Let us kindle then his fire; let us cause them that are sitting in darkness to be delivered from their error. And tell me not, "I have a wife, and children belonging to me, and am master of a household, and cannot duly practice all this." For though you had none of these, yet if you be careless, all is lost; though you are encompassed with all these, yet if you be earnest, you shall attain to virtue. For there is but one thing that is wanted, the preparation of a generous mind; and neither age, nor poverty, nor wealth, nor reverse of fortune, nor anything else, will be able to impede you. Since, in fact, both old and young, and men having wives, and bringing up children, and working at crafts, and serving as soldiers, have duly performed all that is enjoined. For so Daniel was young, and Joseph a slave, and Aquila worked at a craft, and the woman who sold purple was over a workshop, and another was the keeper of a prison, and another a centurion, as Cornelius; and another in ill health, as Timothy; and another a runaway, as Onesimus; but nothing proved an hindrance to any of these, but all were approved, both men and women, both young and old, both slaves and free, both soldiers and people. (Homily 43.7, Mt 12:38–39).

In his homilies on the Gospel of St. Matthew, Chrysostom often uses the term *agora*, "marketplace" (see Homilies 1, 3, 4, 5, 6, 13, 15, 16, 19, 32, 33, 37, 66, 68, 73, 88, and 89) to mean the place where business is done or just the public space. Chrysostom emphasizes the importance of a consistent life: to behave properly not only when in Church, but also when out in the marketplace. Christians "ought to be distinguished not by their place, but by their way of life" (Homily 4, echoing the *Letter to Diognetus*); they are to behave properly "at home, abroad, and in the market, and in church" (Homily 19).[36] For Chrysostom, the marketplace is where Christians are to practice the teaching of Christ—and he would like to preach this teaching "continually, in church, in the marketplace and everywhere" (Homily 9). In summary, the marketplace, in these homilies, is the place where the citizens are to seek holiness. The city and the marketplace are mentioned together not only in the introductory homily but in many others (see, for instance, Homilies 13 and 36), and in a sense they are seen as expressions of the same concept, of the secular society; certainly, the city is present all through these ninety homilies preached by St. John Chrysostom to the citizens of Antioch. A further quotation seems relevant:

For even one dwelling in a city may imitate the self-denial of the monks; yes, one who has a wife, and is busied in a household, may pray, and fast, and learn

---

36. The marketplace is a place where one can help someone ill-treated (Homily 15) but can also be a place where one can show off out of vanity (Homily 3).

compunction. Since they also, who at the first were instructed by the apostles, though they dwelt in cities, yet showed forth the piety of the occupiers of the deserts: and others again who had to rule over workshops, as Priscilla and Aquila. (Homily 55)

The same teaching is found elsewhere in Chrysostom's writing. Thus in his homily on the book of Genesis that he preached in Antioch in 388 (that is, before the *Homilies on the Gospel of St. Matthew*), he said:

Where are now those who say that it is not possible to preserve virtue who live in the midst of the city, but that it is necessary to retire and live in the mountains? As if it were not possible to be virtuous who governs a house and has a wife and takes care of his children.[37]

Yet, though the preaching of Chrysostom—that those living in cities should practice a life of prayer—is clear, his frequent references to monks dwelling in the mountains are striking, though they can be more easily understood in their historical context. After the Edict of Milan, many Christians seeking a rigorous spiritual combat left the cities for the desert (particularly in Egypt) and the mountains (in Syria). Antioch was one of the largest and most important cities of the empire, with a large Christian population. Chrysostom acknowledges that many have left for the mountains, and he admonishes the citizens to seek holiness where they are—in the city—and in the midst of their business, public duties, and ordinary work—in the marketplace.

Chrysostom had firsthand knowledge of the life of those dwelling in the mountains because after his baptism and a period of study, he spent four years with the hermits on Mount Silpius, up above the city, and a further two years alone under the guidance of an old hermit. His biographer explains that he had to return to Antioch to follow his true vocation, as priest, preacher, and bishop. He himself wrote later that were he to have to choose between the troubles of church government and the tranquility of monastic life, he would prefer pastoral service a thousand times over,[38] for it was to this that he felt called, rather than to "occupy the mountains."[39] The reference to withdrawing to the summits of the mountains could be

---

37. *In Genesim Homilia* 43, 1 (PG 54, col. 396).

38. St. John Chrysostom, *On the Priesthood*, bk 6, ch. 7. Grocyn had a copy of this work, which was acquired later by John Claymond, who donated it to Corpus Christi College, Oxford; it is contained in the college's MS. 21. (The same is true of MSS. 22, *Chrysostomi homiliae in Psalmos, grece*, and 25, *Chrysostomi questiones in evangelia*.) See Wilson, *Greek Manuscripts of Corpus Christi College*, MSS. 21, 22 and 25, and pl. 2, 3, and 7.

39. Chrysostom, *On the Priesthood*, bk 6, ch. 4.

read with an almost Morean sense of humor; but whether Chrysostom intended the irony or not, it is evident that for him, the ordinary setting for his audience to practice Christ's teaching was in the city and in the marketplace.

Given the parallel between More's reference to the city and the marketplace and Chrysostom's introductory homily on the Gospel of St. Matthew, it is not impossible that the former may have been aware of the use the latter makes of those terms in his homilies. More, it seems, chose to seek holiness in the city and in the marketplace, and in this he followed closely the teaching of Chrysostom that the fullness of holiness is to be sought in all states of life, and specifically that most Christians are called to practice such holiness while living in the midst of the world.[40]

St. John Chrysostom's Homilies
on the Gospel of St. Matthew

So far in this chapter I have argued that the reference to the city and the marketplace in More's letter to Colet in <1502–4> echoes the sentence discussed previously: "*Non in urbibus tantum, nec in medio foro*," from the first homily of St. John Chrysostom on the Gospel of St. Matthew, and that he had access to MS 23 belonging to William Grocyn. It is to be assumed that More must have pondered on the whole text of that homily, which in MS 23 appears as ΟΜΙΛΙΑ Α. ΠΡΟΟΙΜΙΟΝ (Homily 1: Introduction) and is an introduction to the sequential commentaries to the Gospel of St. Matthew, which start with Mt 1:1 in Homily 2. Before doing so, however, it is worth making two clarifications.

In the first place, in his prefatory letter of 1506 More stated that St. John Chrysostom introduced a large part of Lucian's *Cynicus* into one of the Homilies on the Gospel of St. John,[41] which he delivered at Antioch after his Homilies on the Gospel of St. Matthew. In these homilies, Chrysostom often mentions the city and marketplace (Homilies 19, 34, 39, 48, 62, 63, 77, and 80), but he does not characterize the *urbs/forum* as the places where Christians are to practice the Lord's teaching. Perhaps this is because the Gospel of St. John is more theological, and Chrysostom's

---

40. See the entry on St. John Chrysostom in Angelo di Berardino, ed., *Nuovo dizionario patristico e di Antichità cristiane* (Genoa: Marietti for Institutum Patristicum Augustinianum, 2006–8), col. 2221.

41. *CW* 3, part I, 3:31–33.

homilies on it are more controversial, against the misuse of St. John by the Arians, while his homilies on St. Matthew are full of moral and ascetical exhortations: that is, the homilies on St. John focus on the truths to be believed, while those on St. Matthew focus on the Christian's behavior. In any case, it seems that More was struck by the introductory homily to the Gospel of St. Matthew, and in fact the language used in that homily is kept up throughout the rest of those homilies. That is why it seems possible to posit that the Greek MS of 1499 may have had some impact on the young More. He might have worked at it while learning Greek between 1501 and the time he wrote the letter of October 23, <1502–4>, even though he may not have looked at the Greek homilies on the Gospel of St. John much before tackling the translations from Lucian in 1506.

A second clarification is that although in 1506 More wrote that St. John Chrysostom was the most learned of Christians, he does not seem to single Chrysostom out in the same way in his later writings. The reason is simple: in his apologetic and polemical writings More usually brings in the Fathers of the Church to defend the Church's Tradition against heretical opinions, and, to this end, he prefers to cite the Fathers together or in groups.[42] Thus, for example, in the *Dialogue* of 1529 he declares that Gregory, Augustine, Jerome, Eusebius, Basil, and Chrysostom all spoke in favor of devotion to saints, veneration of images, and going on pilgrimages.[43] In other passages of the same work he lists Jerome, Augustine, Basil, Chrysostom, and Gregory;[44] Jerome, Augustine, Eusebius, Basil, Ambrose, Gregory Nazianzen, and Chrysostom;[45] Augustine, Jerome, Ambrose, Gregory, Cyprian, and Chrysostom;[46] Augustine, Jerome, Ambrose, Chrysostom. and Gregory;[47] so that Chrysostom figures in six of out ten lists of Fathers given in the *Dialogue* of 1529.[48] Chrysostom also appears in the two lists given in the *Responsio ad Lutherum* (1523)[49] and again later in *The Confutation of Tyndale's Answer* (1532–33). In a different context, in the Letter to Oxford <1518>, More speaks of the need to have Hebrew, Greek, and Latin

---

42. William P. Haugaard, "Renaissance Patristic Scholarship and Theology in Sixteenth-Century England," *Sixteenth Century Journal* 10, no. 3 (Autumn 1979): 40, notes that both Catholics and Protestants cited the Fathers in their controversies.

43. *CW* 6, 90.

44. *CW* 6, 238.

45. *CW* 6, 407.

46. *CW* 6, 420 and 434.

47. *CW* 6, 432.

48. *CW* 6, 528fn2.

49. *CW* 5, 417, and 521.

in order to study the writings of Jerome, Ambrose, Cyprian, Chrysostom, Augustine, Gregory, and Basil.[50]

But in the last of More's books published in his own lifetime, *The Answer to a Poisoned Book*,[51] a reply to *The Souper of the Lorde*,[52] he again singles out Chrysostom in defense of the Real Presence in the Eucharist, citing, among others, his homilies on the Gospel of St. John, but especially his homilies on the First Letter to the Corinthians; this may reflect More's awareness that for this topic, he could not rely as much as usual on his mainstay, Augustine. Hence it might be said that at the end of his life, More could well have repeated his assertion that Chrysostom was the most Christian of the learned.

—

In the prefatory letter of 1506 introducing the translations from Lucian, More wrote that St. John Chrysostom was in his opinion the most learned of the Christians. We have seen the correspondence between Chrysostom's introductory homily on the Gospel of St. Matthew (to which More had access since the arrival of Grocyn's new Greek MS in 1499) and the letter he wrote to Colet in <1502–4>. Other features of St. John Chrysostom's Homilies on the Gospel of St. Matthew can also be seen reflected in More's works:

1. St. John Chrysostom starts by pointing out that the Word of God— communicated to Noah, Abraham, Job, Moses, etc.—preceded the written word.[53] This is an argument that More develops later in his *Dialogue* of 1529 and in his disputes with Tyndale.

2. In the introductory homily, section 13, Chrysostom says that the Heavenly City is the subject of the Gospel of St. Matthew (and indeed he speaks of it throughout the homilies). He thus brings up a topic that is to be amply developed by St. Augustine; and it is surely not a coincidence that More lectured on St. Augustine's *City of God* at St. Lawrence's while Grocyn was the parish priest there: he must have invited him to do so. In Grocyn's library there were many works by St. Augustine, including two printed editions of *De civitate Dei*, one of them with commentaries.[54] This is another indication of the possible influence of this homily on More's future work.

50. *CW* 15, 141.
51. *CW* 11.
52. Perhaps by George Joye.
53. Homily I, no. 1.
54. *Collectanea*, nos. 1 and 86.

3. Chrysostom says that the apostles brought us a "new principle of life, another manner of living: both in wealth and poverty, in freedom and in slavery, in life and in death, changing all, our world and our polity. Not like Plato, who composed that ridiculous *Polis*." This can be seen as reflected in the *hexastichon*, the six lines of verse with which More introduces *Utopia*, which include the lines: *Nunc ciuitatis aemula Platonicae / Fortasse uictrix*.[55] More's use of the word *civitas* rather than *respublica* brings him closer to the word used by Plato and Chrysostom: πολιτεια.

After he had preached his Homilies on the Gospel of St. Matthew addressed to the citizens of Antioch, Chrysostom was appointed archbishop of Constantinople in 397; there in his Homilies on the Acts of the Apostles he proposed the model of the primitive Church, based on Acts 4:32–37, as an "ideal city." The old Greek idea of the *polis* gives way to the new idea of a city inspired by Christian faith. More took up the discussion of the *polis* in *Utopia* (1516), though More's *Utopia* was "pre-Christian," for the Utopians had built up their commonwealth without knowledge of Christianity. (In fact, as More points out, the Utopians did not know the classical authors, either.)

4. It seems that there is also a parallelism between the beginning of the letter of October 23, <1502–4>, and the opening of the *Republic*. In his letter More writes, "Recently [*dudum*], while I was walking through the marketplace, your servant [*puer tuus*] made his appearance." The *Republic* starts with Socrates saying that when he went down to the port of Piraeus with Glaucon, Polemarchus saw them and sent his servant, who caught hold of Socrates's coat. An early translation of the *Republic* by the Italian humanist Uberto Decembrio (d. 1427) reads, "*Heri … ad nos puero … vestem meam puer apprehendit*." The *dudum / puer tuus* of More's letter may echo the "*Heri / ad nos puero … puer*" of the *Republic*, which suggests that More may have been aware of Plato's text prior to <1502–4>. There is no evidence, however, that More had any knowledge of that Latin translation. Ficino's 1484 or 1491 editions of the Latin translation of the works of Plato may have reached England by the beginning of the sixteenth century, but for *puero / puer*, the Greek text has *paida / pais*, which can be translated as "boy" or "servant," and Ficino does indeed use *servus* and *servulum* instead of *puer*. Therefore, More was not following Ficino's Latin here. It is more likely that he had read the Greek manuscript of Plato's *Republic*

---

55. *CW* 4 (1965), 21, translates, "I am a rival of Plato's *republic*, perhaps even a victor over it." But *CU* 19 has "with Plato's *state* I can compare"; and Prévost, *Utopia* (Paris: Mame, 1978), 330, reads, "Émule à présent de la platonicienne *cité*," following a more literal translation of the Latin.

that Grocyn possessed.[56] It seems, therefore, that there there may be traces of Chrysostom's introductory homily in More's letter of October 23, not only in the *urbe/foro* combination, but also possibly in a resonance with the start of the *Republic* that Chrysostom mentions.

5. Just a few lines before the reference to the *urbe/foro* as the place to practice the fullness of Christian teaching, Chrysostom states that this is to be learned and practiced by all: the farmer and the smith, the master builder and the ship's pilot (*agricola, vel aerarius faber vel architectus aut gubernator*),[57] each without leaving his trade or honest toil.[58]

6. Chrysostom goes on to declare that the inhabitants of that new *polis* become children of God (Homily 1, 6). He speaks of the Fatherly love of God toward his children in a number of his homilies, repeatedly using the phrase "tender care" or the adjectival "tender loving" (*philostorgos*).[59] The awareness of being a child of God was reflected in More's adaptation of the *Life of Giovanni Pico* by his nephew Gianfrancesco. Gianfrancesco finishes his piece with a prayer of Giovanni Pico that ends, "*Non dominum sed te sentiat esse patrem.*"[60] More, instead of translating it for "not a lord but a Father,"[61] wrote, with a particular stress,

> not as a lorde: but rathir
> As a *very tender loving* fathir.[62]

St. John Chrysostom vs. St. Ambrose

I have suggested that More may have taken from Chrysostom's first homily on the Gospel of St. Matthew an understanding that the fullness of Christian life could be practiced in the city and marketplace without having to flee to the mountains. The opposite attitude to the city, the marketplace,

56. Oxford, Corpus Christi College, MS. 96, Catalogue of 1589, no. 27. The manuscript contains four works by Plato, the *Republic*, *Timaeus*, the *Laws* and *Epinomis*, and the commentary on Plato's *First Alcibiades* by the neo-Platonic philosopher Proclus.

57. Homily I, 5 (11).

58. In teaching that Christian life can be learned and practiced without leaving one's trade, Chrysostom contrasts this with Plato's *Republic*, where the philosopher has to undertake a program of studies and training for many years (*The Republic*, part 8, bk 7); he asks how they are supposed to maintain themselves during that long period of years. More addresses the question in *Utopia*: Utopians work at their trade for only six hours a day, and so have time and opportunities for study and further education in their spare time.

59. Chrysostom uses the phrase "tender loving Father," referring to God, several times in his homilies on the book of Genesis.

60. *CW* 1, 380, l.77.

61. Translation of the original Latin text suggested by Clarence H. Miller, in *CW* 1, 381.

62. *CW* 1, 123, ll. 10–11.

and the mountain is found, however, in another Church Father, St. Ambrose. He writes that

Christ is not found in the marketplace or in the streets [*In foro aut in plateis Christus non reperitur*]. Christ is not a man-about-town. Christ is peace, but the marketplace is for dispute. Christ is justice but the marketplace is for iniquity. Christ is a worker and the marketplace is for empty idleness.... Let us shun the marketplace, let us get away from the streets.[63]

And Ambrose goes on to declare that "we must seek Christ" in the mountains, for Christ flees from the streets, the meeting-places of men, and the noise of the marketplace—this last phrase, *strepitus fori*, is very close indeed to the *forenses strepitus* in More's letter of October 23, <1502–4>.

These words of St. Ambrose are found in his book *De Virginitate*, which is essentially a phrase-by-phrase commentary on the Song of Songs. But when he comes to the verse *Surgam, et circuibo civitatem; per vicos et plateas quaeram quem diligit anima mea*—"I will rise and go about the city; in the streets and in the squares, I will seek him whom my soul loves,"[64] he gives it an allegorical interpretation:

The search must be in the city, in the marketplace, and on the streets: in the city, that is, of our God; in the marketplace where the Judge of divine law sits; in the streets from which were collected those who came to the Lord's supper.[65]

This contrasts with Chrysostom's reference to the actual physical place where people live and work and relate to others. We thus have different readings of mountain, city, and marketplace as the places to encounter Christ in the reflections of the Fathers and in the history of spirituality. Chrysostom was aware of the contrary reading to his own when he referred, in the passage from Homily 68 on the Gospel of St. Matthew quoted previously, to those who had abandoned their ordinary circumstances in order to choose a "life in the hills" separate from "the lot of common men." Of course, the variant interpretations were intended for different audiences: Ambrose was preaching to the women of Milan who had chosen to follow Christ in virginity and something close to a religious life, while Chrysostom was reminding the ordinary citizens of Antioch that they had the obligation to practice the fullness of Christ's teachings where they were, in the city and in the marketplace.

Of the two readings, More seems to have followed Chrysostom's as the setting for his life, but St. Ambrose's reading is also echoed in More's letter

63. *De Virginitate* 46.
64. Song 3:2.
65. *De Virginitate* 89.

of October 23, and so it is worth considering More's attitude to St. Ambrose. He would have seen something of Ambrose in St. Augustine's *De doctrina Christiana*, as the latter gives examples of the style of St. Ambrose's *De Virginibus*.[66] Much more significantly, More would have had access to two printed collections of the works of St. Ambrose in Grocyn's library. And St. Ambrose was something of a favorite of Erasmus: he mentions him (together with St. Augustine and St. Jerome) in the 1495 manuscript of *Antibarbari*[67] and praises him in his *De ratione studii*, which was published in 1511 but based on lessons given in 1496–98. Here Erasmus recommends reading the sources directly; among the philosophers he mentions Plato, Aristotle, Theophrastus, and Plotinus, and he goes on:

Among theological writers, after the Scriptures, no one writes better than Origen, no one more subtly or attractively than Chrysostom, no one more devoutly than Basil. Among the Latin Fathers, two at least are outstanding in this field: Ambrose who is wonderfully rich in metaphors, and Jerome who is immensely learned in the sacred Scriptures.[68]

More first cites St. Ambrose by name, however, in his *Letter to Dorp* (1515). In order to know theology, More argues, it is not necessary to be familiar with the modern scholastics: enough to know the teachings of St. Jerome, St. Ambrose, and St. Augustine.[69] In his *Letter to Oxford* (1518), as we have seen, he urges knowledge of Hebrew, Greek, and Latin for the study of theology, because she (theology) dwells "on holy scripture as her proper home, from which she makes her pilgrimage through all the cells of the oldest and holiest Fathers," specifically Augustine, Jerome, Ambrose, Cyprian, Chrysostom, Gregory, and Basil. In his *Letter to a Monk* (1519), More points to the fact that differences of opinion can be found among the writings of Jerome, Augustine, and Ambrose as an argument in defense of Erasmus's freedom to interpret scriptures,[70] and he goes on to praise the eloquence of Jerome, Cyprian, and Ambrose.[71] He also cites St. Ambrose's *De fide orthodoxa contra Arianos* and *Expositio evangelii secundum Lucam* against the interpretations of his addressee.[72]

But it is in his polemical writings in defense of the Church that More makes the most extensive use of St. Ambrose: the *Responsio ad Lutherum*

---

66. See *De doctrina Christiana*, bk IV, ch. 21.

67. Hyma, *The Youth of Erasmus* (1930), 285, 307, and 322.

68. *CWE* 24, 673:3–12.

69. *CW* 15, 46 and 62.

70. *CW* 15, 212:19–214:21.

71. *CW* 15, 222:18.

72. *CW* 15, 240:23–24 and 248:27–28.

(1523), the *Dialogue against Luther and Tyndale* (June 1529), *The Supplication of Souls* (September 1529), *The Confutacyon of Tyndales Answere* (bks I–III in 1532, bks IV–VIII in 1533), the *Apology* (1533), *The Answer to a Poisoned Book* (1533), *A Treatise Upon the Passion* (April 1534), and *De tristitia* (April 1534–June 1535). In all these books More gives lists of Fathers as authorities of tradition against the novelties of the Reformers; at times, the lists include also other more recent doctors of the Church. The Fathers most cited, apart from St. Ambrose, are St. Augustine, St. Jerome, St. Gregory the Great, St. Basil, St. John Chrysostom, St. Cyprian, and Eusebius.

Ambrose is singled out a number of times. Luther had mocked Ambrose in his book against the king, saying that according to him the accidents of the Eucharist disappear. More points out that Luther has misquoted Ambrose and provides an accurate citation of his words:

Licet figura panis et uini, in altaris uideatur: nihil tamen aliud quam caro et sanguis Christi credendum est.[73]

Where, More asks, does Ambrose say that the accidents have disappeared? If he is supposed to be saying that the accidents have disappeared, how does he say that the appearance of bread and wine remains? Indeed, how could he have said more clearly that the accidents remain and the substance is changed, than saying that the appearance of bread and wine is seen on the altar, but that nothing at all remained that was either bread or wine?[74]

In the *Dialogue* of 1529 More gives ten lists of Fathers and includes Ambrose in five of them. In the *Supplication* he gives a list of six names—St. Augustine, St. Jerome, St. Ambrose, St. Gregory the Great, St. John Chrysostom, and St. Basil—each as an authority refuting one of the Reformers:

> saynt Austayn agaynst frere Luther/
> saynt Hyerom agaynst frere Lambert[75] /
> saynt Ambrose agaynst frere Husken[76]/
> saynt Gregory agaynst preeste Pomeran[77]/
> saynt Chrisosteme agaynst Tindale[78]/
> saynt Basyle agaynst ye beggars[79] proctor.[80]

---

73. *CW* 5, 446:1–2: "Although the appearance of bread and wine is seen on the altar, yet nothing else must be believed to be there but the flesh and blood of Christ."

74. *CW* 5, 440–48, *De Transubstantione*.

75. François Lambert (1486/7–1531), a Franciscan of Avignon who became a follower of Zwingli's.

76. Johann Hausgen (1482–1531), also known as Oecolampadius.

77. Johannes Bugenhagen (1485–1558), a close companion of Luther's.

78. William Tyndale (c. 1494–1536).

79. Simon Fish (d. 1531), the author of *A Supplication for Beggars*, to which More was responding.

80. *CW* 7, 209:14–18.

The pairing is not arbitrary, for Hausgen denied the genuineness of two works attributed to Ambrose and clearly supporting the Real Presence.[81] In his *Treatise upon the Passion*, in defense of faith in the Eucharist, More gives not just a list of authorities but long quotations in Latin and in English from Fathers and other ancient writers, including Ambrose.[82]

—

In the prefatory letter to his translations from Lucian, More wrote only of St. Augustine and St. John Chrysostom. Later on, when defending Erasmus (*Letter to Dorp, Letter to the University of Oxford*, and *Letter to a Monk*), he suggested that to know theology we must appeal to the Fathers in general; and in his polemical writings he followed his own advice. But here the focus is on More's early choices, and here he chooses St. John Chrysostom's approach: the teaching of Christ is to be practiced in the city and the marketplace. In conclusion, it can be said that Thomas More followed the teaching of St. John Chrysostom. Of course, for Chrysostom the city and the marketplace are not just the physical setting but have a theological implication: the decision to follow Christ is a choice to be realized in an attitude of service in whatever job one has (Chrysostom lists the farmer, the smith, the builder, the ship's pilot, stressing the ordinary): work is the contribution that everyone makes to society, the means by which service is made real. This idea, transferred onto a different plane, can help to explain why in More's *Utopia*, everyone works.

81. *CW* 11, xlix.

82. *A Treatise Upon the Passion*, the second lecture upon the blessed sacrament, *CW* 13, 137–74. The other authorities quoted are St. Ignatius of Antioch, St. Justin Martyr, St. Irenaeus, Tertullian, Origen, St. Cyprian, St. Hilary, Eusebius, St. Basil, Hesychius of Jerusalem, St. John Chrysostom, St. Jerome, St. Cyril, St. Augustine, St. Gregory the Great, St. Bede, Theophylact, and St. Anselm.

4

Early Poems

The Lamentation of Queen Elizabeth

Chapters 2 and 3 introduced Erasmus and St. John Chrysostom with the occasion of events in 1499. At that first meeting of Thomas More and Erasmus, the young More composed a poem addressed to Prince Henry, who was staying at Eltham with the other royal children (apart from Arthur, Prince of Wales);[1] it is likely that the Queen, Elizabeth of York, was also with them. The next poem written by More for a royal occasion, as far as is known, was to commemorate the death of Queen Elizabeth four years later, on February 11, 1503, of post-partum fever after giving birth to her last child, Katherine, who was born prematurely on February 2 and died a few days afterward. The poem seems to have been written as an immediate response to Elizabeth's death.

It seems likely that the poem addressed to the eight-year-old Prince Henry in 1499 was in Latin, because around that time "the learned youth Thomas More [he was twenty-one years old]" wrote the Latin epigrams introducing and concluding John Holt's Latin grammar, *Lac Puerorum*; and of course, Latin was the language More used in the presence of Erasmus. *The Lamentation of Queen Elizabeth* and the *Pageant Verses* are More's first poems in English to have reached us.

In the *Lamentation*, More uses the conceit of having Queen Elizabeth—already lying dead—address her husband, children, sisters, and household, exhorting them to think of death, since wealth, power, and pleasure are of no avail when death comes. The remembrance of death or

---

1. Prince Arthur may have been at his manor house of Tickenhill, near Bewdley, where he had celebrated his proxy marriage with Catherine of Aragon on May 19.

95

memento mori, a commonplace of late medieval piety, was a recurring topic for More; it was, naturally enough, the theme of the first chapter of his book on the *Four Last Things* (1522), whose proper title is, "A Treatyce uppon these words of holye Scrypture, *Memorare nouissima, & in eternum non peccabis*, Remember the last thynges, and thou shalt neuer synne."

The *Lamentation* is made up of twelve stanzas in technically difficult rhyme royal (seven lines in iambic pentameters): the last line of each stanza ends with the phrase "Lo, here I lie," giving a dramatic tone to the voice of the dead queen. The first stanza begins:

> Ye that put your trust & confidence,
> In worldly riches and frail prosperity,
> That so live here as ye should never hence,
> Remember death & look here upon me....[2]

The second stanza considers Elizabeth's own royal lineage, her riches, honor, wealth, and ancestry, but ends like the first: "Lo, here I lie." The third stanza focuses on the queen's fame, good name, and veneration by the people, but ends likewise,

> But good god, what avails all this gear?
> When death is come, thy mighty messenger,
> Obey we must, there is no remedy;
> Me hath he summoned. Lo, now here I lie.

The fourth stanza criticizes the predictions made by the royal astrologer, for the year 1503 was meant to be full of blessings.

> O false astrology and divining,
> Of god's secrets making thyself so wise.
> How true for this year thy prophecy?
> The year yet lasted & lo, now here I lie.[3]

The first four stanzas privilege the serene voice of the dead queen, who exhorts those surrounding her to remember their own death while witnessing hers. In the fifth stanza, however, her own sadness comes through. "O brittle wealth, always full of bitterness"—even in this life wealth brings bitterness, and each single pleasure is paid for with doubled pain: "Thy sin-

---

2. The text quoted here is slightly modernized in order not to interrupt the flow: for the original text see *CW* 1, 9–13, together with its commentary and glossary. See also the extensive analysis of this poem in Willow, *Analysis* (1974), chapter 4, 139–73.

3. The final line means, "The year has not finished, but behold I lie here dead." Astrologers are often mocked and criticized in More's Latin poems: see, e.g., his Latin Poem no. 101 (*CW* 3, part II).

gular pleasure ay doubled is with pain." Her high position does not bring happiness: "For all my honour, endured yet have I, more woe than wealth, & lo here I lie."

In the sixth stanza the dead queen evokes to the king their castles and towers and their palace at Richmond; she tells him that she will not see the works finished that he is building at Westminster Abbey, but prays to God that her husband and their children may enjoy it. Her place is now not in castles or towers or palaces: "My place bilded is [My tomb is built], for lo here I lie."

In the following stanzas the queen takes leave of her family; in the first place her husband whom she entrusts the role of mother for their children. She says,

> Into your hands here I clean resign,
> To be bestowed upon your children & mine.
> Before you were father, and now you must supply
> The mother's part also. Lo, here I lie.

Next, she takes leave of her daughter Margaret. She had grieved that the daughter was going to leave her, as she was engaged to the king of Scotland; but now the mother departs first, for "Lo, here I lie."

In the ninth stanza she addresses the king's mother, Lady Margaret Beaufort, and Prince Arthur and his betrothed, Princess Catherine of Aragon, and asks them all, "Pray for my soul, for now lo, here I lie." In the tenth, she speaks to her other children, Henry, Mary, and the little newborn babe, Katherine, who will not know her mother, "for lo here I lie." Then she addresses three of her sisters, Cecily, Anne, and Katherine, and finally her youngest sister, Bridget, who had joined the Dominican Order: More makes use of this to praise Bridget for having fled from earthly folly and loved heavenly things. The queen asks Bridget to pray for her, "for lo here I lie."

More ends the poem by portraying Queen Elizabeth making a more general farewell— "Adewe my lords & ladyes all, Adewe my feythfull seruauntes everychon, Adewe my comyns"—and commending herself to the mercy of God:

> Wherfor to the alone,
> Immortal god very three in on,
> I me commend. Thy infenyte mercy,
> Shew to thi seruaunt now for lo here I lie.

The lamentation echoes Boethius's *Consolation of Philosophy* on the vanity of honors and wealth in the face of death;[4] but it is more serene, and the message is straightforward: remember death, the queen tells those around her, now that you see me lying dead; do not place your confidence in wealth, honors, ancestry, or fame. This message is repeated in *Pageant Verses*, just as Queen Elizabeth's last address to the "Immortal god" is parallel to the Poet's address to the "permansuro deo" in the last line of the *Pageant Verses*.

In the last stanzas of the *Lamentation*, Queen Elizabeth remembers with tenderness the members of her family; this can bring to the reader's mind Thomas More's recommendations to his children in his last letter from the Tower, dated July 5, 1535. In this letter, which is addressed to his "good daughter" Margaret, he asks the Lord's blessing for her and her husband, and their little boy, and "all yours and all my children and all my godchildren and all our friends." In striking contrast to the *Lamentation*, where the queen acknowledges that riches, honor, wealth, and ancestry count for nothing in the face of death, More—who has habitually remembered death—sees the small material objects he mentions as details of affection: a handkerchief for Cecily, a picture in parchment for Elizabeth, the algorism slate for Margaret Clement. And rather than advising his children to remember death, he tells them that he longs to go to God, and that the following day, the eve of the feast of St. Thomas Becket and the Octave of the feast of St. Peter, would be very appropriate and convenient for him.[5]

Pageant Verses

In his edition of the *English Works*, William Rastell wrote that

Master Thomas More in his youth devised in his father's house in London, a goodly hanging of fine painted cloth, with nine pageants, and verses over every one of those pageants: which verses expressed and declared, what the images in those pageants represented and also in those pageants were painted, the things that the verses over them did (in effect) declare, which verses here follow.[6]

---

4. Elizabeth McCutcheon, "Boethius's *De Consolatione Philosophie* and More's *Dialogue against Tribulation* and Other Writings," *Moreana*, nos. 193–94 (December 2013): 160.

5. *Correspondence* [218].

6. *CW* 1, 1. Note that in *CW* the poem is called "Pageant Verses," while William Rastell in the *English Works* (1557) speaks of the "nine pageants" referring to the drawings, and other authors call the poem a "Pageant of Life."

That More was fascinated with the visual arts is shown by the number of his Latin poems that dealt with paintings and sculptures (see Poems 17, 18, 26, 87, 88, 92, 93, 94, 97, 98, 185, 186).[7] The nine paintings of the pageants and their corresponding verses are entitled *Childhood, Manhood, Venus and Cupid, Age, Death, Fame, Time, Eternity,* and *The Poet.*[8] In synthesis, the content of the four first stanzas is:

Childhood: The child's whole mind is on playing, with a throwing disc, a cock-stick, a ball, or a spinning top. The child despises learning: "But would to God all these hateful books were in a fire burnt, that I might lead my life always in play."

Manhood despises childhood, but the man plays like a child, not with toys but with hunting and riding, "but after all his reason is not better."

Venus and Cupid: A man considers that he has not grown up if he does not know the power of Venus and her little son Cupid; but the man, for all his great pride, has been enslaved by Cupid, and he who despised little children has become a child again himself.

Age: Old age is the best part of our short life, wise and discreet, occupied in helping to rule the public weal: these grave matters require leaving behind Cupid, childish games, and idle business. Willow suggests that More probably had his own father "whom he loved, feared, and revered, in mind when he added wisdom and discretion to the above portrayal." But the achievements contained in the pageants need to be treated with a pinch of salt, because each is dethroned by the next one; thus human wisdom, "a wise brain" in *Age*, is called "pride" in the pageant of *Death*. In fact, neither "wise" nor "discreet" appears in the description of John More given by his son in his epitaph of 1532 (see Appendix), where he appears as "affable, charming, irreproachable, gentle, merciful, fair, and upright."

The sentiments expressed in these first stanzas imply that the author has outgrown childhood, can speak of manhood, knows about human love, respects the wisdom given by age, and values serving the commonwealth.

In the stanzas that come after, *Death* follows old age; *Fame* may follow

---

7. *CW* 3, part II.

8. For this section I am in debt to the magnificent study of Willow, "Nyne Pageauntes: Reflections on Man's Life," in *Analysis* (1974), 73–138; as well as Robert Coogan, "Petrarch and Thomas More," *Moreana*, no. 21 (February 1969): 19–30; Robert A. Duffy, "Thomas More's Nine Pageants," *Moreana*, no. 50 (June 1976): 15–30; Elizabeth McCutcheon, "Homo Viator," *Moreana*, no. 164 (December 2005): 25–28; Travis Curtright, "Annotations to a Modernised Text of the Pageant of Life," *Web Library of the Thomas More Studies Center* (www.thomasmorestudies.org); and Anthony S. G. Edwards, "Introduction: English Poems," *CW* 1, xvii–xxvi. The text of the *Pageant Verses* is given in *CW* 1, 1–7.

death, but, even so, *Time* shall destroy it; *Eternity*, however, lasts forever. These were traditional themes; nevertheless, given what More had to say through *The Poet*, it would be interesting to ascertain more precisely the date of these verses.

—

More's nine pageants have been linked to the Triumphs or *Trionfi* of Petrarch (1304–74).[9] Petrarch's *Trionfi* included the themes of *Love, Chastity, Death, Fame, Time,* and *Eternity*; to these, it is suggested, More added the two first stanzas, *Childhood* and *Manhood*, and the last one, *The Poet*. The parallel between the *Trionfi* and More's pageants has been drawn, however, not so much on account of Petrarch's text but more because of the pictorial tradition it inspired. The *Trionfi* were very well known in the fifteenth century: over three hundred surviving manuscripts (many lavishly illustrated) and numerous printed editions (the earliest dating from 1470) attest to its popularity and widespread diffusion, and it was a favorite subject of tapestries, engravings, paintings, and so on; the triumphs were depicted as classical triumphal processions with a figure sitting in a chariot being drawn by animals or people. This pictorial tradition is remarkable for its homogeneity, and not less so for the fact that much of the imagery is extraneous to Petrarch's text. More's depictions, however, do not follow the pictorial tradition, and so Robert Duffy urges caution in ascribing any precise influence of the *Trionfi* on More's treatment. A better case, he suggests, might be made for one of Petrarch's Latin prose works, *De Remediis Utriusque Fortunae.* A passage in the Preface to book II of *De Remediis* anticipates not only More's subject matter but his stages of life structure:

The parallels become evident in terms of the general outlines of More's scheme of life: the child in rebellion against his schoolbooks; the youth at first enflamed with love of the hunt, later subjugated by lust; the old man eschewing lust in his ambition to serve the state, and then falling from power at the hands of death.[10]

J. B. Trapp, in a more recent study of the issue, finds no definitive solution to the problem of sources to explain More's linking of the description of the Ages of Man with the motive of triumph, or indeed to the question of More's knowledge of the *Trionfi* of Petrarch. More's combination

9. A copy of the *Franciscus Petrarcha Memorandum* printed before 1500 was in Grocyn's library, according to Linacre's catalogue: *Collectanea*, no. 65. This may be the copy printed in Basel, 1496, donated by John Claymond to Corpus Christi College, Oxford, and included in the College library catalogue of 1589, no. 180.

10. Robert A. Duffy, "Thomas More's Nine Pageants," 15–35.

of triumph and the Ages of Man, Trapp concludes, is apparently peculiar to More.[11]

Rastell's phrase "in his youth" is usually taken as meaning that More wrote the pageants before he married (c. 1505). Anthony Edwards suggests that the most likely periods for composition are 1492–94 and 1496–1501,[12] and Elizabeth McCutcheon accepts that suggestion without trying to be more precise.[13] But Edwards considers that they are not to be dated while More was in Oxford and assumes that he was there from 1494 to 1496. In fact, a more likely chronology of More is that he was in Oxford from 1492 to 1494, moved to New Inn in London in 1494, and was admitted in Lincoln's Inn on February 12, 1496.

Mary Willow writes that More may have been sixteen years old when he produced the pageant,[14] which would indicate the year of composition as 1494. This was the year that More met the Elizabeth mentioned in one of his Latin poems[15]—"Sixteen years I had lived," he wrote twenty-five years later, and he gives, as the poem's theme, "He Expresses His Joy at Finding Safe and Sound Her Whom He had once Loved as a Mere Boy." However, Willow's detailed study makes clear that the content and treatment of these verses are not the work of an adolescent but of a young man who has already reflected on the meaning of life.

There is, moreover, a striking parallel between the two last verses of *Childhood*—"might I lead my life always in play/which life God send me to mine ending day"—and a phrase in More's letter of November <1501> to Holt: "I am living my life just as I desire; so please God, may my desires be good." A third possible factor for dating More's *Pageant* is the ceremonial entrance of Princess Catherine of Aragon into London that November, which More describes to Holt and which would probably have been an occasion for displaying pageants. I would like, then, to suggest—tentatively—that, in the first place, the verses were written by More not as early as the age of sixteen, but probably in 1501 or soon after. The youthfulness of More painting the nine pageants in his father's house can also be hinted in the letter to Holt of November <1501>: that whole letter exudes youthfulness.

---

11. J. B. Trapp, "Petrarch's "Triumph of Death in Tapestry," in *Thomas More ... and More*: Liber Amicorum *for Hubertus Schulte Herbrüggen*, ed. Christoph M. Peters and Friedrich-K. Unterweg (Frankfurt on Main: Peter Lang, 2002), 151–82; reproduced in Trapp, *Studies of Petrarch and His Influence* (London: Pindar Press, 2003), 171–200.

12. *CW* 1, xviii.

13. McCutcheon, "Homo Viator," 25.

14. Willow, *Analysis* (1974), 95.

15. *CW* 3, part II, Poem no. 263.

Another clue that might help to date the composition of More's verses is the resemblance between his depiction of Venus and Cupid and the painting of *Venus and Mars* (c. 1483) by Sandro Botticelli.[16] It has been argued that Botticelli's composition may be based on Lucian's description of a painting by the Greek painter Echion or Aetion, which portrayed *Alexander the Great and the Persian Princess Roxane* and showed cupids playing with Alexander's spear and armor. The description is found in Lucian's *Heredotus and Aetion*,[17] which More may have known when working on his translations from Lucian in 1506 or possibly even earlier.

It is true that More uses the allegory of Venus freely in his Latin poems, not only in his *Coronation Ode* of 1509 but in seven other short compositions, so the depiction of Venus and Cupid in the *Pageant* is not an isolated reference. The seven poems in which Venus appears, however, are all undated.[18] In two of them, More introduces the allegory of Venus and Mars: in one he writes, "Venus is busy with Mars, and Mars with Venus" (Poem 65), while in the other Venus addresses Mars, "The spear is yours, and the sword; but I claim the apple" (Poem 129), implying her victory over him. In other poems, Venus stands for self-indulgence and lust (Poem 8); for desire for marriage (Poem 47); for the beauty that attracts lovers (Poem 54); and for unfaithfulness (Poems 62 and 253). Lastly, Poem 97 deals with the painting of the *Birth of Venus* by the Greek painter Apelles.

The allegory of Venus and Mars appears at the beginning of the *De rerum natura* by the Roman poet and philosopher Lucretius.[19] The book was to be found in Grocyn's library[20] and was well known to the Italian humanists of the period, especially in Florence; it is extant in some fifty manuscripts and many early printed editions. Lucretius is mentioned by More in his letter dedicating his translations of Lucian, as one of those (Lucian is another) who maintains errors such as the mortality of the soul; but "what difference does it make to me," More comments, "what a pagan thinks about those articles contained in the principal mysteries of the Christian faith," if their works are profitable for teaching that we should put no trust in magic and should eschew superstition?[21] The description

16. For a recent study on the painting, see Frank Zöllner, *Sandro Botticelli* (Munich and New York: Prestell, 2009).

17. Fowler and Fowler, *Works of Lucian*, 2:90–93.

18. *CW* 3, part II, 11n4.

19. Lucretius, *De rerum natura*, 1.29–40, trans. W. H. D. Rouse, ed. Martin Ferguson Smith, (Cambridge, Mass.: Loeb Classical Library, Harvard University Press, 1975), 5.

20. *Collectanea*, no. 98.

21. *CW* 3, part I, 5, ll. 18–20.

of Venus and Mars in *De rerum natura*, however, differs greatly from that portrayed by Botticelli, and Lucretius cannot be claimed as Botticelli's only source of inspiration;[22] in fact, Botticelli's composition has much more in common with Lucian's *Alexander and Roxane* than Lucretius's *Venus and Mars*.

Botticelli's painting shows a warrior who is usually identified as Mars, the god of war, lying asleep, perhaps tired from fighting, while several cupids play with his armor; Venus, elegant and richly dressed, reclines next to him. Commentators have seen in Botticelli's painting a reference to Marsilio Ficino's *De amore*, a commentary on Plato's *Symposium*.[23] Ficino writes that Mars stands foremost in strength, for he makes men stronger: yet Venus masters him. She can tame Mars, "But Mars never masters Venus." If Ficino's views influenced Botticelli in his composition, it would explain why the figure of Venus is depicted as alert and watchful, while Mars is in deep sleep. Ficino was the tutor of Lorenzo di Pierfrancesco de Medici, cousin of Botticelli's patron, Lorenzo de Medici, and so the influence of Ficino is not impossible. When Linacre returned to London, he might have brought news of the painting and of its relationship with Lucian and Ficino; more concretely, he may have brought with him a copy of *Fichinus in convivium Platonis*, printed in 1496 and included in the catalogue of Grocyn's books.[24]

I am not suggesting that More based his depiction of Venus on the painting by Botticelli; indeed, there are important compositional differences between the two. In More's representation Venus is standing on the young man as he lies on the ground, while in Botticelli's she sits beside him; and instead of the several cupids playing in Botticelli, More has a single Cupid standing next to Venus and piercing the man's side with a dart. Nevertheless, we can say that all the influences that art historians ascribe to the painting of Botticelli's *Venus and Mars* were available to the young More, even though he—as always—produced his own composition. Of course, whatever the influences on Botticelli's painting, it can be said that painters and Italian humanists such as Angelo Poliziano and Marsilio Ficino were

---

22. See G. D. Hadzsits, *Lucretius and His Influence* (New York: Cooper Square, 1963), 264–65; E. Wind, *Pagan Mysteries in the Renaissance* (Oxford: Oxford University Press, 1980), 110n1; C. Dempsey, *Journal of the Warburg and Courtauld Institutes* 31 (1968): 251–73, cited in *De rerum natura*, Loeb Classical Library, 436n.

23. Marsilio Ficino, *Commentary on the Symposium: De Amore* (Dallas, Tex.: Spring), Oratio V, chapter 8.

24. *Collectanea*, no. 40.

very familiar with classical figures, as were English humanists such as Grocyn and Linacre who had traveled in Italy; it is no great surprise to find
such allegories in More.[25]

There is a difference between the style and content of More's *Pageant
Verses* and his miscellaneous Latin poems. The Latin poems are exercises;
most of them are translations or arrangements "from the Greek" (Poems 8,
47, 54, 65, 129) or variations, trying different ways of saying the same idea
(Poems 62, 65). In the English verses of the *Pageant of Life*, however, there
is a genuine message that More wants to convey; according to Mary Willow, in the concluding stanza he hides behind the Latin verses to open the
intimacy of his heart: "In the last stanza, that is written in Latin, the youthful More takes off his mask and speaks to us in his own voice." She adds,
"[More] was adept in using this medium [Latin] for the expression of his
innermost thoughts and convictions."[26]

At present, there is no data to ascertain when these Latin poems were
written, but it is reasonable to assume that at least some of the practice
translations were produced during the initial period when More was beginning to study Greek, after his encounters of 1499, or around the time of
his reference to learning Greek in his letter of November <1501>, or even
while he was working with Lily, as he mentions in his letter to Colet of
October 23, <1501–4>. Certainly these possibilities do not invalidate the
tentative conclusion I proposed earlier: that the *Pageant Verses* were produced c. 1501.

Although our investigation of the circumstances surrounding Botticelli's *Venus and Mars* has been of minimal help in dating the *Pageant Verses*,
pinpointing possible influences can help us to understand how More depicted such a topic. If, as art historians suggest, *Venus and Mars* is based
on Ficino's *De amore*, it seems likely that the painting may also have been
known in Ficino's circle. So it is not entirely out of the question to suggest
that Linacre might have reported on Botticelli's painting when he returned
from Florence in 1499 and that More might have known of it.

---

25. Grocyn owned a copy of Boccaccio's treatise on the Greek and Roman gods, *Genealogia deo-
rum gentilium* (Venice, 1494), which Linacre might have brought him in 1499: see the 1589 Catalogue
of the Library of Corpus Christi College, Oxford, no. 167: Liddell, Library of Corpus Christi College, Oxford (1958), 401 (for books that belonged to Grocyn); *Collectanea*, 324.

26. Willow, *Analysis* (1974), 133. Willow similarly affirms that the twelve verses of the stanza
"synthesize More's view on life" (73); that the Poet "epitomizes [the meaning of life] with the assertion
that 'joys, praise and honour, all retire on a speedy foot and only love of God remains'" (78); and that
he "mirrors Thomas More's own philosophy of life and depicts him as a true Christian humanist, who
considered not only man's mind but also his soul" (95).

The first pageant stanza mentions a *child playing*;[27] the last but one is that of *Eternity*. In Lucian's *Philosophies Going Cheap*, one of the customers asks Heraclitus, "Eternity? What's that?" Heraclitus replies, "A child playing with its toys, and flinging them about the nursery."[28] This parallelism suggests that More was probably acquainted with Lucian's works by the time he was writing the *Pageant of Life*.

In chapter 3 we considered St. John Chrysostom's influence on More, and we can note here that in one of his last homilies on the Gospel of St. Matthew Chrysostom also speaks of the different stages of man's life, comparing it to a ship journeying through various seas. The first sea we meet, he says, is that of our childhood, which is stormy because of a child's foolishness and changeability: for this reason, the child has guides and teachers, like the ship's pilot. After this age there follows the sea of youth, where the winds are as violent as in the Aegean on account of lust. Next comes the sea of manhood, subject to heavy and frequent showers of household cares. In our earliest age we learn nothing salutary; in youth, we do not practice sobriety; in manhood we do not conquer covetousness; and so we come to old age with our hold full of bilge water, and with the ship of our soul weakened and the planks sprung by many shocks. Thus we shall arrive at the harbor of eternity bearing much filth instead of spiritual merchandise.[29]

More, however, did not expand on the moral advice given by Chrysostom; his stanzas were rather short and descriptive. When he wrote them, the author was still close to *Childhood* and to his "first love," but was old enough to have reflected on all the situations that he portrayed. There is unity in the text and in the paintings; each stanza is linked to the previous one. The same is true of the paintings, as explained by William Rastell. The first pageant shows a boy playing with a top and whip; in the second pageant, an attractive young man rides upon a fine horse, with the boy of the first pageant lying underneath the horse. In the third pageant the pleasant young man is lying on the ground, and upon him stands

27. McCutcheon, "Homo Viator," 27, suggests fittingly that the *play* progressed through out the stanzas for—for More—everyone's life "*is* a play of sort."

28. Lucian, *Satirical Sketches: Philosophies Going Cheap*, trans. Paul Turner (New York: Penguin, 1961), 155. In the same piece, as mentioned earlier, Lucian makes Socrates speak of "Nowhere" (157). If More's reading of Lucian's work is reflected in the *Pageant Verses*, as is suggested here, it also places a likely influence on *Utopia* within the period.

29. Homily 81, 5.

Venus, the goddess of love, and Cupid by her side. In the fourth is an "old sage father"[30] sitting in a chair, with the image of Venus and Cupid lying under his feet, and in the fifth, the figure of Death, with the old man under his feet. Lady Fame is painted in the sixth pageant, and under her feet the picture of Death; in the seventh the figure of Time—with hourglass in hand—and under his feet the picture of Fame. "In the eighth pageant was pictured the image of Lady Eternity, sitting in a chair under a sumptuous cloth of estate, crowned with an imperial crown, and under her feet lay the picture of Time."[31] Last of all, says Rastell:

In the ninth pageant was painted a Poet sitting in a chayre. And ouer this pageant were there written these verses in Latin folowyng.

The Poet

Has fictas quemcumque iuuat spectare figuras,
Sed mira veros quas putat arte homines,
Ille potest veris, animum sic pascere rebus,
Vt pictis oculos pascit imaginibus.
Namque videbit uti fragilis bona lubrica mundi,
Tam cito non veniunt, quam cito pretereunt.
Gaudia laus & honor, celeri pede omnia cedunt,
Qui manet excepto semper amore dei.
Ergo homines, leuibus iamiam diffidite rebus,
Nulla recessuro spes adhibenda bono.
Qui dabit eternam nobis pro munere vitam,
In permansuro ponite vota deo.[32]

Whoever delights in gazing at these imaginary figures and even thinks them to be real people because of the marvellous artistic skill, can feast his mind on the real things they represent just as he feasts his eyes upon the painted images. For he will see that the elusive goods of this perishable world do not come so readily as they swiftly pass away. Joys, praise, honour, and all things quickly disappear except the love of God, which endures for ever. Therefore, men, henceforth place no trust in trivial matters and no hope in a fleeting good. Place your longings in the eternal God who will grant us the gift of eternal life.[33]

In all the stanzas of the *Pageant Verses* but the last, More follows the classical treatment of the Ages of Man. But in this last stanza, the Poet re-

---

30. *CW* 1, 4:46.
31. *CW* 1, 6:91–94.
32. *CW* 1, 6–7:105–20, and *CW* 3, part II, 292.
33. For other translations, see, e.g., that of Clarence H. Miller (1984) in *CW* 3, part II, 293; Willow, *Analysis* (1974), 95; and Stapleton, 5. Stapleton, however, quotes only the first six lines of the Latin stanza.

flects on the transitory nature of earthly realities: all things will pass away except for the love of God, which endures forever.[34] This insight would guide More to the radical determination to love God above all things—a determination that he developed in the material he added to his *Life of Pico.*

The Epitaph for Thomas More's Mother

Having considered More's *Lamentation of Queen Elizabeth* written soon after her death in 1503 and the *Pageant Verses*, dated circa 1501, it is necessary to transcribe the Latin epitaph carved on the tomb of More's mother, Agnes, and her brother Abel, in the Church of St. Michael, in Basinghall Ward, three minutes' walk from Milk Street. The parish was incorporated into that of St. Lawrence Jewry, where More's father was buried. His mother died in 1499 when More was twenty-one. Though not included among the Latin poems in the Yale Edition of the *Complete Works of St. Thomas More*, Marc'hadour attributes it to More,[35] and this has recently been accepted.[36] In translation it reads:

> Come here, wayfarer, and measure with your eyes
> How small an urn holds the enclosed two.
> What you are today, this man once was, and so was this woman.
> Now each of them is part of this frosty soil.
> His name was ABEL, MORE his surname, and at Exeter
> City was he once a doctor of Civil Law.
> AGNES was the other's name, and she was the wife of JOHN
> MORE, the brother of this ABEL here.
> As you wish that the living should do to you after your interment
> So you, now, whoever you are, utter this short prayer:
> May this ABEL in the first place and this AGNES be relieved by the Lamb
> Who previously washed the sheep in his "agnine" blood.
>
> ABEL died in 1486, AGNES in 1499.
> May their souls through the mercy of God rest in peace.

34. Elizabeth McCutcheon, in "Wings and Crosses: Boethius's *De Consolatione Philosophie* and More's *Dialogue of Comfort against Tribulation* and Other Writings," *Moreana*, no. 193–94 (December 2013): 151–86.

35. Marc'hadour, "The Death-Year of Thomas More's Mother," *Moreana*, no. 63, part 2 (December 1979): 13–16. The length of the Latin poem is exactly the same as that of More's epigram commenting on his epitaphs for Henry Abyndom who died in 1497 (*CW* 3.II, Poem 161).

36. Peter Ackroyd, *The Life of Thomas More* (London: Chatto and Windus, 1998), 9; and Guy, *A Daughter's Love* (2008), 77.

To remember death and to pray for the dead are themes from which the young More did not recoil. The topics are common of the time; but, through the medium of poetry, playful pageants, and his mother's epitaph, More puts across his ever-present awareness of the afterlife. More returned to the same topics frequently in later writings such as *A Treatise upon these words of holy Scripture, Memorare novissima, & in aternum non peccabis—Remember the Last Things, and you shall never sin* (1522), the *Supplication of Souls* (1529), and his own epitaph written in 1532, among others.

A recent author mentions the first four verses of the epitaph for More's mother to emphasize the acceptance of death,[37] while another, writing about More's way of thinking, sees the moralizing content of the early poems, which in the case of the *Pageant Verses* show that, "by acknowledging [the] succession of 'triumphs' and by focusing on the triumphant Eternity, who stands above them all, people can look past the pride that each inspires, allowing worldly things to pass away without attachment."[38] The point, however, underlined here is not so much that of learning detachment but of being thrilled by "the love of God which endures for ever," as the Poet proclaims,[39] and the blood of the Lamb who gives salvation.

The Lamb and the blood of the Lamb—*agnino sanguine*—appear often in one of More's last writings, *A Treatise upon the Passion*.[40] The last two verses of the epitaph introduce a play of words not strange to More:

> Hic ABEL primo hic AGNES relevetur ab AGNO,
> Qui prius agnino sanguine lavit oves.

37. Guy, *A Daughter's Love* (2008), 77.
38. Paul, *Thomas More* (2017), 21.
39. *CW* 3.II, Poem 272.
40. *CW* 13: 62, 80, 92, 120–35.

5

The Life of Pico

A Clear Path: "The First Point Is to Love but One Alone"

After years of study and spiritual searching, Thomas More was "set to place his love unto God." This apt phrase comes from his book *The Life of Pico*, an English work based on the Latin biography of the humanist Giovanni Pico della Mirandola (1463–94) by his nephew Gianfrancesco, first published in 1496.[1] The work by More includes the life of Pico, three of his letters, his commentary on Psalm 15, three duodecalogues—that is, three poems each comprising twelve exhortations—titled "The Twelve Rules of the Spiritual Battle," "The Twelve Weapons of the Spiritual Battle," and "The Twelve Properties or Conditions of a Lover"—and, to conclude, a translation of "A Prayer of Pico Mirandola unto God."

"The Twelves Rules of the Spiritual Battle" by Pico occupy two full pages of Latin prose, seventy-six lines, in the *Complete Works of St. Thomas More*,[2] text that More paraphrases into twenty-three stanzas of rhyme royal English verse. Pico gave just the title of each of "The Twelve Weapons of the Spiritual Battle," and, using those titles, More wrote twelve original English stanzas, one for each one of the weapons. Similarly, Pico gave a brief apothegm for each property of the lover, which More used to compose his own ballade in which he speaks of the love of God, comparing it to human love. This manner of speaking of the love of God in the language

---

1. The text of More's *Life of Pico* is given in *CW* 1, 51–123, and in the *Essential Works of Thomas More*, 61–94. More's Latin sources for the *Life of Pico* is included as Appendix A in *CW* 1, 281–384. The *Essential Works* mark within the text itself whether More is translating from the biography by Gianfrancesco or adding his own knowledge; this information is generally given in the Commentary included in the *CW*.

2. *CW* 1, 372 and 374.

of human love was, of course, traditional among Christian spiritual writers and is to be found in the Fathers of the Church in commenting upon the Song of Songs and other texts of sacred scripture.[3]

More's ballade is the main topic of this chapter. Like his *Lamentation of Queen Elizabeth* and the two previous pieces, the ballade is in rhyme royal. It comprises thirteen sections, each one made up of two stanzas. The two stanzas of the first twelve sections develop the property proposed by Pico: the first stanza describes that property as it characterizes a youthful and fervent love, while the second stanza applies that property to the love of God. Mary Willow suggests that the speaker in the poem is More himself, who assumes the disguise of an experienced lover in the first stanza of each of the twelve sections. "In the second stanza he throws off his disguise and speaks to his addressee in his own voice, which is characterized by sincerity and conviction."[4]

The thirteenth section of the ballade is a paraphrase in English verse of a Latin paragraph in prose that Gianfrancesco placed at the end of Pico's list of the twelve properties of a lover.[5] In fact, that Latin paragraph has its particular interest because the first sentences (*CW* 1, 378, lines 1–6), which are the base for More's first stanza of this thirteenth section, give three reasons for the lover to serve the beloved without thought of reward, while the following sentences (*CW* 1, 378, lines 6–14), which correspond to More's second stanza, apply those three reasons to the lover of God. This seems to be an invitation to apply all twelve properties to the lover of God, and this is what More goes on to do composing his own ballade.

The first property given by Pico was, The first point is to love but one alone. More's two stanzas read:

> *First stanza:*
> The first point is to love but one alone,
> And for that others to forsake
> For anyone who loveth many loveth none:
> The flood that is in many channels take,
> In each of them shall feeble stream make;
> The love that is divided among many
> Hardly sufficeth that any part have any.

---

3. See, for instance, St. Hippolytus, Origen, St. Gregory of Nyssa, and St. Gregory the Great, and later commentaries by St. Bernard and St. Bonaventure.

4. Willow, *Analysis* (1974).

5. *CW* 1, 378.

> *Second stanza:*
> So thou that hast thy love set unto God
> In thy remembrance this imprint and engrave:
> As He in sovereign dignity is unique,
> So will He in love no parting fellows have:
> Love Him therefore with all that He thee gave
> For body, soul, wit, cunning, mind and thought,
> Part will He none but either all or naught.[6]

(For the rest of the ballade, unless stated, I will give only the second stanza of each property, so as to focus on what More had discovered with regard to the lover of God.) From the first verse it is clear that More is proposing an ideal for himself, "thou that hast thy love set unto God." And the advice is to "love Him … with all that He thee gave … body, soul, wit, cunning, mind and thought." Fundamentally, this is simply to follow the First Commandment, but it implies an awareness that More engraved in his mind as he was recommending: "Imprint and engrave this in thy remembrance."

In the sixth verse, to the gospel formulation, "with all your heart, and with all your soul, and with all your mind, and with all your strength" (Mk 12:30 and Lk 10:27),[7] in his typical fashion More adds "wit" and "cunning," including his sense of humor and his passion for letters, Greek and Latin—and indeed, he lists also "body," relevant for one who was to seek holiness in marriage.

The second property listed by Pico is "to think himself unhappy if he is not with his love"—*Infelicem putare eum qui non est cum amato*. More adds:

> So should the lover of God esteem that he
> Which all the pleasure has, mirth and disport,
> That in this world is possible to be,
> Yet till the time that he may once resort
> Unto that blessed, joyful, heavenly port
> Where he of God may have the glorious sight,
> Is void of perfect joy and sure delight.

Engraving the love of God on one's mind includes also the hope of heaven and looking forward to having "of God the glorious sight." Erasmus wrote in a later letter (1519) that when More "talks with friends about

---

6. The modernized English version given here is based on that given in *A Thomas More Source Book*, ed. Gerard B. Wegemer and Stephen W. Smith (Washington, D.C.: The Catholic University of America Press, 2004), 164–70, and in *The Essential Works of Thomas More*, with slight variations. More's original text is available in *CW* 1, 114–20.

7. Mt 22:37 reads, "With all your heart, and with all your soul, and with all your mind"; Deut 6:4, "With all your heart, and with all your soul, and with all your strength."

the life after death, you recognize that he is speaking from conviction, and not without good hope."[8] In the ballade, however, More speaks also of the "mirth" of this world, even though it is "void of perfect joy." Faith and the love of God imply the conviction that the world is good because it came from the hands of God: he created it and looked at it and "saw that it was good" (Gn 1:4, 10, 12, 18, 21, 25)—indeed, "very good" (Gn 1:31). Thus, for More, enjoyment of this world is not incompatible with hope in the life to come, but *perfect* joy and *sure* delight are in heaven, in the vision of God. "Heaven" is one of the words that appears most frequently in More's writings, right up to his very last letter, where he expresses the wish "that we maie merily meet in heaven."[9]

The third property mentioned by Pico was *Omnia pati cum illo sit, etiam mortem*, but More changes the order with the fourth property, *Ornare se ut illi placeat*—"to dress up to please the beloved." He adds:

> So thou that wilt with God get into favour
> Garnish thyself up in as goodly wise
> As comely be, as honest in behaviour,
> As it is possible for thee to devise:
> I mean not hereby that thou should arise
> And in the glass upon thy body look eagerly
> But with fair virtue to adorn thy soul.

This being "honest in behaviour," as a consequence of the desire to please God, is a recurrent theme in More's writings; see, for instance, his *Letter to a Monk*[10] and his *Confutation of Tyndale's Answer*.[11] So far More has spoken of the love of God above all things— "either all or naught" (first property) and the hope of heaven (second property), but loving God implies being "honest in behaviour" and a constant struggle to grown in virtue. More considered the theme of growth in virtue in rendering and his additions to "the Twelve rules of John Pico, Earl of Mirandola partly exciting partly directing a man in spiritual battle."

Being "honest in behaviour" and growing in virtue are characteristics of a unity of life between what one believes and what one practices. More writes that it is not a matter of looking at one's bodily and human qualities

8. *CWE* 7, Ep. 999:298–300.

9. "Heaven" appears 750 times in the *English Works*, and more than 150 in his *Latin Works*. It is by far preceded by "God," 5,575 times in the *English Works*, and more than 700 in the *Latin*. See www.thomasmorestudies.org/concordance.

10. *CW* 15, 279:7–13.

11. *CW* 8, 833:6.

as in a mirror to tickle one's self-esteem, but of adorning one's soul to please God. More here echoes the Letter of St. James: "Be doers of the word, and not hearers only, deceiving yourselves. For if anyone is a hearer of the word and not a doer, he is like a man who observes his natural face in a mirror; for he observes himself and goes away" (Jas 1:22–24). This idea is picked up by More in the *Confutation* (indeed, he quotes the first verse),[12] and he follows St. James's development of his thought that the person who hears the word of God needs to put it into practice by good works: otherwise, his religion is vain (Jas 1:24–27). Quoting St. James,[13] More underlines that together with faith, hope, and charity, the Christian must also practice good works.[14]

For his fourth property, as noted earlier, More takes Pico's third property of the lover: "To suffer all-thing, though it were death, to be with his love."

> Thus should of God the lover be content
> Any distress or sorrow to endure,
> Rather than to be from God absent,
> And glad to die, so that he may be sure
> By his departing hence for to procure,
> After this valley dark, the heavenly light,
> And of his love the glorious blessed sight.

Once again More speaks of the hope of heaven and of being "glad to die" in order to procure "the heavenly light." More's own readiness to endure distress and sorrow even to death rather than to be separated from God would in the end be sealed by his martyrdom, a confirmation that he meant what he had written.

This reference in the ballade to being ready to endure any distress or sorrow rather than deny God has an exact parallel in *De tristitia*, where More wrote:

If anyone is brought to the point where he must either suffer torment or deny God, he need not doubt that it was God's will for him to be brought to this crisis. Therefore, he has very good reason to hope for the best. For God will either extricate him from the struggle, or else He will aid him in the fight and make him conquer so that He may crown him with the conqueror's wreath. For God is trustworthy, the apostle says.[15]

---

12. *CW* 8, 842:16–17.
13. See, for instance, *CW* 8, 688:3 and 780:2.
14. *CW* 8, 1033:34
15. *CW* 14, 69:2–8.

The fifth property proposed by Pico is "to desire also to suffer shame and harm for his love, and to think that hurt sweet." More comments:

> Thus shouldest thou, that lovest God also,
> In thine heart wish, covet and be glad
> For Him to suffer trouble, pain and woe:
> For Whom, though thou be never so surrounded by sorrow,
> Yet thou shalt not sustain (be not frightened)
> Half the dolour, grief and adversity
> That He already suffered has for thee.

The lover of God is thus ready to suffer, bearing in mind all that Christ suffered for him—a theme that More developed in *A Treatise upon the Passion, Dialogue of Comfort against Tribulation*, and *De tristitia*. For him, the love of God is not an abstract concept; it is manifested in good works (third property) and is nourished by contemplating the Passion of Jesus Christ (fifth property).

The first sentence of More's *Treatise upon the Passion* is a quotation from the Letter to the Hebrews (Heb 13:14): "*Non habemus hic civitatem manentem, sed futuram inquirimus*"; We have not here a dwelling city, but we seek the city that is to come. In the brief introductory paragraph addressing the reader, More goes on to say that many men often forget this truth and, "alack," that applies to him as well. After a prologue on the necessity of the Passion, the *Treatise* contains four chapters, but it was left unfinished when More was imprisoned in April 1534; hence, he did not write beyond the institution of the Eucharist. The prologue and the four chapters are each divided into several lectures, most of them finishing with a prayer. The main content of the *Treatise* is exemplified in the initial prayer of the first chapter:

Good Lord, give us Thy grace, not to read or hear this gospel of Thy bitter passion with our eyes and our ears in manner of a pastime, but that it may with compassion so sink into our hearts that it may stretch to everlasting profit of our souls.[16]

In *A Dialogue of Comfort against Tribulation*, the last chapter is entitled, "The consideration of the paynefull deth [of] Chryst";[17] and this consideration, More argues, should be sufficient to make us happy to suffer a painful death for his sake. And More continues his contemplation of Christ's Passion in his last book, *De tristitia tedio pavore et oratione Christi*

---

16. *CW* 13, 52:26–30.
17. More, *A Dialogue of Comfort against Tribulation*, book III, chapter XXVII; see *CW* 12, 312.

ante captionem eius,[18] which follows Christ's prayer from leaving the Upper Room until he was arrested in the Garden.

The sixth property of the lover is "To be with his love ever as he may, if not in deed yet in thought," which is expanded by More.

> Lo in like manner the lover of God should,
> At the least in such wise as he may,
> If he may not in such wise as he would,
> Be present with God and conversant always;
> For certes, whoever wishes, he may obtain it,
> Though all the world wanted to deprive him of it,
> To bear his body in earth, his mind in heaven.

More writes of the need to exercise a constant awareness of God's presence, having God present "if not in deed yet in thought" in all the circumstances of one's life. It implies being "conversant" with God always: while one's body is on earth, one's mind is in heaven, leading a contemplative life in the midst of the world.[19]

For the seventh property I also give the first stanza, because it explains very well the basis for what More has to say about its application to the love of God. The seventh property of the lover is "To love all things that pertain to his love," and More develops it as follows:

> *First stanza*:
> There is no page or servant, most or least,
> That doth upon his love attend and wait,
> There is no little worm, no simple beast,
> Nor none so small a trifle or conceit,
> Lace, girdle, point,[20] or proper glove strait,
> But that if to his love it has been near,
> The lover has it precious, beloved and dear.
>
> *Second stanza*:
> So every relic, image or picture
> That doth pertain to God's magnificence,
> The lover of God should with all busy care
> Have it in love, honour and reverence,
> And specially give them pre-eminence

---

18. *CW* 14, 3:1.

19. More uses the word "contemplative," for instance, in recommending *Scala perfectionis* (see *CW* 8, part I, 37:31), in which Walter Hilton speaks in the same way of being contemplative while engaged in worldly business. See chapter 11.

20. Point: a short cord or lace for (in this case) lacing a bodice.

> Who daily do His blessed body's wurche,[21]
> The quick relics, the ministers of His Church.

More gives a similar defense of images in his *Dialogue* of 1529.[22] Here he adds that the "lover of God" should have special veneration for the ministers of the Church because they are "quick"—living—relics of Christ. The expression "living relics" seems to be an original image of More's, although the same point is made in *The Dialogue of St. Catherine of Siena*, where God speaks to Catherine of the great dignity of priests—whom he calls *My ministers, My anointed ones, My Christs*—because they consecrate the Body of Christ.[23] Campbell and Reed suggest that here "wurche" (work) could have the meaning of "to cause," in which case these lines could be paraphrased as "And especially give reverence to the ministers of his Church; they are living relics for they cause daily his Blessed Body to be made" (that is, they consecrate Christ's body in the Eucharist).

Pico's eighth property is "To covet the praise of his love, and not to suffer any dispraise":

> The lover of God should covet in like wise
> To hear His honour, worship, laud and praise,
> Whose sovereign goodness no heart may comprise,
> Whom hell, earth, and all the heaven obey,
> Whose perfect lover ought by no manner ways
> To suffer the cursed words of blasphemy
> Or anything spoken of God unreverently.

The lover's ninth property is "To believe of his love all things excellent, and to desire that all folk should think the same."

> Of God likewise so wonderful and high
> All thing esteem and judge his lover ought,
> So reverence, worship, honour and magnify,
> That all the creatures in this world wrought
> In comparison should he set at nought,
> And glad be if he might the means devise
> That all the world would thinken in likewise.

---

21. *Wurche* // work.

22. Cf. *CW* 6, 47, ll. 19–31; see Frank Mitjans, "Thomas More on Venerating Images, Devotion to Saints and Going on Pilgrimages," Conference of the Centre of Thomas More Studies, Dallas, 2007, www.thomasmorestudies.org/tmstudies/DCH_Mitjans.pdf.

23. These terms appear often in *The Dialogue of Saint Catherine of Siena*, trans. Algar Thorold (London: Burns, Oates, and Washbourne, 1925), 235–46 (repr.: London: Baronius, 2008), 163–74.

These two stanzas imply that the lover of God is keen to have others love God too: his zeal for God leads him to a constant concern for souls, somewhat as we saw in More's appeal to Colet: "London needs you!" In later life, More spent many a night writing in defense of the Church.

The tenth property of the lover is "To weep often with his love: in presence for joy, in absence for sorrow." More's reflection on the lover of God does not focus specifically on weeping for God, but rather on his perpetual "remembrance":

> Here should the lover of God ensample take
> To have Him continually in remembrance,
> With him in prayer and meditation wake,
> While others play, revel, sing, and dance:
> None earthly joy, disport, or vain pleasure
> Should him delight, or anything remove
> His ardent mind from God, his heavenly love.

The eleventh property is "To languish ever and ever to burn in the desire of his love."

> Like affections feeleth increase the breast
> Of God's lover in prayer and meditation:
> When that his love liketh in him rest
> With inward gladness of pleasant contemplation,
> Outbreak the tears for joy and delectation;
> And when his love wishes afterwards to depart from him,
> Outbreak the tears again for pain and woe.

In these two properties, More once again refers to the example of human love: God's lover keeps God "continually in remembrance," and is always "in prayer and meditation wake," writes More. In his last book he writes instead of the sleeping apostles, pointing out,

Notice here how much greater one love is than another, Notice how Christ's love for His own was much greater than the love they gave Him in return, even those who loved Him most.[24]

More speaks again of "prayer and meditation" in the tenth property—the only time he repeats a phrase word for word. Erasmus wrote that More had fixed hours for meditation,[25] but these two properties are intended to convey the reality that the lover of God prays all the time and that fixed

24. *CW* 14, 157.
25. *CWE* 7, Ep. 999:297.

hours of prayer and meditation can lead to a constant contemplation, as More explains in *De tristitia Christi*, writing

that those words of Christ "You should pray always and not cease" were not spoken figuratively but in a simple and straightforward sense, and that in fact they are actually and literally fulfilled by good men.[26]

Finally, the twelfth property of the lover is "To serve his love, nothing thinking of any reward or profit."

> So thou likewise that hast thine heart set
> Upward to God, so well thyself endeavour,
> So studiously that nothing may thee let
> Not for His service any wise dissever:
> Freely look also thou serve that thereto never
> Trust of reward or profit do thee bind,
> But only faithful heart and loving mind.

As explained at the beginning of this chapter, More's thirteenth and concluding section comes from paraphrasing in two stanzas the prose paragraph that follows the list of the twelve properties in the original Latin text.[27]

> *First stanza:*
> Wageless to serve, three things may us move:[28]
> First, if the service itself be desirable;
> Second, if they whom we serve and love
> Be very good and very amiable;
> Thirdly, as is reasonable that we be ready to serve
> Without striving after anything more
> To those who have done much for us before.

> *Second stanza:*
> Serve God for love, then, not for hope of reward
> What service may so desirable be
> As where all turns to thine own success?
> Who is so good, also so lovely as He
> Who hath already done so much for thee,
> As he that first thee made, and on the rood[29]
> Afterwards thee redeemed with His precious blood?

---

26. *CW* 14, I, 325:4–7.
27. *CW* I, 378, 1–14.
28. Three things may move us to serve without wages (wageless = without pay).
29. Rood // cross.

This last stanza emphasizes that the love of God leads to serve him, as More points out in his *Letter to a Monk*. The ballade ends with a reference to Christ, who "first made thee" (an idea More develops at the beginning of his *Treatise on the Passion*), and then "on the rood afterwards thee redeemed." The ballade is not mere poetry; contemplation is not an abstraction. For More, the way is Christ, as he wrote in the *Dialogue of Comfort against Tribulation*. More's Christology and theology of prayer, which are developed in *The Treatise on the Passion*, *The Dialogue of Comfort against Tribulation*, and *De tristitia*, are already evident in the properties of the lover.

In this ballade More appears as a man determined to love God above all things and to become a contemplative in the midst of the world. This awareness determines his life from then on.

Note on Chronology from the *Life of Pico*

Thus far I have been considering the conceptual process of Thomas More's growing awareness of his path to holiness, rather than its chronology. I have been exploring how he became aware that, as a Christian, he ought "to love but one alone" and have his "love set unto God" (see his ballade). The following chapters sketch out how this could be done in a secular environment (as the Church Fathers already assume), and as a married layman. Of course, some might reach this awareness after marriage, but I argue that More became aware of it before he decided to marry, after a period of intense prayer and study. The *terminus ad quem* of this process would thus be his decision to marry, which can be dated no later than January 1505. The earliest evidence we have of his readiness to respond to God's will is his letter to Holt, tentatively dated November <1501>. Between these two events, however, it is not easy to give specific dates to the stages of his thought process.

The first edition of More's translation of the *Life of Pico* was printed in London by More's brother-in-law John Rastell. It is undated, but John's son, William, declares in the table of contents to the 1557 edition of More's *English Works* that More translated the *Life of Pico* in about 1510. From this statement we can assume that the first edition was produced then.

Stapleton, however, links More's decision to marry with his translation of the *Life of Pico*,[30] for after stating that he had taken this decision, he adds

30. Stapleton, 9.

that More looked for the example of some prominent man *ex ordine La-icorum*[31] on which he might model his life, and finally fixed on John Pico because he was famous for his piety and virtue. This statement is echoed by Cresacre More; and Arthur W. Reed, one of the editors of *The English Works of Sir Thomas More* (London, 1931), concluded that More had completed his *Life of Pico* before he married, and that the dedicatory letter in which he offered the book to Joyeuce Leigh as a New Year's gift should be dated January 1, 1505,[32] or shortly before. This date is accepted by Chambers (1935) and most subsequent scholars.

Anthony S. G. Edwards, however, in the Introduction to the *Life of Pico* in volume 1 of the *Complete Works of St. Thomas More*, published in 1997, states instead that "there is no solid evidence or logical necessity for a date of composition earlier than about 1510."[33] Edwards's conclusion seems to be based on two considerations: first, in spite of what Stapleton wrote, it is unlikely that More considered Pico della Mirandola as a model of holiness for a married layman who had chosen the active life of service to the commonwealth; and second, if this is true, we should follow William Rastell's statement that the *Life* "was translated oute of latin, into Englishe by master Thomas More, about the year of our Lorde 1510," as he and his father were closely connected with the More family.

The argument for the first consideration seems obvious: as James McConica points out, "Pico made the contrary decision to that made by More."[34] In translating the *Life of Pico* More reshaped it in a variety of ways, omitting a number of aspects (such as Pico's interest in esotericism and the occult) and adding his own devotional compositions. Indeed, the most explicit and sustained Christian passages come in More's own verse; and More does not shy away from recording the ambivalences of Pico's own life.[35] In summary, a comparison between More's *Life of Pico* and its Latin source[36] makes it obvious that, on the whole, Pico was not an exemplar for More. Pico thought he had a call to a religious vocation but delayed

---

31. Thomas Stapleton, *Tres Thomae, … D. Thomae Mori Anglae quodam Cancellari Vita* (Duaci [Douai, now in France; then in Burgundy]: Ioannis Bogardi, 1588), item kept in the British Library, 19, line 21.

32. *Correspondence*, Letter [4].

33. *CW* 1, xxxix.

34. James McConica, "The Patrimony of Thomas More," in *History and Imagination: Essays in Honour of H. R. Trevor-Roper*, ed. Hugh Lloyd-Jones (London: Duckworth, 1981), 65.

35. Anthony S. G. Edwards, "Introduction," *Life of Pico*, *CW* 1, xxxvii–lix.

36. Clarence H. Miller gives "More's Latin Sources for the *Life of Pico*," including the full Latin text of the *Life* by Gianfrancesco Pico, as Appendix A of *CW* 1, 279–381.

responding to that call, and so the original text written by his nephew Gianfrancesco goes so far as to place Pico in purgatory after his death: for he had remained an unmarried layman not out of a desire to follow God's will in that condition, but out of procrastination, and to be able to dedicate himself to his studies.

This is by no means to deny that More drew profitable ascetical lessons for himself from his work on Pico; and he published it thinking it would be "godly prosperous" for his readers[37]—specifically for Joyeuce Leigh, to whom he dedicated it after she had joined the convent of the Poor Clares in London.

Such is the conclusion reached by reading what More said about Pico. As regards Stapleton's statements on the matter, we must bear in mind his own treatment of the *Life of Thomas More*. He is often the main source for the letters and facts he supplies, and we can hardly do without him; but he often added his own, not wholly reliable interpretations.

—

Dating is another matter. When Pico della Mirandola died in 1494, most of his works were still unpublished; it was his nephew Gianfrancesco who edited his *Opera omnia*, which were published at Bologna in 1496, prefaced by Gianfrancesco's own rather gushing life of his uncle.

The early biographies give no indication about how More might have acquired the Latin *Life of Pico* and the other texts he translated. It has been asserted that Colet might have been the link,[38] as he had studied in Italy from 1492 to 1495 and knew some of Pico's works well; he used the *Oratio* (1486), *Apologia* (1487), *Heptaplus* (1489), and perhaps *Adversus astrologiam divinatricem* (1491) in his own writings.[39] But Colet had returned to England before the first edition of the *Life* was published. Frederic Seebohm suggested that William Lily had probably brought the *Life*[40] on his way back from Jerusalem and Rhodes as he visited Rome and Venice; but that, too, is unlikely because as far as we know he returned to England in about 1495.

Clarence H. Miller, in his study of More's Latin sources for the *Life*

<hr>

37. See Gerard B. Wegemer, *Thomas More: A Portrait of Courage*, Chapter 3, "More's First Handbook on Spiritual Combat."

38. Edwards, Introduction, *Life of Pico*, *CW* 1, xli and n. 3.

39. See J. B. Trapp, "John Colet (1467–1519," in *ODNB*, accessed July 2014.

40. Frederic Seebohm, *The Oxford Reformers: Colet, Erasmus and More* (1867), ed. Hugh Seebohm (1914; repr. London: Dent and Sons, 1929), 92.

of Pico,[41] identifies fourteen printings prior to 1510 (five of Pico's *Opera omnia*,[42] eight of the letters, and one of the *Life* without the letters). He concludes that errors and omissions in the editions make it highly unlikely that More used either of the two *Opera omnia* of 1496, the *Opera omnia* of 1506, the separate edition of the *Life*, or the separate editions of the letters. He suggests that More probably used the *Opera omnia* of Strasbourg, 1504, although he does not exclude the possibility that he might have used the Venice 1498 edition. In fact, the 1504 edition was set from the 1498 one, and the internal evidence provided by Miller does not allow us to determine which edition More used, or even which is the more likely of the two.[43]

We know, however, that Thomas Linacre spent several years in the period up to 1499 in Venice to assist in the publication of the Greek Aristotle at the Aldine Press; that same year Aldus printed Linacre's translation of Proclus's *De sphaera*. It seems almost certain that Linacre would have known of the publication of Pico's *Opera omnia* in 1498, even though it was produced by another Venetian printer, Bernardinus Venetus, because Linacre was a close friend of another nephew of Pico's, Alberto Pio,[44] and it is possible that he brought a copy of the 1498 *Opera omnia* to England in 1499. Linacre is mentioned together with More, Colet, and Mountjoy by Erasmus in his letter of December 5, 1499,[45] and—as we saw previously—More calls him his master of learning in his letter of October 23, <1502–4>. It seems possible, therefore, that from 1499 More had access to the copy of the Venice *Opera omnia* of 1498, if Linacre did in fact bring it.[46]

41. *CW* 1, Appendix A, 281–91.

42. Bologna 1496, Lyon 1496, Venice 1498, Strasbourg 1504, and Reggio 1506.

43. *CW* 1, 291.

44. See Aldus Manutius's dedicatory letters to Alberto Pio of October 14, 1499, and November 1, 1495, in *The Greek Classics*, ed. N. G. Wilson (Cambridge, Mass.: Harvard University Press, 2016), 81, para. 2; 15, para. 5. Aldus dedicated five editions of Aristotle's works to Alberto Pio from 1495 to 1498; see Wilson, *Greek Classics*, prefaces III, VII, VIII, IX, and XII. Aldus was also close to Giovanni Francesco Pico della Mirandola and dedicated a Greek grammar to him in January 1498: see Wilson, *Greek Classics*, preface XI.

45. *CWE* 1, Ep. 118.

46. Two copies of Pico's *Opera*, including his *Life* by his nephew and some of his letters, feature in the register of the books at Syon Abbey made by Thomas Betson (d. 1516): Mary Bateson, ed., *Catalogue of the Library of Syon Monastery* (Cambridge: Cambridge University Press, 1898), page 145, items O.41 and O.42; and Vincent Gillespie and A. I. Doyle, eds., *Corpus of British Medieval Library Catalogues*, vol. 9, *Syon Abbey with the Libraries of the Carthusians* (London: British Library, 2001). Betson's register specifies that the two books were donated by Richard Reynolds (a Brigittine priest executed May 4, 1535) but does not identify the edition; it does give the catchword for the second gathering of one of the books, which Doyle notes agrees with the Strasbourg 1504 edition of the *Opera*. This edition was set from the Venice 1498 edition, so it is possible that the Syon volume might

Erasmus mentions Pico in a long letter from Paris addressed to Lord Mountjoy [in June 1500],[47] claiming that he is said to be among the greatest of modern authors by virtue of his amazing intellectual powers. Erasmus had gone to Paris directly from London, so whatever opinion he had of Pico in June 1500 he had already had it in London by December 1499 or had acquired it in Paris (Pico's *Opera omnia* had been reprinted in Lyon from the Bologna first edition of 1496). It seems likely, then, that Pico had arisen in conversation between Erasmus, Mountjoy, Colet, More, and Linacre in London in 1499.

So although there is no certainty about when More first had access to the Latin *Life*, it is possible that Linacre brought a copy of it when he returned to England in 1499 and that More had access to it from that time.[48]

—

Apart from his contribution to Holt's *Lac Puerorum*, the first of More's works to be published were his translations of Lucian in November 1506; the publication was Erasmus's work, as he was the main author of the volume. The opportunity for publishing More's *Life of Pico* may have come from the beginnings of More's brother-in-law John Rastell[49] in the printing business: it was the first book Rastell printed, and More may have given him the manuscript without much revision.[50]

One last point regarding William Rastell's claim in the *English Works* of 1557 was that the *Life of Pico* "was translated out of latin, into Englishe by master More, about the yeare of our Lorde 1510." Edwards points out that this suggests publication followed swiftly upon composition.[51] But the dates of composition given in the 1557 edition are not always reliable. For example, as Katherine Rogers points out, Rastell asserted that *A Treatise on the Passion* was written entirely during More's imprisonment in the Tower, but More's letter of April 5, 1534, to John Harris from Willesden suggests

---

be of the Venice 1498 edition, which could have been brought by Linacre from Venice in 1499, as suggested in the body of the text.

47. *CWE* 1, Ep. 126:150–68. The other great modern authors Erasmus mentions are Ermolao Barbaro and Angelo Poliziano.

48. There is a copy of the *Opera* in Corpus Christi College donated by John Claymond (1468–1536), first president of the college. This seems to be the reprint in Lyon of the Bologna first edition of 1496. Even though Claymond had connexions with More and Linacre, there is no evidence that this copy was handled by More, and Miller's study does not support the likelihood of the text of Bologna 1496 being the source of More's translation.

49. *CW* 1, cxx, "The Texts of the Life of Pico," by Clarence H. Miller.

50. *CW* 1, xxxix, Edwards, "Introduction."

51. *CW* 1, xxxvii.

that More had revised it before his arrest.[52] Stapleton cites William Rastell as one of his sources, and the two of them were living in Douai in 1588, when Stapleton published his *Life of More*. He may therefore have ascertained from Rastell that More translated his *Life of Pico* around the time of his marriage, even though we need not follow Stapleton's interpretation of More's motives for such a work.

In addition, More mentions his state as a married man in a number of works he wrote after his marriage—*Translations of Lucian* (1506), *Latin Poems* (1496–1516), *Utopia* (1516), and *Dialogue* (1529). The fact that he does not mention it in the *Life of Pico* suggests that he may have written it before he married.

In conclusion, accepting with Edwards that the argument given by Stapleton linking the dates of the *Life of Pico* with More's marriage is not reliable, I suggest, however, that More composed it during his period of study, from 1499 to 1504, prior to marriage.

The Life by Thomas More: Additions and Omissions.

We have seen what More added to his translation of the *Life of Pico*, but he also omitted a considerable amount of material; this needs to be considered here. The complete title given in the 1557 edition of More's *English Works* is:

The Life of John Pico, Earl of Mirandola, a great lord of Italy, an excellent cunning man in all sciences and virtues of living, with divers epistles and other works of the said John Pico full of science, virtue and wisdom, whose life and works are well worthy and fitting to be read and to be remembered often.

The 1498 Venice edition[53] includes the *Heptaplus*, *Apologia*, *De ente et uno*, *Oratio*, and *Adversus astrologiam*, together with some seventy-five letters and some other material;[54] from this More translated only the *Life*, three letters, and few brief works that appear in the *English Works* of 1557 as:

---

52. *CW* 1, lx, fn 1.

53. As we have seen, this edition is considered because it seems to be the one most likely to have been used by More.

54. For a full description of the contents, see the Bodleian Incunable Catalogue, http://incunables .bodleian.ox.ac.uk/record/P-288.

Commentary on Psalm 15.
– The twelve rules partly urging, partly directing men in their spiritual battle.
– The twelve weapons in the spiritual battle, which should always be kept
   ready to hand—when the urge to sin infiltrates the mind.
– The twelve qualities of a lover.
– A prayer to God asking for mercy.[55]

More's translation omitted some parts and expanded on "the twelve
weapons in the spiritual battle" and "the twelve qualities of a lover"; he also
added a dedicatory letter. Leaving aside the major works in the *Opera omnia*, the omissions are of two kinds. The first is of the personal comments
Gianfrancesco makes in writing the *Life* of his uncle, such as "my uncle
Giovanni Pico,"[56] "with my own eyes … I have often seen,"[57] "I remember
that when I was staying with him at Ferrara,"[58] and other family details.
The larger omission, a quarter of the entire *Life*,[59] comprises references to
Pico's philosophical and esoteric studies: material from the Kabbalah and
exercises in numerology,[60] Pico's *Heptaplus* on the six days of creation,[61]
his arguments reconciling Plato with Aristotle, Averroes with Avicenna,
and Aquinas with Scotus.[62] More also omits reference to Pico's early opposition to Aquinas and his treatment of the neo-Platonist *Celestial Hierarchy* by Pseudo-Dionysius.[63]

Jennifer Summit's study of these omissions leads her to argue that More
manifests serious disagreement with Pico's project of establishing the essential unity of human and divine knowledge,[64] and this conclusion seems
sound. But she then concludes that "More's *Life of Pico* brings humanism
into England, we could say, by losing it."[65] I would say, on the contrary, that
there is little evidence for that reading of More's English *Life of Pico*.

55. In Pico's Latin version, the "Twelve rules" take up eighty-one lines; the "Twelve weapons"
and the "Twelve qualities of a lover" take up a single line each, but in the latter case the final quality
is expanded into a paragraph, giving three arguments for that quality and explaining that the three
arguments also apply to the love of God; the prayer for mercy is in thirty-one couplets. See *CW* 1,
Appendix A.
56. *CW* 1, 295.
57. *CW* 1, 323.
58. *CW* 1, 327.
59. *CW* 1, 305–15, 337–41; see "The Missing Library in More's *Life of Pico*," in Jennifer Summit,
Memory's Library: Medieval Books in Early Modern England (Chicago and London: University of
Chicago Press, 2008), 62–71.
60. *CW* 1, 299.
61. *CW* 1, 305.
62. *CW* 1, 307–15.
63. *CW* 1, 339.
64. Summit, *Memory's Library* (2008), 66.
65. Summit, *Memory's Library* (2008), 71.

More's study of the Latin *Life of Pico*, possibly at the suggestion of Colet, his spiritual director, moved him to write his own stanzas about the love of God, expanding on the "Twelve properties of the lover." But having studied Pico's life and letters, More concluded that he did not share the Italian's ideal of the ivory-towered life of the humanist withdrawn in his library—"I prefer my little house, my study, the pleasures of my books, and the peace of my mind";[66] instead, he decided on the active life of service to society. When publishing his translation, More omitted whatever might cause confusion to his readers, his friend Joyeuce Leigh, and the general public. What was the point of bringing up the Hebrew Kabbalah and numerology, or the *Heptaplus*, which contradicted St. Thomas Aquinas in important points concerning the Creation, or attempted reconciliations of Plato and Aristotle? Pico's study of the *Celestial Hierarchy* may have led Colet to preach on it, under the impression that it was indeed a work by the Dionysius the Areopagite of the Acts of the Apostles (Acts 17:34). More's decision to omit it may have been based on an understanding, shared by Grocyn, that it did not come from the disciple of St. Paul.

More does, in fact, name Pseudo-Dionysius in his replies to Luther and Tyndale. In his *Responsio ad Lutherum* (1523), he notes that Luther admitted that the sacrament of Order was mentioned by St. Dionysius, whom Luther did not deny was very ancient.[67] And in the second part of his *Confutation of Tyndale's Answer* (1533), More quotes Tyndale's claim[68] that churchmen have written false books and pretended that they came from St. Jerome, St. Augustine, St. Cyprian, St. Dionysius, and other holy men; his long reply[69] mentions St. Augustine, St. Thomas Aquinas, St. Bernard, St. Bonaventure, and St. Anselm, but does not name Pseudo-Dionysius except in quoting Tyndale's paragraph again.[70] Thus in these two cases, More mentions Pseudo-Dionysius only because Luther and Tyndale named him.

More also quotes Pseudo-Dionysius on his own initiative in the first part of the *Confutation* (1532), when he points out that "St. Dionysius" states in the *Celestial Hierarchy* that the teachers of Christian faith taught many things, to be kept partly by written instructions and partly by unwritten ones. This is an important argument within More's concept of the

---

66. *CW* 1, 87 and 351, and Summit, *Memory's Library* (2008), 67.
67. *CW* 5, 68:20.
68. *CW* 8, 706:20–707:13.
69. *CW* 8, 707–714.
70. *CW* 8, 712:4.

tradition of the Church against Tyndale and occurs within a long section citing Origen, St. John Damascene, St. Cyprian, St. Hilary, Theophylact, St. Jerome, St. Leo, St. Cassian, St. Polycarp, St. Ambrose, and particularly St. Augustine and St. John Chrysostom.[71] Pseudo-Dionysius's argument is as relevant as those of the others, but he is not singled out: in fact, More refers in passing to St. Polycarp as a "disciple of St. John," but avoids mentioning Dionysius as a disciple of St. Paul. More also mentions Pseudo-Dionysius in the longest list of early holy men in the *Confutation*,[72] but not in any of the many other lists of ancient Christian authors included in the *Dialogue* of 1529, the *Confutation*, and other works.

The inclusion of Pico's *Heptaplus* and his appeal to the authority of Dionysius the Areopagite would have served no purpose in More's *Life of Pico*. More's study of Pico's life and work helped him to formulate his own life project, and what he published was meant to help others. He mentions Pico's appreciation of great libraries, his knowledge of the Church Fathers, and his praise of "Thomas Aquinas above all the others as more solidly based than the others on a foundation of truth," as well as his knowledge of Hebrew, Chaldean, and Arabic. He also retains Pico's references to Plato and Apollonius, Pythagoras and the hermetic writers Trismegistus and Orpheus, and to Seneca and to Poliziano. He shows his freedom of mind with regard to Pico and others, just as he did throughout his life with regard to the influence of figures like Colet, Erasmus, and even St. Augustine.

Another significant omission by More from the *Life of Pico* is a reference to "Ambrose, Augustine, Martin, and others who fled from the dignity of the episcopate when it was offered to them."[73] The example of these "holy men"[74] is given by Gianfrancesco to justify Pico's refusal to be involved in Church affairs, choosing to pursue his studies instead of accepting the active life of service to the community. More knew, however, that the example was inaccurate, because although Sts. Ambrose, Augustine, and Martin were indeed reluctant to accept the office of bishop, they did in fact accept it in the realization that it was what they were being asked to do for the sake of others; or, to put it another way, they knew that they had a vocation to the active life in the service of the Church. The example of the three saints occurs within a paragraph in the *Life* that deals with both sec-

71. *CW* 8, 368–76.
72. *CW* 8, 727:19.
73. *CW* 1, 325:4–24.
74. *CW* 1, 324:14–15.

ular and ecclesiastical dignities[75] and that finishes with the phrase, "Pico was fully persuaded that it is not praiseworthy for a man of philosophy to accumulate riches *or to seek honours*, but rather to renounce them." More omitted the words "or to seek honours": to refuse honors can also be to refuse an opportunity to serve.

75. *CW* I, 322:31–324:24.

6

Some Books Recommended by Thomas More

In the "Preface addressed to the Christian Reader" at the beginning of book I of *The Confutation of Tyndale's Answer*, written by Thomas More while he was lord chancellor of England and published in 1532, the author advises the "unlearned" that in order to learn how to answer the heretics they should read neither their books nor those by him, but rather

occupy themselves, apart from their other business, in prayer, in good meditation, and in reading such English books as may nourish and increase devotion. Of which kind is Bonaventure on the *Life of Christ*, Gerson on the *Imitation of Christ*, and the book on devout contemplation of the *Scale of Perfection*, together with others like them.[1]

Perhaps it could be suggested that these works, which he sees as suitable for the unlearned, also influenced More in his youth.

⁓

The *Life of Christ* attributed to St. Bonaventure was one of the most popular religious books of the late fifteenth and early sixteenth centuries. More may have read it in his youth in Latin—*Meditationes vitae Dom. nostri J. Cristi*—as there was a printed copy dated 1468–93 in Grocyn's library[2] available to him, possibly from 1496. But as he is recommending an "English book," it is most likely that he is referring to the immensely popular

---

1. *CW* 8, part I, 37:30.

2. *Collectanea*, no. 66. There are also several fourteenth- and fifteenth-century English MSS extant: see *Meditaciones vitae Christi, olim S. Bonaventuro attributae*, ed. M. Stallings-Taney, Corpus Christianorum, Continuatio Mediaevalis 153 (Cambridge, Mass.: Medieval Academy of America, 1997), xi–xviii. *The Universal Short Title Catalogue* lists more than forty-nine printings from 1468 to 1505. Most (twelve) were printed in Paris, the others (two) in Augsburg, Barcelona, Lyon, Montserrat, Pavia, Rouen, Strasbourg, Ulm, and Venice, but not in England.

abridged translation by Nicholas Love, *The Mirror of the Blessed Life of Jesus Christ*, which had been authorized as early as 1408 by the archbishop of Canterbury Thomas Arundel, for the edification of the faithful and the confuting of heretics.[3] When More was recommending the *Mirror* in 1532, it had recently been reprinted (on February 8, 1530) by Wynkyn de Worde at Fleet Street, London; and there were numerous earlier printed editions by Caxton (Westminster, 1484, 1486, and 1490), Richard Pynson (London, 1494), and Wynkyn de Worde (London, 1494, 1507, 1517, and 1525).[4] Nevertheless, if we want to trace the possible influences on More's early choices, it may be best to consider the Latin work,[5] and we can indeed look at all of St. Bonaventure's work that could have influenced More. It is worth starting by noticing that St. Bonaventure was canonized in 1482, which may have contributed to his popularity at the time. André Prévost considers the works of Bonaventure (or those attributed to him) as one of the sources of the permanent intimacy with Christ that is present all through More's writings, from the *Dialogue* of 1529 to his last works in the Tower.[6] Grocyn also owned the *Opera* of Bonaventure (printed in 1482), his *Comentarii super libros Sententiarum Petri Lombardi*, and his *Sermones de Tempore*.[7] Bonaventure's philosophical and theological doctrine is eminently Christocentric; for him, Christ is the Exemplar of God.[8] Prévost, taking this reference from Bonaventure, defines More's philosophy as "ontological exemplarism" and sees an important manifestation of this in More's spiritual exemplarism, which leads him to identify the Christian with the feelings and thoughts of Christ—as shown particularly in More's last works, the *De tristitia* and the *Dialogue of Comfort against Tribulation*.

The Latin *Meditationes vitae Domini nostri Iesu Christi* survives in more than a hundred manuscripts, in several versions; the long version includes a hundred short meditations on the life of Christ. It was long supposed

---

3. *CW* 8, part III, 1474, comment to *CW* 8, 37:30.

4. In addition, there are more than sixty-five manuscripts extant.

5. For the study of the *Meditationes*, therefore, we have a number of sources: (1) The critical edition in CCCM, ed. M. Stallings-Taney; (2) Translations of the text: *Meditations on the Life of Christ*, trans., ed. Isa Ragusa (Princeton, N.J.: Princeton University Press, 1961); and *Meditations on the Life of Christ*, trans., ed. F. X. Taney, Anne Miller, and Mary Stallings-Taney (Asheville, N.C.: Pegasus Press, 2000); (3) Early printed versions published abroad; (4) The English translation by Nicholas Love, *The Mirror of the Blessed Life of Jesus Christ*; critical ed. Michael G. Sargent (Exeter: University of Exeter Press, 2004); and (5) Early printed versions of Love's *Mirror*.

6. Prévost, *Thomas More et la Crise de la Pensée Européenne*, 51–52, 77, 157, 232, and 353.

7. *Collectanea*, nos. 15, 51, and 60.

8. For an introduction to St. Bonaventure see Étienne Gilson, *The Philosophy of St. Bonaventure* (London: Sheed and Ward, 1940), in particular "The Man and the Period," 1–86, and "The Spirit of St. Bonaventure," 470–96.

to have been written by St. Bonaventure, but the real author (sometimes referred to as pseudo-Bonaventure) is now widely accepted to be John of Caulibus, a fourteenth-century Franciscan from San Gimigniano.[9] The author starts his prologue by saying that St. Cecilia, a Christian martyr married to St. Valerian, "always carried the Gospel of Christ hidden in her bosom,"[10] which, he explains, means that she meditated on the life of Jesus, as shown in the gospel, day and night with pure and undivided heart; and so the author recommends the continuous contemplation of the life of Jesus Christ. This, he states, is the purpose of the meditations that follow: though based on the text of scripture, they are at times the fruit of his own or others' imagination and do not have to be taken as true stories; if they are not confirmed by the words of scripture they can be used if they are found helpful or otherwise put aside. St. Cecilia's example in contemplating the gospel scenes is mentioned repeatedly through the book, and in the last chapter the author advises the reader to "converse freely with the Lord Jesus and, in imitation of the Blessed Cecilia, strive to place His life, as she did the Gospel, inseparably in your heart."[11]

Little is known about the history of St. Cecilia, although pious romances about her were widely disseminated, and there is a rich pictorial tradition. Her feast has been celebrated in the Roman Church since the fourth century, and her name appears in the Roman Canon of the Mass from at least the end of the fifth century,[12] following which it was incorporated into the Canon of the Sarum Missal widely in use in England until 1549.[13]

In the *Canterbury Tales* (1380s), Chaucer writes that one of the meanings of the name "Cecilia" is a combination of the contemplative and active lives:

> Or elles Cecile, as I writen fynde,
> Is joyned, by a manere conjoynynge
> Of "hevene" and "Lia"; and heere, in figurynge,
> The "hevene" is set for thoght of hoolynesse,
> And "Lia" for hire lastynge bisynesse.[14]

---

9. M. Stallings-Taney, ed., *Meditaciones vitae Christi*, ix–xi.

10. Ragusa, *Meditations on the Life of Christ* (1961), 1.

11. Ragusa, *Meditations on the Life of Christ* (1961), 388.

12. Joseph A. Jungmann, SJ, *The Mass of the Roman Rite: Its Origins and Development* (New York: Benziger Bros., 1955), 2:253.

13. *Ordinary and Canon of the Mass according to the use of the Church of Sarum*, trans. John Theodore Dodd (1872), 15.

14. "Or else Cecilia, as I find written, is joined by a sort of combination of 'heaven' and 'Leah'; and here, symbolically, the 'heaven' refers to her holiness of mind, and 'Leah' for her constant

The meditations conclude with advice on how to meditate:

You ought to know that it is enough to meditate only on what the Lord did or on what happened concerning Him or on what is told according to the Gospel stories, feeling yourself present in those places as if the things were done in your presence, as it comes directly to your soul in thinking of them.[15]

More also used this imaginative way of contemplating Christ's life; when he recommended it in 1532, it was because he had practiced it himself. That much is evident from reading *De tristitia*, where More places himself in the scene and invites the reader to do the same, as André Prevóst shows.[16] The author's teaching is illuminating, though he still seems to lack an appreciation of the unity of life implied in the idea of being a contemplative in the midst of the world.

The author of the *Meditationes* recommends that meditation on the life of Christ should be undertaken daily and distributes the main events of Christ's life among the seven days of the week.[17] This method is followed by Nicholas Love, who similarly arranges the sixty-four chapters of his *Mirror* into seven parts, corresponding to the days of the week.[18] The first part, Monday, starts with "a devout meditation of the great council in heaven for the restoration of man and his salvation"—which, perhaps significantly, coincides with one of the first themes considered by More in the Introduction of his *Treatise Upon the Passion*, under the heading "The determination of the Trinity for the restoration on mankind."[19] The meditations for Monday also include, unsurprisingly, the "Incarnation of Jesus" and the "Feast of the Annunciation," as well as the journey of Mary "with her spouse Joseph" from Nazareth to visit her cousin Elizabeth,[20] the dream of St. Joseph, the Nativity of Jesus Christ, and the Epiphany; it ends with the "feast of the Purification that is called Candlemas."[21]

The second part, Tuesday, covers the flight into and return from Egypt and Jesus' "hidden life" in Nazareth; it ends with the baptism of Jesus by

---

activity"; Chaucer, "The Second Nun's Prologue," vv. 94–98. Chaucer may have derived his etymology from the life of St. Cecilia in Jacobus de Voragine's *Aurea Legenda*.

15. Ragusa, *Meditations on the Life of Christ* (1961), 387.

16. See Prévost (1969), "The Core of the Mind of More: The Person of Christ," in *Thomas More et la Crise de la Pensée Européenne*, 343–58.

17. Ragusa, *Meditations on the Life of Christ* (1961), chapter 100, 387.

18. See Love, *Mirror of the Blessed Life of Jesus Christ*, ed. Sargent, Table of Contents, 3–6.

19. *A Treatise upon the Passion*, Introduction, the third point, *CW* 13, 25:8–9.

20. Jean Gerson similarly asserts that St. Joseph accompanied Mary in his poem *Josephina*, ed. G. Matteo Roccati, Laboratoire de médiévistique occidentale de Paris (LAMOP) (Paris: University of Paris, 2001), v. 1163.

21. Love, *Mirror of the Blessed Life of Jesus Christ*, ed. Sargent, 50.

St. John the Baptist. The public life of Christ is distributed between Wednesday and Thursday, starting with the temptations in the desert; most of the fourth part, Thursday, is focused on scenes related to the institution of the Eucharist, starting with the multiplication of the loaves and fishes (chapter 25) and ending with the Last Supper (chapter 39). The relationship between the active life of Martha and the contemplative life of Mary is also dealt with in this fourth part, in chapter 33, which summarizes a scene that occupies fourteen meditations in the original *Meditationes* and ends with a recommendation to read the work of Walter Hilton.[22]

The fifth, sixth, and seventh parts follow the traditional arrangement to consider the Passion and Death of Jesus (Friday), "what our Lady & others with her did on the saturday" (chapter 49, a single chapter, for Saturday), the Resurrection and Ascension of Jesus Christ, and "the sending and coming of the Holy Spirit" (Sunday), ending with a final chapter (chapter 64), "On that excellent & most worthy sacrament of Christ's blessed body." Thus, Love's work also incorporates a robust response to the teachings of the Lollards, and More could recommend it in his *Confutation of Tyndale's Answer* because Tyndale objected to the traditional teaching of the Church in the same points that the Lollards had done a century earlier.

The content of at least one of the meditations is puzzling. The author, in the chapter on the "Conversion of water into wine at the marriage feast," starts by saying:

Though it is uncertain whose marriage it was that was celebrated at Cana of Galilee, let us, however, for meditation sake, suppose it to be St. John the Evangelist, as St. Jerome seems to affirm in his preface upon St. John.

And he adds, after the miracle,

when the feast was ended, Jesus took John apart by himself and told him, "Leave this woman whom you have chosen for your wife and follow me." Whereupon he immediately left his wife and followed Christ and became his disciple.

This consideration makes nonsense of the traditional teaching that Jesus Christ manifested the holiness of marriage, and even established it as a sacrament, by attending the wedding at Cana; this teaching is explicitly mentioned by St. Augustine, who notes in his commentary on this passage of St. John's Gospel that Jesus attended the wedding "to assure us that marriage was his own institution."[23]

---

22. Love, *Mirror*, 122.
23. St. Augustine, *Commentaries on the Gospel of John*, Tract 9.2.

The account appears with slight variations in the manuscripts of the Latin *Meditationes*,[24] the early printed versions, and Love's English version.[25] For instance, in the Paris 1490 edition it reads:

Quamuis dubium sit cuius fuerint nuptie facte in chana galilee: tamen fuerit meditemur fuisse iohannis euangeliste: ut in prologo iohannis hieronimus affirmare videtur.[26]

And one of the earliest editions of Love's *Mirror*, that printed by Wynkyn de Worde in 1494, gives the phrase as follows:

There is doubt whose bridal it was. But we at this time shall suppose after the common opinion that it was John evangelist as Saint Jerome also tells in the prologue of the gospel of John.[27]

The Latin author—followed by Love—notes that he based his interpretation on St. Jerome's commentary. But in fact, St. Jerome nowhere mentions this idea in his lectures on the Gospel of St. John: not in his comments on the Prologue of St. John (Lectures 1–3), nor in his comments on the wedding at Cana (Jn 2:1–12, Lectures 8–9); he does not even suggest it in the biographical sketch of St. John in his biographical dictionary of (mainly) important Christian writers, *De viris illustribus*, chapter IX.

Mary Stallings-Taney's critical edition of the *Meditationes* sheds some light on the question. Her text, which is based on eleven manuscripts of the fourteenth and fifteenth centuries, reads:

Quamuis dubium sit cuis fuerint nupcie facte in Chana Galilee [sicut magister in Historia scholastica tangit], nos tamen meditemur fuisse Ioannis Euangeliste et sicut in Prologo super Ioanne Hieronymus affirmata uidetur.[28]

The text coincides with the early editions (for instance, those of 1487, 1490, and 1493), but includes an addition between square brackets: "as mentioned by the Master of the *Historia Scholastica*." This addition appears in seven of the manuscripts but is omitted from the other four. Peter Comestor's *Historia Scholastica*, a twelfth-century abridged version of Bible history with patristic commentaries, was a standard textbook in the

---

24. Ragusa, *Meditations on the Life of Christ* (1961), chapter 20, 140–51.

25. Love, *Mirror of the Blessed Life of Jesus Christ*, ed. Sargent, chapter 27, 78–81.

26. BL IA.40283, chapter XX. The text is very similar to that of those printed in Ulm, 1487, chapter XX, and in Barcelona, 1493, chapter XIX.

27. BL IB.55167, similar to the earlier printing by Caxton, c. 1489–90, BL IB.55119.

28. Of the eleven MSS, A–M, AEG are of English provenance; BDJH are Italian; CFIM are German. ABDGJM are dated fourteenth century and CEFHI fifteenth century. The words between square brackets appear only in BDEGHJM.

University of Oxford.[29] It survives in a great number of manuscripts and early printed versions and was translated into French and other languages (though not English). The wedding at Cana is described in chapter 38 of the section narrating Gospel history, "De mutatione aque in vinum," which in some versions reads:

Quidam autumant has nuptias fuisse Ioannis evangelistae, et ideo vocata Maria, quia matertera eius, et Dominus, quia consobrinus eius. Et dicunt, quod Dominus eum volentem nubere, ex his nuptiis vocaverit, quod certum non est.

This could be translated as follows:

Some allege that this wedding was that of John the Evangelist, and so Mary was invited as his maternal aunt and the Lord as his cousin. And they say that the Lord called him, who wanted to marry, out of this wedding, which is not certain.

In this reading, the text is divided into two sentences, and the subclause "quod certum non est" qualifies grammatically only the second sentence, "Et dicunt." This is ambiguous, because in fact the second sentence is not independent of the first: if it is not true that the Lord dissuaded John from marrying, how it can have been his wedding?

But punctuation and sentence division in manuscripts and early print editions are notoriously unstable and very largely dependent on the vagaries of copyists and typesetters. The version in blackletter by Johannes Amerbach at Basel, dated November 25, 1486, punctuates the passage in question quite differently. It reads:

Quidam autumant has nuptias fuisse iohannis euangelistę·& ideo vocata est maria·quia matertera eius·& dominus quia consobrinus eius & dicunt quod dominus eum volentem nubere·ex his nuptijs vocauerit:quod certum non est.[30]

In this reading, there is a single sentence from "Quidam ... " to "quod certum non est," and the assertion "quod certum non est," which follows the colon, qualifies the whole sentence and makes the meaning clear:

Some allege that this wedding was that of John the Evangelist, and that Mary was invited as his maternal aunt, and the Lord as his cousin and say that the

---

29. James Willoughby, "The Provision of Books in the English Secular College," in *The Late Medieval English College and Its Context*, ed. Clive Burgess and Martin Heale (Woodbridge: Boydell and Brewer, 2008), 157.

30. Petrus Comestor, *Historia scholastica* (Basel: <Johannes Amerbach>, 1486, after the feast of St Catherine, November 25), 356 (available online from the Biblioteca Virtual del Patrimonio Bibliografico, bvpb.mcu.es). The same reading appears in the thirteenth-century Tarragona, Biblioteca Pública del Estado, MS 155, f. 203v (also available at bvpb.mcu.es).

Lord called him who wanted to marry, out of this wedding: [all of] which is not certain.

The difference between this reading and that found in other manuscripts and early printed editions may explain why some manuscripts of the *Meditationes* mention the *Historia scholastica* in support of the assertion that St. John was the bridegroom at Cana, while others omit the reference. Yet it is still surprising that More should recommend a work that—although it admitted that there was doubt about the allegation—was still ready, "for meditation['s] sake," to suggest that the wedding could be imagined to be that of St. John.

Whatever reservations More may have had about "Bonaventure on the *Life of Christ*," he is not afraid to cite Bonaventure in his refutation of Tyndale. Nevertheless, he appears only four times in the *Confutation*, always together with St. Anselm, St. Bernard,[31] and St. Thomas Aquinas,[32] and plays a relatively minor role in the arguments of the *Confutation* compared with many Fathers and other theologians.[33] He appears in no other work by More.

—

The third work recommended by More at the beginning of *The Confutation of Tyndale's Answer* is *The Scale* (or *Ladder*) *of Perfection*, a work written by the Augustinian mystic Walter Hilton (1340–96) in two books. Nothing is known of Hilton's place of birth or early life, but it seems that he studied at Cambridge University and gained a bachelor's degree in civil law by 1371 and in canon law by 1376 before becoming a clerk of Thomas Arundel, then bishop of Ely since 1373 (Arundel became archbishop of York in 1388 and archbishop of Canterbury in 1396). Hilton became a recluse around 1384 but quickly found that that life did not suit him, and c. 1386 he entered the Augustinian Priory of Saint Peter at Thurgarton, near Southwell, Nottinghamshire, and probably died at the Priory on the Eve of the Annuncia-

---

31. St. Bernard's two sermons commenting on the wedding at Cana make no reference to St. John as the bridegroom, even though one sermon deals mainly on the spiritual espousals between Christ and the church. See St. Bernard, "First and Second Sermon for the First Sunday after the Octave of the Epiphany," in *Sermons* (Dublin: Browne and Nolan, 1923), 2:35–54.

32. Aquinas's commentary on John 2:1–11 in the *Catena Aurea* cites Chrysostom, Alcuin, Augustine, Bede, and Hilary, none of whom support the idea of St. John as the bridegroom: see St. Thomas Aquinas, *Expositio Continua super Quatuor Evangelistas simul ac Catena Aurea* (Avignon, 1851), 130–42.

33. Most important are Polycarp, Irenaeus, Origen, Tertullian, Cyprian, Basil, John Chrysostom, Hilary, Ambrose, Jerome, Augustine, Leo the Great, Anselm, Bernard, Gregory the Great, and Thomas Aquinas.

tion 1396. It has also been suggested that he was in touch with the Carthusian Order and that perhaps he died a Carthusian rather than a Canon Regular. Hilton seems to have been connected with the upsurge of interest in Carthusian spirituality in late medieval England, and indeed two of the forty English manuscripts of his *Scale of Perfection* belonged to the London Charterhouse; one was copied there.[34] There were at least four print editions of the work in the fifteenth century, by Caxton (1486, 1490), Wynkyn de Worde (1494), and Pynson (1494), and a number of other editions of the *Scale* had appeared before More's *Confutation of Tyndale's Answer* in 1507, 1519, and 1525. Another important writing by Hilton, his *Treatise of Mixed Life*, was added at the end of the *Scale* in a number of manuscripts and in nearly all the early print editions (1494, 1507, 1519, and 1525). So when More was recommending in 1532 "the book on devout contemplation of the *Scale of Perfection*," he was in effect advising the reader to read not only the *Scale* but also the *Treatise of Mixed Life* in any of those printed editions. The *Scale of Perfection* and the *Mixed Life* would, of course, have been available to More before his decision to get married, not only from the early editions but also, potentially, from the manuscripts at the London Charterhouse.

Book I is addressed to a nun (whether a real person or a literary device). Hilton explains that "there are two ways of life in Holy Church through which Christians may reach salvation; one is called active and the other contemplative" (chapter 2), and he goes on to say that his book has been written only for those who seek contemplation and "forsake all worldly riches, honours, and outward affairs, and devote themselves body and soul to the service of God in spiritual occupations" (chapter 3). So much is this the case that he ends book I clarifying: "Lastly, what I have written does not apply to anyone living the active life, but only to you and others who live the contemplative life" (chapter 93).

From the text it is evident that some time elapsed between the completion of book I and the writing of book II.[35] John Clark writes that in book II,

Contemplation is seen as the means of perfecting humility, with openness to grace and charity, and as such is no longer to be seen as an "extra," but as some-

---

34. See Darrel W. Bargen, "The English Manuscripts of Walter Hilton's *Scala perfectionis*: An Assessment of Reception," Ph.D. thesis, University of Alberta, 2017, 31–32, 50.

35. Walter Hilton, *The Ladder of Perfection*, ed. Leo Sherley-Price (London and New York: Penguin, 1957), "Introduction," xvii.

thing that may and should be sought by all Christians, whatever their state in life.[36]

Nevertheless, although in book II Hilton deals with the spiritual life in more general terms, focusing on faith, God's grace working in the soul, the need for repentance, the sacraments, and so on rather than on specifically monastic practices, the book is presented as directed to those same people to whom book I was addressed: "Since you have asked to hear more" (book II, chapter 1); and Hilton continues to contrast "those leading the active life" with "the contemplatives" (chapter 5).

The *Treatise of Mixed Life*, which is published in the early print versions as a third book together with the two books of the *Scale*, begins however with a short Foreword that reads:

This is the start of a little book written for a man of authority in the world, to teach him how in his position he should behave with well-ordered love towards God and his fellow Christians.

Clark suggests that

Mixed Life is congruous in outlook with *Scale, Book One*, and must have been completed at the same stage in Hilton's development. It does not go as far as *Scale, Book Two*. As its title implies, it deals with the mixed life of action and contemplation. Since the time of Gregory the Great with his *Pastoral Rule*, this pattern of life, exemplified above all in the life of Christ, had been seen as the model for pastors. Hilton is innovative in applying the principles which Gregory set out for clergy to lay people with temporal responsibilities—including care for others—living in the world.[37]

The approach of *Mixed Life* was, indeed, innovative for its time. At times its reading is quite attractive to a lay person:

You must mix the tasks of active life with the spiritual labours of the contemplative life, and then you will do well. For at one time you must be busy with Martha, managing and directing your household, your children, your servants, your neighbours, and your tenants: if they do well, support and help them in their work; if they do wrong, teach them to reform, and correct them. You must also find out and take careful heed that your possessions and worldly goods are properly kept by your servants, managed and distributed faithfully, so that you can the more liberally do acts of kindness for your fellow Christians. Another time you must with Mary leave the activities of the world and sit down at our Lord's feet

36. Walter Hilton, *Mixed Life*, ed. John Clark (Oxford: SLG Press, 2001), "Introduction," vi.
37. Hilton, *Mixed Life*, vi.

in prayer and holy thoughts, contemplating him according to the grace he gives you. So you will pass from one to the other with profit, and fulfil both: and then you will keep the true order of charity.[38]

What Hilton suggests here, however, falls short of More's vision discussed previously of being contemplative in the world, of seeking holiness in service to the *polis*, and of marriage as a path to sanctity. Hilton does not propose to his reader an image like that of the "lover of God" who appears in More's ballade mentioned in chapter 5; but the doctrine put across in *Mixed Life* does affirm that the contemplative life is not the preserve of those who have withdrawn from the world, and suggests that those involved in worldly affairs can keep up a life of prayer by having fixed times for it.[39] Indeed, Hilton specifies, "At other times they should give themselves to contemplation by devotion, in prayer and meditation."[40]

He goes on to point out that this mixed life, following St. Gregory's advice in his *Pastoral Rule*, "belongs especially to men of holy church such as bishops and other pastors: those who have the care and direction of others," and he adds:

Moreover, this way of life is in general right for certain men with high temporal rank and large holdings of worldly assets, and a kind of authority too over others to direct and support them: as a father has over his children, a master over his servants, and a landed proprietor over his tenants, these men also have received grace of devotion by the gift of our Lord, and—in part—a taste for spiritual occupation. To them too this mixed life belongs, which is both active and contemplative.[41]

What about those without authority over others? Hilton does not say: he is not talking about a universal call to the contemplative life in the ordinary circumstances of ordinary people, because he is answering a specific inquirer. In Section 7, which is entitled, *The kind of life most suited to the man for whom this book was made*, he explains:

In my opinion, this mixed life is the most appropriate for you. For our Lord has deliberately set you in so great a position of power over others ...; in addition you have through the mercy of our Lord received grace in order to have some knowledge of yourself, with spiritual longing and a joy in his love.[42]

---

38. Hilton, *Mixed Life*, 6.
39. For the fixed times of prayer practiced by More, see Erasmus to von Hutten, Ep. 999.
40. Hilton, *Mixed Life*, 9.
41. Hilton, *Mixed Life*, 8.
42. Hilton, *Mixed Life*, 11.

Hilton's proposition is not aimed at a young man seeking his own path to holiness, but it does not exclude the possibility that the fullness of the Christian life can be practiced by a father with children and a man with responsibilities; indeed, to be fair to Hilton, he offers in Sections 12–28 copious useful advice for fostering the spiritual life in the midst of the ordinary duties of work. He points out that the desire for God can be present in all occupations throughout the day:

It may sometimes happen that the more troubled you have been outwardly with active work the more fervent your desire will be for God and the clearer your view of spiritual things. (Section 12)

Furthermore, he states that those practicing the "mixed life" can be full of love of God, quoting the Lord's words (Lk 12:49), "Ignem veni mittere in terram, et qu[i]d [volo] nisi ut ardeat,"[43] and he comes close to making an explicit affirmation of the universal call to the contemplative life when citing St. Augustine to say that "the life of every Christian is a continual desire for God" (Section 14).[44]

Hilton's *Mixed Life* was well known to the London lawyers. Hilton himself is thought to have obtained the degree of Bachelor of Civil Law at Cambridge before he embraced the religious life, and his letters reveal that he renounced a promising legal career. His writings reflect his clear legal mind and interest in moral theology, as well as his wide grasp of spiritual theology, in the tradition of St. Augustine and St. Gregory the Great.

Another popular book dealing with the active and contemplative life, once thought to be also by Hilton but now otherwise attributed, is *The Cloud of Unknowing*. The London Charterhouse had a copy of this work from around 1500, so it may have been accessible to More. Paradoxically, although it is explicitly written for religious, its approach is closer to St. Augustine's teaching that "contemplative life and active life are joined in ghostly kinship and made sisters, after the example of Martha and Mary" (*The Cloud of Unknowing*, chapter 21).

More's mention of Hilton highlights a feature of Christian practice in England, where the fourteenth and fifteenth centuries witnessed an extensive and consistent process of assimilation by the laity of techniques and materials for spiritual advancement that had historically been virtually the

---

43. Hilton, *Mixed Life*, 18. Hilton habitually quotes scripture in Latin, as can be checked in the *Treatise of Mixed Life*, Lambeth Palace MS. 472, ed. S. J. Ogilvie-Thomson (Salzburg, 1986), line 458.
44. Hilton, *Mixed Life*, 16–29.

preserve of religious orders.[45] There was a notable production of spiritual works in English (either original compositions or translations from Latin); significant authors include not only Walter Hilton, Nicholas Love, and the author of the *Cloud of Unknowing*, but also Richard Rolle (c. 1300–1349), Julian of Norwich (1342–1416), and the writer of the *Fervor Amoris*. These books were read by an educated laity that was appearing on the scene, and by the end of the fifteenth century they were being printed in London. In this context, it seems likely that More was recommending specifically the works of Hilton and Love, rather than those of others, because both wrote following the guidelines of Archbishop Arundel in defense of the Church.

The second book recommended by More is *The Imitation of Christ*, a work associated with the Dutch Brethren of the Common Life; it is now generally ascribed to Thomas à Kempis but was then commonly thought to be by Jean Gerson. The book was very popular; although, like the *Cloud of Unknowing*, it was explicitly aimed at those embracing the religious state, from the beginning it was read by layfolk seeking to practice a fervent spiritual life in their own circumstances. Rather than a rule for the monastic life, it is a series of considerations about growing in virtue, contemplating the life of Christ, practicing humility, seeking friendship with Christ, loving the cross, reading holy scripture, fostering personal meditation, and so on. In book I the author states:

Habit and tonsure change a man but little; it is the change of life, the complete mortification of passions that endow a true religious. (chapter 17.2)

This is of course a late medieval commonplace; but it indicates an attitude that explains why the *Imitation of Christ* was found useful for the interior life of people both inside and outside the cloister. It is likely that More had read it in his youth in Latin. He seems to refer to the *Imitation of Christ* in the *Dialogue of Comfort against Tribulation* attributing the passages to Gerson.[46] The recommended English edition would have been possibly the first English translation that was made by William Akinson and Margaret Beaufort, mother of Henry VII and patron of Bishop John Fisher, and printed in 1503 by Pynson and in 1528(?) by Wynkyn de Worde;

---

45. See, e.g., Vincent Gillespie, "Vernacular Books of Religion," in *Book Production and Publishing in England, 1375–1475*, ed. Jeremy Griffiths and Derek Pearsall (Cambridge: Cambridge University Press, 1989), 317.

46. See *CW* 12, 98:16–19 and 153:28–30.

that translation was made from the French and mentions Gerson as the author of the book.

More cites Gerson also in several books written toward the end of his life, for Gerson was a tireless worker for the unity of Christendom, and as chancellor of Notre-Dame and of the University of Paris played an active role in the Council of Constance (1414–18), which ended the Great Schism of the West (1378–1418).[47] In June 1392 he preached for a joint action of the kings of France and England to achieve ecclesiastical reunion. In December that year he defended his mastership in theology on the topic *De jurisdictione spiritali* concerning the validity or otherwise of resignation of spiritual authority as a way of allowing for a new election of a single head. In 1395 he was appointed chancellor, and he kept giving sermons and addresses and writing tracts on the subject. Together with a determination to promote unity, Gerson showed a flexibility of approaches in particular with regard to Benedict XIII, the Avignon pope, first with *De substractione obedientiae* or *De substractione schismatis*,[48] 1395, appearing as a moderating influence, and *De schismate, vel de papatu contendentibus*, 1397, favoring *via discussionis*. Then in the *Acta quedam de schismata tollendo*, 1406, he suggested several possible solutions, including a council and a new election by the united cardinals. The Council of Pisa (1409), however, elected a third pope, Alexander V (1409–10); it was an attempt at a solution, but it did not solve the situation.

Following the failure of Pisa the aim of the Council of Constance was again to return to the unity of the papacy and the reform of the Church. At the start of the council there were simultaneously three reigning popes: John XXIII (elected at Bologna in 1410 to succeed Alexander V and deposed by the Council on May 29, 1415); Gregory XII (elected at Rome in 1406, resigned on July 4, 1415); and Benedict XIII (elected at Avignon in 1394 and deposed by the Council in 1417). The Council was attended, among others, by cardinals, archbishops and bishops, abbots and generals of religious orders, professors of theology and canon law, and envoys of kings, princes, cities, and universities. When John XXIII fled on March 20, 1415, Gerson's sermon *Ambulate dum lucem habetis* was of crucial impor-

47. For Jean Gerson and the papacy see, e.g., *History of the Church*, ed. Hubert Jedin and John Dolan (London: Burns and Oates, 1980), 4:352–89, 401–72, and 573–79; R. N. Swanson, *Universities, Academics and the Great Schism* (Cambridge: Cambridge University Press, 1979).

48. Swanson, *Universities, Academics and the Great Schism*, 97; and Brian Patrick McGuire, *Jean Gerson and the Last Medieval Reformation* (University Park: Pennsylvania State University Press, 2005), 70.

tance in the decision to continue with the assembly. Gregory XII officially convoked the Council again through a delegate; and finally, the College of Cardinals elected Martin V (1417–31) as the sole pope. Gerson therefore was instrumental to a return to the unity of Christendom.

Gerson was also an eager contributor to the late medieval movement of spiritual and mystical literature in vernacular forms that could be read by lay Christians. He maintained that everyone was called to practice contemplation, and he taught a type of contemplation rooted in piety and in practice of the human virtues, writing, for instance, that

there is no contemplative person who has no need for any labour. Thus in one person it is always necessary that Martha be with Mary, and Mary with Martha.[49]

More had great admiration for Gerson's loyal opposition to ecclesiastical corruption and his emphasis on personal piety.[50] Gerson's works were first printed at Cologne in 1483; by 1521 there were nine editions of his collected works. In More's *Treatise on the Passion* and *De tristitia* he uses the texts of the gospels from Gerson's *Monotessaron*;[51] and again in *De tristitia* and in the *Dialogue of Comfort against Tribulation* he cites from Gerson's *De Oratione et eius Valore*[52] and *De Probatione Spiritum*.[53] These two pieces were included in Gerson's *Opera*—for instance, in that published in Strasbourg in 1482. A copy of the *Opera* is listed in the catalogue of Grocyn's books;[54] it was therefore available to More. In his last work, *De tristitia*, he calls Gerson an outstanding scholar,[55] a most learned and virtuous man,[56] and a remarkable man.[57]

In the *Apology* and *The Debellation of Salem and Bizance*, both from 1533, More answers the use made of Gerson by his opponents, "The Pacifier" and Christopher St. German, by saying that Gerson was writing in Latin and was not addressing the general public when he criticized the clergy.

---

49. Jean Gerson, *Early Works*, ed. Brian Patrick McGuire (New York: Paulist Press, 1998), 91.

50. *CW* 1, lxxvii; *CW* 9, 338, Commentary to *The Apology* 60:11.

51. In the *Treatise upon the Passion*, More writes, "I will rehearse the words of the evangelists … in Latin word by word after my copy as I find it in the work of that worshipful father, Master John Gerson, which work he entitled *Monotessaron*, that is to wit, 'one of all four'"; *CW* 13, 50:6–10. For *De tristitia*, see *CW* 14, 623.

52. *CW* 14, 327.

53. *CW* 12, 133:5–8.

54. *Collectanea*, no. 53.

55. *CW* 14, 315.

56. *CW* 14, 325.

57. *CW* 14, 623.

The need to defend Gerson seems to have compelled More to a deeper study of Gerson's works.

Thus More found in Gerson not only a man who worked tirelessly for the unity of Christendom and who taught how to be contemplative in the midst of ordinary occupations, but also a sound director of consciences. Confronted with the papal schism, Gerson could not base his obedience on legalistic arguments; it seems that he coined the term "moral certainty" for precisely this situation.[58] Equally, More could not rely on the traditional arguments for obedience to the king, but had to act in conscience. In *De tristitia* More writes that Gerson was "a gentle handler of troubled consciences";[59] and perhaps More himself had found consolation in Gerson.

We have seen that in 1532, Thomas More recommended works of spiritual reading that were well known at the time and widely available in print to "nourish and increase the devotion" of the reader faced with literature produced by heretics. His recommendations do not, however, tell us much about what influenced him personally when he became aware of the need to search for holiness as a married man following both a contemplative Christian life and an active life of service to the *polis*. The doctrine that can be found in Love's *Mirror*, Hilton's *Treatise of Mixed Life*, and *The Cloud of Unknowing* attests that it was at least possible for him to strive to be a contemplative in the midst of the world.

—

While St. Bonaventure (assumed author of *Meditationes*), Gerson (assumed author of the *Imitation of Christ*), and Walter Hilton are all mentioned together by More in his *Confutation of Tyndale's Answer*, another figure is mentioned several times in *The Confutation*. Tyndale (as quoted by More) writes:

Likewise as the Jews had set up a book of their Talmud to destroy the sense of the Scriptures, so the Church had set their Dunce [Duns Scotus], their Thomas, and a thousand like dregs, to establish their lies through falsifying the Scripture.[60]

More replies with a wholehearted praise of the

holy doctor saint Thomas, a man of such learning that all the great excellent minds and the most learned men that the Church of Christ has had since his days have esteemed him and have called him the very flower of theology, and a

58. Rudolf Schüssler, "Jean Gerson, Moral Certainty and the Renaissance of Ancient Scepticism," *Renaissance Studies* 23, no. 4 (September 2009): 445–62.

59. "*Mitissimus attrectator affictae conscientiae*": *CW* 14, 315:5–6.

60. *CW* 8, 713:1–4.

man of such truly perfect faith and Christian living as well, that God himself has testified his holiness by many great miracles and has honoured him here in His Church on earth, as He has exalted him to great glory in heaven.[61]

More mentions Aquinas in the *Confutation* above all as an authority in the exegesis of sacred scripture, together with St. Anselm, St. Bernard, and St. Bonaventure;[62] all four of them also appear in the company of a long list of Fathers of the Church, as "seed" sent by God to feed his Church:

Now look upon the seed, with which the flock of the Catholic Church has been always fed from age to age, and that seed you find St. Ignatius, St. Polycarp, St. Dionysius {107}, St. Cyprian {48}, St. Chrysostom, St. Basil, St. Gregory Nazianzus, St. Irenaeus, St. Eusebius, St. Athanasius, St. Hilary, St. Cyril, St. Sixtus, St. Leo, St. Jerome {20}, St. Ambrose {9, 85, 92}, St. Augustine {1, 35, 59, 86, 88, 97}, St. Gregory the Pope, St. Bede, St. Bernard, St. Thomas {7, 80}, St. Bonaventure {15, 60}, St. Anselm {14}, and many other holy men of every age since the Apostles' days which were all left by God for seed in the known Catholic Church.[63]

The "holy doctor saint Thomas" is also mentioned on his own as an authority elsewhere in the *Confutation*,[64] in the *Dialogue Concerning Tyndale* (1529),[65] and in the *Dialogue of Comfort*.[66] More's use of Aquinas's works has been thoroughly explored by scholars;[67] the question here is how much he knew of Aquinas's teachings when making his early choices. Morales[68] wrote of the possible influence of St. Thomas Aquinas in More's early years at Oxford and London, in particular the books he had available at Lincoln's Inn; and if we allow that the references to Bonaventure and Hilton in the *Confutation* may point to an influence in his early years, the same can be said of the references to Aquinas in the same work. But there are a couple of more direct early pointers.

If More shared in Erasmus's project as mapped out in the *Antibarbari* that it is assumed Erasmus showed to More in 1499,[69] it is worth men-

61. *CW* 8, 713: 21–28.

62. *CW* 8, 716:9.

63. *CW* 8, 727. The numbers between braces are those given in *Collectanea* for the catalogue of Grocyn's library.

64. *CW* 8, 711.

65. *CW* 6, 223:19.

66. *CW* 12, 82:18.

67. Germain Marc'hadour, "Fathers and Doctors of the Church," Introduction to *A Dialogue Concerning Heresies, CW* 6, 526–34.

68. José Morales, "La formación espiritual e intelectual de Tomás Moro y sus contactos con la doctrina y obras de Santo Tomás de Aquino," *Scripta Theologica* 6, no. 2 (July–December 1974): 439–89.

69. *CWE* 23, 3.

tioning that in that work Erasmus praised Aquinas as one of his supporters, writing:

That most noble writer Thomas Aquinas brought out commentaries on the pagan philosopher Aristotle, and even in his theological Questions, where he is reflecting about the first principle and about the Trinity, he offers evidence from Cicero and the poets.[70]

Aquinas is also acclaimed in the *Life of Pico*, where More translated that Pico "regularly praised Thomas Aquinas above all the others as more solidly based than the others on a foundation of truth,"[71] while omitting from the same paragraph that Pico, when he was young, opposed the opinions of Aquinas. Thomas Stapleton wrote that the fact that More

had carefully read St. Thomas is proved by a story told by John Harris, his secretary. Once a pamphlet recently printed by a heretic was brought to More's notice while he was travelling by water from his home at Chelsea to London. When he had read a little he pointed out with his finger some passages to Harris. The arguments (said he) which this villain has set forth are the objections which St. Thomas puts to himself in such and such a question and article of the *Secunda Secundae*, but the rogue keeps back the good Doctor's solutions.[72]

The reference to the *Secunda Secundae* is particularly interesting, because of the works of Aquinas, the catalogue of Grocyn's library includes only his Commentary on the *Sentences* and the *Secunda Secundae* of the *Summa Theologiae*. This does not mean that More did not know other works of St. Thomas by then, but undoubtedly he could at least have come across those two.[73]

It is in the *Secunda Secundae* that St. Thomas deals with the *Active and Contemplative Life* (qq. 798–). He follows the terminology of St. Gregory the Great (q. 179, a. 1), but the main arguments are based on Aristotle's teaching:

Since some men especially dedicate themselves to the contemplation of truth while others are primarily occupied with external activities, it follows that human living is correctly divided into the active and the contemplative. (*ST* II-II, q. 179, a. 2)[74]

---

70. *CWE* 23, 112:4–8.

71. *CW* 1, 317.

72. Stapleton, 35.

73. *Collectanea*, 320–22nn37, 80.

74. St. Thomas Aquinas, *Summa Theologiae*, vol. 46, *Action and Contemplation*, ed. Jordan Aumann (London: Eyre and Spottiswoode for Blackfriars, 1966), 5.

Here the editor adds a reference to Aquinas's Commentary on the *Sentences*, the other book by Aquinas in Grocyn's library:

Cf. III *Sent.* 35, I, where it is shown that an ordered human life requires intellectual operations, and since these are operations of the intellect as such or of the lower faculties directed by the intellect, it follows that man's life is either contemplative or active.[75]

In a. 2, ad 2, a life both "active and contemplative" is included; in a. 2, ad 3, St. Thomas makes it clear that he is not speaking of two types of men but

if directed to the needs of the present life in accordance with right reason, all endeavours of human action belong to the active life [while] human strivings that are directed to the consideration of truth belong to the contemplative life.

Later on Aquinas points out that "it is evident that when a person is called from the contemplative to the active life this is done not by way of subtraction but by way of addition" (q. 182, a. 1, ad 3). In the following question (q. 183, a. 3), he considers whether the contemplative life is hindered by the active life, and in reply concludes that, on the contrary, "the practice of the active life is conducive to the contemplative life."

We should be careful not to confuse references to contemplative and active lives with references to *states* of life. Aquinas deals with the states of life in II-II, qq. 186–89, while qq. 179–84 investigate the kind of life being led by the individual person, regardless of his or her state in life.[76] Aquinas argues that there are two aspects to the life of every man: our life on earth is a journey toward a goal, but this requires first a vision of the goal being sought (contemplative aspect) and then a movement toward that goal by carrying out human acts (active aspect). This follows from the fact that man is an intelligent being, endowed with speculative and practical intelligence (q. 179, a. 2).

Applying these ideas to the specifically Christian life, we can say that both the active and the contemplative are found in Christ, and so the division of life into contemplative and active should not be pushed to the point of opposition between the two. Thus, action can dispose for contemplation; or action can proceed from contemplation; and there may be an alternation between contemplation and action. This means that action can

---

75. *Summa Theologiae*, 46:5fnf.
76. *Summa Theologiae*, 46, Appendix I, 85.

have an ascetical value, in relation to the mystical state of contemplation,[77] or may have a mystical value, as an expression of love of God for his glory and in his service.

—

Love's *Mirror*, the *Imitation of Christ*, and Hilton's *Scale of Perfection* and *Mixed Life* all deal with the Christian's ascetical life and specifically the relationship between the contemplative and active lives; the same is true of Aquinas's *Summa Theologiae*, specifically the *Secunda Secundae*. At first sight, these four authors—all of whom are mentioned by More in the *Confutation*—are simply dealing with an ascetical topic of the Christian spiritual life. However, the teaching that they contain has other dimensions that could have been influential on More's own thinking at this crucial juncture of his life.

1. Aquinas, though he takes his terminology from Gregory the Great, who permeated all the spiritual theology of the Western Church in the Middle Ages, bases his study on the teaching of the Greeks and thus gives it a broader context: action and contemplation are not to be applied only to Christians, but are aspects of the life of every man. Plato's *Republic* already indicates how the practical and the speculative activities of life should alternate in the life of one and the same man,[78] and St. Augustine writes that Plato understood that action and contemplation were to be practiced by the individual philosopher-guardian.[79] Aristotle speaks of the political and the contemplative life; as a political animal, man should concern himself with the right way of living, how to raise his children, and how to serve the *polis*—an important issue for the Renaissance humanists. Origen[80] speaks of the active and contemplative life in a more specifically Christian way, moving away from a purely philosophical attitude;[81] he was also the first to use Martha and Mary as types of the active and contemplative life,[82] introducing a typology later taken up by Augustine and Gregory the Great. Thus, when humanists such as Pico speak of the active and contemplative life and of the figures of Martha and Mary, they are using Christian paradigms for a philosophical issue expressed by Aristotle as the political and contemplative aspects of man's life.

77. *Summa Theologiae*, 46, Appendix I, 86.
78. *Summa Theologiae*, 46, Appendix II, 90.
79. St. Augustine, *The City of God*, book VIII, chapter 4, trans. William Babcock (New York: New City Press, 2012), 246.
80. Grocyn's library included "*Origenes* in print," *Collectanea*, no. 72, but without specifying which works. The editor of *Collectanea* states that the *Homilies* were printed in 1475 and *Opera* at Paris in 1512.
81. *Summa Theologiae*, 46, Appendix II, 94.
82. *Summa Theologiae*, 46, Appendix II, 95.

2. In Love's *Mirror*, St. Bonaventure,[83] the *Imitation of Christ*, Hilton's *Mixed Life*, and Aquinas's *Secunda Secundae*, More would have found corroboration of the principle that the contemplative life of the Christian was to be practiced by all the faithful and that the active and contemplative were two aspects of a person's single Christian life.

—

Finally, in recommending Nicholas Love's *Mirror of the Blessed Life of Jesus Christ* and the works of Walter Hilton, More was doing in 1532 what these two authors had done a hundred years before: to work for the edification of the faithful. This is not evidence that these two authors influenced More in his youth; nevertheless, we can speak of More's contribution to the "continuity of English prose."[84] Immersed in a rich and lively literary tradition, More worked at his prose drawing from the works available to him, which would have included those of Rolle, Hilton, Love, and the *Cloud* author. Of course, when looking for influences we cannot limit More's outlook to what reached him in his mother tongue; like every other writer in England from Chaucer and even before, More was very much open, not only to the Fathers, but also to other Continental authors.[85]

83. Works by Bonaventure also featured in Grocyn's library: *Collectanea*, nn. 15, 60.

84. See R. W. Chambers, "On the Continuity of English Prose from Alfred to More," Introduction to Harpsfield, xlv–clxxiv.

85. Peter Ackroyd, *Albion: The Origins of the English Imagination* (London: Chatto and Windus, 2002), writes, "There has never been a time, in fact, when European scholarship and cultivation did not materially affect the fabric of English life" (197). This sentence comes near the beginning of the chapter dealing with Grocyn, Linacre, Colet, and More.

7

Λαϊκός (*Laikós*)—A Layman

Letter to Budé, <1518>

More knew a number of European humanists who were, like himself, married laymen: these included the Flemish Frans van Cranevelt, the Spaniard Juan Luis Vives, and the Frenchman Guillaume Budé. Budé (who had nine children) was the most distinguished Greek scholar of his time in Europe. His first contact with More took place in July 1517, when he wrote to him to praise the recently published *Utopia* and its author. His letter was included in the second edition of the book, and the two humanists corresponded from then on; they first met in 1520, at the Field of Cloth of Gold, when More was in Henry VIII's entourage and Budé in Francis I's.

The first letter we have from More to Budé, <c. August 1518>, has a particular interest; it is in Latin, but for emphasis he writes two words—λαικὸν and λαόν—in Greek. The letter ends:

quod hic tam utilis labor in literis, omnes tibi mortales obstringit, vel quod tam incomparabilis eruditio, quae peculiaris olim cleri gloria fuerat, tibi faeliciter obtigit uxorato. Nam λαικὸν appellare non sustineo, tam multis, tam egregiis dotibus, tam alte subuectum supra λαόν.[1]

Λαικὸν is the accusative of λαϊκός (*laikós*), "layman," and λαόν the accusative of λαός (*laós*), "people." Following is Philip E. Hallet's translation, but to capture the emphasis given by More I give the Greek words as More did, and I translate λαόν as "ordinary people," thus:

You have earned the gratitude of all men for your useful literary labours: though *a married man* you have happily acquired a degree of learning that was once the

---

1. *Correspondence* [65], 18–22.

exclusive possession of the clergy. Indeed, I am hardly content to call you a λαικὸν ("layman"), when by your splendid gifts you are so highly raised beyond the level of the λαόν ("ordinary people").[2]

The word λαός was used in classical Greek simply to refer to the people, without further qualification (for instance, by Herodotus and Plutarch), or the people who were not members of the ruling elite, or soldiers as opposed to their chiefs. In Homer and Hesiod it meant citizens gathered together, the people at large. Christian authors used it to refer to those who belonged to the Christian people, just as in the Greek Septuagint it was used to refer to those who belonged to the People of Israel. Originally λαϊκός was the adjective related to the substantive λαός, meaning "of the people" or "from the people"; it was used simply to refer to things belonging to the people. It seems that the earliest surviving text in which λαϊκός appears as a substantive is St. Clement of Rome's Letter to the Corinthians (AD 96–98), meaning a person of the Christian people who was not a priest: "The layman is bound by the laws that pertain to laymen."[3] Clement of Alexandria uses it to designate a Christian who was not a cleric;[4] and it is found with the same meaning several times in the works of Origen.[5] More and Budé used Greek words when the Latin equivalent was not common in classical Latin: the Latin form *laicus* is used by Christian writers such as Tertullian and St. Jerome, but not by classical authors.

In his letter to Budé, More points out that on the one hand it is praiseworthy for a married layman to have acquired a degree of learning that was once exclusive to the clergy; but on the other, it cannot be said that Budé was "unqualified." Had More used instead the Latin words *laicus* and *populus*, he would have missed the wordplay and been unable to highlight the relation between λαϊκός and λαός.

Expertise in letters was by no means the exclusive realm of the clergy by 1500, but it is nonetheless true that most of the humanists in More's circle were clerics. Colet, Grocyn, and Erasmus were priests, Linacre a subdeacon (he was ordained a priest in 1520). The great majority of those who taught at the two universities were ordained ministers, although some doctors in medicine and civil lawyers were laymen. The same was true of many of those in royal administration: in More's own time, for instance, the three lord chancellors who preceded him—Cardinal Morton, Archbishop

2. *SL*, 108–9.
3. 1 Clement 40:5.
4. Clement of Alexandria, *Stromata* 3.12.90.1.
5. Origen, *Homilies on Jeremiah* 11:3; *Homilies on Exodus* 11:6; and *Homilies on Joshua* 17:3.

Warham, and Cardinal Wolsey[6]—were all churchmen. Morton had been master of the rolls (one of the senior judges of English law), as had Warham and the bishop of London, Cuthbert Tunstall. Royal secretaries regularly received preferment: Thomas Ruthall was made bishop of Durham, and William Knight became bishop of Bath and Wells. Richard Pace, Henry VIII's chief secretary in 1515, was appointed dean of St. Paul's in 1519 and dean of Salisbury in 1523, holding both positions until his death.

The long tradition in England of clerics—often bishops—in royal administration had an obvious practical reason: that they tended to be the only ones with the necessary intellectual training. Nevertheless, there was also a theological rationale: bishops were not just acting as civil servants or the royal administrators, but by being entrusted with imparting discretionary justice based on reason, conscience, equity, and natural law, which was considered part of divine law, they were performing rightly part of their pastoral office.[7] There were, however, many cases of people following an ecclesiastical training only to pursue an academic or political career. It is obvious that when More decided to follow the path of a "lover of God" as described in his ballade, it was not going to be as a means for a political career.

In More's first letter to Budé, he virtually identifies himself with his correspondent:

Whomsoever I love, you, by good fortune, love also: you possess so many excellent virtues: your temperament, as I judge, hardly differs from mine.[8]

Other letters, no longer extant, must have followed between the two, because in the second surviving letter[9] from More to Budé (written probably from Calais c. June 1520, just after they had met for the first time), More refers to Budé's plan of publishing their correspondence and suggests that he would like first to revise his "remarks upon peace and war, upon morality, marriage, the clergy, the people, etc." It would have been interesting to read those remarks "de moribus, de coniugatis, de sacerdotibus, de populo, etc."[10]

—

6. Indeed, since early Norman times the lord chancellor of England was usually an ecclesiastic; that was very much the rule, though there were a few exceptions, such as Sir Robert Thorp (1371–72); Sir John Knyvet (1372–77); Richard Scrope, 1st Baron Scrope of Bolton (1381–82); Michael de la Pole, 1st Earl of Suffolk (1383–86); Sir Thomas Beaufort (1410–12); and Richard Neville, Earl of Salisbury (1454–55).

7. See Gwilym Dodd, "Reason, Conscience and Equity: Bishops as the King's Judges in Later Medieval England," *History* 99 (2014): 213–40.

8. *SL*, 108.

9. *Correspondence*, Letter [96].

10. *Correspondence*, Letter [96]:20. More could have written "*de laicis*"; instead he chose

The regard for the λαϊκός, the lay person, that More shows in his letter to Budé contrasts strongly with John Colet's views on the matter. For Colet, marriage contained a sacramental principle with respect to Christ and his bride, the Church (Eph 5:32); but, he adds,

now that the Bridegroom has come, the truth of spiritual marriage is fulfilled, there is no longer any necessity for the married state to exist as a figure of that which is to come.[11]

In answer to the obvious objection that, if Colet's ideal is followed, the human race will die out, he argues that there are still plenty of heathen to populate the world and to be converted to Christianity. And in fact, once the whole world becomes faithful and celibate, married only to Christ, then the human race will indeed die out, and the world will end in a state of blissful sanctity.[12] Colet makes a connection between priesthood and matrimony, the latter being an earthly representation of the marriage between Christ and the Church. Through the priestly ministry, the Church is cleansed, illuminated, and perfected and so becomes ready for her marriage to Christ. "Just as Eve was formed from Adam's side, so the Church was born from the blood from Christ's side. Therefore, true matrimony has now been established."[13] And earthly matrimony should disappear. This highly eccentric view, developed by Colet during his years as an academic at Oxford before he took charge of St. Paul's, nevertheless does not go as far as rejecting marriage (a position repeatedly condemned by the Church and clearly at odds with scripture).[14] More clearly did not follow Colet on this. On the contrary, Colet seems to have changed his views, perhaps partly under More's influence: although as dean he put great effort into reforming the clergy of St. Paul's Cathedral, he also promoted the holiness of the laity and tried to influence the secular world by various measures, including the establishment of St. Paul's School (with encouragement from More).[15]

Arnold concludes that "John Colet was a visionary." His ecclesiology

---

"de populo," emphasizing the common condition of belonging to the people, which of course then referred to the people of Christendom or to the Christian people.

11. Jonathan Arnold, *Dean John Colet* (2007), 28.

12. Arnold, *Dean John Colet* (2007), 28.

13. Arnold, *Dean John Colet* (2007), 35.

14. See, e.g., Council of Toledo I (AD 400), c. 16 (DS 206) and Council of Braga (AD 563), cc. 11–13 (DS 461–63), against the Priscillianists and Manichaeans; also Lateran Council II (1139), c. 23 (DS 718); 1 Tm 4:3–4.

15. Other measures included his revival of the Guild of the Holy Name of Jesus in 1507 and the restoration of the Hospital of St. Thomas of Acre. These two, together with the foundation of St. Paul's School, were linked with the Mercers' Company, whose lawyer was More.

was largely based on the neo-Platonist Pseudo-Dionysius: it was other-worldly and absolutist, concerned with an institutional rather than an individual relationship with God. Colet departed from scholastic and even humanist[16] notions of the potential of human reason. The root cause of his over-cerebral theological vision may have been the development of his ecclesiology within an academic rather than a ministerial context.

In contrast, when Thomas More speaks of the Church, he sometimes makes the point that he is speaking of the whole Church—that is to say, not the clergy alone, but the whole congregation of all Christian people, clergy and laity:

that is to wyt not the clargye onely but the hole congregacyon of all crysten people that yf the spyrytualtye were of the mynde to leue it yet wolde not the temporaltye suffer it.[17]

He, as a layman, considered himself fully a member of the Church, even though he recognized the special veneration due to the priest for his unique role in carrying out the Eucharist ("His blessed body works")[18] and in other sacraments.

There is some evidence suggesting that More helped Colet to change his views. In Erasmus's letter of July 23, 1519, he wrote that

John Colet, a sensitive and experienced critic, used to say [referring to More] sometimes in conversation that there was only one able man in the whole of England, though the island is blessed with so many men of outstanding ability.[19]

This remark—proof of Colet's high regard for More—is placed within a paragraph in which Erasmus praises More's powers of disputation, which enabled him to take on even the most eminent theologians in their own field and prove too much for them.[20] As Erasmus certainly considered Colet one of the most eminent theologians in England, he may be intending to imply that More had persuaded Colet of his views on the role of the laity, marriage, and clergy.[21] In 1521, when writing a long posthumous portrait of Colet, Erasmus points to the fact that Colet had placed the finances and all the business side of St. Paul's School under the responsibility

---

16. This can be seen in Colet's rejection of pagan classical authors, in contrast to More's defense of them, for instance in his introductory letter to his translations of Lucian.

17. *CW* 6, 54:20–25.

18. See chapter 5, The love ballad, seventh unit, second stanza, line 6.

19. *CWE* 7, Ep. 999:292–95.

20. *CWE* 7, Ep. 999:289–92.

21. These are the themes—*de coniugatis, de sacerdotibus, de populo*—mentioned in the letter from More to Budé in June 1520.

not of priests or the bishop or the cathedral chapter, but of a number of married citizens, because this was the class of men in whom he found the least corruption,[22] because their natural affection and care for their children and the business of a household seemed to fence them in.[23] As always with the writings of Erasmus, such a portrait of Colet probably represents more the views that Erasmus wanted to convey than Colet's own views; but it is nonetheless true that Colet entrusted his school to the Mercers' Guild rather than to the chapter of St. Paul's Cathedral.

The last two paragraphs of Erasmus's portrait of More in his letter of 1519 to von Hutten deal with More's views on theology and his practice of true piety, and Erasmus ends the portrait saying, "What becomes then of those people who think that Christians are not to be found except in monasteries?"[24] For More lived out his holiness as a married layman in all circumstances— "even at court."[25]

The London Charterhouse and Priesthood

In chapter 6 we considered how Thomas More found himself and others like him, such as Guillaume Budé, as laymen in an environment—that of men of letters and royal administrators—which was very largely a clerical one. The focus must now switch to More's physical environment in 1499–1504 and to what we have received from his early biographers. Both William Roper and Nicholas Harpsfield (who based his biography on Roper's) refer to More's dealings with the London Charterhouse.[26] Roper's testimony is significant not only because he lived with Thomas More, but also because had links (as a benefactor) with the Charterhouse of Sheen, re-established under Queen Mary by the royal charter of January 26, 1557. The Charterhouse of Sheen had been established near Henry VII's palace at Richmond; More mentions it in his *Lamentation of Queen Elizabeth*. The new foundation at Sheen was considered as both a restoration of the pre-dissolution Charterhouse of Sheen and a continuation of the London Charterhouse, because it was undertaken by several of the London monks with the encouragement of some of the relatives of the martyrs from the London Charterhouse.[27]

22. *CWE* 8, Ep. 1211:395–403.
23. *CWE* 8, Ep. 1211:496–99.
24. *CWE* 7, Ep. 999:285–302.
25. *CWE* 7, Ep. 999:300.
26. Roper, 5–7; Harpsfield, 17, l.14.
27. Dom Lawrence Hendriks, *The London Charterhouse: Its Monks and Its Martyrs* (London, 1889), 281.

Roper's testimony is given here with reference to the pages as they appear in the first printed edition:[28]

[p. 5] Whereupon for his better furtherance in learning, he [Morton] placed him [More] at Oxford, where, when he was both in the Greek and Latin tongue sufficiently instructed, he was then for the study of the law of the realm put to an Inn of Chancery called New Inn, where for his time he very well prospered. And from thence was admitted to Lincoln's Inn [February 12, 1496], with very small allowance, continuing there his study until he was made and accounted a worthy utter barrister.

[p. 6] After this, to his great commendation, he read for a good space a public lecture of St. Augustine's *De civitate Dei*, in the Church of St. Lawrence in the old Jewry, whereunto there resorted Doctor Grocyn an excellent cunning man, and all the chief learned of the City of London.

Then was he made reader at Furnival's Inn, so remaining by the space of three years and more.

After which time he gave himself to devotion and prayer in the Charter-house of London, religiously living there, without vow, about four years, until he resorted to the house of one Master Colt, a gentleman of Essex, that had oft invited him thither, having three daughters, whose honest conversation and virtuous education provoked him there specially to set his affection. And albeit his mynde moste served him to the second daughter, for that he thought her [the] fairest and best favoured, yeat when he considered that it would be both great greif and some shame also to the eldest to see her younger sister in marriage preferred before her, ... soon after married her; never the more discontinuing his study of the law at Lincoln's Inn, but applying still the same until he was called to the bench, and had read twice [Lent and Autumn Lectures], which is as [p. 7] often as ordinarily any judge of the Law doth read.

The first problem with Roper's account is that the chronology does not add up. On page 6 he says that "*after* having been *three* years and more as a reader at Furnival's Inn, More spent *four* years in the Charterhouse of London," which is simply not possible: there is not enough time before More's marriage in November 1504 or January 1505. David Knowles suggests that More was at the Charterhouse while he was a student of law;[29] Germain Marc'hadour that he became a barrister in 1501, and then taught at Furnival's Inn the "three years and more" mentioned by Roper and stayed at the Charterhouse while he practiced as a lawyer.[30] That is, Marc'hadour and

---

28. The pages and line numbers correspond to the first printed edition of Roper, *Life of Sir Thomas Moore* (1558; 1935).

29. David Knowles, *Charterhouse* (London: Longmans, 1954), 11.

30. *L'Univers*, 115.

others are suggesting that More stayed at the Charterhouse *while* teaching at Furnival's Inn—which is precisely what Roper does not say.

The documentary sources tell us that after he was admitted at Lincoln's Inn on February 12, 1496 (as registered in the Black Book), More studied there for a number of years. In August 1499, while still a student at Lincoln's Inn, he and Erasmus, together with Edward Arnold, a fellow student of More's, met Prince Henry at Eltham at the invitation of Lord Mountjoy.[31] On April 2, <1500>, Erasmus wrote to Jacob Batt asking him to send his English post to Arnold or to More—and specifying that More was then still resident at Lincoln's Inn.[32] More's letter to Holt is dated from his description of Princess Catherine's entry into London, which took place on November 14, 1501. In October 1502 More was appointed to the Commission of Peace for Hampshire. On January 26, 1503, at Stepney, John Colet resigned the living of Goodeaster in front of two witnesses, one of them being "Thomas More of London, lawyer." That same year More was appointed auditor of Lincoln's Inn; the following year he was elected Member of Parliament and was appointed to the second Commission of Peace for Hampshire.

The second problem is that the "second source"—Stapleton's *Life*—does not mention More's stay at the Charterhouse in his account of the same period:

Thomas More adorned his youth as much with solid virtues and remarkable piety as with his brilliant studies; or, rather, he was far more zealous to become a saint than a scholar. For, even as a youth, he wore a hair-shirt, and slept on the ground or bare boards with perhaps a log of wood as his pillow. At the most he took four or five hours' sleep, and he was frequent in watchings and fastings. Although he was practising such austerities, yet he hid them so carefully that no sign of them could be perceived.[33]

Stapleton seems to rely on the account of Erasmus (who does not mention the Charterhouse, either).[34] Neither does More himself mention the

31. *CWE* 9, Ep. 1341A.

32. *CWE* 1, Ep. 124:27.

33. Stapleton, 8. The first witnesses that Stapleton mentions are John Clement and his wife, Margaret, née Giggs, who went into exile first to Louvain, 1544, and later, 1562, to Louvain and Mechlin (xvii and note 2). She knew More's spiritual exercises well: she kept his hairshirt when she left England (69–70, 192). She was present at More's death and assisted at his burial (188, 191). She was probably the person in More's circle closest to the Carthusians, as she attended, after More's execution, to those imprisoned in Newgate in May 1537.

34. Erasmus writes that More "applied his whole mind to the pursuit of piety, with vigils and fasts and prayer and similar exercises"; *CWE* 7, Ep. 999:172–74. Trapp and Herbrüggen suggest that

Charterhouse when, having resigned as lord chancellor, he lists his previous abodes:

"I have been brought up," quoth he, "at Oxford, at an Inn of Chancery [New Inn], at Lincoln's Inn, and also in the King's Court.... We will not therefore descend to Oxford fare, nor to the fare of New Inn. But we will begin with Lincoln's Inn diet."[35]

It is Cresacre More who brings the Roper-Harpsfield and Stapleton-Erasmus traditions together. He tells us that

When he was about eighteen or twenty years old ... he began to wear a sharp shirt of hair next to the skin.... He added also to his austerity a whip every Friday and high fasting days, thinking that such cheer was the best alms that he could bestow upon himself.... He used also much fasting and watching, lying often upon the bare ground, or upon some bench, laying some log under his head; allotting himself but four or five hours in a night at the most, for his sleep, imagining with the holy saints of Christ's Church.

Cresacre concludes:

For this cause he lived **four years** amongst the Carthusians, dwelling *near* the **Charter-House**, frequenting daily their spiritual exercises, **but without any vow.**[36]

In the last sentence, bold type denotes the information given by Roper, and underlining what has been received from Erasmus-Stapleton, with italics for what Cresacre himself added: that More lived *near* the Charterhouse, rather than actually *in* it. Chambers suggests that Cresacre obtained this information from family tradition. Whether that is the case, or whether it is just that he was familiar with the physical arrangements at the London Charterhouse (as he was familiar with Cheapside), or whether he was simply trying to reconcile his two sources, cannot be known for certain. Before going further, it is necessary to describe briefly the history and circumstances of the London Charterhouse.

~

Erasmus, in his letter to Hutten, leaves it uncertain whether More stayed in the Charterhouse or not, inclining to the view that he lived nearby, as the Inns of Court were no long walk away; J. B. Trapp and Hubertus Schulte Herbrüggen, *The King's Good Servant: Sir Thomas More*, Catalogue of the Exhibition at the National Portrait Gallery (London: National Portrait Gallery, 1977), 28, text to exhibit no. 21. What is certain is that Erasmus does not mention the Charterhouse.

35. Roper, 53.

36. Cresacre More, 24–25.

The General Chapter of the Carthusian Order accepted the proposal to found a Charterhouse in London in 1370,[37] with the title of the House of the Salutation[38]—that is, of the Salutation of the most Blessed Virgin Mary. In 1490 the General Chapter gave permission for laymen to live in a house within the precincts,[39] and so the London Charterhouse included a guesthouse.[40] As the modern Carthusian rule limiting visits and retreats to ten days was not in force,[41] the general opinion is that More lived in the quiet atmosphere of this guesthouse or (according to Cresacre More) nearby, and that there he read the Fathers, learned Greek, prepared his manuscript for his lectures on *De civitate Dei*, and practiced prayer. There he would have had access to the works of Hilton, Love, and Gerson mentioned in chapter 6.[42]

The founders of the London Charterhouse were Sir Walter Manny and Michael Northburgh, bishop of London.[43] The Black Death had reached England in the summer of 1348 and was at its height in London in the early months of the following year. When the capacity of the city graveyard proved inadequate, Sir Walter rented from the Master and Brethren of St. Bartholomew's Hospital some thirteen acres of land known as Spital Croft to be put aside for a graveyard, with the understanding that he should be granted full possession when he could provide the hospital with property of equal value in exchange; within the graveyard a chapel was built wherein masses were to be celebrated for those buried there. The first suggestion of a charterhouse seems to have come from Bishop Northburgh, who had visited the Charterhouse at Paris. He approached Sir Walter with

37. Bruno Barber and Christopher Thomas, *The London Charterhouse* (London: Museum of London Archaeology Service, 2002), 16.

38. Stow, *Survey of London* (1598), 160.

39. E. Margaret Thompson, *The Carthusian Order in England* (London: Church Historical Society, 1930), 311–12.

40. Knowles, *Charterhouse* (1954), 32.

41. Hendriks, *London Charterhouse* (1889), 65.

42. The only booklists belonging to the London Charterhouse to survive suppression were records of loans to other houses of the Carthusians. These loans are published in *Corpus of British Medieval Library Catalogues*, vol. 9 (London: British Library, 2001): they include the loan of Hilton's *Scala perfectionis* and the *Meditationes vitae Christi* to the Charterhouse in Hull (C2, nos. 3 and 4) and the *Imitatio Christi* (Venice, 1483) to the Charterhouse in Hinton (C5, no. 6). I have already mentioned that the *Opera Iohannis de Gersonno* [Gerson] and *Vita Cristi meditationes* were also in Grocyn's library (*Collectanea*, nos. 52 and 66).

43. For an extensive study on the London Charterhouse, see "Religious Houses: House of Carthusian Monks," in *A History of the County of Middlesex*, ed. J. S. Cockburn, H. P. F. King, and K. G. T. McDonnell, *Victoria County* History (London: Institute of Historical Research, 1969), 1:159–69.

the suggestion that they should cooperate in the foundation of a monastery in Spital Croft.

The suggestion was in harmony with a recent change in the policy of the Carthusian Order. The Grande Chartreuse and all early charterhouses had been founded in desert places; this was the case also with the English foundations, which were at Witham, Hinton, and Beauvale. More recently, however, houses had been founded in urban sites such as Paris, Bruges, Cologne, and Liège, where the austere, secluded community served as a living contrast to the worldliness and vice of a great city. Bishop Northburgh hoped for a similar result in London. Sir Walter was agreeable to the proposal, and the bishop approached the priors of Witham and Hinton; once the General Chapter had accepted the new foundation, permission was sought from the king, and on March 28, 1371, came Sir Walter's foundation charter. In 1372 Manny died and was buried, together with his wife, Margaret, before the high altar of the graveyard chapel, now the monastic Church.

The General Chapter of 1371 allowed John Luscombe to resign as the prior of Hinton in order to establish the new foundation; and as Visitor of the province, he was authorized to summon monks from each of the existing houses to become founding members of the new community. The Charterhouse was built as a double house; that is, one of twenty-four cells—rather than the usual twelve—plus one for the prior. It depended for the majority of its income on the gifts, large and small, in cash and in real estate, mainly from Londoners. The names of the founders of the cells have been preserved; they date from 1371 to around 1420. Many of them were rich Londoners; some were Mercers,[44] as were the fathers of Colet and of More. Apart from the tombs of Sir Walter Manny and his wife, the monastic Church contained those of several knights and of Philip Morhan, bishop of Ely (d. 1434); Bartholomew Rede, mayor of London (d. 1505), was buried in the cloister.[45] All these connections made the Charterhouse very much part of the city establishment, and by the end of the fifteenth century it was a center of religious and cultural influence in London,[46] "the pre-eminent centre of lay piety for Londoners [and] it had a nationally renowned library."[47] Sir John More, Thomas's father, bequeathed money

---

44. Knowles, *Charterhouse*, 26.

45. Stow, *Survey of London*, 160–61.

46. Knowles, *Charterhouse*, 11.

47. Guy, *Reputations* (2000), 30.

in his will "to the Charterhouse of London"[48] as well as to each of the four orders of friars "of London";[49] other members of Lincoln's Inn in the period indicated in their wills their desire to be buried at the Charterhouse.[50] And More lists the Charterhouse as one of the important London religious establishments, together with the Franciscans of Greenwich and the Bridgettines of Syon.[51]

The Charterhouse lay halfway between Furnivall's Inn in Holborn and More's family house at Milk Street, about fifteen minutes' walk from one or the other, and the same distance from Lincoln's Inn; the area, outside the walls of the city, was a convenient place of residence for students or lecturers at the Inns of Court. In considering More's life during the period, we must bear in mind that he was both lecturing and practicing as a lawyer in various capacities. Lodgings outside the family home allowed him space for study and prayer, but it is noteworthy that he lectured on St. Augustine at his parish church and that his spiritual guides were secular priests: Colet and, in his absence, Grocyn, who was his parish priest. So the Charterhouse was not the focus of his active involvement, even though it was almost equidistant from the places where he lectured and worked: St. Lawrence, Furnivall's Inn, and Lincoln's Inn.[52]

—

The original plague graveyard was dedicated on the Feast of the Annunciation, March 25, 1349, by the then bishop of London, who preached on the word *Ave*, the "Hail" of the angel Gabriel. This circumstance gave the name that the future monastery was to bear: the House of the Salutation of the Mother of God; the term "Salutation" was commonly given to the angel's greeting at the Annunciation. This is confirmed by the seal of the Charter-

48. Public Record Office, National Archive, PROB 11/23/381: Will of Sir John More, Justice of the King's Bench, December 5, 1530.

49. Presumably the Franciscans, the Dominicans, the Carmelites, and the Austin Friars, which were the main orders of friars in London.

50. Keane, "Thomas More as a Young Lawyer," 58.

51. *CW* 8, 163:12–21.

52. John Bouge, who was looking after the parish of St Stephen Walbrook at the time of the death of Jane, More's first wife, in 1511, described More in a letter as his "ghostly child." The letter was addressed to Dame Katherine Manne in 1535, after More's execution; by then Bouge had joined the Charterhouse of Axholme. Referring to More, he wrote, "He was my parishioner at London. I christened him two godly children. I buried his first wife." The letter does not suggest any connection of More or Bouge with the London Charterhouse. The letter is kept in the Public Record Office, the National Archive of England, and is printed, together with a commentary by James Gairdner, in the *English Historical Review*, VII, Notes and Documents (October 1892): 712–15; available online. A modern English paraphrase of the full letter is included in *Letters and Papers, Foreign and Domestic, of the Reign of Henry VIII, Addenda*, vol. I, part I, printed 1929, Document 1024, 357–58.

house as used at least from 1379 until 1537: a pointed oval showing the angel
and the Blessed Virgin at the Annunciation, and a scroll between the two
figures with the angel's words *Ave Maria*; the legend around the seal reads:
SIGILLUM COMUNE DOMUS MATRIS DEI ORDINIS CARTUSIANORUM
LONDINIARUM.[53]

One of the monks in the London Charterhouse in More's time was
Dom Maurice Chauncy (c. 1513–81), who entered the Carthusians and
was professed there in 1534; he stayed until the monks were expelled in
1538. Shortly afterward he wrote an account of the history of the eighteen
Carthusians who suffered martyrdom from 1535 to 1537. In his account he
gives the dates of execution of the first Carthusians (May 4), of John Fisher,
bishop of Rochester (June 22), and of Thomas More (July 6), all in the
same year of 1535;[54] but he makes no reference to More having any links
with the London Charterhouse. If More had lived in the London Charterhouse, it would be highly surprising that Chauncy—who gives the names
of all the thirty Carthusians there in 1535, and of many others—should fail
to mention it. Even if he had not been aware of such a link when he joined
the community in the early 1530s, More's martyrdom would have made it
a cause of holy pride for all of them,[55] and it seems most unlikely that he
would not have reported it in his *Historia Aliquot Martyrum*. No link is reported until William Roper appears as a benefactor of the reestablishment
of the Sheen Charterhouse in 1557, with Dom Maurice Chauncy, the new
prior, at its head and several London monks under him.[56]

The evidence strongly suggests, then, that we should concur with Cresacre: More stayed *near* the London Charterhouse, rather than *in* it.

More himself does speak of the London Charterhouse, however, in several
of his writings. Apart from references in his *Confutation of Tyndale's Answer*, which we will look at later, in his *Treatise Upon the Passion* (1534) he
writes:

And therefore as touchynge the Paschal Lambe, when our Sauiour sayde, I wyll
from hencefoorthe eate thys no more tyl it be fulfilled in the kyngdome of God,

53. Cockburn, King, and McDonnell, "Religious Houses: House of Carthusian Monks," 159–69.
54. Dom Maurice Chauncy, *Historia Aliquot Martyrum Anglorum, maxime octodecim Cartusianorum* (Mainz, 1550); English translation *The History of the Sufferings of the Eighteen Carthusians
in England* (London: Burns and Oates, 1890), 66.
55. The London community remained there until expelled from the house on November 15, 1538;
Chauncy, *History of the Sufferings*, 71.
56. Hendricks, *London Charterhouse*, 281.

was as muche as to saye, after this I will neuer eate it more. After such manner of speakynge as one myghte saye that looked for too dye, or that were entring into the charter house, I wyll neuer eate fleshe more in thys worlde.[57]

And in his letter of May 2 or 3, 1535, to his daughter Margaret from the Tower of London, he refers to the Fathers of the Charterhouse and Richard Reynolds of Syon Abbey, who had been sentenced to death for treason.[58] Roper, indeed, transcribes his moving words to his daughter Margaret as they watched three Carthusians and Reynolds being taken from the Tower for execution on May 4.[59] The same account is taken up by Harpsfield[60] and Ro: Ba:.[61] From these references of More's, two observations are obvious: his praise of the Carthusians for their life of prayer and penance and the veneration of the Charterhouse by the London citizens. It would been very natural for More, in this context, to have informed the reader that he had been at the Charterhouse—just as he writes in *A Dialogue of syr Thomas More* (1529) that he had previously lived in the "parysshe of saynt Stephens in walbroke in London,"[62] or mentions in his Letter to the Senate of Oxford that he had studied there,[63] or writes in book I of *Utopia* that he was brought up in the household of John Morton at Lambeth,[64] or states in the *Debellation of Salem and Bizance* (1533) that he studied at Lincoln's Inn,[65] or imagines himself as a young man again in one of the Inns of Chancery,[66] or speaks (as we have seen) of the fare at Oxford, New Inn, and Lincoln's Inn. But none of his references to the Charterhouse suggests that he had stayed in the London Charterhouse.

—

But the earlier biographers seem to say more, suggesting that he was thinking of becoming a priest or a religious. Thus, Erasmus writes:

And all the time he applied his whole mind to the pursuit of piety, with vigils and fasts and prayers and similar exercises thinking of the priesthood. In this indeed he showed not a little more sense than those who plunge headlong into so exacting [a] profession without first making [a] trial of themselves. Nor did any-

57. *CW* 13, 122:5–10.
58. *Correspondence* [214].
59. Roper, 80:9–81:15.
60. Harpsfield, 179–80.
61. Ro: Ba:, 223–24.
62. *CW* 6-I, 79:1–2.
63. *CW* 15, 130:24–27.
64. *CU*, 80:28.
65. *CW* 10, 79:21.
66. *CW* 10, 37:35.

thing stand in the way of his devoting himself to this kind of life, except that he could not shake off the desire to get married. And so he chose to be a god-fearing husband rather than an immoral priest.[67]

Erasmus is an exceptional witness to More, and we have gained much precious information from his correspondence. But we also know, from More's letters and other sources, that the two humanists differed in certain of their views: specifically, as to whether More should have devoted himself exclusively to scholarly work rather than to the practice of the law; and, later on, when More was fully involved in royal politics, whether More—as a layman—should have left the question of the king's divorce to the theologians. The last sentence of Erasmus's description almost sounds to me like a Gilbert and Sullivan paradox. Allen emphasizes that the following sentence starts with the conjunction *Tamen*, which, he notes,

suggests that the three previous sentences (which are a characteristic Erasmian sally) were added later than the first composition.[68]

John Guy writes that in these sentences

it is also obvious that Erasmus's language is playful, almost ironical, and his concluding sentiment was proverbial. To say that someone had chosen to be a "chaste husband" rather than a lewd priest was a "merry jest" that had virtually become a colloquialism.[69]

As for what Erasmus says that More was thinking of the priesthood (*sacerdotium meditans*):[70] This follows from the assumption, as described in chapter 6, that those who wanted to pursue a humanistic career had to be clerics. In the same letter Erasmus praises the humanists then at Henry's court:

Had you lived in this court, my dear Hutten, I have no doubt you would ... cease to be a professed enemy of court life, though you too live with as honourable a prince as you could wish, nor do you lack men who look for a better state of things.... But what are the few that you have in comparison with such a company of distinguished men: Mountjoy, Linacre, Pace, Colet, Stokesley, Latimer, More, Tunstall, Clerk, and others like them?[71]

---

67. Letter from Erasmus to Ulrich von Hutten, July 23, 1519: *EE* 4, Ep. 999, lines 160–67, and in *CWE* 7, Ep. 999, lines 172–79.

68. *EE* 4, 18, footnote to Ep. 999, line 168.

69. Guy, *Reputations* (2000), 32.

70. Ep. 999, 162.

71. Ep. 999, 320–21.

All of these, except for More and Mountjoy, were clerics. This topic will be discussed in more detail in chapter 8, but here we can refer to the argument given by John Guy in his book *Thomas More: Reputations*.[72] There he points out that Roper makes no reference to More's considering the priesthood, even though he draws extensively on Erasmus's correspondence elsewhere. Erasmus's vignette is not authoritative: it was not a private letter but designed for publication. Here John Guy cites Lisa Jardine,[73] and he writes, "It is now well understood that Erasmus' career was largely a triumph of image management."[74] Erasmus's objective was to set before Europe not so much a factual description of Thomas More as an idealized depiction of a Christian humanist life: he sought to create a model of decorum in which the clash between "action" and "contemplation" in their Christian and classical settings should be fully resolved. It was essential to Erasmus's own story that More should have carefully tested his vocation before deciding that he was "called" to the active life.[75]

Of the other early biographers, Thomas Stapleton writes that

[More] debated with himself and his friend Lily the question of becoming a priest. For the religious state he had an ardent desire and thought for a time of becoming a Franciscan. But as he feared even with the help of his practices of penance, that he would not be able to conquer the temptations of the flesh that come to a man in the vigour and ardour of his youth, he made up his mind to marry.... Perhaps it was that the circumstances of the time were not propitious to his desire of embracing a stricter life, for our religious communities had become lax, as the utter destruction and desolation of the monastic state, which followed so soon afterward, showed with sufficient clearness. Or perhaps it was that God, for his own greater glory, wished him to remain a layman, to accept the honours and to meet the difficulties of public life, and at the same time wished to keep his servant unspotted and unharmed, and even to lead him to the highest perfection of sanctity. Certainly, when he came to the conclusion that it was not for him to aspire to the more perfect state of life, he at least earnestly resolved never to cease, throughout the whole course of his life, to worship God with most sincere devotion.[76]

72. Guy, *Reputations* (2000), 32–33.

73. Jardine, *Erasmus, Man of Letters*.

74. Guy, *Reputations* (2000), 33.

75. J. B. Trapp also states that Erasmus's description of More included elements of self-portrait: see Trapp, entry on John Colet in *ODNB*, September 2004.

76. Stapleton, 8–9. But James McConica writes, "It was part of More's distinction to confer upon his married career an importance beyond the ideals of Christian asceticism, with its tendency to see marriage as a safety-net for those unable to climb to the heights of consecrated virginity"; McConica, *Thomas More* (1977), 10.

This account largely reflects Stapleton's own views. Cresacre More, himself a married layman, draws on Stapleton and Roper but sees More's choice in a different light:

For this cause he lived four years amongst the Carthusians, dwelling near the Charter-House, frequenting daily their spiritual exercises, but without any vow. He had an earnest mind to be a Franciscan friar, that he might serve God in a state of perfection. But finding that at that time religious men had somewhat degenerated from their ancient strictness and fervour of spirit, he altered his mind.[77]

He is following Stapleton, who refers to the laxness of "religious communities" in England in general terms; but the accusation certainly does not fit the London Carthusians, who were known for their austere and holy lives and who were the first religious to suffer martyrdom for refusing to accept the Act of Supremacy; the same can be said of the Franciscan Observants and the Bridgettines, who followed similarly strict discipline.[78] More specifically defends the monks of the London Charterhouse in his *Confutation* of Tyndale: when Tyndale accuses them of being superstitious, saying that they preferred to die rather than to eat meat, More praises them for their virtuous devotion and points out that in fact, many of them live to a very great age and that he had never heard of any of them dying on account of not eating meat![79] He similarly defends them in his *Apology* against the charge of failing to do what they were established to do, to pray and fast and give alms, as any reader knew well that they did all these things.[80] And in the *Dialogue of Comfort against Tribulation*[81] he again writes highly of the Carthusians, as well as of the Bridgettine nuns of Syon and the Poor Clares who lived outside London Wall, just beyond Aldgate.

Cresacre continues:

He had also, after that, together with his faithful companion Lillie, a purpose to be a priest; yet God had allotted him for another state, not to live solitary, but that he might be a pattern to remind married men how they should carefully bring up their children; how they should love their wives, how they should employ their endeavours wholly for the good of their country, yet excellently

---

77. Cresacre More, 25–26.

78. David Knowles, *The Religious Orders in England*, vol. 3: *The Tudor Age* (Cambridge: Cambridge University Press, 1961), 206–11 and *passim*. The Franciscan Observants were the first to challenge Henry.

79. *CW* 8, 125:34–126:14.

80. *CW* 9, 103:5–19.

81. *CW* 12, 276:23–25.

perform the virtues of religious men, as piety, charity, humility, obedience, yea, conjugal chastity.[82]

Harpsfield, following Roper, does not mention the Franciscans or Lily, though he enlarges on what Roper says:

And all this while was he unmarried, and seemed to be in some doubt and deliberation with himself what kind and trade of life he should enter, to follow and pursue all his long life after. Surely it seemeth by *some apparent conjectures*[83] that he was sometimes somewhat propense and inclined either to be a priest,[84] or to take some monastical and solitary life....

Now, if any man will say that, seeing the contemplative life far exceedeth the active, that he marvelleth why Master More did not follow, embrace and pursue the said inclination, to this I answer, that no man is precisely bound so to do; I answer further, that *were it so* that he had such propension and inclination, God himself seemeth to have chosen and appointed this man to another kind of life, to serve Him therein more acceptably to His divine honour, and more profitably for the wealth of the Realm and his own soul also.[85]

So, it seems that there is no agreement or certainty about the picture the biographers present of this question—apart from the fact that none of them suggest that More considered being a Carthusian, which is what some recent writers assumed. Of course, a young man desiring to do God's will (as More mentions in his letter to Holt) would consider, in general, the various options open to him; but from More's biographers we can say little more.

But Stapleton's and Cresacre's reference to Lily requires further investigation. Stapleton's phrase "*Meditabatur adolescens sacerdotium cum suo Lilio*" appears in chapter II of his *Vita Thomae Mori*.[86] The same chapter, several paragraphs further on, contains the letter to Colet dated October 23, which finishes:

Interea cum Grocino, Linacro, et Lilio nostro tempus transigam, altero (vt tu scis) solo (dum tu abes) vitae meae magistro; altero studiorum praeceptore; tertio charissimo rerum mearum socio.

This is followed by a further reference to Lily as "*adolescentis Mori socius*." And in chapter V, Stapleton mentions him among the "learned and famous men" who were friends of More. The list starts with Colet, Grocyn,

---

82. Cresacre More, 26.
83. Italics my emphasis.
84. Guy, *Reputations* (2000), 33, considers that Harpsfield takes this from Erasmus.
85. Harpsfield, 17–18.
86. Stapleton, *Vita Thomas Mori* (ed. 1689), 18.

and Linacre, all of whom were rather older than More; next come William Lily and William Mountjoy, described as *socios quasi studiorum*. Mountjoy's date of birth is not known, but he is thought to be a close contemporary of More's; Lily, however, is estimated to be about ten years older than More, having been born around 1468.[87] In <1502–4>, when More mentions him as his companion and suggests that the two of them shared projects and ideals, such as a common search for a spiritual life (*charissimo rerum mearum socio*), More was between twenty-four and twenty-six and Lily was perhaps already thirty-six. This significant discrepancy of ages prompts a careful study of their circumstances.

Lily appears to have been elected a demy[88] of Magdalen College, Oxford, in 1486;[89] according to his eldest son, George, before graduating he went on pilgrimage to Jerusalem, on his return trip spending some time in both Rhodes[90] and Italy, where he registered at the English Hospice in Rome on November 4, 1490. It is thought that on his return to England he settled as a schoolmaster in London. In 1510 he was appointed the first high master of the school set up by Colet at St. Paul's.

We have few details of his family life. He married Agnes, with whom he had six children, four boys and two girls.[91] There are two clues for the date of his marriage. The first is the presentation of a "Wilhelmus Lilye, scholaris" to the rectory of Holcot in Northamptonshire on May 24, 1492, by John Kendall, prior in England of the Knights of St. John;[92] the relation with the Knights might be explained by his stay in Rhodes. Lily resigned the benefice in 1495.[93] The other clue is that he appears to have died by December 10, 1522, when a successor at St. Paul's School was appointed; however, a codicil was added to his will in late February 1523, and the memorial stone placed by his son George was dated February 25, 1523. Lily's

87. The estimate of Lily's date of birth is based on his age at death, recorded as fifty-four on his memorial tablet in old St. Paul's, and on the statement that he was eighteen years old at his election in 1486; see entry on William Lily, *ODNB*, online ed., revised by Hedwig Gwosdek in June 2020, accessed December 11, 2021.

88. "Demy" was a term used at Magdalen College for a "scholar" on the foundation—etymologically one entitled to half a fellow's allowance from the founder's bounty.

89. L. W. B. Brockliss, ed., *Magdalen College Oxford: A History* (Oxford: Clarendon Press, 2008), 106.

90. Beatus Rhenanus states that Lily "spent some years on the island of Rhodes" in his dedicatory letter (dated February 23, 1518) introducing the edition of More's Epigrams: *CW* 3.II, 76–77.

91. Emden suggests that they had fifteen children, but this may not be accurate. See A. B. Emden, *A Biographical Register of the University of Oxford to A.D. 1500* (Oxford: Clarendon Press, 1958), 2:1,147.

92. BL, MS Lansdowne 979, f. 32; the date was November 6, 1495.

93. Emden, *Biographical Register*, 2:1147.

epitaph for his wife states that she died on August 11 after seventeen years of marriage, but does not give the year; nevertheless, the record suggests that they married by August 11, 1505, at the latest.

As More went to Oxford around 1492, he could not have met Lily there because Lily had already left; he may have got to know Lily after 1496, when he was admitted to Lincoln's Inn and William Grocyn (Lily's godfather), became rector of St. Lawrence's. It seems likely that Lily was granted the benefice of Holcot to support his studies, as canon law allowed, and as was common practice; this provided him with the means to study in Italy. On his return he resigned his benefice and settled in London as a schoolmaster. By the time of More's letter of October 23, <1502–4>, we find More and Lily working together and discussing their future; More got married to Jane in November 1504 or January 1505 and, no later than August 1505, Lily to Agnes. Their friendship continued; the two of them translated from the Greek and produced their *Progymnasmata*, "exercises by the friendly rivals Thomas More and William Lily," although this seems to have been much later.[94] In a letter to Erasmus dated December 1516, More is still calling his friend *Lilius noster*;[95] Lily wrote a poem to celebrate "the painting belonging to More, containing portraits of Erasmus and Giles," which was sent to More on September 8, 1517.[96]

Where did Stapleton get his information about Lily? One of his sources, John Clement, was educated under Lily at St. Paul's School; he became a member of More's household and married Margaret Giggs, More's adopted daughter. The couple went into exile in Louvain in 1549, returning to England in 1554, but by 1560 they had again left the country, settling first in Bergen op Zoom and then in Mechlin. It may be that when Stapleton left England in 1563 and settled in the Low Countries, the Clements provided him with the two letters from More to Colet that appear in *Tres Thomae* and that John Clement could have got hold of from Lily; indeed, John Clements could also have transmitted Lily's memories of More. Thus the source of the statement *Meditabatur adolescens sacerdotium cum suo Lilio* could be the same as that of More's letters to Colet. It is obvious, however, that Stapleton was copying from Erasmus's letter to Hutten, in which he uses a very similar turn of phrase: *adolescens … sacerdotium meditans*.[97] In fact, Stapleton mentions the letter as one of his sources and gives sev-

94. *CW* 3, II, 12–13.
95. Ep. 499.
96. *CW* 3, II, 421–22.
97. Ep. 999:159, 162.

eral direct quotations from it.[98] The only written source we have, then, is Erasmus's letter, which, as we have seen, does not seem to be reliable. Nor can we give much weight to a possible recollection by Lily transmitted by the Clements, for Margaret died in 1570 and John in 1572, while Stapleton's *Vita Mori* was published in 1588 and contains many factual errors—he places the writing of the *Progymnasmata* when More was a boy, and similarly dates wrongly the writing of *The Four Last Things*; he mistakes a letter from Erasmus to Froben as if it were to More; he confuses the names of William Grocyn, Richard Croke, and William Daunce; he states that Erasmus visited More's house at Chelsea, and so on.[99]

—

It is not surprising to find that a young man who had decided to give his life to God (as shown by his additions to the *Life of Pico*, "to place his love unto God") should consider the attraction of the priesthood; what is admirable is that, in his time and context, he sees that marriage—as shown in St. John Chrysostom's *Commentaries on the Gospel of St. Matthew*—is a path to holiness, the fullness of Christian life.[100]

More's vision of marriage will be dealt with later; but, as it is often the case, More puts across his thought with wit. After his marriage he wrote a 234-verse "advice" poem, *To Candidus: How to Choose a Wife, A Poem in Iambic Dimeter Brachycatalectic*.[101] The argument is simple: in choosing a wife, a man should look not for money or beauty but for virtue, for a wife—More tells Candidus—is meant to be a lifetime companion and a teacher of your children and grandchildren.

You will be glad to leave the company of men and seek repose in the bosom of your accomplished wife.... Then you will be glad to spend days and nights in pleasant and intelligent conversation, listening to the sweet words which ever most charmingly flow from her honeyed mouth.[102]

The poem is not dated. But in the last verses More mentions a series of famous women: Eurydice, the wife of Orpheus, of whom the author suggests that though she was famous for her beauty, the poet would not have made such an effort if she had been an uncultivated woman (*foeminam rusticam*); Perilla, famous daughter of Ovid (*Nasonis inclytam filiam*),

<hr>

98. Stapleton, 8, 59, 69, 88, 89.
99. Stapleton, 5n9; 9n9; 5n10; 39n1; 40n8; 66n10; 87n1.
100. On St. John Chrysostom's teaching on marriage, see chapters 3 and 10.
101. *CW* 3, II, Poem no. 143.
102. *CW* 3, II, Poem no. 143, 187.

who could rival in poetical composition even her own father; Tullia, the daughter of Cicero; Cornelia, the mother of the Gracchi; and Cassandra. These figures of classical antiquity belong to the period in which he "exercised principally in poetry," knew the Greek and Roman authors and mythologies, and composed his Latin poems published in 1518. Tullia, Perilla, and Cassandra do not appear in any other of More's works;[103] Cornelia, mother of the Gracchi, is mentioned also in the "Ode for the Coronation of Henry VIII" (dated 1509). But Eurydice, Orpheus's beloved, appears in More's letter of October 23, <1502–4>, suggesting that perhaps the two pieces might have been written not long apart. While Candidus is unmarried, the author of the poem is already married, as he speaks of his own wife (in v. 215), indicating that the poem was written after More's marriage to Jane, late in 1504 or in January 1505.[104]

James Hutton has suggested that the "maiden" referred to in vv. 183–200 of *To Candidus* could be Princess Catherine, future wife of Henry VIII, who is also mentioned in More's Coronation Ode, "On the Coronation Day of Henry VIII, most Glorious and Blessed King of the British people, and of Catherine his most Happy Queen." In the Coronation Ode, Catherine is introduced by the same rhetorical device as that employed in *To Candidus*.[105] In the latter More writes:

Such a woman was the mother of the two Gracchi [Cornelia]. She taught her sons right principles; she accomplished no less as their teacher than she did as their mother.

Why do I continue to contemplate ancient times? After all, our age … does have one maiden, though it has only one, whom it may set above almost all others and compare with any of those stories come down to us from ages past. Borne high upon the soaring wings of fame, she now gives warning even to remotest Britain, the one and only boast and glory of the whole world.[106]

Of Catherine after her marriage to Henry, More says:

In her you have as wife one whom your people have been happy to see sharing your power.… She it is who could vanquish the ancient Sabine women in de-

---

103. Orpheus is mentioned also in the translation of the *Life of Pico*, *CW* 1, 57:6; the translation of *Menippus*, *CW* 3.I, 31:27; and *CW* 3.II, Epigram 265:32, dated c. 1518.

104. Nevertheless, the editors of the *CW* and James Hutton suggest that the "mea" of v. 216 does not imply that the author of the poem was married. It may refer to a sweetheart or fiancée: *CW* 3.II, commentary to Poem 143, v. 216; or—rhetorically—to a future wife; James Hutton, "A Speculation on Two Passages in the Latin Poems of Thomas More," in *Essays on Renaissance Poetry* (Ithaca and London: Cornell University Press, 1980), 330n2.

105. Hutton, "Speculation" (1980), 336.

106. *CW* 3-II, Poem no. 143:174–98, 191.

votion … half-divine heroines of Greece. She could equal the unselfish love of Alcestis…. The well-spoken Cornelia would yield to her in eloquence.[107]

The "maiden" of *To Candidus* seems to come from afar, but her fame throughout the world vanquishes the heroines of the past. The parallel is obvious, especially if we bear in mind the enthusiasm that More expressed for Catherine in his letter to Holt of November 1501.

It has been objected that in *To Candidus*, v. 184, this exceptional woman is described as "virginem," but "virgo" in classical Latin denotes a young girl free to be married.[108] Catherine was married to Prince Arthur in November 1501, but after his death on April 2, 1502, she was certainly free to marry.

If More was in fact referring to Princess Catherine, it is not impossible that the poem may have been written soon after his own marriage and between Catherine's two marriages.[109] What of the message? If we can establish that the poem was written soon after More married Jane, it would seem appropriate "advice" for More's "friendly rival" William Lily. Having himself married, he can address his elder:

Your time in life, Candidus, is now reaching a point where it suggests that at last … you find a girl to take as wife formally and in mutual devotion.[110]

A plausible scenario might be that after Lily returned from Italy and settled in London as a schoolmaster, he was introduced to More by his godfather, Grocyn, who had got to know More at some stage between 1496 and 1499. After More got married he encouraged Lily to do likewise to avoid becoming a bachelor living only for his studies, as had happened to Pico. More tells him to have children:

Add to your most splendid line. Your father did as much for you. Hand on with increase to your descendants what you have already received from your ancestors. (vv.17–24)

We have very little precise information regarding Lily's age. The present conjecture is based on Lily's age at death, as recorded on his memorial tablet, and these inscriptions have often been found unreliable. But even if

---

107. *CW* 3-II, Poem no. 19:162–72, Coronation ode, 111.

108. It is also used on occasion (e.g., by Virgil) for a young married woman, a young wife.

109. Hutton suggests that the poem was written before Catherine married Prince Arthur and may have been written even before she arrived in England; Hutton, "Speculation," (1980), 330n3. But to me the context suggests otherwise.

110. *CW* 3-II, Poem 143:1–16, 181.

he had been only fourteen when admitted to Magdalen College in 1486, he would have been thirty-two to More's twenty-six years old in 1504.

At the end of the poem, More tells Candidus not to be afraid of his choice of wife. There is no point of imagining a legendary woman "such as those I have mentioned above" (vv. 201–9), because "no man possesses more than he who is content with what he has" (vv. 210–15). The key point, he emphasizes again, is to look for a girl of "virtuous disposition" (v. 225), and he repeats it at the very end: "If she has this virtuous disposition, she would be in my eyes the richer" (vv. 232–33).

Of those women of old the one whom More gives most details is Cornelia, "the mother of the Gracchi. She taught her sons right principles; she accomplished no less as their teacher than she did as their mother" (vv. 174–77). Years later Juan Luis Vives wrote that Cornelia was a model of chastity and taught this virtue to her own children.[111]

In this section I have been considering the conflicting accounts of Erasmus, Roper, Stapleton, and Cresacre and ventured some conclusions. Of course, there is much in their testimonies that coincides; specifically, all five authors wrote that Thomas More in his youth gave himself to prayer and penance. Stapleton is more specific: he says that More was zealous to become a saint, wore a hairshirt, and practiced other mortifications, such as vigils and fastings.[112] Cresacre writes that when More was about eighteen or twenty years old he began to wear a hairshirt next to the skin and "added also to his austerity a whip every Friday and on high fasting days."[113]

Popular imagination has shown surprise at the references to More using a hairshirt and a whip. Though there is not much literature, the use of the hairshirt was certainly common in the period. It is a garment of rough cloth, often called a "cilice" because it was originally made of Cilician goats' hair.[114] The earliest scriptural use of the word in its Latin form occurs in the Vulgate: "Ego autem, cum mihi molesti essent, induebar cilicio" (Ps 34:13),[115] and the term appears in Stapleton: "Adolescens quippe usus est cilicio."[116] Ro: Ba:, who bases his account on Harpsfield and Staple-

---

111. Juan Luis Vives, *The Education of a Christian Woman*, trans. Charles Fantazzi (Chicago: University of Chicago Press, 2000), chapter 4, no. 23.

112. Stapleton, 8.

113. Cresacre More, 24.

114. See *ODNB*, s.v. "cilice."

115. "Sackcloth" in most English translations; "I was clothed in a hair-shirt," in the Wycliffe Bible (fifteenth century) and in the Douay Rheims Catholic translation (1582).

116. Stapleton, *Vita Thomae Mori* (1588, ed. 1689), 18.

ton, writes, "In his youth or tender years he used to were a Cilice or hear-shirt."[117]

The use of the hairshirt as a means of mortification was very common during the early ages of Christianity, even among ordinary lay people, who made it serve as an unostentatious antidote for the outward luxury and comfort of their lives. St. Jerome mentions the hairshirt as being frequently worn under the rich and splendid robes of men in high worldly positions; it continued to be fairly common among lay people in later centuries.[118] The detail of the hairshirt shows that for More, mortification was not to be identified with the asceticism of the Stoics, which aimed at achieving self-control, but was an offering to God for the remission of sin in union with Christ's Cross, far above the natural virtue of temperance.[119] Years later, in his *Confutation to Tyndale's Answer*,[120] More writes that the purpose of fasting and mortification is not to tame the flesh (as the Reformers claimed) but to obtain God's grace. He cites a number of examples from the Old Testament, such as that given in the book of Esther, where the queen asks all the Jews in Susa to fast along with her and her servants (Esther 4:15–16). Earlier on, in his unfinished *Treatise upon these words of Holy Scripture*, Memorare novissima, and in eternum non peccabis, *Remember the last things and you shall never sin*, More writes:

For as the holy doctor Saint Chrysostom saith, though pain be grievous for the nature of the affliction, yet is it pleasant by the alacrity and quick mind of them that willingly suffer it.[121]

Elsewhere he writes of the value of voluntary penance such as "almsgiving, pilgrimages, fasting, discipline,"[122] and other spiritual exercises, which the soul willingly offers to God.[123] And he adds:

117. Ro: Ba:, 25:3.

118. The *ODNB* mentions the use of the hairshirt not only by medieval saints and churchmen, but also by figures such as Simon de Montfort, Earl of Leicester (c. 1208–65); Anthony Woodville, Earl Rivers (c. 1440–83); and Lady Venetia Digby (1600–1633). See also the letter of John Dalgairns to Bl. Dominic Barbieri dated at Littlemore on October 3, 1844, asking him for help in procuring "shirts or girdles of hair cloth" and "a discipline such as ordinary persons would use," given in full in *Dominic Barbieri in England: A New Series of Letters*, ed. Urban Young, CP (London: Burns, Oates and Washbourne, 1935), 218–20.

119. *CW* 8.I:69:8.

120. *CW* 8.I:68.

121. *CW* 1, 134:16–18.

122. "Discipline" was and is a common term for the little whip used for mortification by scourging oneself. It is referred to as "whippes, the cordes knotted" by Roper, 49:9, and Harpsfield, 65:15, and simply "whip" by Cresacre More, 25.

123. *CW* 1, 134:26–32.

And whensoever, as I say, that a man feeleth in this pain a pleasure, he hath a token of great grace and that his penance is pleasant to God. For as the Holy Scripture says, our Lord loveth a glad giver.[124]

Stapleton emphasizes More's discretion in his penances:

Although [More] was practising such austerities, yet he hid them so carefully that no sign of them could be perceived.

In fact, Erasmus probably did not know of More's use of the hairshirt, for he does not mention it in his biographical profile, even though he writes there of his austere meals—"I have never seen a man less particular about his food"[125]—and of his "vigils and fasts."[126] Roper is able to speak of the hairshirt because his wife, Margaret, More's eldest daughter, told him of it:

[More] used also sometymes to punishe his body with whippes, the cordes knotted, which was knowen only to my wife, his eldest daughter, whom for her secrecy abouve all other he specially trusted, causing her, as need required, to washe the same shirte of heare.[127]

And he writes that the day before his execution, More sent his "shirte of heare (not willing to have it seene)" to Margaret, "his deerly beloved daughter."[128] Cresacre More adds that his grandmother, Anne Cresacre, discovered the hairshirt on a hot summer day, as More did not realize that it could be seen because he was wearing only a plain shirt, without collar.[129] Roper and Harpsfield do not indicate when More started to use a hairshirt, but write of it only when speaking of More already as chancellor of England:

And albeit by reason he would not be noted of singularities, he conformed himself outwardly to other men in his apparel, according to his state and vocation, yet howe little he inwardly esteemen such vanities, it well appered by the shirt of heare that he ware secretly next to his body.[130]

Stapleton, as we have seen, says that More used it from his youth, and Cresacre (based on Stapleton and Roper and family traditions) specifies that it was "when he was about eighteen or twenty years old"—that is, when he was studying Law at Lincoln's Inn—and adds in tones of surprise

124. *CW* 1, 134:32–135:2.
125. *CWE* 7, letter 999:62.
126. *CWE* 7, letter 999:173.
127. Roper, 49, 8–12.
128. Roper, 99, 10–13.
129. Cresacre More, 24.
130. Harpsfield, 65:15; cf. Roper, 48, 15–22.

that it was something "which he never left off wholly, no, not when he was lord chancellor of England."[131]

More's private and hidden bodily mortification must be seen within the context of his constant cheerful attitude in life. Erasmus, to their mutual friend Richard Whitford, writes of More's "exceptionally charming disposition" and good-natured wit;[132] and in his long letter to Ulrich von Hutten, he speaks of More's good humor and readiness always to serve others.[133] And the sobriety that Erasmus says he experienced in More's household should be balanced against the testimony of Frans van Cranevelt, who, in thanking Erasmus for introducing More to him, acknowledged Thomas More's "more than Sicilian dinners."[134]

131. Cresacre More, 24.

132. *CWE* 2, letter 191.

133. *CWE* 7, letter 999:111.

134. *CWE* 8, letter 1145, from Bruges, September 19, 1520. The editor of *CWE* explains that "Sicilian dinners" refers to the rich and sophisticated cuisine of the Syracusans, as described in Erasmus's *Adagia*.

8

St. Augustine's *City of God*

Chapter 1 of this book dealt with More's letter to Colet dated <1502–4>, which shows two aspects of More at the time: first, his spiritual concerns, as he sought a life of virtue in the face of the distractions of the city and awaited the return of his spiritual advisor (availing himself of Grocyn's spiritual advice in Colet's absence); and second, More's dedication to the study of Greek together with William Lily and with the help of two Greek scholars, Grocyn and Linacre. The letter also shows More's familiarity with Cicero and Terence and possible acquaintance with Ovid, Virgil, Seneca, and Boethius.

The interest in Greek that More shows in his letter to Colet, as well as in his previous one to John Holt of November 1501, suggested that this study should start with More's first encounter with Erasmus in 1499 and their shared project regarding Greek, the classics, and the Fathers of the Church, and in particular with More's praise for St. John Chrysostom, whom he may have known from the Greek manuscript belonging to Grocyn that is echoed in the letter to Colet. Now let us turn to the other Father of the Church singled out by More, St. Augustine.

Erasmus, Roper, Harpsfield, and Stapleton all agree that, after he had studied law, More spent time in study and prayer and that around this time he gave public lectures on St. Augustine's *De civitate Dei*.[1] The text of these lectures has not reached us, and the first account we have of them is Erasmus's (1519):

---

1. *CWE* 7, Ep. 999:168–74; Roper, 6, ll. 1–10; Harpsfield, 59–62; Stapleton, 7–8.

On St. Augustine's *City of God* he gave public lectures before large audiences while still quite a young man; priests and old men were not ashamed to seek instruction *in holy things* from a young man and a layman, or sorry they had done so.

He is followed by Roper (1558):

He redde for a good space a publike lecture of St. Augustine, *de civitate dei*, in the Churche of St. Lawrens in the old Jury; whereunto there resorted Doctor Grosin, an excellent cunning man, and all the chief learned of the City of London.

Harpsfield (1558) expands on Roper's account:

Master More, being so young ... openly read in the Church of St. Lawrence in London the books of the said St. Augustine *De civitate Dei*, to his no small commendation, and to the great admiration of all his audience. His lesson was frequented and honoured with the presence and resort, as well as of that well learned and great cunning man, Master Grocyn ... as also with the chief and best learned men of the City of London. About the same time the said Grocyn read in the aforesaid City the books of Dionysius the Areopagite,[2] but he had not so frequent and so great an auditory as had Master More.

Stapleton (1588) adds further detail of his own:

At the same period of his life he lectured publicly in London, in the Church of St. Lawrence, on St. Augustine's *De civitate Dei. He did not treat this great work from the theological point of view, but from the standpoint of history and philosophy*; and indeed the earlier books of St. Augustine's work deal with these two subjects almost exclusively. More's lectures were so well attended and highly esteemed that even Grocyn, whose supremacy in letters had hitherto been undisputed, found his audience leaving him for More.[3]

Stapleton's emphasis is quite different from that of Erasmus, who plays with the contrast that a *young man* was lecturing to *priests and old people* (*sacerdotes ac senes a iuuene prophano sacra discere*), adding the paradox that they were learning sacred things (*sacra discere*) from a non-sacred person (*a prophano*).[4] Stapleton certainly knew Erasmus's statement, because he mentions Erasmus's letter to von Hutten in the same paragraph and refers

2. In his letter of <c. November 1501>, More mentions that Grocyn's lectures took place at St. Paul's. Two of Grocyn's Greek MSS., Corpus Christi College, Oxford, MSS. 141 and 163, include works by Pseudo-Dionysius.

3. The letter of <c. November 1501> in which More tells Holt of Grocyn's lectures (BL MS Arundel 249, f. 85v) is not quoted by Stapleton.

4. *EE* 4, Ep. 999, 158–60. Baker-Smith comments that the translation given in *CWE* 7, Ep. 999, 170–72 loses the sharpness of the Latin: Dominic Baker-Smith, "Who Went to Thomas More's

to it again later on.[5] But the letter is not Stapleton's only source, for he mentions that the lectures on St. Augustine were delivered at the Church of St. Lawrence, which Erasmus does not mention; he may have known this from members of More's circle exiled in the Low Countries.

Some have suggested that in chapter II of his biography, Stapleton shows discomfort with More, a layman, lecturing on matters theological. Certainly, his statement that the earlier books of *De civitate Dei* deal almost exclusively with history and philosophy is not really accurate, for St. Augustine deals with theological topics all through his work. Nevertheless, in chapter IV Stapleton not only praises More's apologetic works but writes that More paid such attention to the study of dogmatic theology in them that "a professional theologian could scarcely speak more accurately." And he goes on to say that More's English controversial works did great good and were read and reread by many serious scholars; "Nothing more powerfully strengthened and promoted the Catholic cause than the numerous works of More in English, edited with great care and labour by William Rastell."[6]

In fact, the differences between Stapleton's and Erasmus's descriptions lie mainly in Stapleton's seeming attempt to distance More from Erasmus. Stapleton shows his antipathy toward Erasmus in a number of places of the *Vita*,[7] and this seems to be behind his comment, in chapter IV, that More's love of letters in the early enthusiasm of his youth was excessive:

He was, however, in the first flower of his age, not only a devotee of good literature or polite letters, but even an almost superstitious lover of them.[8]

It is Ro: Ba:, in his *Life of Syr Thomas More* (1599), who helps to elucidate what is at stake here. He writes that his biography is based on those written by Stapleton and Harpsfield,[9] though at times he adds information that shows a considerable knowledge of details of More's family history.[10] With regard to the lectures on *De civitate Dei*, after copying Harpsfield's description he adds,

----

Lectures on St. Augustine's *De civitate Dei*?," *Church History and Religious Culture* 87, no. 2 (2007): 145–60.

    5. Stapleton, 88.

    6. Stapleton, 35–36.

    7. See the editor's notes in Stapleton, chapter IV, 36n17, and chapter V, 47n19.

    8. "Fuit autem in prima sua et florenti aetate bonarum literarum, seu politioris literaturae, non devotus tantum, sed et superstitiosus paene amator"; Stapleton, Thomas, *Tres Thomae, … D. Thomae Mori Anglae quodam Cancellari Vita* (Duaci [Douai, now in France; then in Burgundy]: Ioannis Bogardi, 1588), item kept in the British Library, 54, lines 1–4.

    9. Ro: Ba:, 17:12–13.

    10. Ro: Ba:, Preface, xxv.

More in his reading proued him selfe a diuine [theologian], a philosopher [and] an historian; for he must be furnished with these arts that will read and expound these books of St. Austines as he did.[11]

In this he corrects not only Stapleton's account of More's role, but even his description of the content of *De civitate Dei*.

In his turn Cresacre, who based his account of 1627 on Roper and Stapleton,[12] follows Stapleton, writing that Thomas More

read a lecture in St. Laurence's church at Lothbury, where Sir John More, his father lieth buried, out of St. Augustine's books *De civitate Dei*, not so much discussing the points of divinity, as the precepts of moral philosophy and history, wherewith these books are replenished.[13]

As on other occasions, Cresacre shows his local knowledge, identifying the location (Lothbury, a London street) and also giving the added information that Sir John was subsequently buried there. Perhaps he nuances Stapleton slightly in writing that the books of *De civitate Dei* are full of historical data and of moral philosophy, without going so far as to say that they deal "almost exclusively" with those two subjects. But he does not give any more information; and indeed he seems to have mistaken the chronology, because he places More's lectures on St. Augustine after the publication of *Utopia*.

So it seems that, despite his polished and studied Latin, Erasmus is our best guide, and he reports what he had been told by those known to him who had attended the lectures and the effect they had on those who had gone to listen to the young barrister recently qualified from Lincoln's Inn. And More's role as a lay theologian—which is underlined by Erasmus—is reflected in the way that More himself, years later, quotes early Christian authors who were laymen: St. Justin,[14] Lactantius,[15] and Boethius.[16]

Whether or not Thomas More limited himself to some aspects of *De civitate Dei* in his lectures, there is no doubt that he quotes St. Augustine often in his later works and cites *De civitate Dei* more often than any other of Augustine's writings.[17] In one of his last letters, to the priest Nicholas

11. Ro: Ba:, 23:16–19.

12. Cresacre More, 2.

13. Cresacre More, 53.

14. "Iustius the holy martyr, writing of our faith," in *A Treatise Upon the Passion*, *CW* 13, 161:6–27.

15. More names Lactantius in the *Letter to a Monk*, *CW* 15, 242:6–11 and in the *Dialogue of 1529*, *CW* 6, 66:16, and paraphrases him elsewhere: see *CW* 15, 522 and 609.

16. See Chapter 2. Although we have no positive evidence that Justin and Lactantius were laymen, no reference is ever made to a clerical condition in their cases.

17. See Dominic Baker-Smith, *More's Utopia*, 13.

Wilson, he mentions studying *De civitate Dei* with him.[18] Perhaps more surprisingly, given his interest, More comments in his letter to Martin Dorp of <1515> that he did not agree with everything St. Augustine wrote:

Homo erat, errare potuit—He was human and could make a mistake. I trust him in most things, as much as I do anybody; but I don't trust any one man in all things.[19]

This remark throws light also on the relations of More with other humanists and on the freedom that he exercised in making up his own mind about the matters in question.

De civitate Dei was written by St. Augustine against claims that Christians were to blame for Alaric's sack of Rome in AD 410; in it he ranges across Roman history and produces a theology of world history from the Creation to the Last Judgment and beyond, as he writes of eternal punishment and the eternal happiness of the saints filled and replenished with God's blessing and sanctification.[20] The kernel of the whole vast work is given in the well-known phrase at the beginning of the last chapter (chapter 28) of book XIV, *On the character of the two cities, the earthly and the heavenly.*

The two cities then were created by two kinds of love: the earthly city by a love of self carried even to the point of contempt for God, the heavenly city by a love of God carried even to the point of contempt for self.[21]

But it is worth transcribing the whole paragraph:

Consequently, the earthly city glories in itself while the other glories in the Lord. For the former seeks glory from men, but the latter finds its greatest glory in God, the witness of our conscience. The earthly city lifts up its head in its own glory; the heavenly city says to its God: "My glory and the lifter of my head."[22]

18. *SL* no. 59, addressed to Nicholas Wilson in 1534, when the two were in the Tower of London.

19. Bruges, October 21, <1515>, in *CW* 15, Latin and English translation on 68, ll. 3–5; a different translation is given in *SL*, no. 4. The phrase "Homo erat, errare potuit" appears in St. John Chrysostom, *Homilia XXVI in Matthaeum*, and is used by Colet in *De Sacramentis* (Gleason, *John Colet*, 191, 324). Erasmus uses a similar phrase referring to himself in a letter: "Homo tamen sum, labi possum"; *EE* 3, Ep. 961, 19, May 1, 1519.

20. For a general introduction see, e.g., Christopher Dawson, "The City of God," in *A Monument to Saint Augustine* (London: Sheed and Ward, 1930); Étienne Gilson, Foreword to the *City of God*, Fathers of the Church 8 (Washington, D.C.: The Catholic University of America Press, 1950); MacIntyre, *God, Philosophy, Universities*, 21–32; William Babcock, Introduction to his translation of St. Augustine, *The City of God* (New York: New City Press, 2012); Pierre Manent, *Metamorphoses of the City* (Cambridge, Mass.: Harvard University Press, 2013).

21. Saint Augustine, *The City of God*, trans. Philip Levine (Cambridge, Mass.: Loeb Classical Library, Harvard University Press, 1966), 404–7.

22. Psalm 3:3.

In the one, the lust for dominion has dominion over its princes as well as over the nations that it subdues; in the other, both those put in charge and those placed under them serve one another in love, the former by their counsel, the latter by their obedience. The early city loves its own strength as revealed in its men of power; the heavenly city says to its God: "I will love thee, O Lord, my strength."[23]

The chapter ends:

In the heavenly city, on the other hand, man's only wisdom is the religion [*pietas*] that guides him rightly to worship the true God[24] and awaits as its reward in the fellowship of saints, not only human but also angelic, this goal, "that God may be all in all."[25]

This chapter summarizes the whole of the work. St. Augustine speaks of two cities, the earthly and the heavenly, while acknowledging that at the present time, the citizens of both cities live together in the world; the two cities are enmeshed and interlocked. The citizens of the two cities define themselves by their love: that is, their last end, whether it be on earth or in heaven. This may explain why Erasmus, in his letter of 1519, says that More spoke of heaven with conviction,[26] and why More, at his trial, speaks of his union with all the "holy sainctes in heaven"[27] and also with the "vertuous men that are yeat alive."[28]

The citizen of the heavenly city, says Augustine, loves God even to contempt of self: this is the lover of God as described by More in his ballade discussed in Chapter 5, with his mind in heaven, while at the same time he has his feet on the ground, for St. Augustine does not separate the citizen of the heavenly city from the rest but places the citizens of both city side by side.

The distinction between the two cities is particularly pointed in Augustine's distinction between the *principes* and the *praepositi*:

Illi in *principibus* eius vel in eas quas subiugat nationibus dominandi libido dominatur; in hac serviunt invicem in caritate et *praepositi* consulendo et subditi obtemperando.

---

23. Psalm 18:1.

24. Joseph Ratzinger comments that true worship is the city of God: that is, that to worship God, to give God his due, we must carry out human affairs as described in this chapter: "That is why St. Augustine could say that the true 'sacrifice' is the *civitas Dei*, that is, love-transformed mankind, the divinization of creation and the surrender of all things to God: God all in all"; Ratzinger, *The Spirit of the Liturgy* (San Francisco: Ignatius Press, 2000), 28.

25. 1 Cor 15:28.

26. *EE* 4, Ep 999:273–74, and *CWE* 7, Ep. 999:299–300.

27. Roper, 95:3.

28. Roper, 94:23.

In the earthly city, the lust for dominion has dominion over its *princes* as well as over the nations that it subdues; in the other [the heavenly city], all serve one another in love, *those put in charge* by their counsel, and those placed under them by their obedience.[29]

This distinction seems to be echoed in book I of *Utopia* where Raphael, after describing the government of the Achorians, states that the king should love his people and be loved by them: "Amet suos et ametur a suis."[30] He makes the point while criticizing the futility of a king fighting against another for the sake of aggrandizement; instead, Raphael counsels, he should look after his kingdom, improve it as much as possible, and let other kingdoms alone.[31]

In considering the lover's ballade, we proposed that More reached the conclusion that the Christian had to have his "love set unto God," to be truly contemplative, with his mind in heaven. In *De civitate Dei*, Augustine gives a picture of the love of God that builds up the heavenly city in a way that is not divorced from secular affairs. The Christian is necessarily a contemplative soul, even though he lives in the world and shares all the interests and activities of society.

—

Erasmus's fresh translation of the New Testament in 1516 was not welcomed by everyone; an English Carthusian, John Batmanson, wrote (apparently at the suggestion of Edward Lee, a younger scholar who had had a falling-out with Erasmus) attacking the translation and suggesting that Erasmus would have done better to return to his monastery rather than waste time publishing a new translation of the scriptures.[32] More replied in <1519–20> with a long, polemical letter "to a Monk" defending Erasmus and his project,[33] in which he comments, among other things:

It would probably be not unwholesome for you to feel inwardly doubtful and fearful lest either you do not share Mary's portion or you have chosen Mary's portion mistakenly, since you rank her portion not merely above Martha's office, as Christ did, but even above that of the apostles. You should be afraid that,

29. Levine, trans., *City of God*, 4:405.

30. *CU*, 20:25.

31. *CU*, 20:24–27. McConica, *Thomas More*, 23, points out that More seems to have been concerned with the nature of true kingship from the time of his lectures on the *City of God* onward.

32. Batmanson was apparently known to More and was prior of the London Charterhouse 1529–31: see C. B. Rowntree, "Batmanson, John (d. 1531)," in *ODNB*, published online on September 23, 2004; and Knowles, *Religious Orders in England*, 3:469. No copies of Batmanson's book, *Contra annotationes Erasmi Roterodami*, survive.

33. *Correspondence* [83]; *CW* 15, 197–311.

when you view yourself, too indulgently, as one who has retreated into holy solicitude to escape harmful pleasures, the deeper scrutiny of God, who observes us with more penetration, who explores our hearts more profoundly than we do, and whose eyes discern our imperfections, may find that what you have been doing is avoiding responsibility, dodging work, cultivating the pleasure of repose in the shadow of piety, looking for a way out of life's troubles, and wrapping your talent up in a napkin, thus wasting it inside for fear of losing it out-of-doors.[34]

The figures of Mary and Martha, the sisters of Bethany (Lk 10:38–42), have traditionally been taken as exemplars of the contemplative and the active life, respectively. St. Augustine discusses their cases in his commentaries on the gospels.[35] He points out that both were pleasing to the Lord, both disciples and objects of his love; yet these two women are figures of the life present and the life to come, the life of labor and the life of quiet, life temporal and life eternal. Nevertheless, Augustine does not conclude that the two lives are to be practiced by different people or in different places, but rather that the life of prayer is the basis for a life of service.

Augustine develops the same idea in *De civitate Dei* when speaking about what he calls the "kinds of life" in connection with philosophers who embrace Christianity. In book XIX, chapter 19, he states that

as for the three kinds of life—the leisured, the active, and the combination of both—it is true that anyone, so long as his faith is sound, can lead his life and attain eternal rewards in any one of them. It does matter, however, what he holds back in his love of truth and what he pays out in the duty of charity.[36]

He goes on to say that no one should be so active that he makes no room for the contemplation of God; nevertheless, he sees more danger in the leisured life, for no one ought to be so completely at leisure that he takes no thought for serving his neighbor, and the one who follows the contemplative life is in danger of just such idleness.

More identified Mary of Bethany with Mary Magdalen, to whom he had a special devotion[37] because she accompanied Jesus Christ, assisted

---

34. *Letter to a Monk*, text and translation in *CW* 15, 300:26–302:10; in the last sentence, "*Talentumque tibi creditum involuisse sudario, quod ne foras emitteres, intus perderes,*" the reference is to Lk 19:20, the servant in the parable who kept his talent wrapped up in a cloth instead of trading with it. Rogers, in *SL*, translates "to waste it within the cloister rather than fling it away out in the world."

35. St. Augustine, *Sermones de Scripturis de Novo Testamento*, PL 38, *Sermo* 104: "Tractatus de Martha et Maria significantibus duas vitas"; trans. St. Augustine, *Selected Lessons on the New Testament*, ed. Philip Schaff (Grand Rapids, Michigan: Wm. B. Eerdmans, repr. 1979), vol. VI, Sermon 54, 429–30.

36. *De civitate Dei*, XIX, 19. Here "leisure" (Latin *otium*) is the classically accepted prerequisite for philosophical contemplation.

37. *CW* 6, 49:13. This identification was traditional in medieval Christianity.

him, anointed him, and announced his resurrection to the apostles.[38] This devotion fits in with More's vision of the contemplative in the midst of the world: after spending time in prayer, to accompany Christ in a secular environment. This was choosing the "better part" (Lk 10:42) as More understood it: not practicing the *contemptus mundi* or withdrawal from the world but giving primacy to prayer. There is even a link with the apostles that More hints at in the passage of the *Letter to a Monk*, for he says: "ne foras emitteres": literally, that the servant should *send out* his talent, as the apostles were appointed by Jesus "to be with him and to be sent out to preach" (Mk 3:14).

—

In *De civitate Dei* it is possible to distinguish various different strands of argumentation. It presents a theological and philosophical view of humanity; in doing so, it informs the reader of the history of Roman political thought; it is also a more general discussion of political philosophy. On a personal and practical level, it describes the virtues and the calling of the Christian (or the saint, or the citizen of the city of God)—but also, more specifically, the virtues and vocation of the Christian involved in public life. Of course, Thomas More's future attitude toward those who spread heretical doctrines is beyond the scope of this study, which tries only to elucidate his early choices.[39] But it is fair to ask whether his early formation sheds any light on this issue, and the answer is to be found in *De civitate Dei*. At the end of book XIX, chapter 19, Augustine says that we must accept the burden of governing others if it is imposed on us; a little earlier on, in chapter 6 of the same book, he writes:

In the midst of these dark shadows of the social life, will the wise man serve as a judge or will he shrink from doing so? Clearly, he will serve. The claim of human society, which he finds it unthinkable to ignore, constrains him and draws him to his duty.[40]

For Augustine, whoever accepts the job of governor or judge in the service of society is obliged to carry out the duties of his office. As Richard Rex points out, in More's case the repression of heresy

38. It is for this reason that St. Thomas Aquinas calls her the Apostle of the Apostles: Thomas Aquinas, *Super Ioannem*, trans. Fabian R. Larcher (Albany, N.Y.: Magi Books, 1998), available on the web, paragraph 2,519.

39. For a recent exposition of this matter see Richard Rex, "Thomas More and the Heretics: Statesman or Fanatic?," in *Companion*, 93–115.

40. This reference was pointed out to me by Dominic Baker-Smith during a discussion on the topic.

was first and foremost a function of his public position. Since the time of Henry V, the oath sworn by every man who took office under the crown had included an undertaking to assist the Church in the struggle against heresy.[41]

More would, then, have been aware of his responsibilities when taking office, following St. Augustine's teaching—which he had read and perhaps even taught in his lectures in 1501.

—

In the *City of God* St. Augustine draws heavily on classical writers: Sallust for the history of Rome, Cicero for the definition of a republic that Augustine uses to reject the Roman claim to have been a republic; Seneca for his open denunciation of Rome's traditional gods; Plato and the Platonists (exemplified by Apuleius) as proof of the bankruptcy of pagan values.[42] Sallust, Cicero, Seneca, and Plato are all authors referred to by More in *Utopia* and other writings.

Although the text of More's lectures does not survive, it may be possible to see an echo of them in the work of one of More's friends, Juan Luis Vives, who in 1522 published an edition of *De civitate Dei* with commentaries.[43] In a long letter from Canterbury addressed to Erasmus and dated May 26, 1520, More mentions that he has read several works by Vives and praises him highly, saying that Vives has treated some themes on almost the same lines as he, More, had thought of himself before he had read anything by Vives—even using the same words More was going to use.[44] The letter gives the impression that they had not yet met, as More writes that Vives is a stranger to him;[45] but there is already an evident empathy that is relevant when considering Vives's later commentaries on *De civitate Dei*.

Erasmus introduced More to Vives and Cranevelt, and the four of them stayed at Cranevelt's house in Bruges from July 25 to July 29, 1520.[46] In a letter to Erasmus dated Bruges, September 19, 1520, Cranevelt praises More and thanks Erasmus for the introduction,[47] and from then on More, Erasmus, Vives, and Cranevelt corresponded and sent each other news often.[48]

41. See Rex, "Thomas More and the Heretics," 108.
42. See, e.g., Babcock, Introduction, *City of God*, 1:ix–xxii.
43. St. Augustine, *De civitate Dei*, with commentaries by J. L. Vives (Basel: Johann Froben, 1522).
44. *CWE* 7, Ep. 1106:70–85.
45. *CWE* 7, Ep. 1106:106. On the possibility of More having met Vives before, see *CWE* 4, 274, note to l.16. Jardine argues convincingly that More's letter employs the fiction that Vives was unknown to him: Jardine, *Erasmus, Man of Letters*, 18.
46. *L'Univers*, 295.
47. *CWE* 8, Ep. 1145.
48. On the relationship between More and Vives, see Stapleton, 30, 56, 92, 101; Chambers,

Vives wrote to Erasmus on July 10, 1521, saying that he was staying in Bruges to meet Charles V and More there the following month, in the hope (as he delicately puts it) of seeing how he might live from then on: that is, he was hoping for financial support, either from Charles V or on More's recommendation. He adds in the same letter that he has written to More on the matter already. The rest of the letter deals with his work of finishing the edition of *De civitate Dei*.[49] On August 14, More arrived in Bruges and duly met Vives.[50]

On April 1 the following year Vives wrote another letter to Erasmus from Bruges,[51] telling him of his progress with his *De civitate Dei*; he mentions that he has received a letter from More[52] and that in an earlier letter More had indicated that he was improving from an illness. Three months later, on July 14, 1522, Vives again wrote to Erasmus, this time from Louvain, saying that he has received two letters from More and that he is very well; he tells Erasmus that he has finished *De civitate Dei* and has sent the last five books to him by a messenger.[53] On August 10 Vives wrote to Cranevelt exultant at having Erasmus, Budé, and More as "godparents" of his work and asking Cranevelt to pass on his greetings to More.[54] On August 15 Vives wrote again to Erasmus, anxious to know whether the final books of *De civitate Dei* had reached him;[55] he also mentioned that he had sent off Erasmus's letter to More.

By the end of August 1522, Vives's edition (in two volumes) was already being printed; the introduction on the first page by Froben, the publisher, is dated *Basileae, pridie calendas Septembris* (August 31). On the verso is a letter from Erasmus,[56] and on page aa 2, Vives's Dedication to Henry VIII. This is followed by a preface by Vives in which he mentions that he had met Erasmus and More at Bruges the previous June. A major feature of the

---

Thomas More, 106, 177, 217, 259; *Companion*, 80, 88, 217; and Robert P. Adams, *The Better Part of Valour: More, Erasmus, Colet, and Vives on Humanism, War, and Peace, 1496–1535* (Seattle: University of Washington Press, 1962). Adams (190) suggests that "Vives' commentary [to the *City of God*] is probably as close as it is possible to come to More's own work" [i.e., his lectures on the *City of God*].

49. *CWE* 8, Ep. 1222.

50. *L'Univers*.

51. *CWE* 9, Ep. 1271.

52. *CWE* 9, Ep. 1271:127.

53. *CWE* 9, Ep. 1303.

54. Letter from Vives to Cranevelt, *Literae Virorum Eruditorum ad Fr Craneveldium*, ed. H. de Vocht (Louvain: Librairie Universitaire, 1928), Letter 13, Louvain, August 10 [1522]; also in Juan Luis Vives, *Epistolario*, ed. José Jiménez Delgado (Madrid: Editorial Nacional, 1978), accessible online from "Biblioteca Valenciana Digital," Letter 45.

55. *CWE* 9, Ep. 1306.

56. Included also in *CWE* 9, Ep. 1305.

work is Vives's copious commentaries at the foot of each page. For book II, chapter VII, the title heading reads:

That the Instructions of the Philosophers are weak and ineffectual; not having any divine mark or character. And that the Example of the gods tends more to confirm Men in Vice, than do the Arguments of the Wise to persuade them in Virtue.[57]

And the body of the text by St. Augustine follows:

For, indeed, all the worshippers of the gods, as soon as they were seized by lascivious passions, tainted, as Persius says, with glowing poison, hastened rather to contemplate the filthy deeds related of Jupiter, than read over and meditate on the wise instructions of Plato, or the noble sentiments of Cato. Hence, Terence, a debauched young man, looks at some painting hung against the wall, upon which was represented the fable of Jupiter sending down a shower of Gold into Danae's lap; and from such a great authority he deduces a worthy precedent for his turpitude, when he boasts, that in it he imitates this god! even he who shakes the temples with his divine thunder. And shall not a mean mortal man deign to act in the same manner? I will do so, says he, and that most willingly.

At the foot of the page, Vives adds his commentary to "worshippers of the gods":

We are mostly influenced by the example of those whom we respect, for we always endeavour to imitate them, whether gods or men. The people affect the manners of the prince; the scholars strive to copy the men whom they respect; and mankind invariably aims at the morals of those they reverence as gods. For this reason, our holy religion proposes for our imitation, the example of Christ, and the saints. Plato, 1.ii, *De Republica*, amongst various reasons for not tolerating poets within the commonwealth, he alleges, that in their fables concerning the gods, they give examples most ruinous to the morality of the reader; such as their wars, rapines, seditions, adulteries, thefts, and the like.

Vives's commentary continues with a long quotation taken from one of More's translations of Lucian:

And from this passage are taken the words, which Lucian makes Menippus speak in his *Necromantia*. "Therefore I," says he, "when a boy, hearing Hesiod and Homer relating the wars and seditions, not merely of the demigods, but even of the gods themselves; their adulteries likewise, their violations, tyrannies, expulsion of parents; their marriages of brothers with sisters; by Hercules, I thought all these were good and honourable, and therefore I imitated them most zealously. For I

---

57. Vives, from the translation by Alban Butler, *The City of God by St. Augustine Bishop, Confessor, and Doctor of the Church with the Commentaries of J. L. Vives* (Dublin, 1822), 72–73.

never could suppose, that the gods would themselves become fornicators and adulterers, or would excite quarrels and broils amongst one another, if they had not allowed men to do the same, as good and honourable."

Then Vives adds an explicit reference to More, praising him in what must have seemed embarrassingly fulsome terms:

We have given this version of Lucian in the words of Thomas More, in preference to a translation of our own; to touch whose praise negligently, or whilst intent upon any other subject, were inexcusable, and, in short, a species of profanation, for his merits could scarcely be done justice to in several volumes. Who could speak, as they deserve, of the shrewdness of his wit, the strength of his judgement, the excellence of his learning, his eloquent flow of language, the suavity of his deportment, the probity of his manners, the judicious prudence, his rapidity in execution, his invariable integrity, his equity and faith; unless, in a word, one say, that they are completely perfect, absolute, and exact, in their full proportion! unless he calls them, as they are, each the highest of its sort, and all examples worthy the imitation of all men? I say a great deal of him, and they, who knew no More, will wonder at the extraordinary praise: but they will readily acknowledge the truth of my words, who knew him, who read his writings, who either witnessed his actions, or heard them related. But I will yet have an opportunity of spreading out, in this man's praise, as a ship's sail in an extensive sea, expanded by the prosperous winds, when I shall say of him as highly as my exertions can equal his merits; and that, too, with the full approbation of my readers.

And this is how his commentary on that passage ends.

If Vives takes the occasion of commenting on *De civitate Dei* to praise More in this way, it seems unlikely that the two of them would not have discussed Vives's project when together in the Low Countries and perhaps later by letter, as well. Peter Ackroyd suggests that *De civitate Dei* was a common interest of More and Vives,[58] and indeed More writes that he shares Vives's ideas. The commentary on this chapter of *De civitate Dei* may even have come from a specific conversation between the two. And if the second part of Vives's commentary—the quotation from Lucian—came from More's published work, it is certainly possible that the first part also came from him. Lucian's meaning is clear: the example of the Greek gods is not to be followed. St. Augustine's text says as much: the examples of the gods confirm men in vice; or rather, it says more: the example of the gods tends more to confirm men in vice. In the first part of his commentary, Vives explains that if men imitate those they respect, whether gods or men, Christians must imitate the example of Christ and the saints. Much

---

58. Peter Ackroyd, *The Life of Thomas More* (London: Chatto and Windus, 1998), 236.

later, when writing in the Tower, More refers again the example of Martha and Mary and suggests in a similar way that the reader imitate both of them[59]—that is, Martha's life of service and Mary's attentiveness to prayer.

—

Looking at Thomas More's commentary on *De civitate Dei*, I suggest that More took on board the work's central theme of the two cities and the two loves, as stated in book XIV, chapter 28: "the love of self, even to the contempt of God; … the love of God, even to the contempt of self." Then, seeing the praise of More that Vives inserts in his commentary to book II, chapter 7, after his citation of More's translation of Lucian, I propose that Vives's commentary may have been the result of a conversation between him and More and could possibly even be attributed to—or at least endorsed by—the latter.

What, then, does Vives have to say of that central theme of book XIV, chapter 28? After transcribing the phrase, he comments:

St. Augustine here has expressed, in a few words, all that the great philosophers, who wrote on political government, have considered necessary to a truly free, well-governed and perfect commonwealth. In which the rulers neither use tyranny nor compulsion; and the subjects do not repine or resist. Where the governors are but as sentinels, placed on an eminence, to give warning of danger; or as honoured friends, whose advice is received with gratitude and respect; and where the people are as children, cheerful in their obedience, and affectionate in their respect.[60]

For Vives, what Plato, Aristotle, Cicero, Sallust, Seneca, Plutarch, and others had said about tyranny and freedom is all present here in St. Augustine. Furthermore, it was St. Augustine's *De civitate Dei* that introduced these philosophers to Christianity. And this commentary can also be applied to More himself, for he had come to know these ideas on tyranny and human freedom *not* in the first place because they were part of the common knowledge of fifteenth-century humanists (as they are mentioned, for example, by Erasmus in his *Antibarbari*), but because he had already learned them in his study of *De civitate Dei*. Vives continues his commentary:

Hence, the Magistrates, whom the Romans appointed after the expulsion of their kings, were named consuls, advisers, or providers.

This, of course, is what happened in Utopia, where all the officials are elected: the magistrates (the famous "syphogrants" and "tranibors") and

<hr>

59. *CW* 13, 201:30–202:14.
60. Vives, *Commentaries to the City of God*, 576.

even the prince or principal of each city. Sallust (as quoted in *De civitate Dei*, book III, chapter 16) states that the time of the first Roman consuls was ordered with justice and moderation; but St. Augustine denies this, describing instead the horrors of the year in which the Roman republic inaugurated the office of the consulship. Book XIV, chapter 28 concludes:

[In the heavenly city], there is no human wisdom, but the piety, by which the true God is truly worshiped; and which expects its reward in the society of the holy ones, not only men but angels, as "God is all in all."

And Vives's footnote to Augustine's mention of "human wisdom" reads, in words that might almost be taken out of More's mouth,

Neither philosophy, nor eloquence, nor the other admired arts and disciplines of the world, but this one and perfect art, to know God and serve him.[61]

61. Vives, *Commentaries to the City of God*, 577.

9

IN LITERIS VTCVNQ VERSATVS

The Humanist's Dilemma

Thomas More's passion for letters appears in the very first phrase of his epitaph:[1]

THOMAS MORVS VRBE LONDINENSI
FAMILIA NON CELEBRE SED HONESTA NATVS
IN LITERIS VTCVNQ VERSATVS

Here he calls himself "versed in letters." Rogers translates the phrase in a very self-deprecating fashion: "He engaged to some extent in literary matters," but *utcunque* can also be translated by "always," "in one way or another." I would suggest that a possible translation could be, "Thomas More was born in the city of London, of an honest though not famous family, and was always engaged in letters in one way or another." He loved Latin at school; he improvised speeches while acting in plays in Morton's household; he produced poetry in English and Latin in his youth; "after that," wrote Erasmus in 1519, "came a long struggle to acquire a more supple style in prose by practising his pen in every sort of writing." More read the Fathers of the Church in their original languages; he learned Greek, translating from Greek to Latin as a way of mastering the tongue. He read constantly, even perusing the books Erasmus sent for John Fisher before passing them on to their addressee. He wrote *Utopia* while he had some time to spare during an embassy abroad and had to finish it back at home by stealing hours from sleep. He made use of any opportunity to write let-

1. See Appendix.

ters to his children, from court, even (occasionally) on horseback … he corresponded with his fellow humanists and wrote long letters in defense of Erasmus. Once in the royal court, he became the king's private secretary because of his literary expertise.[2] Asked by the bishop of London to write in defense of the Church, he poured out hundreds of pages of polemic. Even after resigning as lord chancellor, he continued writing: from Chelsea, from Willesden, even from the Tower, checking his sources or, when deprived of books, recalling them from memory, with pen and ink or with a charcoal stick, to the very eve of his beheading.

But this passion for letters could also be an obstacle to a clear sight of the path to follow. Thomas More was determined to fix the love of God as the lodestar of his life and to be a contemplative in the middle of the world. He understood that he could live this dedication to God in a secular environment, in the midst of human affairs, in the hustle and bustle of the marketplace. But he had still to face the dilemma of the humanist.

—

In *De civitate Dei*, book VIII, chapter 4, St. Augustine writes about Plato's philosophy, explaining that

the study of wisdom consists in action and contemplation, so that one part of it may be called active, and the other contemplative—the active part having reference to the conduct of life, that is, to the regulation of morals, and the contemplative part to the investigation into the causes of nature and into pure truth.[3]

He argues that some previous philosophers had excelled in either the one or the other, but Plato managed to combine the two; so it is that in the *Republic* Plato makes the philosophers the rulers of the *polis*.

The attraction that the humanists of the early sixteenth century felt for classical culture and writing expressed itself both in their study of the Greek and Roman philosophers and in their desire to go back to the original works of the Fathers and to the Greek text of the New Testament. But experience showed that humanist studies could all too easily develop into a negative criticism of present-day practice within the Church or society, without any effort to place this knowledge at the service of society in a constructive way. The dilemma of the humanist was defined, using Christian terminology, in terms of the tension between the contemplative life of Mary and the active life of Martha. Pico della Mirandola wrestles with

2. Guy, *Public Career of Sir Thomas More*, 15.
3. Babcock, trans., *City of God*, 246.

the dilemma in his letter of October 15, 1486, to a fellow humanist, Andrea Corneo, that More appended to his *Life of Pico*. Corneo pleaded with Pico, "I want you to embrace Martha without deserting Mary." But Pico, citing his love for liberty, opts to turn his back on public life for the contemplative life of the philosopher.[4]

More gives a vivid description of the humanist's dilemma in book I of *Utopia*. Peter Giles introduces More to Raphael Hythloday, a man whose main interest is philosophy and who is very learned in Greek; Hythloday then tells them about the manners and institutions of the Utopians, and speaks

describing the errors found both among us and in the new world (and there are plenty of them), and he had also touched on the wiser measures adopted by both sides, so depicting the customs and institutions of each land he had passed through as if he had spent his entire life there.[5]

Peter, struck with admiration, tells him:

I wonder, my dear Raphael, that you don't attach yourself to some king. For I can't think of a single one by whom you wouldn't be most welcome, seeing that with your learning and your experience of places and peoples you're equipped not only to divert him but also to instruct him with examples and guide him with counsel. By the same token, you would promote your own interests and prove a support to your relatives and friends.[6]

But Hythloday replies, "Now I live as I will,[7] to which I believe few courtiers can pretend," a perfect summary of Pico's answer to Corneo. But if it would later be applicable to the dilemma More faced when presented with the opportunity to enter royal service, it was no less applicable to the situation he faced earlier.[8]

Hythloday goes on to tell Giles and More various stories pointing to some of the prevalent social evils of the time. Applying capital punishment for theft in England, he points out, simply encourages thieves to commit murder; he then goes on to blame the disorders in France on its custom of

4. *CW* 1, 85:15–88:10.

5. Baker-Smith, trans., ed., *Utopia*, 27.

6. Baker-Smith, trans., ed., *Utopia*, 27.

7. *Atqui nunc sic vivo ut volo*: see *CW* 4, 56:1, and *CU*, 50:29, and notes. This phrase is close to the definition of *libertas* given by Cicero in *De Officiis* I, 70: "cuius proprium est sic vivere ut velis." More uses the same phrase in his earliest extant letter, <c. November 1501>, addressed to John Holt (see chapter 2).

8. Baker-Smith points out that *Utopia* did not grow suddenly out of the prospect of a career in royal service, but out of More's previous reflections, and so what is found in *Utopia* is relevant to "the personal decisions which More had to face in the period 1503–5"; Baker-Smith, *More's Utopia*, 20.

retaining troops of mercenaries and rails against the enclosure of common land in England, which increases the poverty of the many for the sake of the luxury of the few.

Returning to excessive punishment for theft, Hythloday proposes instead the example of the Polylerites, whom he had encountered during his travels in Persia. As their land was surrounded by mountains, they had no interest in extending their frontiers and were protected from any aggression; in consequence, they lived comfortably and at peace. Thieves in this country were not killed or imprisoned but employed doing public works. After this account, More observes dryly:

It seems obvious to me that if only you could overcome your horror of princes' courts, your counsel would be an important asset to public welfare.[9]

Hythloday disagrees. If the king of France wished to aggrandize his territories by war, he argues, he would not welcome any advice Hythloday might have about avoiding war and being content with the lands he already had; likewise, a king who controlled the coinage and the administration of justice for his own benefit would reject the advice of a counselor who pointed out that the prince's duty is to put his people's well-being before his own. And so Hythloday concludes, "There is no room for philosophy in the councils of princes." To which More replies,

That is certainly true. There is no place for that academic philosophy which supposes every topic suitable for every occasion: but there is rather a *political* philosophy which knows its stage and adapts itself to the play in hand, acting out its role fittingly and with due decorum.[10]

More's actual words in the original Latin are significant:

Immo, inquam, est verum, non huic scholasticae que quidvis putet ubivis convenire: sed est alia philosophia civilior quae suam novit scaenam, eique sese accommodans, in ea fabula quae in minibus est suas partes concinne et cum decoro tutatur.

The term *civilior* has been variously translated as "more practical for statesmen,"[11] "better suited for the role of a citizen,"[12] "better suited to public affairs,"[13] or "more attuned to public affairs."[14] But Cicero, Quintilian,

<hr>

9. Baker-Smith, trans., ed., *Utopia*, 43.

10. My translation following Baker-Smith's.

11. *CW* 4, 99:14.

12. *CU*, 97.

13. Translation by Clarence H. Miller included in Wegemer and Smith, eds., *Essential Works of Thomas More*, 171.

14. Baker-Smith, trans, ed., *Utopia*, 49.

Tacitus, and Horace all use the Latin *civilis* as equivalent to the Greek *politicos* (πολιτικος),[15] and so it seems correct to translate it as "political philosophy," though all the translations given here convey a similar meaning. Cicero writes precisely of that philosophy "*quem civilem recte appellaturi videmur (Graeci* πολιτικόν)":[16] that is, the philosophy that the Romans called *civilem*, the Greeks called *politikon*. What we now call "political philosophy" is precisely the kind of philosophy More tells Raphael he should practice.

Hythloday represents the "contemplative" philosopher who does not want to involve himself, while More argues for the need to intervene in the service of the commonwealth rather than keeping knowledge for oneself. It may be that Erasmus did not agree with More's argument, for he wrote:

The second book [of *Utopia*] he had written earlier, when at leisure; at a later opportunity he added the first in the heat of the moment. Hence there is certain unevenness in the style.[17]

The second book is mainly taken up with Hythloday's description of Utopia, while the first consists of a conversation between More, Giles, and Hythloday in which More, as a fictitious speaker, states his position in favor of entering royal service. Two years after the publication of *Utopia*, the real More entered the service of Henry VIII, and Erasmus wrote to him, "Certainly you are a loss to literature, and to us."[18]

Erasmus amended his assessment a year later, however, when he produced his famous pen-portrait of More for Ulrich von Hutten. There he praises the court of Henry for including in his service humanists such as Mountjoy, Linacre, and Colet, as well as More,[19] even though it seems that previously Erasmus would have sided with Raphael, who in *Utopia* despised the courts of princes. Thus, after his change of mind, writing to Budé in 1521, Erasmus says that More was to be congratulated for having been promoted by the king;[20] and he notes that

There is no journey, no business however voluminous or difficult, that can take the book out of More's hand; and yet it would be hard to find anyone who was more truly a man for all seasons and all men, who was more ready to oblige, more

---

15. Charlton T. Lewis and Charles Short, *Latin Dictionary* (Oxford: Oxford University Press, 1962), s.v. "civilis," B.

16. Cicero, *De finibus*, bk IV, ch. II, section 5.

17. *CWE* 7, Ep. 999:284–87.

18. *CWE* 5, Ep. 829:8 [Louvain, April 1518].

19. *CWE* 7, Ep. 999:317.

20. *CWE* 8, Ep. 1233:25.

easily available for meeting, more lively in conversation, or who combined so much real wisdom with such charm of character.[21]

In fact Erasmus kept praising More all through his life, writing that he was "the most upright, fair-minded, friendly, intelligent man on whom the sun has shone for many generations."[22]

In the paragraph from *Utopia* cited earlier, More is dealing with a "political philosophy," one that tries to adapt to the circumstances. This can be further clarified by another text from Cicero concerning "civilis quaedam ratio": "a certain political science." Political philosophy, he explains, cannot be reduced to rhetorical skill; it does require eloquence, but this is to achieve its end, which is the welfare of the political community, just as the duty of a physician is to cure the patient.[23] Or as More puts it in *Utopia*,

Even if you can't eradicate harmful ideas or remedy established evils, you must not therefore turn your back on the body politic: you mustn't abandon the ship simply because you can't direct the winds.... Instead, you must do your best to operate through an indirect approach, and try to handle everything tactfully, so that whatever you cannot turn to good will at least do the minimum of harm.[24]

The opposition between academic or theoretical philosophy and political philosophy that the three men discussed near the end of book I of *Utopia*, just before they broke off for lunch, can already be seen in the Latin "translation" of the four-verse stanza written in the Utopian tongue that Hythloday showed to Giles and that appears among the introductory material of *Utopia*.

Utopus me dux ex non insula fecit insulam.
Una ego terrarum omnium absque philosophia.
Civitatem philosophicam expressi mortalibus.
Libenter imperio mea, non gravatim accipio meliora.[25]

The primary meaning of *civitas* in classical Latin is "citizenship," as seen in Cicero, Livy, Tacitus, and Suetonius, among others. So, this quatrain might be translated:

21. *CWE* 8, Ep. 1233:101–5.
22. *CWE* 9, Ep. 1341A:1047, January 30, 1523.
23. Cicero, *De inventione* I, 6, 5.
24. Here I follow mainly the translation by Baker-Smith, *Utopia*, 50.
25. *CU* 22:24–27.

The leader Utopus turned me from a non-island into an island.
Out of all lands I alone, without philosophy,
have pictured for mortals a philosophical citizenship.[26]
I share my own things freely; not unwillingly I accept better things.[27]

These lines appear on page 13 of the November 1518 edition of *Utopia*. The previous text, the "Hexastichon" (a six-line poem on the island of Utopia, written ostensibly by the Utopian poet laureate Anemolius) shows also an opposition between the Platonic discourse on the body politic and what Utopia has to offer. It reads:

Utopia pricis dicta ob infrequentiam,
Nunc civitatis aemula Platonicae,
Fortasse victrix (nam quod illa literis
Delineavit, hoc ego una praestiti
Viris & opibus, optimisque legibus):
Eutopia merito sum vocanda nomine.

Here More writes "civitatis ... Platonicae," using *civitas* for Plato's *politeia*: that is, More is referring not to the city—for which he uses *urbs*, as we saw at the beginning of this chapter—but to the *polis* or body politic.[28] And so these six lines might be translated:

Remote, in distant times I was called "No-place,"
But now I claim to rival Plato's *polis*,[29]
Perhaps outdo her (for what he only drew in words
I have made live anew in men and wealth, as well as splendid laws):
So "Happy place" I rightly should be called.

Following St. Augustine, as we have seen, the dilemma between dedicating oneself to scholarly work and to the service of the commonwealth was usually framed in terms of the contemplative and the active life. St. Augus-

---

26. Lewis and Short, *Latin Dictionary*, s.v. "civitas," I, note that *civitas* is never used by Cicero for *urbs* or city (see "civitas," I). Therefore; "philosophical city," which appears in some translations of *Utopia*, seems unjustified if we assume that More tried to follow Cicero's usage; *civitas* can also be translated by the body-politic, the state, the citizens united in community (Lewis and Short, "civitas," II), rather than *urbs*. Following the second meaning of *civitas* and bearing in mind that the Island of Utopia included fifty-four cities, "civitatem" here could also refer to the whole body-politic, thus, to "a philosophical commonwealth."

27. My translation based on Baker-Smith, trans., ed., *Utopia*, 8, but in line 2 he writes, "without abstract philosophy"; and in line 3 he writes, "the philosophical city" instead of "a philosophical citizenship."

28. Here More follows normal classical usage. The use of *civitas* in the sense of *urbs* is extremely rare in classical Latin; see Lewis and Short, *Latin Dictionary*, s.v. "civitas," II.B.

29. *CW* 4 translates "civitatis Platonicae" as "Plato's republic"; *CU* translates it as "Plato's state." I prefer *polis*, but it could also be translated as *commonwealth*.

tine, after his conversion to the Christian faith, decided to lead a life totally dedicated to the contemplation of God and of things eternal with some like-minded friends; his intention was to practice a Christian version of the ideal of the contemplative life expressed in the great Greek philosophical tradition, choosing in this way the "better part" (Lk 10:42).[30] But he quickly realized that he was called not to abandon the world but to remain there in the service of others. Looking back on that moment, he writes in his *Confessions*:

I had resolved in my heart, and meditated flight into the wilderness; but you forbade me and gave me strength, by saying: "Christ died for all, that those who live might live no longer for themselves but for him who died for their sake" (2 Cor 5:15).[31]

Of course, More's situation was very different. St. Augustine was called to the exercise of the priestly, and then episcopal, ministry in the city of Hippo. But his lectures on the *City of God* may have led More to realize that his longing to be with Christ could also be fulfilled in a secular environment. Faced with the dilemma of the humanist, between the contemplative life of the philosopher and the active life, More chose both the active life of the service to the city[32] *and* the contemplative life of the Christian.

Immediately after this choice he became involved in many and varied public activities: quite apart from a busy law practice, he was elected to Parliament in 1504, then became financial secretary of Lincoln's Inn (1507); a member of Mercers' Company (1509); member of the House of Commons for the city of London (1510), the same years as he published his *Life of Pico*; under-sheriff of London (1510–18); autumn reader at Lincoln's Inn (1511); governor of Lincoln's Inn (1512); and so on. All this activity, however, is beyond the scope of this monograph.[33]

More understood that the dilemma between the contemplative life of the philosopher and the active life in the service to the city was not the case

30. This interpretation is inspired by Benedict XVI, *Spe Salvi* (2007), no. 28.

31. St. Augustine, *Confessions* X, 70.

32. The first chapter of James McConica's *Thomas More* is entitled "Called to the Service of Christendom." There he writes, "What is clearest from his youthful ideals is his calling to the service of Christendom through scholarship and the renewal of the commonweal" (10).

33. Guy, *Reputations*, Chapter 2, "Action or Contemplation?," is an excellent treatment of this question, and it also sets out the positions of assorted biographers on More's choice. See also John M. Headley's review of Guy's book: "John Guy's Thomas More: On the Dimensions of Political Biography," *Moreana*, nos. 143–44 (December 2000): 81–96, which argues that at least in More's case, the answer to the question of action or contemplation was not "either-or" but "both-and" (93).

at the level of his relation with God; that, in fact, a Christian was called to be a contemplative soul, a man of prayer always. That what is suggested earlier—that More chose the active life of the humanist and the contemplative life of the Christian: they are two different planes, though of course intimately and deeply related; More's contemplative life is the unifying force for all his activity.

Indeed, More's choice is described in *De civitate Dei* with regard to the philosophers who joined the faith. St. Augustine addresses them in book 19, chapter 19, and his words can be applied to the humanists of the Renaissance:

As to their three modes of life, the contemplative, the active, and the composite, although, so long as a man's faith is preserved, he may choose any of them without detriment to his eternal interests, yet he must never overlook the claims of truth and duty. No man has a right to lead such a life of contemplation as to forget in his own ease the service due to his neighbour; nor has any man a right to be so immersed in active life as to neglect the contemplation to God.

And although St. Augustine starts that chapter addressing the philosopher, his conclusion is that all Christians must practice contemplation. And he goes on to say that in the active life, it is not honors and power that should be sought, but the welfare of society.

—

Thus, faced with the dilemma of the humanist between the active life of service to the commonwealth and the scholarly work of the philosopher, More opted for the active life of service. In this he followed—or, at least, was in tune with—the life described by Cicero in *De Officiis*. More's familiarity with *De Officiis* can be seen in his paraphrases from it in his first two extant letters, that of 1501 to Holt (*vivimus ut volumus*, I am living my life just as I desire),[34] and that of <1502–4> to Colet (*cetarios, lanios, coquos, fartores, piscatores, aucupes, qui materiam ventri ministrant*).[35]

In *De Officiis* Cicero writes that to be drawn by study from the active life is contrary to moral duty, for the whole glory of virtue is in activity; besides, activity may be interrupted, and there are many opportunities for returning to study.[36] Cicero compares the lives of men in retirement—*otiosus*—with that of those involved in public service, and concludes that the career of those who apply themselves to statecraft is more profitable

---

34. *De Officiis*, book I, section 70. The references follow Miller's translation of Cicero, *De Officiis*.
35. *De Officiis* I, 150.
36. *De Officiis* I, 19.

to mankind.[37] Perhaps Cicero's use of *otiosus* in *De Officiis* is echoed in More's letter to Colet of <1502–4>: "*inter aliena negotia ocianti.*" In the following paragraph Cicero goes on to say that those who refuse public service claim it is because they do not care for glory: "In reality, however, they seem to dread the toil and trouble and, perhaps, the discredit and humiliation of political failure and defeat"—words that could be applied to Pico della Mirandola. He then adds that those whom Nature has endowed with a capacity for administering public affairs should put aside all hesitation and enter the race for public office.[38] This choice of the career is what Cicero, in the translator's words, calls a "vocation." He emphasizes that each one has to choose his own vocation[39] and that youth is the time appointed by Nature for every man to choose the path of life on which he would enter: a decision that involves choosing between the path of Pleasure and the path of Virtue (*duas vias, unam Voluptatis, alteram Virtutis*).[40] It is not only a matter of considering each individual act as occasion may present, but also of ordering the whole course of one's life; and for this great care must be taken so that "we may be true to ourselves throughout all our lives and not falter in the discharge of any duty."[41]

In the paragraphs that follow, Cicero considers the care to be taken in choosing a career and in following "our calling in life,"[42] and each individual's vocation in life (*vitam institutam*[43] or *institutio vitae*[44]). The vocation of the humanist to the service to the commonwealth, as described by Cicero, was a typical topic of the sixteenth-century European Renaissance; a topic of which More was well aware and that interested him, too.

—

Another perspective on the vocation of the humanist is given by Aldus Manutius. In a letter to Aldus dated August 27, 1499,[45] Grocyn tells him that his best friend, Thomas Linacre, has recently returned to Britain and thanks him for his services to Linacre—for, as Terence and Cicero wrote, "all things ought to be common among friends." He then goes on to thank Aldus for the noble service he is providing to all humanists by publishing

37. *De Officiis* I, 70.
38. *De Officiis* I, 72.
39. *De Officiis* I, 116.
40. *De Officiis* I, 118.
41. *De Officiis* I, 119.
42. *De Officiis* I, 120–21.
43. *De Officiis* II, 30.
44. *De Officiis* II, 39.
45. Manutius, *Greek Classics*, 284–87.

the Greek authors, and particularly for publishing Aristotle ahead of Plato, as well as for "planning a still more remarkable work," the printing of the sacred scriptures in the original languages. Several months later, on December 5, 1499, Erasmus mentions Colet, Grocyn, Linacre, and More together, and in his letters of 1501 and <1502–4> Grocyn and Linacre appear as More's Greek teachers. Perhaps significantly, while Erasmus emphasizes Plato's influence in his letter, Grocyn in his letter agrees with Aldus in placing Aristotle ahead of Plato:

In this matter I too certainly take your view, since I feel that the difference between these two greatest of philosophers is simply—forgive me, everyone—the difference between a polymath and a "polymyth."[46]

More may have also appreciated this difference between Colet and Grocyn, and it seems he sided with Grocyn. Aldus's project of publishing the Greek and Latin text of the New Testament is prior to any known contact with Erasmus; so is his praise, in his preface to his edition of Proclus's *Sphaera* (translated by Linacre), of the "Britons"—Grocyn and Linacre—as leading scholars of Greek and Latin for the Italians to imitate.[47]

More was well acquainted with Aldus's work. When Hythloday relates that he had provided the Utopians with a number of Greek books, he specifically mentions Sophocles "in the small Aldine type" (*minusculis Aldi formulis*)[48] that was published by Aldus in August 1502 and described in its preface as *parva forma*;[49] Hythloday remarks that the Utopians admired the books printed by Aldus. All the works mentioned by Hythloday in that section of *Utopia*[50] (apart from Galen's *Ars medica*, the works of Hippocrates,[51] and Lucian's *Dialogues*[52]),[53] were published by Aldus, who wrote prefaces to each one of his editions. In order of appearance in *Utopia* they are: most of Plato's works and several of Aristotle's; Theophrastus's *On Plants*, Lascaris's *Grammar*, and the *Grammar* by Theodore Gaza that Raphael did not take to Utopia; and the works of Hesychius and Dioscorides,

---

46. I.e., a fabulist, a teller of many tales. Manutius, *Greek Classics*, 285n32.

47. Manutius, *Greek Classics*, 78–81. Aldus referred to the Britons also in his preface to Aristotle, *Moral Philosophy*, dated June 1498 (cf. Manutius, *Greek Classics*, 64).

48. *CW* 4, 183:4.

49. Manutius, *Greek Classics*, 104.

50. *CW* 4, 181:4–183:5.

51. Galen's *Ars medica* and the works of Hippocrates are mentioned in *CW* 4, 183:7–8.

52. *CW* 4, 183:2.

53. Aldus wanted to publish Galen's works: see Manutius, *Greek Classics*, 45. The Aldine Press published Hippocrates's *Opera Omnia* in 1526; Lucian's works were first published by Lascaris in Florence, 1496.

Plutarch, Aristophanes, Homer, Euripides, Thucydides, Herodotus, and Herodian.[54]

The first published of these works was Constantine Lascaris's *Grammar*; Aldus's preface is dated March 8, 1495. In it, the vocation of the humanist comes across very clearly: Aldus writes that his aim is to make Greek widely available and that he has decided to devote his whole life to benefiting mankind in this way. "God is my witness," he writes, "that I wish for nothing more than to help humanity." And he takes up Cicero's idea of the vocation of activity in the service of others. This view pervades the rest of Aldus's prefaces. Thus in the last one he wrote before Linacre's return to England, his preface to Dioscorides's *Materials of Medicine* (July 8, 1499), Aldus speaks of his determination to persevere in his aim in spite of the difficulties: "Do not give way to adversity, but oppose it with greater courage." He is ready to spend time, the most precious thing of all, and to suffer himself in order to be of benefit to others. Twice in those early prefaces Aldus writes that youth is the time given by Nature to choose which path to follow, the arduous path leading to virtue or the easy path of pleasure[55]—a topos that, as we have seen, is used by Cicero in *De Officiis*.[56] And in his first preface Aldus writes that man is born to work, echoing the Bible's "Man is born to work, and the bird to fly" (Job 5:7).[57] The phrase by Aldus clearly has a vocational meaning:

For although we can lead a quiet and undisturbed life we have nevertheless chosen one that is busy and full of occupations, since man is not born for pleasures that are unworthy of the good and educated person, but to work and to be engaged always in something worthy of man.[58]

Vocation, as described by Cicero in *De Officiis*, is determined by the talents received by Nature and the circumstances presented by Fortune, but it also involves a choice that, once made, requires perseverance, determination, and courage in the face of the difficulties, as he comments in book I:

54. These authors were published by Aldus as appears in Manutius, *Greek Classics*, for Plato, 234; Aristotle, 10, 36, 46, 50, 62; Theophrastus, 126; Lascaris, 2; Gaza, 16; Hesychius, 258; Dioscorides, 74; Plutarch, 170, 200); Aristophanes, 68; Homer, 162, 166; Euripides, 112; Thucydides, 98; Herodotus, 106; Herodian, 118.

55. Manutius, *Greek Classics*, 21 and 53.

56. Cicero, *De Officiis* I, 118.

57. This is the Vulgate text, *Homo nascitur ad laborem et avis ad volatum*. Most modern translations do not convey this vocational idea but read instead, "Man is born to trouble, as the sparks fly upward."

58. Manutius, *Greek Classics*, 7, para. 4.

Since the most powerful influence in the choice of a career is exerted by Nature, and the next most powerful by Fortune, we must, of course, take account of them both in deciding upon our calling in life.... If, therefore, anyone has conformed his whole plan of life to the kind of nature that is his (that is, his better nature), let him go on with it consistently—for that is the essence of Propriety.[59]

In this way Cicero identifies five elements in the choice of man's vocation. First come the "talents received from Nature." Second are the circumstances of time and place, which Cicero identifies as the work of Fortune, a common medieval topos. The third and—in Cicero's view—main element is the personal decision to follow a particular calling or career, which should provide a clear path in the face of difficulties. Fourth comes perseverance in the struggle to follow one's calling: this is what makes an act virtuous, and (again according to Cicero) makes a man behave with propriety or *integrity*—a word first used in English by More. Fifth, Cicero points out that the plan for one's life is to be chosen in one's youth. And, as has been mentioned, Cicero advises that man should follow the vocation to the active life in the service to the commonwealth.

For Cicero the Stoic, Fortune cannot be identified with the Roman goddess of Fate, against whom man is powerless, for Nature is much more stable than Fortune. More's vision of Fortune coincided with Cicero's, as can be seen from the poem included by William Rastell in the *English Works* under the rubric "Certain meters in English written by master Thomas More in his youth for the boke of Fortune, and caused them to be printed in the begynnyng of that boke." It is not clear which book is being referred to, but the *Book of Fortune* was a common title at the time whether in Italian, French, or English. It might well be that More was not prefacing a book invited by its printer but was in fact criticizing the content of the book.[60] He describes Fortune as mighty, variable, inconstant, evasive, flimsy, and full of treason.

The 314-verse poem is divided into a prologue and three parts. In the first part, Fortune speaks to the people; in the second and third parts More addresses "them that trust in Fortune" and "them that seek Fortune." At the end of the second part he advises the reader:

59. *De Officiis* I, 120. Newton (2016) translates, "Since nature has the greatest force, followed by fortune, both must be thoroughly considered when choosing a way of life, but nature more so; for nature is firmer and more constant.... Therefore, he who directs all his thoughts on how to live according to what sort of nature he has ... exhibits constancy."
60. *CW* 1, xxix.

> Therefore, if you surely want to stand,
> Take poverty's part and let proud Fortune go,
> Receive nothing that comes from her hand.
> Love moderation and virtue, because they are the two things
> That inconstant Fortune cannot take from you.
> Then you may boldly despise her turning chance:
> She can neither hinder you nor advance.
>
> But if you must needs meddle with her treasure,
> Place not your trust in it, but spend it liberally.
> Behave not proudly, nor take anything out of measure,
> Build not your house high up to the sky:
> None falls far, but he that climbs high.
> Remember Nature sent you here bare,
> The gifts of fortune count them borrowed ware.[61]

More's *Fortune Verses* show that for him, as for Cicero, the changing turns of fortune are to be reckoned with, but they are not the main factors to guide man's life project. The *Fortune Verses* were written with a Stoic approach, but in the Tower he smiled at Lady Fortune[62] and repeated the lesson of his verses:

Aye, flattering fortune, though you look never so fair and begin to smile pleasantly as though you would repair my ruin, you shall not beguile me during this life. I shall trust God to enter in a while his sure and firm haven of heaven. After your calm I ever expect a storm.[63]

And afterward he continued writing:

> Long was I, Lady Luck, your serving man,
> And now I have lost again all that I had got;
> Wherefore, when I think of you now and then,
> And in my mind remember this and that,
> You may not blame me though I have reversed your plans for me,[64]
> But in faith I bless you again a thousand times,
> For lending me some leisure to make rhymes.[65]

The idea of vocation found in Cicero needs to be revised in the context of the Christian tradition of the late Middle Ages. The choice of terminology has been considered already; at times the humanists use the figures of

---

61. *CW* 1, 40–11, vv. 250–63, modernized English.
62. Willow, *Analysis* (1974), 210.
63. Roper, 82:1–7, and *CW* 1, 45.
64. The original has "I beshrewe your catte": see note to *CW* 1, 46:6 in *CW* 1, 208.
65. *CW* 1, 46.

Mary and Martha to refer to the contemplative life of the philosopher and the active life of service to the city. In a Christian context, however, the contribution to society is for the sake of God. As Aldus mentions in the prefaces to his editions, his eagerness to continue providing Greek texts comes from a desire to serve Christendom.

James McConica writes of More that

what is clearest from his youthful ideals is his calling to the service of Christendom through scholarship and the renewal of the commonweal.[66]

Of course, the "calling" identified by McConica cannot be equated with the vocation that Cicero defines in terms of Nature and Fortune. A Christian calling implies the conviction that God is the one who calls, and the decision required is a personal response to this calling—once one is aware of the calling. This is what we can see so far in considering the early writings of Thomas More. And we can say that More, faced with the dilemma of the humanist, chose both the active life of service to the city as proposed by Cicero *and* the contemplative life of the Christian as described by Chrysostom, Augustine, Bonaventure, and others.

It is outside the scope of this book to analyze More's activity beyond his awareness of the calling. Such activity—as a lawyer, undersheriff of London, and in royal service, his work in defense of humanism and of orthodoxy—has been dealt with by numerous biographies and other studies on More. But insofar as it is part of More's awareness of his calling, I agree with Baker-Smith that we should look to

a key passage in Augustine (*City of God*, book XIX, c. 6) where he raises the question, "Given that social life is surrounded by such darkness, will the wise man take his seat on the judges' bench, or will he not venture to do so? Clearly, he will take his seat; for the claims of human society, which he thinks it wicked to abandon, constrain him and draw him to his duty." I believe that this is a hugely important passage for More: rather than … being dragged by his insensitive father from his literary studies, we can see him as drawn by a steady sense of vocation to commit himself to God's work through this mixed life. Erasmus never quite grasped this. The passage itself seems to echo one in Plato's *Republic* which has importance for *Utopia* and which argues that the wise man will not be active in "the city of his birth." Following Augustine, More reverses this in a Christian acceptance of an imperfect social order which can be ameliorated by charity. And his career is that progress; first as a socially aware lawyer and then as a courtier/counsellor whose major achievement in his own view (see the epitaph

66. McConica, *Thomas More* (1977), 10.

on himself that he sent to Erasmus) was his part in the achievement of peace at the treaty of Cambrai in 1529.[67]

In the previous paragraph of the same letter Baker-Smith refers to the mixed life mentioned by Walter Hilton, and he adds:

Only when his [More's] active role is blocked after 1532 does he retire to a life of prayer—though even then he is hard at work on controversy. I think that it all adds up to a very consistent whole, which matches Hilton's ideal.

As Baker-Smith writes, More's "active role" in Parliament ceased when he submitted his resignation as lord chancellor to the king. On June 14, 1532, he wrote to Erasmus that his wish "of being relieved of all public duties and eventually being able to devote some time to God alone and myself; at long last this wish has come true."[68] But as has been seen so far, More's life of prayer was evident from his early writings and from his biographical profile by Erasmus. It did not start when he retired from public duties.

The concept of the "mixed life" considered by Hilton and taken up by Baker-Smith comes from a different starting-point, that of dividing Christians into those who follow the contemplative life and those who follow the active life; faced with such a division (which, admittedly, was never proposed as an absolute), Hilton, following St. Gregory the Great, points naturally to the option of a mixed life. This coincides with the Christian life presented by St. John Chrysostom and St. Augustine and other Fathers and doctors of the Church, such as St. Thomas Aquinas: for them, all Christians had to practice the contemplative life (that is, the life of prayer) in whatever circumstance. This is what Chrysostom preached to the citizens of Antioch, and this is what Augustine expressed when saying that the attitudes of both Martha and Mary were to be practiced by all Christians. Faced with the dilemma of the humanist between scholarly work and a life of service to society in the tradition of Cicero, More, as opposed to Pico, chose the active life of service, but, this was not More's dilemma as a Christian. Therefore, we can say that he chose the life of service to society *and* the contemplative life of a Christian.

---

67. Baker-Smith, private correspondence, July 6, 2016, quoted by Mitjans in "In Memoriam of Dominic Baker-Smith," *Moreana* (December 2016): 11–12.

68. *SL*, Letter 44.

10

Marriage

A Holy Knot

Having decided to dedicate himself fully to God in a secular environment, following the path of holiness by being a contemplative in the midst of the world, More chose to marry. This choice clearly shows that he did not share John Colet's views on marriage; instead, his view coincides with that found in *De civitate Dei*, book XIV, chapter 22, which deals with "on the conjugal union as originally instituted and blessed by God." St. Augustine points out that God blessed marriage:

For no sooner had Scripture said, "male and female He created them" than it immediately continues, "God blessed them, and God said to them, 'Be fruitful and multiply, and fill the earth and subdue it.'"[1]

And he notes that Christ confirmed this blessing, saying,

"Have you not read that He who made them from the beginning made them male and female, and said, 'For this reason a man shall leave his father and mother and be joined to his wife, and the two shall become one flesh?' (Gn 2:24). So they are no longer two but one flesh. What therefore God has joined together, let not man put asunder" (Mt 19:4–6).

We do not have More's thoughts on this passage of *De civitate Dei*, but we do know that he met Juan Luis Vives while the latter was engaged in writing his own commentary, as has been discussed in chapter 8. The meeting was in Bruges in August 1521. Vives was twenty-nine years old

---

1. *De civitate Dei*, bk XIV, ch. 22.

and unmarried; Frans Cranevelt, who was also there, was thirty-six, and, having married in 1509, he was father already to several of his eleven children; More was forty-three. Under the circumstances, the topic of Vives's commentary to *De civitate Dei* must have come up in conversation, and indeed it would have been natural to discuss the issues that More had studied when lecturing on *De civitate Dei* in 1501, when he was younger than Vives was in 1521.[2] To the text of Genesis quoted earlier, "male and female He created them," St. Augustine adds the consideration,

Although these latter sentences may not unfitly be applied spiritually, yet "male and female" cannot properly be applied to anything spiritual in man; not even to that which rules, and that which is governed. But, as evident in the real distinction of sex, they were made male and female, to bring forth fruit by generation, to multiply and fill the earth. This is so manifest a truth, that none will contradict it, but the most silly.

And Vives reinforces St. Augustine's statement, commenting,

There is nothing in the Scriptures but may be spiritually applied; yet we must preserve the true and real sense, or otherwise we should make a great confusion in religion.[3]

Arguably, then, Vives may be reflecting More's own attitude in this realist approach: God blessed the union of man and woman in marriage; Jesus confirmed that blessing, therefore marriage was willed by God and was a path to holiness; to depart from the true and real sense of scripture was, in the words of St. Augustine, silly.

More and Vives remained in touch after their meeting in Bruges. On July 14 the following year, Vives mentioned to Erasmus that he had received two letters from More,[4] and on August 10 he sent greetings to More through Cranevelt.[5] In September he visited England for three or four months.[6] During this time he got to know the daughters of Thomas More—Margaret, Elizabeth, and Cecily, as well as Margaret Giggs—and he mentioned them in *De institutione feminae Christianae*, which he finished

2. Adams, *Better Part of Valor*, 190, argues that since More's lectures on the *City of God* are lost, Vives's commentary (that of a humanist sharing ideals very close to More's) is probably as close as we can come to More's own work.

3. Butler, trans., *City of God by St Augustine with the Commentaries of Vives to "De civitate Dei,"* book XIV, chapter XIII, 1522.

4. *CWE* 9, Ep. 1303.

5. De Vocht, ed., *Literae Virorum Eruditorum*, Cra 13/32–35; Spanish translation in Biblioteca Valenciana Digital, *Epistolario de Juan Luis Vives*, carta 45.

6. *CWE* 9, Ep. 1306:41–46.

back in Bruges in April 1523. In it he once again praises More[7] and speaks of the holiness of marriage, instituted by God at the beginning, when humankind kept its original purity and integrity, and sanctified by Christ's presence at Cana.[8] Although this is an entirely conventional view, Vives's closeness to More at the time suggests that this view of marriage coincided with More's.

St. Augustine wrote about marriage on several occasions. In his treatise *On the Good of Marriage* (AD 401), he defended the Christian view of marriage: against those who said that it was a Manichean approach, he argued that, on the contrary, the union of man and woman is the first natural bond of human society; that it is good and honorable; that its goodness is confirmed by the gospel; and that husband and wife should be aware that

it was said to all the faithful, "Do you not know that your bodies are a temple of the Holy Spirit within you, Whom you have from God?" (1 Cor 6:19) Therefore the bodies also of the married are holy, as long as they keep faith to one another and to God.[9]

Nevertheless, John Colet might have found the basis for his less positive approach in the same treatise, for we also find St. Augustine saying that "if all men should abstain from all sexual intercourse ... much more speedily would the City of God be filled" (§10). But in his later *Retractations* he refers directly (in chapter 48) to *On the Good of Marriage*, admitting that certain things said there could be misunderstood and declaring that he had spoken of them "at a later time in other writings": this is probably an oblique reference to *De civitate Dei*, which he had finished shortly before.[10]

More would have known the treatise *On the Good of Marriage*, at least from John Colet. However, he must also have known also *The Retractations*; not only were they widely available in England at the time,[11] but the chapter of *The Retractations* that deals with *De civitate Dei* (bk II, ch. 69) was included at the beginning of *De civitate Dei* in many fifteenth-century editions.[12] It is likely, therefore, that More would have come across the

---

7. Vives, *De institutione feminae Christianae*, bk I, ch. 4.

8. Vives, *De institutione feminae Christianae*, bk II, ch. 1.

9. St. Augustine, *The Good of Marriage*, Fathers of the Church 15 (Washington, D.C.: The Catholic University of America Press, 1955), 26.

10. St. Augustine, *The Retractations*, trans. Mary I. Bogan, Fathers of the Church 60 (Washington, D.C.: The Catholic University of America Press, 1968), 164n2.

11. See, e.g., Coates, *English Medieval Books*, 145, 196; and Augustine, *Retractations*, xviii–xix.

12. See, e.g., Augustine, *De civitate Dei*, the editions of Rome, 1468, 1470, 1474; Mainz, 1473; and Basel, 1479. In most cases the source is cited: *Argumentum operis totius ex libro retractationum* in

chapter when preparing his lectures on *De civitate Dei*, and this might have alerted him to look into the rest of *The Retractations*. The complete two books of *The Retractations* first appeared in print as a separate work in 1486, and they were included in the first comprehensive printed edition of St. Augustine's works c. 1499. It is one of the works mentioned in the *Antibarbari*.[13]

In summary, Thomas More could not but have taken Colet's opinion seriously, but, having studied the matter for his lectures on *De civitate Dei* and in his reading of other Fathers of the Church, St. John Chrysostom in particular, he concluded that marriage was indeed a path to holiness, that husband and wife are called to sanctify their married life and to sanctify themselves in it. Or in the words of James McConica, "The brilliant and idealistic young husband understood marriage as a vocation."[14]

⁓

While considering More's views on marriage it is worth bearing in mind what Erasmus wrote on the subject at the time of More's decision to get married. In February 1503 Erasmus published what he called the *Lucubra-tiunculae*, a miscellany of works pertaining to *pietas* (as he classified them later in his letter to Hector Boece of March 15, 1530),[15] and he sent a copy of it to John Colet in December 1504;[16] this was the first edition, the only one published before Thomas More's marriage. The main text of this volume was Erasmus's *Enchiridion militis christiani*,[17] a phenomenally popular work: by the end of the sixteenth century there had been more than seventy editions of the Latin text and innumerable vernacular translations.[18]

The *Enchiridion* is addressed to "A FRIEND AT COURT" who had asked Erasmus for a guide to living worthily for Christ and—in view of the difficulties of his position—even wondered whether he should leave court

---

the editions of Rome 1470 and 1474; *Sententia beati Augustini Episcopi ex libro retractationum* in the editions of Maiz and Basel. It is without a title in the 1468 Rome edition.

13. *CWE* 23, 96:27.

14. McConica, *Thomas More* (1977), 14.

15. *EE*, vol. VIII, Ep. 2283:120; cf. *CWE* 66, ix.

16. See Ep. 181:49–50. The title translates as "Nightly jottings," a diminutive of *lucubratio*, which is any work done by night.

17. The *Enchiridion* is accompanied by a letter dated from the monastery of St. Bertin, Saint-Omer, 1501: Ep. 164, *CWE* 2, 52–53 (sixty-three lines). In the first edition the whole of Ep. 164 is given at the beginning, but in subsequent editions only the first sixteen lines of Ep. 164 are given at the start of the *Enchiridion* and the rest of the letter (lines 17–63) are placed at the end.

18. See *CWE* 66, 4. From 1518 onward, the *Enchiridion* was published with a sixteen-page Prefatory Letter (*CWE* 66, 8–23) dated Basel, Eve of the Assumption, August 1518. Much of the letter is a critique of contemporary religious congregations, although Erasmus also praises the zeal of the great founders and quotes the Fathers in defense of monasticism.

and withdraw from the world. The setting, therefore, is not dissimilar to that of Walter Hilton's *Treatise on Mixed Life*.

Erasmus's reply is a lengthy (110-page) exposition of what he later defined as "the pattern of a Christian life."[19] In his covering letter to John Colet he explains that he composed the *Enchiridion*

> in order to counteract the error of those who make religion in general consist in rituals and observances of an almost more than Jewish formality, but who are astonishingly indifferent to matters that have to do with true goodness. What I have tried to do, in fact, is to teach a *method of morals*, as it were, in the manner of those who have originated fixed procedures in the various branches of learning.[20]

Hence the use of the word *Enchiridion*, meaning "handbook." Erasmus starts by telling his addressee:

> First of all you ought to bear constantly in mind that the life of mortals is nothing else but an unremitting *warfare*, according to the testimony of Job, a tried and unvanquished soldier.[21]

The *Enchiridion militis Christiani* thus fits into the long tradition of works treating of "spiritual combat."[22] The full title of the treatise as it appeared with three companion pieces in the *Lucubratiunculae* of 1503 reads, *Enchiridion militis christiani saluberrimis praeceptis refertum contra omnia vitiorum irritaementa efficacissimis et ratio quaedam veri christianismi*—that is, "the handbook of the Christian soldier, replete with most salutary precepts of much efficacy against all the allurements of vice, and a model of true Christianity,"[23] and indeed, most of the *Enchiridion* treats of precepts or "rules" (*canones* in the original) against specific vices, particularly the capital sins.

What Erasmus reiterates throughout the *Enchiridion* is that the fullness of Christian life, and thus holiness, is not to be practiced only by some people who have withdrawn from the world but by all Christians, because all are bound to follow Christ: "Our commitment to Christ springs from the sacraments," Erasmus writes (*CWE* 66, 26), meaning primarily bap-

---

19. See Ep. 337:94.

20. Ep. 181:53–60.

21. *CWE* 66, 24.

22. The image of spiritual combat, derived from St. Paul, is present in the Fathers: see, e.g., St. John Chrysostom, *Commentary to the Gospel of St. Matthew*, Homily 15. St. Thomas Aquinas mentions spiritual combat in *ST* III, q. 72, a. 5. Erasmus's *Enchiridion* had a wide impact and influenced such classical spiritual writers as St. Ignatius of Loyola and Lorenzo Scupoli.

23. Charles Fantazzi, Introductory note to the *Enchiridion*, *CWE* 66, 3–4.

tism and confirmation. Confirmation makes the person who receives it a "Christian soldier" (hence the text's title), but above all Erasmus stresses baptism, which he describes as a "treaty struck with God" (*CWE* 66, 25) at "the life-giving font" and a "promise" made to Christ (*CWE* 66, 26). Erasmus argues that there is no vow more religious than baptism (*CWE* 66, 58), for at baptism the person swears to be a Christian (*CWE* 66, 75), and that this applies to everyone, to the man of the world—young or old, married or single, poor or rich, even courtier or prince—as much as to the priest or the monk (*CWE* 66, 57): "This is the common profession of all Christians" (*CWE* 66, 58).

Not long before, in <March> 1499, Erasmus had written a letter (also published in the *Lucubratiunculae*) to the ten-year-old Lord of Veere, Adolph of Burgundy, admonishing him to practice an all-encompassing *pietas*: "Let it be one of your firmest convictions that nothing so well becomes the noble and well-born as piety," despite those who think and say that Christ's teaching (*Christi doctrinam*) should be left to priests and monks (Ep 93:107–9).[24] In the *Enchiridion* he addresses also the married man, advising him to love his wife "above all because you perceive in her the image of Christ" (*CWE* 66, 53); "no longer love her in herself but in Christ, or rather Christ in her" (*CWE* 66, 54). But the *pietas* that Erasmus proposes is not exclusively for the laity but all Christians, whatever their state in life. Thus when speaking of the virtue of chastity he writes:

If you are a priest, bear in mind that you have been totally consecrated to the celebration of divine rites (*CWE* 66, 116).... If you are married, consider how worthy of respect is an unsullied marriage-bed and make every effort possible that your marriage imitates the hallowed wedding of Christ and the church, of which your marriage is a reflection, and therefore should be as free as possible of all immorality and filled with fecundity (*CWE* 66, 117).

And Erasmus goes on in the same paragraph: "If you are young.... If you are a woman.... If a man.... If an old man...."

After stating that life is a warfare and that all Christians are committed to this struggle by virtue of their baptism, Erasmus goes on to encourage the Christian, who is aware of the enemy's powers, to be "conscious also of the presence of [the] divine helper" and of the weapons available for the struggle. "These two weapons are prayer and knowledge" (*CWE* 66, 30); "Prayer is the more effective of the two, since it is a conversation with God, but

---

24. To be found in *Lucubratiunculae*, Strasbourg, 1516, 175 (BL 3837, c. 34); *EE* 1, *Ep.* 93; and in *CWE* 1, letter 93; see also Charles Fantazzi, Introductory note to the *Enchiridion*, *CWE* 66, 2.

knowledge is no less necessary." This "knowledge," for Erasmus, is the study
of scripture; but—in line with what he had written in the *Antibarbari*—
he adds,

I should certainly not disapprove a kind of preliminary training in the writing
of the pagan poets and philosophers... These writings ... provide an admirable
preparation for the understanding of the divine Scriptures. (*CWE* 66, 33)

In summary, Erasmus proposes in the *Enchiridion* that Christian *pietas*
(often translated as "holiness," or simply "Christian life"),[25] which is to be
practiced by all, consists not so much in specific religious practices as in the
exercise of the Christian virtues, which are to be lived in all states of life,
including marriage and worldly affairs; and in the struggle to do so, the two
weapons are prayer and learning—mainly the knowledge of scripture, but
also of classical pagan authors.

Although Thomas More shared this vision, we can hardly conclude
that his marriage in 1505 was a direct consequence of reading the *Lucubratiunculae*. The *Enchiridion* is dated in 1501, but "the germination and
maturation of the work in the mind of its author can be traced to some
extent between the early months of 1499 and the publication of the *Lucubratiunculae* in February 1503."[26] Erasmus may have discussed his ideas
with Colet and More during his stay in England in 1499. Indeed, arguably
in this More was not a disciple but a real "exemplar" of Erasmus's vision, so
that in his prefatory letter to the 1518 edition he writes that

among those who have married twice [a clear reference to More], there are some
whom Christ thinks worthy of the first circle [of holiness]. (*CWE* 66, 16)[27]

And of the twenty-two rules that Erasmus offers in his *Enchiridion*, the
first two are very much in tune with More's later behavior:

---

25. The classical virtue of *pietas* (cf. Virgil's *Aeneas*) is reverence toward one's parents and relatives
(as used by Erasmus of More in his letter of July 23, 1519: see Ep.999: 196), toward one's Fatherland,
and toward the god. Erasmus uses the words *pius* or *pietas* over 100 times in the *Enchiridion*, rendered
in fifty different ways in one of the first English translations (1534): "godliness," "holiness," "charitable
living," "virtuous" or "devout life," and "genuine piety" are equivalents suggested by John O'Malley in
his Introduction to *CWE* 66, ix–xxv, where he analyzes the different nuances given by Erasmus. In its
most elevated meaning, *pietas* refers to the unity between one's faith and one's behavior; and in this
sense Erasmus refers to More as an example of true piety (*verae pietatis*: Ep.999: 271) and someone
who applied his whole mind to the pursuit of piety (*ad pietatis studium*: Ep.999: 160); that is, ulti-
mately a total identification of a man with the will of God, for him.

26. Charles Fantazzi, Introductory note to the *Enchiridion*, *CWE* 66, 2.

27. In addition, his editor considers that Erasmus's views were probably influenced by his friendship with More: see John W. O'Malley, Introduction to the books on *Spiritualia*, *CWE* 66, xxxv.

The first rule should be to understand fully what the Scriptures tell us about Christ and his Spirit, and to believe this not only by mere lip service, not coldly or listlessly or hesitantly, as does the common lot of Christians, but with your whole heart. (*CWE* 66, 55)

The second is that you enter upon the road of salvation not hesitantly or timidly, but with resolute purpose, wholeheartedly, and with a trusting and, so to speak, gladiatorial heart, ready to suffer the loss of your fortunes or your life for Christ's sake. (*CWE* 66, 56).

—

The view of marriage proposed in the previous paragraphs may have been Thomas More's conclusion from studying *De civitate Dei* and from his knowledge of the teaching of St. John Chrysostom and other Fathers of the Church. What is striking is that More refers often to his marriage in his letters and other writings and shows a deep appreciation of marriage and, in particular, of his choice of wife.

A good example of this tendency can be seen in More's letter to Thomas Ruthal, in which he dedicates to him his translations of Lucian's dialogues from Greek into Latin. The translations were done, as we have seen, together with Erasmus while Erasmus was staying in More's house in the city, and More describes these Latin versions of Lucian as the "first fruits" of his Greek studies. It might have been expected that these exercises would remain in the realm of the scholarly work of the two humanists, or even as their joint hobby. Yet in the very first paragraph of the letter, More writes:

For just as among girls [*e virginibus*] all men do not love the same one, but each has his own preference as fancy dictates and adores not the one he can prove is best but the one who seems best to him—so of the most agreeable dialogues of Lucian, one man likes a certain one best, another prefers another.

Does this not sound as if More—while writing about Lucian—was thinking of Jane Colt, his own "best choice"? The same implication can be detected in More's poem advising Candidus, "How to choose a Wife":

> Nec quisquam habet magis
> Quam qui sibi satis
> Quodcunque habet, putat.

"No man," he says, "possesses more than he who is content with what he has." And immediately More refers to his own wife:

> Sic nunc me amet mea,
> Ut nil ego tibi,
> Amice, mentiar.

"May my own wife cease to love me if I am not telling you the truth, my friend."[28]

Similarly, More mentions his wife in all three of his three extant letters to Peter Giles.[29] Two of them are especially relevant because they are "public letters" published in *Utopia*: one serves as preface in all the early editions, and the other was included at the end of the second edition (Paris, 1517). Likewise, at the beginning of his first book of apologetics, the *Dialogue* of 1529,[30] More makes a point of stating that he had married twice.

I do not intend to write here about Thomas More as husband and father: this is a subject that I have already mentioned (albeit only in passing) in a study published in *Moreana*.[31] My point here is simply that More seems keen to state that he is a married man, even when writing about other, apparently unrelated, topics.

This is very evident in his letters to his friend Frans van Cranevelt, in which he often mentions Cranevelt's wife in terms that only a married man can address another:

As for my lady your wife, or rather your lady my wife since I betrothed myself to her there long since—and seriously, she is a woman of the highest dignity, complete adorned with the ornaments by giving birth and that your family has been increased by offspring....

But he corrects himself and returns to speaking of—"my lady, your wife"—and ends up asking his friend to give warmest regards to "your most charming wife" (Letter LCB 49/B 50, April 9, <1521>).[32] He continues in the same vein in other letters: "Give my regards to our lady and wife" (Letter LCB 93/B 95, November 12, <1521>); though on other occasions he just writes, "greet your most excellent wife" (Letter [135], August 10, <1524>);[33] but continues jokingly, "farewell, together with the wife who is mine by day and yours by night; but the lady of us both" (Letter [139], June 6, <1525>); "Give best regards to your lady wife, and likewise mine" (Letter [142], February 22, <1526>). Ending the series of letters that have reached us, he again corrects himself: "Please give my regards to my lady,

---

28. Poem no. 143, in *CW* 3, II.

29. *Correspondence*, letters [25], [41a], and [47].

30. *CW* 6, 53, l, 1.

31. Mitjans, "*Non sum Oedipus, sed Morus,*" 12–67.

32. See letters edited by Clarence H. Miller, in *Moreana*, no. 117 (March–April 1994), 3–66, and Hubertus Schulte Herbrüggen, "More to Cranevelt," in *Supplementa Humanistica Lovaniensia* (Leuven: Leuven University Press, 1997), 141–96. Herbrüggen uses the LCB series numbers, while Miller follows the old B series.

33. In this letter More also mentions Vives, who had married on May 26 of that year.

your wife (for I do not dare to reverse the order again)" (Letter [163], June 10, 1528).

More's jovial references to his married state can be found even in his epitaph, which reads:

> Here lies Joanna, the beloved little wife of Thomas More,
> I intend that this same tomb shall be Alice's and mine, too.
> One, my wife in my youthful years,
> has made me father of a son and three daughters;
> the other has been as devoted to her stepchildren
> (a rare achievement in a stepmother)
> as very few mothers are to their own children.
> The one lived out her life with me, the other still lives with me:
> I cannot decide whether I did love the one or do love the other more.
> O, how happily we could have lived all three together
> if fate and religion permitted.
> The grave will unite us however,
> and I pray that heaven will unite us too.
> Thus death will give what life could not.[34]

Another recurrent topic in More's reference to marriage is the good of having children and bringing them up for the benefit of society. The poem to Candidus on how to choose a wife has already been cited; there he writes, "Let her be fruitful and add sweet children to your most splendid line. Your father did as much for you."[35] In *Utopia*, he writes of those who choose marriage because they consider that they "owe children to their country."[36] And writing to Frans van Cranevelt in 1524, More says:

I offer hearty congratulations that your family has been increased by new off-spring, and indeed I do so not only for your sake but also on behalf of the commonwealth, to which it is very important which parents enlarge it with the most numerous progeny, for from you only the best can be born.[37]

In chapter 9, More's decision to follow the active life of the humanist was illustrated with reference to a passage from *Utopia*. But he started writing *Utopia* when on a royal mission to the Low Countries in 1515, while I have suggested that his decision was taken before he married in January 1505.

34. According to Rastell, it was written c. 1512: see Appendix: "Two Epitaphs in Chelsea Old Church."

35. *CW* 3.II, Poem no. 143, 17–20.

36. *CW* 4, 227.

37. *Moreana*, no. 117 (March–April 1994), Letter no. 115, trans. Miller.

As Edward Surtz notes in the introduction to *CW* 4, the sources of *Utopia* are innumerable. The main classical sources are Plato and Plutarch, but the influence of Cicero, Seneca, Lucian, and Tacitus can also be seen, as well as, among patristic works, St. Augustine's *City of God*. More lectured on the latter work c. 1501. As we saw, a knowledge of Lucian's *Philosophies Going Cheap* can be ascertained in the *Pageant Verses* <1499–1505>, and with it the word "Utopia" in Socrates's mouth. More specifically, I argued that *Utopia* is a response to St. John Chrysostom's reference to Plato's *Republic* in his *Commentaries on the Gospel of St. Matthew*; and we have seen the parallel between the first paragraph of *Utopia* and the first paragraph of More's letter of October 23, <1502–4> discussed in chapter 1. So I think it is safe to state that More became acquainted with most of his sources for *Utopia* during his period of study between 1499 and his marriage in January 1505.

More wrote on marriage much later in defense of the Church's teaching, first under a pseudonym in his *Responsio ad Lutherum* in 1523 and then in his own name in his *Dialogue against the teachings of Luther and Tyndale* in 1529 and his *Confutation of Tyndale's Answer* of 1532. In these three books he emphasizes that marriage is a sacrament included in the New Testament together with baptism, confirmation, and the other sacraments.[38]

The most extensive reference to marriage is to be found in book I of the *Confutation*, in which More deals systematically with the seven sacraments, quoting Tyndale's arguments one by one and refuting them.[39] He begins with the statement that "this holy sacrament of matrymonye was bygone by god in paradyse" (Gn 2:24; Mt 19:4–6). He goes on to explain that God instituted it to signify both the union ("coniunccyon") between God himself and the soul and that between Christ and his Church; for this reason, St. Paul describes it as a great sacrament (Eph 5:32), and it has always been accepted as such by the Church. He also makes the rather less conventional comment that, although God gives more grace to the souls of those who refrain from matrimony for his sake, "yet in that couplying of matrymonye (yf they couple in hym) he couplet hym selfe also to theyr soules wyth grace": that is, through grace, God also unites himself to the souls of the spouses when they marry, as long as they are doing so for holy reasons. The

---

38. See, e.g., *CW* 5, 220, 286, 382, 622, 664, 666, 668, 670; *CW* 6, 190; *CW* 8, 12:18, 15:18, 86–87, 296–98, 306–7, 843:25–28.

39. *CW* 8, 86–87.

sacramental grace helps to make their marriage virtuous and helps also in the bringing up of the children "as shall come bytwene them."[40]

All this is a reply to Tyndale's *Answer*. Tyndale—as More is fair enough to quote, though in abbreviated form—does acknowledge some positive aspects of marriage as instituted by God for the increase of the human race and for the mutual help of the spouses with all love and kindness; but he denies that it is a sacrament or that it was called a sacrament in scripture.[41] More, in his reply, emphasizes that marriage is a sacrament, being called such in St. Paul's Letter to the Ephesians, and so is a means of union with God. While Tyndale sees only that spouses do not sin in the marriage act, More points out that matrimony is a channel of grace.

More goes on to say that God's blessing given to our first parents in paradise was effective "not in the bodye onely of reasonable folke, but mych more effectually to excercyse his strength in the reasonable soule," conveying the idea that marriage is a union not only of bodies but also of souls; and that to those who bind themselves in the "holy knot" of matrimony, God gives them the grace to keep it, and decrees that they should do so.

This vision of married couples searching together for holiness we can, perhaps, see echoed by Erasmus in his letter to Margaret Roper of Christmas Day, 1523:

God will not … despise the singing of praises by such a married pair, whose life shows such innocence, such concord, such tranquillity, so much so that it would be unlikely to find people who profess virginity[42] who would dare to compare themselves with you. A rare sight, especially in this age of ours; but I foresee it soon spreading more widely. In your own country you have a queen who might be the Calliope of your saintly choir, and in Germany too there are families of no mean station who practise with success the life of which you have given hitherto such a successful example. Farewell, not least among the glories of your generation and your native England, and mind you give my greetings to all the members of your choir.[43]

It is clear, then, from his references to St. John Chrysostom and St. Augustine, his correspondence and other writings, and his replies to the writings of Luther and Tyndale that More considered marriage not just as the ordinary setting for the *faithful folk* (as he puts it in the chapter on mar-

40. *CW* 8, 86:7–22.

41. Tyndale's text as quoted by More is in *CW* 8, 85:30–86:5; the full text is given in the Commentary, *CW* 8, 1,495.

42. The original, *virginitatis professores* (*EE* 5, Ep.1404.22), means "those who profess" or "make a public declaration" or "take a vow" of virginity, as translated in *CWE*.

43. *EE* 5, *Ep.* 1404, my translation taking into account that given in *CWE* 10, *Ep.* 1404.

riage in the *Confutation*) to practice their Christian lives with God's blessing (as it is also assumed by Luther and Tyndale), but a means of union with God, and therefore a path to holiness. It is interesting to note also that when More attempts to give a more complete exposition on marriage he points out that through the grace of the sacrament God helps the spouses toward the good education and upbringing of their offspring.

11

Life's Pilgrimage

Ever since the death of Thomas More, there has been a constant flow of people who considered him a saint; both in England and throughout Europe, they have ensured the continuity of his memory as a scholar and a man of integrity.[1]

It is probably true that More's family did not understand his attitude at the time of his trial and death. Even Margaret, his eldest daughter and confidante, took the oath her father refused. Immediately after the execution, however, the news was known in London and elsewhere, specifically through *The Paris News Letter* produced in French[2] dated in Paris on July 23, 1535, just seventeen days after More's beheading. *The News Letter* was translated into German and Spanish as well as in Latin—*Exposition fidelis de morte D. Thomae Mori et quorumdam aliorum insignium virorum in Anglia*. The Latin version was published in Paris in August 1535, and by Froben in Basel that same year. It was reprinted in Antwerp in 1536. Already around 1540, just five years after More's execution, Dom Maurice Chauncy speaks of John Fisher and Thomas More as saints in his history of the Carthusian martyrs.

Dr. John Clement, who had married Margaret Giggs, adopted daughter of Thomas More, seems to have been the first of More's circle to go into exile under Edward VI; he fled in July 1549 to Louvain, where he was joined in October by his wife, and in December by their daughter Winifred and her husband, William Rastell, More's nephew. One of More's closest

---

1. See James McConica, "The Recusant Reputation of Thomas More," *Canadian Catholic Historical Association*, Report 30 (1963): 47–61, and John Guy, *Reputations*, chapter 1.

2. The *Paris News Letter* is reproduced as Appendix II in Harpsfield, 253–66.

friends in London, Antonio Buonvisi, had taken flight to Antwerp by September 25 of the same year and later settled in Louvain, where his house became effectively the center of those who kept More's memory alive.[3] Nicholas Harpsfield joined them in 1550 and thereby learned about More.[4] Winifred died in 1553; her husband and her parents (William Rastell and the Clements) returned to England in 1554. Buonvisi chose to remain in Louvain; he died in December 1558. Rastell had prepared More's *English Works* during his stay in Louvain and published them in London in 1557; and Harpsfield wrote his biography of More in England. After the accession of Elizabeth I, Rastell and the Clements again went into exile in Louvain; they were joined by John Harris, More's secretary, who had married Dorothy Colley (Margaret Roper's maid) and had been the head of a school in Bristol after More's death. Rastell prepared the publication of More's *Latin Works*, first printed in Louvain in 1565.

John and Margaret Clement, William and Winifred Rastell, John and Dorothy Harris, and Antonio Buonvisi had known More for many years and had a firm conviction of his holiness. For them, however, he was not a saint because he was a martyr; rather, he had received the gift of martyrdom because all his life he had tried with God's grace to seek holiness, to be a lover of God. Recent scholars have reached the same conclusion: thus the last lines of John Guy's *The Public Career of Sir Thomas More* (1980) are:

Yet by suffering torment for the truth he had discovered, More gave posterity an assurance that it was not an illusion. When the axe finally fell on July 6, 1535, "the king's good servant" also earned his place among the very few who have enlarged the horizon of the human spirit.[5]

Gerard Wegemer, in the introduction to his biography of Thomas More, suggests (following Erasmus, Roper, and Stapleton) that More trained himself from an early age to grow in virtue and that he persisted in that training throughout his life. What he did is the focus of Wegemer's book *A Portrait of Courage*. Rather less ambitiously, I have tried only to show the origins and meaning of that early training, with the suggestion that Thomas More became aware first that every Christian is called to seek the love of God even to the contempt of self, and second that in his case this seeking was to take place in a secular environment, as a married

3. Frederick E. Smith, "'A Fownde Patrone and Second Father' of the Marian Church: Antonio Buonvisi, Religious Exile and Mid-Tudor Catholicism," *British Catholic History* 34, no. 4 (2018): 222–46.

4. Hitchcock, Introduction to Harpsfield, clxxx.

5. Guy, *Public Career of Sir Thomas More*, 203.

man, and in service of the commonwealth. I have not intended in any way to consider More's successes or failures with regard to the plan of life he mapped out for himself, but only to ascertain the choices he made in his early life: he became aware of the need to search for holiness as a married man, choosing both the active life of the humanist in service of the city *and* the contemplative life of a Christian.

It is not easy to find an explicit statement of this awareness in the writings of a layman: the contemplative life of a layman tends to pass unnoticed on account of his very condition. In a young man these aspirations may be discovered in his poetry; and this is, in fact, the case of the Latin verses of the Poet that end More's *Pageant Verses* and his additions to the *Life of Pico*: "The first point is to love but one alone." More's spiritual life becomes more visible at the end of his life, and we can see a particular manifestation of it in his last work, *De tristitia tedio pauore et oratione Christi ante captionem eius*, written in the Tower of London. More starts his book with a paraphrase of the words of the gospel: "When Jesus had said these things, they recited the hymn and went out to the Mount of Olives"; and he comments that Jesus went up a mountain to pray,

teaching us by this sign [*significans*] that, when we prepare ourselves to pray, we must lift up our minds from the bustling confusion of human concerns to the contemplation of heavenly things (fol. 2ᵛ–3).[6]

For More, going up the mountain in this passage has a spiritual significance. In his letter to Colet of October 23, <1502–4>, he had appeared confused by the *forenses strepitus*; in *De tristitia* he wrote similarly of the *tumultum rerum humanarum* (fol. 2ᵛ–3), but he knew now that, as taught by St. John Chrysostom, going up the mountain does not imply a change of physical setting, because the Christian is to practice Christ's teaching in the *forum et urbs*, in the marketplace and in the city; indeed, More quoted Boethius on the need of "raising the mind to heaven, lest the soul look downwards to the earth."

More goes on to note that after Jesus had spoken of holy things at the Last Supper he went out to the Mount of Olives to pray, as was his custom (fol. 2ᵛ), implying the need to dedicate set times to prayer (as Erasmus tells us was in fact More's practice). But he adds in the following pages that he wishes that

6. Citations from *De tristitia* are given from the Valencia holograph manuscript as it appears in *CW* 14, ed. Clarence H. Miller, and in Tomás Moro, *De Tristitia Christi*, ed. Francisco Calero (Valencia: Ayuntamiento de Valencia, 1984).

whatever our bodies may be doing we would at the same time constantly lift up our minds to God (which is the most acceptable form of prayer). For no matter where we may turn our steps, as long as our minds are directed to God, we clearly do not turn away from Him who is present everywhere (fol. 34^v–35).

In this context More wrote that the Christian can pray while walking: *quacumque nos "ambulando" uertimus* (fol. 35: 2–3), and *istas ita dictas "ambulando" preces* (fol. 35: 10–11), phrases that connect again with the start of his letter of October 23, <1502–4>: *Ambulanti mihi dudum in foro.* Was he then praying on what his choice had to be? Clearly, he was searching for it. But while he writes that the Christian has to be always at prayer whatever else he is doing, he returns to the need of spending specific periods of meditation, "for which we prepare our minds more thoughtfully" (*ut tali meditatione preparetur animus,* fol. 35:12–13); without such set times of prayer, a constant awareness of God's presence is not possible. And it is the example of Christ's prayer that is the main topic of More's last written work.

Here, however, More refers to Jean Gerson, a man he considered "an outstanding scholar and a most gentle handler of troubled consciences" (fol. 79), and he takes up an example given by Gerson in his book *De oratione et eius valore*: that of a man setting out on pilgrimage to the shrine of St. James in Compostela. More explains that the pilgrim is journeying and at the same time meditating on the saint's life and the purpose of the pilgrimage, and so throughout this whole time is continuing his pilgrimage by a double act, namely (here More says that he is using Gerson's own words) a "natural continuity" and a "moral continuity": natural, because he is actually and in fact moving toward the shrine; moral, because his thoughts are occupied with the matter of his pilgrimage.

By "moral" Gerson refers to the moral intention by which the act of setting out—which is neither good nor bad in itself—is perfected by the pious reason for the journey. Sometimes, of course, the pilgrim walks along considering other matters, without thinking at all about the saint or the shrine; then the natural act of walking is informed and imbued with moral virtue because it is implicitly accompanied by the good intention formed at the beginning, since all this action follows from the first decision. At other times the moral act takes place when there is no natural act: for example, when the pilgrim thinks about his pilgrimage when he is perhaps sitting and not walking. Finally, it also happens that both kinds of acts are missing: for example, when the pilgrim is asleep, for then he is performing neither the natural act of walking nor the moral act of meditating on the pilgrimage. But even then, the moral virtue remains as a habitual virtue, just as long as it is not deliberately renounced. So the pilgrimage is never actually interrupted in such a way that its merit does not persist, unless the pilgrim makes an opposite decision, either to give up the pilgrimage entirely or at least to put it off until another time.

And so, More concludes, from this image Gerson draws the same consideration about prayer—namely, that once it has been begun attentively it will not afterward be so interrupted that the virtue of the first intention does not persist, as long as it is not relinquished by making a decision to stop. Hence More writes that Gerson says that Christ's words, "You should pray always and not cease," were not spoken figuratively but literally, and they are actually and literally fulfilled by good men. Gerson supports his opinion with the well-known adage, "Whoever lives well is always praying";[7] the adage is true, More explains, because whoever follows St. Paul's precept "whether you eat or drink, or whatever you do, do all to the glory of God" (1 Cor 10:31), once he has begun praying attentively, never afterward interrupts his prayer (fol. 79v–81v).

The editor of *De Tristitia Christi* points out that More probably had the text of Gerson's *De oratione et eius valore* before him as he wrote,[8] and also notes that, covering almost exactly the same ground, More wrote over twice as much as Gerson,[9] which suggests that he was very much taken by the analogy. We know that More did go on pilgrimage himself (always on foot, Stapleton recounts),[10] and he defends the practice in his *Dialogue* of 1529. If the life of prayer is similar to going on pilgrimage, which is not interrupted even when the wayfarer stops and sits down or sleeps, then the image also applies to being a contemplative in the midst of the earthly occupations. As Thomas Aquinas teaches in the *Secunda Secundae* (a work well known by More),[11] "The term 'contemplative' is applied not to those who simply contemplate, but to those who dedicate their whole lives to contemplation,"[12] who direct all their actions to God; and that contem-

---

7. The Explanatory Note given in *CW* 14 reads, "*Glossa ordinaria* on 1 Thess 5:17 cites Augustine: *Iustus enim nunquam desinit orare: nisi desinat iustus esse: semper orat qui semper bene agit.* The same saying also appears in *Glossa ordinaria* on Luke 18:1. Bonaventure (*Opera Omnia,* 7, 448b) cites the gloss on both passages."

8. *CW* 14, 765n1.

9. *CW* 14, 765n2.

10. Stapleton, 64.

11. Stapleton, 35.

12. *ST* II-II, q. 81, a. 1 ad 5: *"contemplative" dicuntur, non qui contemplantur, sed qui contemplationi total vitam suam deputant.*

plation is not interrupted by dealing with other occupations, provided that they are done for God's glory—just as More says in *De tristitia*.

More had already made use of the simile of the pilgrimage in a previous work, *A Treatise upon the Passion*,[13] which he began in English and left unfinished when imprisoned in April 1534. The *Treatise* starts quoting the Letter to the Hebrews: *Non habemus hic civitatem manentem, sed futuram inquirimus* ("Here we have no lasting city, but we seek the city which is to come" [Heb 13:14]).[14] And More writes that, in order

> to regard much the world to come, we need to consider that in that world we shall be forever at home and that in this world we are but wayfaring folk.

He goes on to pray that we might "reckon ourselves for no dwellers but for pilgrims upon earth, that we may long and make haste … to come to the glorious country,"[15] and consequently,

> as no man can come to Canterbury by the bare knowledge of the way there if he will sit still at home, so by knowing the way to heaven we can never the more come there but if we will walk therein.[16]

In More's analogy between the life of prayer and the pilgrimage, he points out that the value of the pilgrimage comes from faithfulness to the "good intention formed at the beginning, since all this motion follows from the first decision" (fol. 80^v)—that is, in the case of More, from his early choice to be a wholehearted lover of God. To start off on a pilgrimage, according to More in *De tristitia*, you need first to decide to do so.

In considering Thomas More's choices with regard to his spiritual life, we can distinguish a number of stages. First, there was his early piety, which came from his background and environment and the education he received at school and under the guidance of Morton, and which showed itself, for instance, in his early verses in which he speaks of the love of God that endures forever: *Qui manet … semper amore dei*. Next came a genuine desire to do God's will, as can be seen in his letter to Holt. This readiness to seek out what God's will was for him led him to prayer and study and to make use of personal spiritual guidance from such men as John Colet and William Grocyn. After this, once he had undertaken a demanding spiritual path, he became aware that he was being asked to set his love "unto God,"

---

13. For this text I use a modernized version based on Garry E. Haupt, ed., *The Tower Works* (New Haven: Yale University Press, 1980).

14. Haupt, *Tower Works*, 4.

15. Haupt, *Tower Works*, 103.

16. Haupt, *Tower Works*, 113.

that God was asking him for complete self-surrender: "Part will He none, but either all or naught" (Ballade 1:7). Through prayer and study—specifically, I have suggested, by his study of *De civitate Dei* and other works of St. Augustine and of St. John Chrysostom—he realized that this self-surrender was to take place in secular surroundings: called, like all Christians, to a contemplative life, he was to respond to that call in the middle of the world, as a layman.

More's love of letters was an important crux for him. Dedicating himself to the scholarly work of the new Christian humanism together with his friends, Colet, Erasmus, Linacre, Lily, and others, was a very attractive proposition: after all, it was through this scholarship and these friends that he had become aware of his call to holiness. He faced and resolved the dilemma between the contemplative life of the philosopher, as exemplified by Pico della Mirandola, and the active life of service to the city. The dilemma, formulated famously by St. Augustine both in *De civitate Dei* when speaking of Plato and in the *Confessions* when speaking of himself, More portrayed in his description of the attitude of fictional Raphael Hythloday in book I of *Utopia*. More chose service to the city *and*, no less, the contemplative life of a Christian in the midst of the world.

With this determination clearly engraved on his mind, as he wrote in his love ballade, Thomas More married, formed a family, and became fully involved in the service of the city. He faced a number of choices—first of all, the daily ones arising from the commitments acquired with his wife, family, and the practice of his profession.[17] Some of these had greater repercussions: how to look after his family when his first wife died, for instance, or how to respond to the invitation to enter royal service. Nevertheless, he remained very much in control of his life. Whether to marry again or not was a matter he would have to consider in conscience, thinking over the various pros and cons; but in the end it was up to him, an issue in which he had freedom of choice. But at some stage he was confronted with other options, in which he maintained his freedom, but his choice had already been made: "Part will He none, but either all or naught": he had to renounce his position as lord chancellor, to accept martyrdom, and thus enter the heavenly city:

In that city, then, there shall be free will.[18]

17. See letter to Peter Giles that prefaces *Utopia*.
18. Augustine, *De civitate Dei*, last chapter: bk XXII, ch. 30.

The Calling of the Common People

Throughout this study, I have been considering the early writings of Thomas More to try to gain an insight into his early choices. My reading has suggested to me that More felt he had received a call to serve Christendom as a humanist, as part of his wider call to holiness as a Christian and as a married layman. The response to one's vocation as a life project has a definite starting point, as Cicero notes, with his remark that the choice usually takes place in youth,[19] even if it changes over time.[20] From a Christian perspective, rather than a simple choice based on nature and fortune or circumstances (as in Cicero's *De Officiis*), vocation implies awareness of a calling that requires a free response by the one called; and that awareness is largely the fruit of a life of prayer and, in More's case, also of the study of the Fathers.

More's awareness of his calling is seen in the first line of the first stanza of his ballade, the *Twelve Properties of a Lover*:[21] that "The first point is to love but one alone." In his second stanza he applied this "point" to the love of God:

> So thou that has thy love set unto God
> In thy remembrance this imprint and engrave:
> As He in sovereign dignity is unique,
> So with He in love no parting fellows have.
> Love Him therefore with all that He thee gave
> For body, soul, wit, cunning, mind and thought,
> Part wills He none but either all or naught.

More's understanding of vocation comes through in these seven lines. To respond to God's call implies loving God in the totality of one's being, "body, soul, wit, cunning, mind and thought"; the sovereign God has a right to demand that one love him wholeheartedly, without sharing that love with others. This is the consequence of the determination made to have "thy love set unto God": if you have made that resolution, says More, then engrave it in your memory. To this initial determination and consequent remembrance, a third element is involved in the awareness of vocation—that is, perseverance, which is what More describes as going on pilgrimage having always the end in mind. Cicero emphasizes this aspect

19. Cicero, *De Officiis*, bk I, xxxii, no. 117.
20. Cicero, *De Officiis*, bk I, xxxiii, no. 120.
21. The *Twelve Properties of a Lover* are further discussed in chapter 5.

in the passage of *De Officiis* already cited, writing that once a person has chosen his plan of life—*deligendo genere vitae*—he should stick to it consistently.[22]

More's view of the Christian vocation, however, comes across more clearly and in more detail in his *Letter to a Monk* (1519), in which he speaks of the calling of the "common people."[23] He begins by praising the religious orders:

I have no doubt at all that there is no good man anywhere who does not feel a great deal of heartfelt esteem for all the religious orders, and certainly I myself have always regarded them not only with love but also with the utmost reverence.[24]

Nevertheless, his reverence does not prevent him from delivering a forceful rebuttal to the anonymous monk's virulent attack on Erasmus's life and works.[25] In the course of his reply, More points to the active life of the apostles;[26] he notes ironically that the essence of holiness does not consist in staying glued to one rock all the time, like an oyster or sponge;[27] and he also criticizes those religious who do not practice the way of life proper to their state. In this context More emphasizes what is

common to the whole Christian people, such as those common virtues of faith, hope, charity, fear of God, humility, and others of similar kind.[28]

These are the "common virtues of Christianity,"[29] he explains, and adds:

A truly Christian faith through which Christ Jesus' name is truly uttered in the spirit, a truly Christian hope which despairs of its own merits and put all its trust in the generosity of God, and a truly Christian charity which is not puffed up, which does not become angry, which does not seek its own glory, are not to be had, however, by anyone except through God's grace and gratuitous favour alone.[30]

Thomas More was an outstanding scholar, writer, and statesman, and he died a martyr: he can hardly be called an "average man"—and yet, when

---

22. Cicero, *De Officiis*, bk I, xxxiii, no. 120.
23. *CW* 15, 280:11.
24. *CW* 15, 274:31–276:3.
25. See *CW* 15, xli.
26. *CW* 15, 294:25, 302:1.
27. *CW* 15, 294:18–20.
28. *CW* 15, 280:10–13.
29. *CW* 15, 302:22–23.
30. *CW* 15, 302:17–22.

speaking of the Christian vocation, he considers it the lot of the common people.

Comforting Those in Need

An overview of some of More's written works is required in order to grasp More's concern for the common people. In *Utopia* More reflects over the active life versus the contemplative life of the philosopher. "The contemplative life was a life of pride and self-interest. The active life, on the other hand, demonstrated attention to what was held in common,"[31] and More, in *Utopia*, advances a "political philosophy" for the pursue of the common good.

Most of the subsequent works published by More were in response to the works and requests of others. The first one in his name against the reformers is his reply to the Lutheran John Bugenhagen (1526). Bugenhagen, also known as Pomeranus, had addressed his letter "To the Saints in England," and More starts his answer saying:

I am against my will, as far removed from those who truly deserve such noble title as I am glad to remove myself from the only ones you regard saint, Pomeranus. For I see that nothing is sacred to you except the Lutheran sect.[32]

And goes on to point out to Bugenhagen that there are no grounds to speak of a new reception of the gospel; for the gospel of Christ is what the four evangelists wrote, all the ancient leaders of the Church interpreted, and the "whole Christian world for more than fifteen hundred years has understood and taught as the gospel."[33]

To the petition of the bishop of London to write in defense of orthodoxy he responded by writing his *Dialogue* of 1529, which was answered by William Tyndale, and More replied with *The Confutation of Tyndale's Answer*, books I–III, addressed to the "Christian reader."[34] To Simon Fish's *Supplication for the Beggars* he answered with *The Supplication of Souls*, addressed "To all good chryten people."[35] In these works More spoke of the "common consent of the Church."[36] In the words of Eamon Duffy, More

31. Paul, *Thomas More*, 57.
32. *CW* 7, 12:12–16.
33. *CW* 7, 14:23–32.
34. *CW* 8, 3:1.
35. *CW* 7, 111:1.
36. *CW* 6, 169:32; Brian Gogan, *The Common Corps of Christendom: Ecclesiological Themes in the Writings of Sir Thomas More* (Leiden: Brill, 1982); Paul, *Thomas More*, chapter 4, "The Common Corps of Christendom."

"comes forward as the champion of the religion of ordinary Christian men and women."[37] More wrote them with the authority of being at the service of the king, first as chancellor of the Duchy of Lancaster and, from October 1529, as lord chancellor of England.

On May 16, 1532, More resigned as lord chancellor, but he continued writing in the same vein. In the early months of 1533 he completed the publication of *The Confutation of Tyndale's Answer*, books IV–VIII. To Christopher St. German's *A Treatise concerning the Division between the Spirituality and Temporality*, More replied in the *Apology* (Eastertide 1533); St. German answered with his *Salem and Bizance*, and More replied again in turn with *The Debellation of Salem and Bizance* (October 1533). And finally, More's *Answer to a Poisoned Book* in December 1533 is a confutation of George Joye's *Super of the Lord*, which is the last of his polemical works against heresy. All these responses were addressed to the Christian reader.[38]

—

The beginning of 1534 marked a new turn in More's life. In July 1533 Elizabeth Barton, known as the Holy Maid of Kent or the Nun of Kent, was taken to the Tower.[39] She was one of the most influential English religious figures of the day. Having been cured of epilepsy, she was credited with miraculous and prophetic powers and became the leader of a sort of Catholic revivalist movement. She had many followers, and the rich and powerful sought her advice. She predicted that if Henry VIII divorced Catherine he would lose his throne. On September 7 Pope Clement VII excommunicated Henry VIII. By then the king was in a rage, and in January 1534 he ordered that John Fisher and Thomas More be included in the Bill of Attainder against those who were supposed to have supported the nun. Around February 25 and again at the beginning of March, More wrote to Cromwell asserting his innocence from allegations that he had been involved with the Nun of Kent.[40] Early in March More appeared in front of a commission made up of Thomas Cranmer, archbishop of Canterbury, Thomas Cromwell, secretary of the Council, the Duke of Norfolk, and Sir Thomas Audley, lord chancellor, accused of involvement with the nun, which More denied.[41] On March 5 More wrote to the king declar-

37. Duffy, *Reformation Divided*, 74.
38. *CW* 9, 3:2; *CW* 10, 3:27; *CW* 11, 3:3.
39. Cf. Richard Rex, *Henry VIII* (Stroud, Gloucestershire: Amberly, 2009), 61–62, 68–72.
40. *Correspondence* [195 and 197].
41. Roper, 64:12–71:9.

ing his innocence from any involvement with her.[42] On Friday, March 6, the House of Lords refused to approve the Bill of Attainder and suggested to Henry that he withdraw the name of More. The following Thursday, March 12, after the name of More had been withdrawn, the lords accepted the Bill of Attainder, and Cromwell told William Roper to communicate the good news to More.[43] The bill was approved by the Commons on March 17, and Elizabeth Barton, together with her alleged accomplices, were executed in April at Tyburn.

On March 23 the Act of Succession was passed, and on March 30, Monday in Holy Week, before the Easter recess, it was given the royal assent, and a commission to administer the oath was issued to the archbishop of Canterbury, the lord chancellor, and the dukes of Norfolk and Suffolk.[44] On Monday, April 13, More was asked to swear the oath required by the act. He refused and was delivered into the custody of the Abbot of Westminster Abbey; on April 17 he was sent to the Tower of London. Thus, from the beginning of 1534 to Easter that year, More was not in a position to write in defense of orthodoxy with the authority he had had hitherto, insofar as he could not claim the king's favor any longer. In those circumstances, rather than ceasing to be concerned for others, he devised the plan of writing on the Passion of Christ, starting with *A Treatise upon the Passion*, for the edification of the ordinary Christian reader. The full title given by More is eleven lines long and reads:

A treatise historical, containing the bitter passion of our Saviour Christ, after the course and order of the four evangelists, with an exposition upon their words, taken for the more part out of the sayings of sundry good old holy doctors [ending] in the committing of His blessed body into His sepulchre.[45]

The treatise was to have a brief introduction (dealing with the creation and fall of the angels and of mankind, and the Holy Trinity's plan for the restoration of mankind) and several chapters, each divided into various lectures. But More did not finish it. A few days before his arrest, on April 5, 1534 (which was Easter Sunday), he wrote from Willesden to John Harris, his secretary, asking him to make some corrections to the manuscript: he had not brought it with him but left it in his house in Chelsea. He was aware of the danger of being arrested; when told in March that his name

---

42. *Correspondence* [198 and 199].

43. Roper, 71:9–16.

44. Richard Rex, *Henry VIII and the English Reformation*, 2nd ed. (Basingstoke: Palgrave Macmillan, 2006), 13.

45. *CW* 13, 3:4–14.

had been withdrawn from the Bill of Attainder against those accused of having supported the Nun of Kent, Elizabeth Barton, he commented to his daughter Margaret, "*quod differtur non aufertur*" (what is delayed is not taken away). Nevertheless, having begun work on his treatise in February, at the end of March[46] he put it aside to undertake what Peter Ackroyd describes as his "last pilgrimage."[47] He visited first his daughters Elizabeth and Cecily in Willesden (and presumably also visited the shrine of the Blessed Virgin there, which he mentioned in the *Dialogue* of 1529). On the following Sunday, April 12, he listened to a sermon at St. Paul's[48] and visited Margaret Giggs and her husband, John Clement, in London; on the way there he was summoned to appear the following day at Lambeth Palace to take the oath of the Act of Succession. As a result, More was unable to cover the whole account of the Passion, death, and burial of Christ as he had planned, but wrote only the four first chapters, ending with the preparation and institution of the Eucharist.

The *Treatise upon the Passion* has often been classified among the "Tower works," but it was not written in the Tower of London; on the contrary, it can be said with some confidence that More worked on it in Chelsea from the "Vigil of the Purification of our Blessed Lady," February 1, 1534, to the end of March and left it at Chelsea when he traveled to Willesden. Once in the Tower he wrote the long *Dialogue of Comfort against Tribulation*, as well as the brief *Treatise to Receive the Blessed Body of Our Lord Sacramentally and Virtually* and his last text, *De tristitia*. In the edition of the *English Works of Sir Thomas More* prepared by Rastell (1557), the *Treatise Upon the Passion* is placed after the *Dialogue of Comfort* and the *Treatise on the Blessed Body*, and all three of them are identified by Rastell as having been "made in the yere of our lorde, 1534, by syr Thomas More knyghte, while he was prysonner in the tower of London." This statement is not accurate, as we have seen.

Louis L. Martz suggests that the *Treatise on the Blessed Body* could be considered as completing the third lecture in chapter 4 of the *Treatise upon the Passion*, as that lecture is clearly unfinished. Nevertheless, even if this were the case, the *Treatise upon the Passion* would still be hardly more than a beginning of More's plan as described in his title. What seems clear is that

---

46. The Act of Succession entered into force on March 30, and a commission to administer the oath required by the act was issued to the archbishop of Canterbury, the lord chancellor, and the dukes of Norfolk and Suffolk; Rex, *Henry VIII and the English Reformation*, 13.

47. Peter Ackroyd, *The Life of Thomas More* (London: Chatto and Windus, 1998), 350.

48. Stapleton, 145.

he did not in fact try to complete the *Treatise upon the Passion*; instead, once in the Tower, he embarked upon a much larger but very different project, *A Dialogue of Comfort against Tribulation*.

In the *Dialogue of Comfort* More tries to give comfort to those who faced persecution for their faith in the face of the imminent tyranny of those who wanted to impose a new religion. More devised an imaginary setting for the *Dialogue* to avoid being identified as referring to the state of affairs in England in 1535 and in the following years, but also to be able to touch on many topics in a conversational way rather than as an academic treatise. This was the literary device used personally by Erasmus in the *Antibarbari* and by More himself in *Utopia* and the *Dialogue* of 1529. The fictional *Dialogue* takes place in the city of Buda, Hungary, between Anthony, a wise old man, and his nephew Vincent, who approaches his uncle faced with the feared coming persecution by the Turks, which in fact took place in 1529. More speaks through the mouth of Anthony. Interestingly in the first question put by Vincent he addresses Anthony in terms similar to those used by More in addressing Colet in his letter of <1502–4>. Vincent tells Anthony that since he will be going to God soon, he is going to leave his family and friends as a group of sorrowful and comfortless orphans, for by his good help, counsel, and comfort he had long been a great support to him, Vincent, and all his family, relatives, and friends; as cited at the beginning of this book, More had written to Colet thirty years earlier "what could be more grievous to me than to be deprived of your most pleasant companionship, whose prudent advice I enjoyed, by whose most delightful company I was refreshed, by whose powerful sermons I was stirred"; we see here that while years before he was seeking the comfort of his spiritual guide, now he is ready to give advice and comfort to his readers. And in his first reply to Vincent he says:

As for your taking so hard my departure from you, as that of someone you recognize out of your goodness as having given you much help and comfort, I wish to God that I had done for you, and for many others, half as much as I think I should have done. But for you to think that when God takes me you will then be comfortless, as though your chief comfort resided in me ... it is not I but God who is and must be your comfort. And a sure comfort he is. For as Christ said to his disciples, never would he leave his servants as comfortless orphans ... he also assured them that to the very end of the world he himself would constantly live with them.[49]

49. Translation taken from Thomas More, *Dialogue of Comfort*, modernized English by Mary Gottschalk (Princeton, N.J.: Scepter, 1998), book 1, preface, 18.

More states clearly his motivation for writing: no one with a spark of Christian love in his heart can fail to think and care about others, so the fictional Anthony tells Vincent, his nephew, that "we shall concern ourselves not just with the harm that this persecution may happen to you or me, but with all the harms in general, or as many as we can call to mind, that may happen to anyone," for, he says, "God has given everyone care and charge of his neighbour." Temptation against faith, More argues, is the most dangerous, and he advises his readers to be aware of it rather than to avoid thinking of it for Christ himself spoke often and plainly about it, saying that everyone must "confess our faith even if people take us and try to drive us, through dread of death to the contrary." More reminds the reader that no one can serve two masters (Mt 6:24). It is not possible to serve both Christ and his enemy. Though all through the *Dialogue* More is speaking of the danger of the Turk, he is explicit in referring to Henry VIII when he writes, "I have known him and his father before him to break promises." In the last of the three books of the *Dialogue* More states that the greatest comfort is to have our hearts in heaven and rely on God, for "everything works for good with those who love him" (Rom 8:28), knowing that Christ suffered and that he told the two disciples going toward the village of Emmaus that it had been necessary for Him to suffer. So in the last chapter he concludes that the consideration of the Passion and Death of Christ should be enough to make us content to suffer a painful death for his sake; he encourages readers to rely on God's help in preparing themselves for the coming persecution; he ends writing, "And if we were full of faith, we would be spurred on even more by a deep consideration of the joys of heaven, of which the Apostle says, 'The sufferings of this present time are not worth comparing with the glory that is to be reveal to us'" (Rom 8:18).[50]

Whether the *Treatise on the Blessed Body* was written before or after the *Dialogue* is not known, but it is obvious that it is closely related to the *Treatise upon the Passion* and *De tristitia*, in that all four works sprang from More's desire to bring his readers closer to Christ. In the introduction to the *Treatise upon the Passion* he wrote,

This may be a warning to every man in this world to do the utmost that he possibly can to keep every other man from hurt. For as the Holy Scripture says: *et mandavit illis unicuique de proximo suo*, God has given every man care of his neighbour (Eccl 17:12).[51]

---

50. *CW* 12, 319:18–23.
51. *A Treatise upon the Passion*, Introduction, *CW* 13, 21:12–16.

And in the treatise he constantly addresses the "good Christian reader," often using "we" as a way of identifying himself with the common Christian people. But once in the Tower, it seems, More left aside his project of writing an elaborate exposition on the Passion and resolved to write more briefly and practically for the benefit of readers on how to receive the Blessed Sacrament properly and on the need to pray. Nevertheless, his unfinished treatise shares the same purpose as those other works: to help the reader to focus on Christ's Passion and to walk confidently toward heaven.

This idea of walking to heaven, our life on earth being a state of pilgrimage, is, of course, a commonplace in Christian spiritual writing.[52] But it also reflects Thomas More's understanding of his Christian vocation as a journey that has a definite beginning and leads toward the future, exactly as indicated by the quotation from the Letter to the Hebrews that makes up the first lines of the *Treatise upon the Passion* already mentioned;[53] the idea is repeated even more explicitly in the prayer at the end of chapter 2:

and so to reckon ourselves for no dwellers but for pilgrims upon earth, that we may long and make haste, walking with faith in the way of virtuous works, to come to the glorious country.[54]

It is perhaps no great surprise to find that this sense of life being a pilgrimage toward heaven, "seeking the city which is to come," appears even more strongly in More's last work, *De tristitia*.[55] There he writes that the Christian follows in the footsteps of Christ (fol. 64), advantages successfully, and presses on through all obstacles (fol. 27), firmly confident (fol. 27), calm and hopeful (fol. 18).

The manuscript of *De tristitia* is, in fact, the only extant long autograph of Thomas More, and its 155 folios give an insight into how he composed it. He wrote it in a hurry, sentence after sentence, correcting it as he went along, crossing out a word or full sentence here and there, adding another in places. Though it has a clear structure, it branches in different directions: More followed a line of thought and then expanded the same in another.

52. It is mentioned in the Fathers; St. Augustine speaks frequently of the "terrena peregrinatio" (see, e.g., *Enarrationes in Psalmos* 76, 4). The idea also appears in Erasmus's *Adagia* IV, X, 74: *Vita hominis peregrinatio*. "Παρεπιδημία τίς ἐστιν ὁ βίος, id est Peregrinatio quædam est vita." And he adds, "Haec enim sententia frequenter occurrit in sacris voluminibus, vitam hanc esse exilium, esse incolatum et peregrinationem"; see, e.g., 2 Cor 5:6, 1 Pt 2:11.

53. "Here we have no lasting city, but we seek the city which is to come" (Heb 13:14), cited in the first three lines of *A Treatise upon the Passion*; *CW* 13, 3:15–17.

54. *CW* 13, 100:12–15.

55. For an introduction to *De tristitia*, see Mitjans, "*De tristitia tedio pavore et oratione christi ante captionem eius*: The Last Work by St. Thomas More," *Annales Theologici* 35 (2021): 11–58.

It is very much a personal meditation but addressed to the reader, whom he names every so often. It is a meditation exhorting the reader to pray. It is also very much an autobiographical text that he writes aware of his own circumstances, expecting to be executed at a moment's notice.

De tristitia tedio pavore et oratione christi ante captionem eius is like no other work by More. The letters to Dorp, to a Monk, to Lee, and to the Masters of Oxford University were written addressing specific individuals or groups. The settings of *Utopia*, the *Dialogue* of 1529, and the *Dialogue of Comfort against Tribulation* were a mixture of fiction and nonfiction. *Utopia* is a conversation between *Morus* and the fictional traveler Raphael Hythloday, introduced one to the other by More's friend Peter Giles after Sunday Mass at the Church of St. Mary in Antwerp and continued in More's also fictional house in that city, about a nonexistent isle found nowhere. In the *Dialogue of Comfort against Tribulation*, More, imprisoned in the Tower of London, portrayed himself as old bedridden Anthony who advised his young nephew Vincent confronted by an imminent invasion by the Turks, which historically took place in 1529, though in fact the author is referring to the imminent threats truly present in England in 1534. In the *Dialogue* of 1529 against Tyndale and Luther the real More welcomes into his house in Chelsea the fictitious student confused by ideas he had heard; this gives More the freedom to confront what he considers to be the arguments of the reformers, while in all other writings in defense of orthodoxy he is tied up, as mentioned already, with answering specific written objections.

De tristitia is different. There is no fictional device, no academic treatment. In *De tristitia* More opens his heart and his mind, he prays, he meditates on the gospel, he exhorts his readers to pray. In the Tower, a few weeks before his execution, there is no need to use any device: he can play it straight. He had also expressed what was in his heart in that stanza in Latin in his early youth while joking in English through the previous stanzas.

From the start of *De tristitia* it is evident that More had his mind constantly focused on heaven. Erasmus in his biographical profile of More wrote that when More talked "with friends about the life after death, you recognize that he [was] speaking from conviction, and not without hope."[56] More's hope of heaven is evident right through *De tristitia*, from considering that the sufferings of this time are by no means worthy to be

----

56. *CWE* 7, Letter 999, line 300.

compared to the future glory[57] that will be revealed in those who loved
God so dearly that they spent their very life's blood for his glory (fols.
27 and 61) to saying, by the end of the book, that he has not the slight-
est doubt that the young man who followed Christ that night and could
not be torn away from him until the last possible moment, after all the
apostles had fled, lives with Christ in everlasting glory in heaven, and that
he—More—hopes and prays that we—More and his readers—will one day
live in heaven with the young man: "Then he himself will tell us who he
was, and we will get a most pleasant and full account of many other details
of what happened that night" (fols. 145ᵛ–46).

Having our hope in heaven, however, does not take away the difficulties we encounter, and More saw in the toponyms given in the text from
Gerson's *Monotessaron,* "*in montem Olivarum, trans torrentem Cedron in
villam cui nomen Gethsemani,*"[58] a reference to the need of going through
the sufferings of this life before reaching the joys of heaven. He writes that
the stream of Kedron lies between the city of Jerusalem and the Mount of
Olives, where the orchard of Gethsemane is; that *cedron* means "sadness,"
and Gethsemane a "most fertile valley" or "valley of olives"; and therefore,
that while we are exiled from the Lord we must surely cross over a valley
of tears and a stream of sadness whose waves can wash away the blackness
and filth of our sins before we come to the fruitful Mount of Olives and
the pleasant estate of Gethsemane, an estate most fertile in every sort of
joy. This, he writes, is the salutary lesson contained in these place-names
(fols. 3–5ᵛ). The parallel between going through Kedron to reach Gethsemane and through suffering to reach glory is found in the *Catena aurea*
from Alcuin commenting on John 18:1.

As a whole, and as has been commonly said, *De tristitia* deals throughout, almost from beginning to end, with three themes: the contemplation
of Christ's agony in the garden; an exhortation addressed to all Christians
to pray; and a discussion of martyrdom. Although the last-mentioned has

---

57. St. Paul's words, 2 Cor 4:17, found on fol. 27, are similar to Rom 8:18, which is cited on fol. 61.

58. Mt 26:30 reads in the Latin Vulgate, "Et hymno dicto, exierunt in montem Oliveti"; and
Mt 26:36, "Tunc venit Jesus cum illis in villam quae dicitur Gethsemani"; Mk 14:26, "Et hymno dicto
exierunt in montem Olivarum, and Mk 14:3232, Et veniunt in praedium, cui nomen Gethsemani";
Lk 22:39, "Et egressus ibat secundum consuetudinem in montem Olivarum"; Jn 18:1, "trans torrentem
Cedron, ubi erat hortus." Gerson's *Monotessaron* brings together the "torrentem Cedron" mentioned
by John and "Gethsemani/montem Olivarum" from the synoptic gospels, into a unified reading:
"Haec cum dixisset Iesus, & hymno dicto, exierunt in montem Oliveti. Et egressus ibat secundum
consuetudinem in monthem Olivarum, trans torrentem Cedron, in villam, cui nomen Gethsemani";
cf. Gerson, *Monotessaron,* edition published in Cologne by Ludwing van Renchen in 1546.

autobiographical undertones, *De tristitia* is "a work entirely consistent with the rest of More's lifelong dedication not merely to the inner workings of the self but to 'the whole corps of Christendom.'"[59]

The point here is that although this whole book has focused on More's awareness and corresponding response to seek the contemplative life of a Christians in his circumstances, this of course is the calling of all Christians as taught, for instance, by St. John Chrysostom addressing the *Homilies on the Gospel of St. Matthew* to the citizens of Antioch, and as More himself maintained in all his works addressed to Christian readers. This is further illustrated in *De tristitia* where More emphasizes that all fatherhood proceeds from God both in heaven and on earth (fol. 38) and that Christ taught us to call him "*our* Father" rather than have any individual addressing him as "*my* Father" (fol. 45^v), because that way of addressing belongs to the Son alone, while all of us are brothers; he had in mind that the reformers claimed a direct relationship with God without the Church, or a "Church of the elect," as when Bugenhagen sent his letter "to the Saints in England."

De tristitia: More's Last Book

Having considered in *De tristitia* More's vocation as a pilgrimage and his concern for the common people, it is worth focusing on other aspects he brings up in his last book so that we better understand his mind and feelings while waiting execution. Indeed, reading of the *Dialogue of Comfort* and *De tristitia* has helped us to define Thomas More's vocation as a pilgrimage, but of course such a pilgrimage has a beginning—the awareness of the calling—and an objective, which in the case of More, as Erasmus wrote and has been apparent all through this chapter, was the afterlife, or rather the love of God in the afterlife, as More wrote in the Second Property of a Lover:

> Yet till the time that he *may once resort* [can finally go]
> Unto that blessed, joyful, heavenly port
> Where he of God may have the glorious sight[60]

That is, More mentions the "pilgrimage" in the *Dialogue* and *De tristitia*; but reversely, "the image of the pilgrimage" requires focusing on More's works at the end of his life, the *Dialogue* and *De tristitia*.

59. Katherine G. Rodgers, "The Lessons of Gethsemane: *De Tristitia Christi*," in *CU*, 259.
60. *Life of Pico*, "Second Property of a Lover," second stanza, *CW* 1, 114:28.

As said, *De tristitia* deals with the agony of Christ from when he arrived with his disciples in Gethsemane, right up to his capture. More points out that the place-names mentioned by the evangelists harmonize very well with the immediate context of Christ's passion for the prophet predicting that Christ would work out his glory by means of inglorious torment. "Then—More writes—the meaning of the stream He crossed, 'sad,' was far from irrelevant as He Himself testified when He said, "My soul is sad unto death" (fols. 5ᵛ–6ᵛ).

The words of Jesus, "My soul is sad unto death," are found in Mt 26:38 and Mk 14:34, but not in John's Gospel, where many of the events recorded in the synoptics are assumed to be already known to readers. The reference to Kedron—meaning sad—is hint enough of the agony of Christ in John's account and lets John go on to describe Christ's control of the situation (Jn 18:4–11). Further on in the text (see fols. 102–15) Thomas More wrote about how Jesus confronted those who were seeking him; in the first folios, however, he focused on Jesus's prayer and on how that of his disciples should be.

More writes of "Christ's holy custom of going together with his disciples to that place—Gethsemane—in order to pray" (fol. 7ᵛ), that he had the habit of spending whole nights praying without sleep (fol. 8ᵛ). On that occasion, "He began to feel sorrow and grief and fear and weariness," and "said to them, 'My soul is sad unto death. Stay here and keep watch with me'" (fol. 10). More continues writing:

[Christ] suddenly felt such a sharp and bitter attack of sadness, grief, fear, and weariness that He immediately uttered, even in their presence, those anguished words which gave expression to His overburdened feelings: "My soul is sad unto death" (fol. 11–11ᵛ).

Christ, More, argued, suffered in Gethsemane because he had present in his human soul the physical suffering that he was going to undergo in his body from the blows, thorns, nails, and horrible tortures up to the crucifixion; he suffered from the treacherous betrayer and bitter enemies; but over and above these, by the abandonment of his disciples, the loss of the Jews, and finally—More wrote—by the "ineffable grief of His beloved mother" (fol. 12ᵛ).

He went on to explain that Christ, truly God and truly man, had as a man the ordinary human feelings; he experienced hunger, thirst, and sleep; and equally he had the capacity to suffer and chose to experience sadness, dread, weariness, and fear of tortures and thus to show by these very real signs of human frailty that He was really a man. Moreover [More wrote] because He came into the world to earn joy for us by His own sorrow, and since that future joy of ours was to be fulfilled in our souls as well as our bodies, so, too, He chose to experience not only the pain of torture in His body but also the most bitter feelings of sadness, fear, and weariness in His mind [*in animo*] partly in order to bind us to Him all the more (fol. 24ᵛ).

Fear is the suffering of the soul engendered by foreseen future events, and More emphasizes that Christ's soul suffered in Gethsemane for all the physical pain his body was to feel up to his death on the cross. St. John Henry Newman was later to emphasize that "the agony, a pain of the soul, not of the body, was the first act of His tremendous sacrifice."[61]

While Matthew and Mark report the words of Jesus, "My soul is sad unto death," and John gives just a hint of the agony, Luke amplifies the scene and gives a further abundance of details; he is the only one who mentions that Jesus sweated blood (Lk 22:44). Luke's Gospel is more tender and conveys especially the mercy of God. He is the one who relates the infancy of Jesus, the parables of the prodigal son and the good Samaritan, and the repentance of the good thief. More writes that Christ was overwhelmed by mental anguish more bitter than any other mortal has ever experienced from the thought of coming torments, even to the point that a bloody sweat broke out all over his body and ran down in drops to the ground (fol. 58ᵛ). And similarly, Newman preached three centuries later that Christ shed blood in Gethsemane; that his agonizing soul broke up his framework of flesh and poured it forth:

His passion [has] begun from within. That tormented Heart, the seat of tenderness and love, began at length to labour and to beat with vehemence ...; the foundations of the great deep were broken up; the red streams rushed forth so copious and fierce as to overflow the veins, and bursting through the pores, they stood in a thick dew over His whole skin; then forming into drops, they rolled down full and heavy, and drenched the ground.[62]

More goes on to write, however, that Christ's sadness, fear, and weariness did not prevent him from obeying his father's command (fol. 21ᵛ). He addressed him saying, "Abba, Father, to you all things are possible. Take this cup away from me," but continued, "yet not what I will, but what you will" (fol. 28).

<hr>

61. J. H. Newman, *Discourses to Mixed Congregations* (London, 1892), discourse 16, 325.
62. Newman, *Discourses*, discourse 16, 340.

A Discussion on Martyrdom

The discussion on martyrdom starts with the consideration of Christ's suffering in his pre-passion, which More considered to be greater than it "has been to anyone else" (fol. 58), "more painful than the suffering of any of all martyrs, of whatever time or place, who underwent martyrdom for the faith" (fol. 57). Then, More speaks of two types of martyrs, those who embrace martyrdom eagerly and those who do so reluctantly, which was to be very much his own case. He went over and over again in his mind the different aspects of this matter, and what he wrote was clearly autobiographical. He did not consider himself to have the vocation of a martyr.

The whole drift of the present discussion finally comes to this: we should admire both kinds of most holy martyrs, we should venerate both kinds, praise God for both, we should imitate both when the situation demands it, each according to his own capacity and according to the grace God gives to each (fol. 62ᵛ).

And he concluded by saying:

In our agony remembering His (with which no other can ever be compared) let us beg Him with all our strength that He may deign to comfort us in our anguish by an insight into His; and when we urgently beseech Him, because of our mental distress, to free us from danger, let us nevertheless follow His own most wholesome example by concluding our prayer with His own addition: "Yet not as I will but as you will" (fol. 63ᵛ).

The Church, Bishops, Priests

More considered himself very much a member of the Church; the Church is made up of all the faithful, those on earth and those who have preceded us and are in heaven or undergo purification in purgatory, to whom he dedicated a full book, *The Supplication of Souls*. For More the laity are fully members of the Church. In *De tristitia* he calls the Church repeatedly the mystical body of Christ (fols. 25, 87, and 111ᵛ) and Christ the head of the Church (fol. 111ᵛ). In all his writings More had in mind that the Holy Spirit plays an essential role in the Church, as Christ promised that the Holy Spirit will guide the Church into all truth (Jn 16:13); in *De tristitia* he writes that the Holy Spirit taught the apostles after the resurrection what they would not have been able to bear had it been told them a short time before (fol. 3).

More's awareness of his belonging to the Church leads him to pray for all the faithful. He quotes Terence,[63] "Since I am a man, I consider nothing human to be foreign to me"; likewise, More suggests that because we are Christian we need to be interested in all Christians, and we must all pray for those in need. In the context of the sleeping disciples, he writes, "How could it be anything but disgraceful for Christians to snore while other Christians are in danger?" (fol. 87[v]).

In contemplating the sleep of the apostles in Gethsemane, More reflects on the attitude of many bishops:

Why do not bishops contemplate in this scene their own somnolence? Since they have succeeded in the place of the apostles, would that they would reproduce their virtues just as eagerly as they embrace their authority and as faithfully as they display their sloth and sleepiness! For very many are sleepy and apathetic in sowing virtues among the people and maintaining the truth, while the enemies of Christ in order to sow vices and uproot the faith (that is, insofar as they can, to seize Christ and cruelly crucify Him once again) are wide awake—so much wiser (as Christ says) are the sons of darkness in their generation than the sons of light (fol. 65).

The previous paragraph contrasts with More's apologetic writings in which he defended bishops and priests against the attacks of the reformers. In 1526, in his Letter to Bugenhagen, More wrote that the bishops of England were not going to be influenced by the doctrines of Luther.[64] Alas! The tables had been turned. Seven years later the bishops in Convocation,[65] by the statute of the Submission of the Clergy of May 15, 1532, relinquished their authority and recognized Henry VIII's royal authority over all Church legislation, thereby opening the door to the royal supremacy and to breaking with Rome;[66] the following day, May 16, More resigned

63. In *De tristitia* More calls him "the comic poet": Terence was a Roman playwright (c. 186– c. 159 BC). Miller mentions him a dozen times in commenting on More's Latin in *De tristitia*; cf. *CW* 14, II.

64. *CW* 7, 27:10–12.

65. The Convocations of Canterbury and York were the synodical assemblies of the bishops and clergy of the two provinces of the Church in England. At the time they included the bishops and other members of the clergy.

66. The declaration of the Royal Supremacy proceeded in stages. From the beginning of the session of Parliament that started in October 1529, the king attempted to control the Church but found clear opposition in Parliament. The House of Lords, which included Thomas More as lord chancellor and William Warham as archbishop of Canterbury, refused to pass the Submission of the Clergy Act. and Henry dismissed Parliament on May 14, 1532. The bishops in Convocation accepted the Submission of the Clergy on May 15, 1532. More resigned the following day, and the archbishop of Canterbury died that summer. By the Submission of the Clergy, the bishops accepted that they would not make new canons without the king's license and ratification and that they would submit prior canons to a royal revision. This declaration was probably meant for putting pressure on the pope, rather than for a definitive break with Rome. (For a detailed account of More's resignation, see, for

as lord chancellor. In describing the attitude of the sleeping bishops, he used words that he had written in his letter of October 23, <1502–4> addressed to John Colet. There, he wrote about the "stuff for the belly and the world and for the world's lord, the devil."[67] In *De tristitia* he writes that some of the sleeping bishops *"multo plures quam vellem,"* far more of them than I would wish, "are numbed and buried in destructive desires; that is, drunk with the new wine of the devil, the flesh, and the world, they sleep like pigs sprawling in the mire" (fol. 65–65ᵛ). And he uses the image he placed on the lips of the quasi-fictional *Morus* in replying to Raphael Hythloday: "You must not abandon the ship in a storm because you cannot control the winds."[68] In *De tristitia* he writes:

If a bishop is so overcome by heavy-hearted sleep that he neglects to do what the duty of his office requires for the salvation of his flock—like a cowardly ship's captain who is so disheartened by the furious din of a storm that he deserts the helm, hides away cowering in some cranny, and abandons the ship to the waves— if a bishop does this, I would certainly not hesitate to juxtapose and compare his sadness with the sadness that leads to hell; indeed, I would consider it far worse, since such sadness in religious matters seems to spring from a mind which despairs of God's help (fol. 66).

Some authors have suggested that More used strong words in *De tristitia* because, writing in Latin, he was addressing a more erudite audience. This does not seem to be the case. The reality is that the bishops in England had abdicated their responsibility in the face of the king's oppression. *De tristitia* is addressed to them and the clergy and to the common people who could read Latin, not just to a select few.

More goes on to speak of two other categories of bishops. "The next category, but a far worse one, consists of those" moved by ambition who "do not sleep like Peter" but "make his waking denial" (fol. 66–68). Here More seems to have had in mind the case of Cardinal Wolsey, who not only submitted to the king's desires, but out of his own ambition worked actively to achieve the divorce of Henry from Catherine. And finally, the third group is made up of "those that not merely neglect to profess the

---

instance, Guy, *Public Career of Sir Thomas More,* "The Events of 1532," 175–203). In March 1533, however, by the Act in Restraint of Appeals, Henry VIII was declared head of the Church. By the Act of Submission of the Clergy of March 1534, Parliament formalized the 1532 Convocation statute, and all appeals in Church law were to be addressed to the King's Court of Chancery. The Acts of Succession and Royal Supremacy followed. Thomas More and Bishop John Fisher refused the oath to the Act of Succession on April 13, 1534, and were taken to the Tower of London. The Act of Royal Supremacy was passed in November 1534 when the two of them were already in the Tower.

67. *Correspondence* [3:26].

68. *Utopia,* book I, *CW* 4, 99:34–35.

truth out of fear" but preach false doctrine "whether for sordid gain or out of a corrupt ambition, such a person does not sleep like Peter, does not make Peter's denial, but rather stays awake with wicked Judas and like Judas persecutes Christ" (fol. 68ᵛ). This was the case of Thomas Cranmer, who not only tried to please the king but, as archbishop of Canterbury, granted the annulment, allowed the marriage to Anne Boleyn, conferred on her the crown, and introduced Lutheran doctrines in England. More continues reflecting on the state of the clergy:

At this juncture another point occurs to us, that Christ is also betrayed into the hands of sinners when His most holy body in the sacrament is consecrated and handled by unchaste, dissolute, and sacrilegious priests (fol. 88).

Again, strong words from the pen of Thomas More, but he had already written of the marriage of Luther to a nun and of that of other Continental reformers earlier;[69] closer to home, people were aware of the illegitimate son of Cardinal Wolsey. Archbishop Cranmer also brought a wife from his stay in Germany, though this was kept secret, and it was perhaps not known by More.[70] On the following folio More speaks of those who deny the real presence of the body of Christ in the sacrament, though they call it by that name, *Corpus Christi* (fol. 89). In the unfinished *Treatise upon the Passion* he wrote a most extensive defense of the real presence, citing in Latin and English from nineteen Latin and Greek Fathers of the Church and other ancient Christian writers, from St. Ignatius of Antioch to Theophylact of Bulgaria;[71] and later on, probably soon after arriving at the Tower, he wrote the brief *Treatise to Receive the Blessed Body of Our Lord, Sacramentally and Virtually Both*.[72] Those pages are evidence of the love and veneration More had for the Eucharist.

Psalm II

It is interesting to note that More cited Psalm II a couple of times: first with reference to the reformers who claimed to be able to interpret scrip-

---

69. *The Confutation of Tyndale's Answer*, *CW* 8, 41:31.

70. Sometime between March and August 1532 Cranmer got married in Nuremberg. He left his wife in Germany while continuing his diplomatic mission on the Continent, but at the death of Warham he was recalled to be consecrated archbishop of Canterbury. The consecration took place in January 1533. Sometime later Cranmer's wife slipped into England. Although she bore a daughter, the marriage remained hidden through most of Henry's reign. It is not unlikely, though, that by 1534 More knew of the marriage.

71. *A Treatise upon the Passion*, chapter 4, lecture 2, *CW* 13, 136–74.

72. *CW* 13, 191–202.

ture without the help of the old doctors or the tradition of the Church (fol. 110ᵛ), and later when Jesus replied to his captors, "This is your hour and the power of darkness," Lk 22:53 (fol. 133ᵛ). Psalm II was recited by the first Christians when the Apostles Peter and John, who had been arrested by the Jewish authorities, the chief priests, and the elders, were released after proclaiming Jesus Christ; the disciples understood Psalm II as a manifestation of their trust in God in front of the opposition of earthly authorities (Acts 4: 23–31). More places in the mouth of Christ that "this hour and this power of darkness are not only given to you now against me, but such an hour and such brief power of darkness will also be given to other governors and other caesars against other disciples of mine" (fol. 135). More sees those words fulfilled in the case of Nero and others who persecuted Christ's disciples from the beginning of the Church and for centuries to come, including in this, his own situation; and he paraphrases the words of the Psalm:

Although the nations have raged and the people devised vain things, although the kings of the earth have risen up and the princes gathered together against the Lord and against His Christ, striving to break their chains and to cast off that most sweet yoke which a loving God, through His pastors, places upon their stubborn necks, then He who dwells in heaven will laugh at them and the Lord will deride them.... He will establish His Christ, the son whom He has today begotten, as king on His holy mountain of Sion (fols. 136–38ᵛ).

The picture described by More from folios 64 to 138 is really grim: bishops and clerics in England, and those in authority and illustrious men, had deserted Christ. But not all was lost. Bishop John Fisher kept the faith, and the Carthusians, and other religious: his friend and fellow scholar Richard Reynolds, a Bridgettine priest, and three Carthusian priors, died martyrs on May 4, and the rest of the London Charterhouse was resisting Thomas Cromwell's attempts to gain their submission (up to eighteen of them were to die martyrs; the others submitted and abandoned the house, which was taken over).[73]

Another source of consolation for More was his friend Antonio Buonvisi, to whom he wrote his last-but-one extant letter,[74] probably after finishing *De tristitia* because, though *De tristitia* was written in ink, tradition-

---

73. M. Chauncy, *The History of the Sufferings of Eighteen Carthusians in England*, written in Latin in 1539, was published in English in 1890 by Burns and Oates, London.

74. His last extant letter was addressed to his daughter Margaret on July 5, 1535, the day before his execution on Tower Hill.

ally it is assumed that the letter to Buonvisi was written with a coal.[75] He started it saying:

Since my mind has a presentiment (perhaps a false one, but still a presentiment) that before very long I will be unable to write to you, I have decided, while I may, to show by this letter, at least, how much I am refreshed by the pleasantness of your friendship now that fortune has abandoned me.[76]

More goes on to write that the happiness of a friendship so faithful and constant against the contrary blast of fortune is a higher good arising from the loving-kindness of God.

Faithful also were his adopted daughter, Margaret Giggs, and her husband, John Clement, and his secretary, John Harris, who married Dorothy Colly, the maid of Margaret Roper, eldest daughter of Thomas More. Margaret Roper, Margaret Giggs, and Dorothy Colly brought More's headless body from Tower Hill to be buried in the Tower. Margaret Giggs succoured the imprisoned Carthusians. And faithful at the time were most common people, most of the religious, and most of the clergy. More found consolation in the company of all the Church in Christendom and of the saints in heaven.

But, of course, his main comfort was God himself, and More finished his meditation on Psalm II with the following words, which he placed on the lips of Christ:

Thus, when they have taken up their cross to follow me, when they have conquered the prince of darkness, the devil, when they have trod underfoot the early minions of Satan, then finally, riding aloft on a triumphant chariot, the martyrs will enter into heaven in a magnificent and marvellous procession. (Fol. 137ᵛ)

75. This would date the letter between June 12, 1535, when he was deprived of writing utensils, and July 1, when he was sentenced to death. William Rastell, editor of the *English Works of Sir Thomas More*, 1557, placed the letter to Bonvisi and the letter of July 5 to Margaret last among the letters of Thomas More, *English Works*, pages 1,455 and 1,457 respectively, and they are preceded by a paragraph in which the editor says that they were generally written "with a coal" because More did not have "pen or ink." From this grew a family tradition that More in the Tower had to write with a piece of coal. Rodgers considers this to be an exaggeration (cf. *Companion*, 240), and, in fact, the Valencia manuscript itself disproves it. The editor of the *English Works* mentions using a coal only for the last two letters, and charcoal pencils were, and are, a normal medium for drawing (used, for instance by Holbein in the sketch of Thomas More's family) and not uncommon for writing. Rather than saying that he used a coal, perhaps it is more accurate to say that More used a *pencil* (a charcoal pencil) for those his last two letters.

76. The letter was written in Latin, translated into English by E. McCutcheon, "'The Apple of My Eye': Thomas More to Antonio Bonvisi, a Reading and a Translation," *Moreana*, nos. 71–72 (November 1981): 55–56. Most collections of letters of Thomas More give the English translation published in the *English Works* of 1557, rather than a fresh modern translation from the Latin.

The Flight of the Apostles and the Capture of Christ.

At the end of folio 115v Thomas More lists three topics that he is going to develop in the rest of the text:

> *De amputate Malchi auricula*
> *Apostolorum fuga*
> *et captione christi*
>
> The severing of Malchus' ear [fol. 116–38v],
> the flight of the apostles [fol. 139–53],
> and the capture of Christ [fol. 154–55v].

These three final sections are the only ones that clearly have been given headings in More's own handwriting on the folios of the manuscript, as if, until then, More had been writing in haste, following his train of thought with everything he had in mind, and, in finishing folio 115, he had stopped and had wanted to ensure that he covered those three last topics. These three headings appear well centered at the top of each of the respective folios, 116, 139, and 154.

At the bottom right of folio 138^v, he wrote the heading of the following page; it appears on top of folio 139: *De fuga discipulorum.*[77] The first lines of this section continue to be clearly autobiographical:

"Then all the disciples abandoned him and fled." From this passage it is easy to see how difficult and arduous a virtue patience is. For many can bring themselves to face certain death bravely provided they can strike back at their assailants and give vent to their feelings…. But to suffer without any comfort from revenge, to meet death with a patience that not only refrains from striking back but also takes blows without returning so much as an angry word, that, *I assure you*, is such a lofty peak of heroic virtue.

I would suggest that staying in the Tower from April 17, 1534, to July 6, 1535, and keeping his calm all the while was a real trial for Thomas More's *patience.*

The last heading, *De christi captione*, appears in the final title of the book, as well as in a previous attempt, *De oratione ante captionem christi.* There has been some discussion as to whether More intended to write further, but, from the list of those three topics, it is obvious that, at least

---

77. On fol. 115^V he wrote *Apostolorum fuga*; but on fol. 138^V and on top of fol. 139, he wrote, *De fuga discipulorum*, in concordance with the following line of fol. 139: *Tunc discipuli relicto eo omnes fugerunt* (Mt 25:56).

from the moment he reached writing folio 115, the *De christi captione* was going to be the end of his narrative, which he finished with the few lines describing the capture of Christ—which took place, he writes, after Christ had twice addressed those who had come to apprehend him and had announced to them that they then had permission to do what they had not been able to do before—to take him captive, that is, after all the apostles had escaped by running away, after the young man who had been seized but could not be held had saved himself by his active and eager acceptance of nakedness—only then, after all these events, did they lay hands on Jesus (fol. 155).

The Gentleness of Thomas More

At this stage, it seems necessary to focus on what might be called the gentleness of Thomas More that is apparent throughout *De tristitia*. Early in the book More points out that Christ used to eat with sinners, calmly and kindly helping them to reform their lives (fol. 9). In discussing the words of Our Lord, "Are you sleeping and taking your rest? It is enough" (Mk 14: 41), More says that he was not unaware that there are various interpretations and states that everyone is free to choose, as he is not an arbitrator (fol. 76). Similarly, by the end of the work, More comments that he differs from the interpretation adopted not only by many celebrated doctors of the Church but also approved by that "remarkable man John Gerson" whom he had generally followed in his work (fol. 154^v–55). In these comments, More's freedom of mind in giving his own opinion comes through, but also his honesty in mentioning other interpretations and his gentleness in praising those who held opposite views.

After criticizing those prelates who had actively denied Christ out of fear, he suggests that most of them will eventually repent (fol. 68), which was in fact the case under Mary Tudor. One of those who repented was Bishop Stephen Gardiner (c. 1495–1555). Gardiner had served under Wolsey in the attempt to obtain the divorce of King Henry VIII and Catherine of Aragon. Henry appointed him bishop of Winchester in 1531; though he opposed the king in 1532, he was among those who accepted the royal supremacy and defended it in his book *De vera obedientia*. Under the following king, the young Edward VI, Gardiner sought the return of the kingdom to the Catholic Church, and he was imprisoned in the Tower of London. He was released at the accession of Queen Mary in 1553 and appointed her lord chancellor. He backed her in her efforts for a Catholic restoration. It was reported that on his deathbed, listening to the gospel narrative of Peter's betrayal of Christ, the bishop, weeping bitterly, said, "*Ego exivi sed non dum flevi amare*"—"I have gone out, but as yet I have not wept bitterly."[78]

With regard to those who had preached false doctrine, he points out that, since there is no limit to the mercy of God, Christians had to pray humbly and incessantly that with God's help they should return to their senses and rectify (fol. 70ᵛ). More had also spoken about unfaithful priests and went on to advise that people had to pray more earnestly for priests, for it will be much to the advantage of the people if bad priests improve (fol. 88ᵛ).

It has been mentioned in the preceding section that More made reference to Psalm II, "He who dwells in the heaven laughs to scorn these wicked and vain attempts of [the bad theologians]"; but More goes on to write, "But I humbly pray that he may not so laugh them to scorn as to laugh also at their eternal ruination, but rather that he may inspire in them the health-giving grace of repentance" so that they "may retrace their steps to the bosom of mother Church and so that all of us together, united in the true faith of Christ and joined in mutual charity as true members of Christ, may again attain to the glory of Christ our Head" (fol. 111ᵛ).

All through the book Thomas More contemplated the passion of Christ who suffered as no other man had suffered, but he emphasized that Christ did so because he wanted to, and specifically, focusing in the account of John, that he went freely to meet those who sought to capture him (Jn 18: 4–8) and that he was in command of the situation (fol. 64 and 102), so much so that those who went to take him fell to the ground at his word (Jn 18: 6). This gave More a deep trust in Jesus Christ, and he ended his narrative full of confidence, calm, and joy.

Youthful Love

He also returns to his determination to embrace the "first point" of his ballade, "to love but one alone." And so it is that he focuses in a special way on those figures in Christ's Passion who have their "love set unto God"

---

78. Cited in the entry of Stephen Gardiner, in the *ODNB*, online version of January 3, 2008, accessed on December 21, 2020. The source of this quotation was Stapleton (July 1535–98), biographer of St. Thomas More. He was educated at Winchester College and graduated from Oxford in 1556, the year after Gardiner's death. He was a canon of Chichester under Mary but was deprived of the prebend in the next reign on refusing the Oath of Supremacy in 1563. He emigrated to the Continent and was later a professor at the English College in Douay and at the University of Louvain.

wholeheartedly. The first one undoubtedly was the Blessed Virgin Mary, for in speaking of Jesus' agony, More writes that he suffered also because of "the ineffable grief of his beloved mother" (fol. 12[v]), whom More mentioned again as Jesus's "most loving mother" on fol. 39 and on fol. 48a[v].[79] He had already mentioned Christ's "Immaculate mother" in the *Dialogue of Comfort*.[80] Next after her comes John, the young apostle, whom More commends for following Christ all the way to the place of crucifixion and for standing by the cross with Christ's mother, "two pure virgins standing together" (*virgo purus cum virgine purissima partier*), and accepting Mary as his own mother when Christ commended her to him (fol. 142).

In this, his last work, More did not want to omit mentioning Mary Magdalen to whom Jesus appeared after his resurrection (fol. 105[v]). He had written of her in 1529 in his first dialogue in defense of orthodoxy: Christ promised that St. Mary Magdalen would be venerated through the world because she bestowed that precious ointment upon his blessed head;[81] from the example of that holy woman and from the words of our Savior, More wrote, we learn that God delights in seeing the fervent heat of the heart's devotion bubble out through the body and do him homage.[82] He had praised her previously in his Letter to Bugenhagen.[83] He wrote of her also in the *Treatise upon the Passion*[84] before being taken prisoner, and again, already in the Tower, in *A Dialogue of Comfort against Tribulation*;[85] in these two books he identifies Mary Magdalen with Martha's sister.[86]

More's excitement is at its best, however, when speaking of the young man who followed Jesus when all the disciples had abandoned him and run away (fol. 143).[87] More tells us how he would imagine the situation. He suggests that the young man had heard of Christ's fame, and, as may have happened, he was serving at table during the Last Supper when he was

79. More inserted two additional folios after fol. 48, which in the transcription given in *CW* 14 are called fol. 48a and 48b.

80. *CW* 12, 315:24.

81. *CW* 6, 49:13–15. "shold be worshypped thorow the worlde and have here an honorable remembraunce"; Christ's words in Mt 26:13 and Mk 14:9 do not in fact say that she will be venerated, but only that she will be remembered wherever the gospel is preached.

82. *CW* 6, 49:29–32.

83. *CW* 7, 92:23.

84. *CW* 13, 76–77 and 157.

85. *CW* 12, 146 and 185.

86. The identification of the three Maries, Mary Magdalen, Mary the sister of Martha, and Mary who washed the feet of Jesus in Bethany, was common in the pictorial and liturgical tradition at the time; cf. Rex, *Theology of John Fisher*, Chapter 4, "The Magdalene Controversy," 65–77.

87. This young man is also mentioned in the *Dialogue of Comfort*; *CW* 12, 246:24.

touched by a secret breath of the spirit and felt the moving force of charity. Then, impelled to pursue a life of true devotion, he followed Christ when he left after dinner and continued to follow him. When all the apostles had escaped in terror, this young man, More suggests, dared to remain behind, with all the more confidence because he knew that none as yet was aware of the love he felt for Christ.

But how hard it is to disguise the love we feel for someone! Although this young man had mingled with that crowd of people who hated Christ, still he betrayed himself by his gait and his bearing, making it clear to everyone that he pursued Christ, now deserted by the others, not as a persecutor but as a devoted follower (fol. 144ᵛ).

Thomas More continued to consider the example of this young man. He managed to escape when they tried to catch him, but he did not abandon Christ out of fear; he escaped out of necessity when he was able to do so without betraying Christ; and—More writes—he avoided being caught because he was not attached to material things. Here More brings up the example of another young man, "the holy and innocent patriarch Joseph" (Gn 39:12), who left to posterity a notable example, teaching that one should flee from danger of falling into sin (fol. 152).[88] More, almost at the end of his narrative, reveals once again his inner self:

If we patiently endure the loss of the body for the love of God, then, just as the snake sloughs off its old skin (called, I think, its *senecta*) by rubbing it against thorns and thistles, and leaving it behind in the thick hedges comes forth young and shining, so too those of us who follow Christ's advice and become wise as serpents will leave behind the thorns of tribulation suffered for the love of God, and will quickly be carried up to heaven, shining and young and never more to feel the effects of old age (fol. 153).[89]

These words—like many other passages of this, his last work—suggest that at the end of his life, awaiting execution, Thomas More looked back to his early years and experienced a renewal of his youthful love, an ardent love for Christ like that of the young man who followed Jesus without being hindered by earthly attachments: with the fervent heat of Mary Magdalen's heart, the purity and zeal of John, the beloved apostle.

---

88. Also in the *Dialogue of Comfort*; *CW* 12, 279:12.

89. *CW* 14, 615:4–617:5. The simile is found in St. Augustine's *De doctrina Christiana* II, 16, 24.

Conclusion

This book started looking at Thomas More's early writings in order to discover the choices that mapped his life, and it is suggested that he became aware that "the first point is to love but one alone," as he added to his own translation of the *Life of Pico*. We can speak of More's vocation to seek the contemplative life of a Christian as a married layman and in the active life of service to society. The contemplative life of a Christian focuses, of course, on the contemplation of the life of Christ as reflected on the two major works of More in the Tower of London awaiting execution, the *Dialogue of Comfort against Tribulation* and *De tristitia tedio pavore et oratione christi ante captionem eius*—a meditation on the agony of Christ before he was apprehended. The topic of these two works could give the false impression of focusing on the inner self. On the contrary, the last lines of the *Dialogue of Comfort* make clear that the work was written for the benefit of readers. The book, in a fictional setting, is a conversation between Anthony, a bedridden old man, and his cousin Vincent, who asks for Anthony's advice. At the end of the book, Vincent prays that God will give him and all other readers the grace to follow the advice contained in the book,[1] and similarly *De tristitia* is constantly addressing the reader.

It could not be otherwise. In the *Dialogue of Comfort* More says that God has given everyone care of his neighbor, and specifically he writes of the love for others that burns in the heart of the Christian: "spark of christen love & charite in his brest."[2] The phrase brings to mind Hilton's Latin citation in his letter on *Mixed Life*: *Ignem veni mittere in terram, et quid volo nisi ut ardeat*—"I have come to cast fire upon the earth; and would that it were already kindled!"[3] The Christian, More writes, should be

1. *CW* 12, 320:16–17.
2. *CW* 12, 202:29.
3. Hilton, *Mixed Life*, 18.

concerned with all those in need.[4] This attitude of More's toward others is shown first in More's letter to Colet in <1502–4> in which he tells Colet that he is needed in London to preach and look after those who require his spiritual advice. In general terms More shared Erasmus's project of re-vitalizing Christendom. In a more personal way, More's concern for others is shown in his friendships, as reported, for instance, by Erasmus, the Italian scholar Niccoló Sangundino,[5] Frans van Cranevelt, Peter Giles, and Juan Luis Vives. But in the *Dialogue of Comfort* More emphasizes that the Christian "needs to care and take thought, not for his friends only but also for his worst foes."[6] This concern for others led him to accept the commission of writing in defense of orthodoxy while he had the authority for doing so, and—when he no longer enjoyed that authority—to continue writing for the benefit of those in need of his spiritual advice.

Thus, the awareness of the Christian vocation implies a mission toward others. There is, however, a third element: though such awareness requires a personal and individual response, "the first point is to love but one alone," it brings with it, at least in the case of More, the realization that such a vocation is "common to the whole Christian people."[7]

4. *De tristitia*, fol. 87ᵛ.
5. *CWE* 4, letter 339:73–86.
6. *CW* 12, 203:1–2.
7. *CW* 15, 280:10–13.

Two Epitaphs by Thomas More

The Sources

There have been references to the two epitaphs engraved on the tombstone of Thomas More several times in this monograph. The epitaphs evidence his life as a Londoner and a man of letters and his love for his two wives. It is worth therefore looking at the sources we have for this engraving. In fact there are two distinct elements in the texts: a thirty-two-line long epitaph in prose (*Thomas Morvs vrbe londinensi*)—in which he speaks of his resignation— and a short epitaph in verse: a twelve-line poem on his two wives (*Chara Thomæ*).

Thomas More resigned as lord chancellor of England on May 16, 1532. Soon afterward he wrote the epitaph for his tombstone in Chelsea parish church, and sometime later he sent a letter to Erasmus saying that he was going to forward him a copy of the epitaph.

The standard edition in Latin of the letter from Thomas More to Erasmus, including the two epitaphs, has been published in *Opus Epistolarum Des. Erasmi Roterodami,* ed. P. S. Allen, H. M. Allen, and H. W. Garrod (Oxford: Oxford University Press, 1906–58), 12 volumes. This work is commonly known as *Erasmi Epistolae,* which is the title that appears on the spine of the twelve volumes, and it is abbreviated as *EE.* The letter in question is in volume X, Letter 2831, <June 1533>.[1] The English translations most accessible are those published in *Selected Letters,* (1961), no. 46, 178–83; *The Essential Works of Thomas More,* Letter no. 191 (2020), 370–72; and *The Collected Works of Erasmus,* vol. 20 (2020), Ep. 2831, 80–86.

---

1. The transcription of the letter is not included in *Correspondence,* although there the letter is assigned number [191].

On August 31, 1533, Erasmus sent the text of the epitaph to Boniface Amerbach, informing him that he intended to publish it together with some letters.[2]

The *EE*'s version is somehow similar to the text of the letter and the two epitaphs found in a book published in 1536 by John Cochlæus and known as *Antiqua … Epistola Nicolai Papa I*, Leipzig (British Library shelf mark 851.i.10). The main differences between the two texts are as follows:

1. The letter from Thomas More to Erasmus in *Antiqua* (1536) starts in line 29 of letter 2831 as it appears in *EE*: *Quod in epistola priore scribes.*

2. The editors[3] of volume X of *EE* emphasize the phrase in line 90, "*Quam superi pacem firment faxintque perennem*," as it is at present emphasized in the engraving, line 12 (2008), by centering it within the text; there is no emphasis given to the phrase in *Antiqua* (1536).

3. At the end of the whole text the editors add *Epitaphii finis*; this phrase does not appear in *Antiqua* (1536) or on the tombstone.

In transcribing Ep. 2831 the editors of *EE* stated that their source was "*De præparatione ad mortem*, 112–15"; in a footnote to the aforementioned Ep. 2865, from Erasmus to Boniface Amerbach, of August 31, 1533, they wrote that "Erasmus published More's epitaph (not with Emmeus, but with Froben) together with More's letter (Ep.2831) … in the *De præparatione*, <c. Jan> 1534." *EE*, volume X, page 258, and the Brief Table of Editions of Erasmus' Letters given in the same volume X, page xiii, state that Ep. 2831 is to be found in *De præparatione ad mortem* (Basel: H. Froben and N. Episcopius, <c. Jan.> 1534).

De præparatione ad mortem is a treatise written by Erasmus and dated December 1, 1533. It ran through some twenty Latin editions in six years.[4] Some of them included other works, and the text of the epitaph was presumably to be found in one or more of those editions.[5] I have checked the following editions of *De præparatione ad mortem* published during Erasmus's life:

Frobenium, Basileæ, 1534, 167 pages, British Library 4411.e.16, 125 x 190 mm, entitled: *De præparatione ad mortem, nunc primum & conscriptus & Æditus. Accedvnt aliquot epistolæ seriis de rebus, in quibus item nihil est no[n] novum ac recens.* As stated in *EE*, it includes the letter from Thomas More (Ep.2831) on page 112, but the two epitaphs are not placed after Ep. 2831 as in *EE*, but before it. Ep. 2659 from Thomas

---

2. *EE*, vol. X, Ep. 2865:27.

3. P. S. Allen died in 1933. Volume X was published in 1941; the editors were his wife, H. M. Allen, and his friend H. W. Garrod.

4. *CWE*, 70, xxvi.

5. In *CWE*, 70, there is a translation of the *De præparatione ad mortemi*, but the editors did not include the text or any reference to the epitaph.

More to Erasmus, dated June 14, 1532, in which he tells Erasmus of his resignation, is also included before the epitaphs. The arrangement is:

pp. 103–8: Ep. 2659, June 14, 1532
pp. 109–11: Long epitaph introduced as "*Tabula affixa ad sepulchrum Tomæ Mori*"
p. 111: Short epitaph introduced as "*Epitaphium inibi fixum*" and ended by
 "*Epitaphii Finis*"
pp. 112–15: Ep. 2831

Antverpiæ, 1534, 88 pages, British Library 697.b.11, 95 x 145 mm, as previously, with the following pagination:

pp. 24–29: Ep. 2659, June 14, 1532
pp. 30–32: Long epitaph introduced as "*Tabula affixa ad sepulchrum Tomæ Mori*"
p. 32: Short epitaph introduced as "*Epitaphium inibi fixum*" and ended by
 "*Epitaphii Finis*"
pp. 33ff: Ep. 2831

Antverpiæ, 1534, 88 pages, British Library G.11982. (2.), as British Library 697.b.11
Eucharius Cervicornus, Coloniæ, April 1534, British Library, 3021.a.18.5

The volume—British Library shelf mark 3021.a.18/1–5—includes several books; number 5 is *De præparatione ad mortem, liber unus*. It does not include the two letters from Thomas More or the epitaphs.

Rogers's is a translation from *EE*'s composition, while the version given in *A Thomas More Source Book*, edited by Gerard B. Wegemer and Stephen Smith, pp. 305–10, follows faithfully that given in *Antiqua*—that is, starting at *Quod in epistola priore scribes*, without emphasizing *Quam superis pacem*, and without adding *Epitaphii finis*.

—

In 1557 within the *English Works*, pp. 1,419–1,421, Rastell published a Latin transcript of the two epitaphs and his own translation.[6] After transcribing the Latin text of the long epitaph he wrote, "Under this epitaphy in prose [shown previously], he caused to be written on his tomb this latten epitaphy in versis folowing, which himself had made XX years before."

The two epitaphs appear also in *Thomæ Mori Omnia Latina Opera*. There are at least three printings of the same composition:

1. *Lovanni, Apud Ioannem Bogardum sub Biblijs Aureis, Anno 1565* (British Library VOYN 134)—this is the best kept printing of the three.

2. *Lovanni, Apud Petrum Zangrium Tiletanum sub Fonte, Anno 1565* (British Library 3936.i.15)

3. *Lovanni, 1566* (British Library 632.1.8)

6. Rastell's translation was reproduced in *The Life and Writings of Sir Thomas More*, by T. E. Bridgett (London: Burns and Oates, 1891), 248–52.

In these three printings of 1565 and 1566 the *long epitaph* appears on the first page—p. Aij—after the title page, and occupies the full page; it is called: *Epitaphivm Thomæ Mori.* The *short poem—Chara … vita, dabit—*appears on the reverse of the same first page, under the heading *Altervm Epitaphivm ab eodem huius poftea adiecta, licet antea coscriptum.*

The letter to Erasmus is not included in these *English Works* (Rastell 1557), 1565, and 1566 printings.

Finally, the letter to Erasmus and the long epitaph appear in the *Opera Omnia Latina* published in 1689, Epistola XII (*Opera Omnia Latina*, 1), pp. 318–19; but the short poem appears in the same edition within the *Epigrammata*, p. 253, under the heading *"Epitaphium in Sepulcro Johannæ, olim uxoris Mori, destinantis idem sepulchrum & sibi & Aliciæ, posteriori uxori."*

Two conclusions can be drawn:

1. In 1534 Erasmus published Ep. 2831 with the two epitaphs. In the letter Thomas More wrote, "You will receive a copy of my Epitaph—*Epitaphium meum accipies.*" From this phrase it is not crystal clear whether a copy of the epitaph was sent with the letter or whether Thomas More intended to send it in the near future; in any case, Erasmus had received it by August 31, 1533. He published the two epitaphs in 1534 after the letter of June 14, 1532 (in which More told him about his resignation as lord chancellor) and before Ep. 2831. Subsequently, those who published Ep. 2831 included the text of the epitaphs after it: *Antiqua* (1536), *Opera Omnia Latina* (1689), and *EE* (1906–58). These introduced the first epitaph at the end of the letter writing: Tabula Affixa ad Sepvlcrum Thomæ Mori; and the second: Epitaphium in Sepulcro (1689) or Epitaphivum inibi Fixvm (*EE*, 1906–58).

2. But others published the epitaphs without mentioning the letter, just trying to reproduce what was on the tombstone: *English Works* (Rastell 1557), and *Omnia Latina Opera* (1565 and 1566).

Following this second group, the Latin text on the tombstone is given as an Appendix to the *Vita Thomæ Mori*, by Thomas Stapleton, *Francofurti ad Moenum* 1689, facsimile 1964, page 76, and (together with references to the Thomas More's *English Works*) as Appendix IV of Harpsfield's *Life of More*, edited by Elsie Vaughan Hitchcock and published for the Early English Text Society, by Oxford University Press, London, 1932.

Of the first biographies, Roper (1558) did not mention the epitaph, nor any of Thomas More's writings. Harpsfield (1558) and Stapleton (1588) mentioned the epitaph. The two of them referred to Sir John More's qualities as described in the epitaph in the first paragraph of their biographies of Thomas

More. Harpsfield described the epitaph explicitly within his section on Thomas More's *Resignation*. Neither of the two mentioned the letter of Thomas More to Erasmus referring to the epitaph.

Cresacre More (1627), following Stapleton—as he acknowledged—mentions the epitaph in chapter I, paragraph 1, of his *Life of Thomas More*, in describing the virtues of his father, Sir John More (p. 9), and elsewhere (pp. 10, 70, 126, and 211). On p. 211 he quoted the letter to Erasmus in which Thomas More mentioned the epitaph, but Cresacre More did not infer explicitly that the epitaph was sent accompanying the letter.

From what is said, though we have to be especially grateful to the editors of *EE* and to Elizabeth Rogers for making the epitaphs on the tombstone and their translation widely available, the texts supplied by them are a bit confusing. A proper critical edition of this material should contain three different sets of texts without mixing them:

1. The texts engraved on the tombstone at Chelsea Old Church, with whatever references we have of previous versions and of the same texts as found in the Latin transcription given in the *English Works* (Rastell 1557) and in *Thomæ Mori Omnia Latina Opera* (1565 and 1566) and their translation.

2. The composition found in *De Præparatione ad mortem* and its translation, that is:

> Letter from Thomas More to Erasmus, June 14, 1532, telling him of his resignation;
> The two epitaphs;
> Letter from Thomas More to Erasmus, <June? 1533>

3. The composition found in *Antiqua* (part of the letter and the two epitaphs) and its translation as done in *A Thomas More Source Book*, pp. 305–10.

The Engraving in Chelsea Old Church

Additional Short Titles

In discussing and transcribing the engraving in Chelsea Old Church the following short titles are used:

English Works (Rastell 1557)	Latin transcription of the two epitaphs given in the *English Works*, pp. 1419–21, published by Rastell in 1557
Engraving, Chelsea Old Church	Transcription of the engraving taken at Chelsea Old Church on June 22, 2008
Epigrammata, poem 258 (1518)	Short epitaph as included in the *Epigrammata,* poem 258, published in 1518 as described in the *CW* 3, part II, p. 6; footnotes on p. 270; and commentary on 410–11
Epigrammata, poem 258 (1520)	Short epitaph as included in the *Epigrammata,* poem 258, published in 1520 as described in the *CW* 3, part II, p. 7; footnotes on p. 270; and commentary on pp. 410–11
Epistola XII (*Opera Omnia Latina,* 1689)	Letter to Erasmus and the long epitaph as published in *Opera Omnia Latina,* 1689, Epistola XII, pages 318–19
Erasmus, *De præparatione ad mortem* (1534)	Latin transcription of the two epitaphs as published by Erasmus in *De præparatione ad mortem* and as per the copies in the British Library 4411.e.16 and 697.b.11
Harpsfield	Transcription of the engraving as edited by Elsie Vaugham Hitchcock as Appendix IV of *The Life and Death of Sr Thomas Moore,* by Nicholas Harpsfield, published for The Early English Text Society, by the Oxford University Press, London, 1932, 277–81
Thomæ Mori Omnia Latina (1565)	Transcription of the two epitaphs in *Thomæ Mori Omnia Latina Opera, Lovanni, Apud Ioannem Bogardum sub Biblijs Aureis, Anno 1565* (British Library VOYN 134)— this is the best printing of the three editions kept at the British Library. The three have the same composition.
Vita Thomæ Mori (1689)	Latin transcription given on page 76 at the end of the *Vita Thomæ Mori,* by Thomas Stapleton, published Francofurti, 1689

Transcription of the Present Engraving on the Tombstone in Chelsea Old Church[7] ANNO. 1532.[8]

1   THOMAS MORVS[9] VRBE[10] LONDINENSI FAMILIA NON CELEBRI SED
HONESTA NATVS IN LITERIS[11] VTCVNQ[12]

7. The Latin transcription given here and in the body of this essay has been taken directly from the inscription as it stands at Chelsea Old Church as checked on June 22, 2008.

EE, vol. 10, page 260, note 61, says that the monument was restored in 1644 and in 1833. Underneath the tombstone there is an inscription that reads, "This monument having become dilapidated was restored by voluntary subscription in the year 1833." Thomas Faulkner reported in *The Gentleman's Magazine* (December 1833): 485–86 on the restoration of the monument by Mr. J. Faulkner, statuary of Chelsea. Rogers, in *SL*, page 181, added, "The monument was much damaged in the bombing of Chelsea Old Church, but has been most carefully restored." An inscription in the entrance porch of the church states that it was destroyed in the bombing on April 16, 1941, and reconsecrated on May 13, 1958. That is, the engraved text on the tombstone studied by Hitchcock in 1932 may differ from the present engraving (2008), though it does not seem that it was much damaged apart from two big cracks, which do not interfere much with the wording.

In *English Works* (Rastell 1557) it is written that Thomas More "caused [the epitaph] to be made in the parish church of Chelsea (where he dwelt) three miles from London. The copy of which epitaph here follows." In *Vita Thomæ Mori* (1689), at the top of page 76, the text of the Epitaph is preceded by the following lines:

EPITAPHIUM
THOMÆ MORI,
QUOD PAULO POST ABDICATUM
CANCELLARII MUNUS
ipse sibi composuit, & sepulchro suo in parochiali sua
Ecclesia affixit.

while in (1534) there is no mention of the church in Chelsea. Therefore, it seems that *English Works* (Rastell 1557) and *Vita Thomæ Mori* (1689)—as well as *Thomæ Mori Omnia Latina* (1565)— were not dependent on (Erasmus, *De præparatione ad mortem* [1534]).

8. This date is carved on the white stone under the arch above the black marble tombstone. It does not appear in any of the other versions of the text of the epitaph considered in the text: Erasmus, *De præparatione ad mortem* (1534), *Antiqua* (1536); *English Works* (Rastell 1557); *Thomæ Mori Omnia Latina Opera* (1565, 1566, and 1689), and *Vita Thomæ Mori* (1689). Therefore, it is not clear whether the engraving is original. It seems odd that it does not include the initials A.D. or a similar reference. Harpsfield's *Life*, published in 1932 for the Early English Text Society, was reprinted in 1963; in this reprinting there is a photograph in which the present (2008) arrangement—"ANNO. 1532."—appears but the transcription of the engraving has only "1532." Therefore, it is not clear what the real situation in 1932 was, either.

9. The engraving on the tombstone of the first epitaph (lines 1–32) and the transcription given by Hitchcock (Harpsfield) are done in Roman lapidary writing (all capitals, use of V for U, etc.). In the *English Works* (Rastell 1557) and in *Opera Omnia Latina* (1689) lower and upper case are used: "*Thomas Morus vrbe Londinensi, familia non celebri, sed honesta natus, in literis utcunque versatus.*" The engraving of the twelve-line poem on the tombstone is done using upper and lower case.

10. Erasmus, *De præparatione ad mortem* (1534); *Thomæ Mori Omnia Latina* (1565); and *Vita Thomæ Mori* (1689): "urbe"; *English Works* (Rastell 1557) and *EE* (1941): "vrbe"; Epistola XII (*Opera Omnia Latina*, 1689): "urbi."

11. Erasmus, *De præparatione ad mortem* (1534), *English Works* (Rastell 1557): litteris; *Vita Thomæ Mori* and Epistola XII (*Opera Omnia Latina*, 1689): literis

12. Erasmus, *De præparatione ad mortem* (1534); *Vita Thomæ Mori* (1689); Epistola XII (*Opera Omnia Latina*, 1689); and *EE* (1941): utcunque;

2   VERSATVS:[13] QVVM ET[14] CAVSAS ALIQVOT ANNOS[15] IVVENIS
     ECISSET[16] IN FORO ET[17] IN VRBE SVA PRO SHIREVO[18] IVS

3   DIXISSET[19]; AB INVICTISSMO[20] REGE HENRICO OCTAVO[21]
     (CVI VNI REGVM OMNIVM[22] GLORIA PRIVS INAVDITA

4   CONTIGIT VT FIDEI DEFENSOR QVALEM ET GLADIO SE ET CALAMO
     VERE[23] PRÆSTITIT, MERITO VOCARETVR)

5   ADSCITVS IN AVLAM EST DELECTVSQ; IN CONSILIVM ET CREATVS
     EQVES PROQVÆSTOR PRIMV, POST CANCELLARIVS

6   LANCASTRIÆ, TANDEM ANGLIÆ MIRO PRINCIPIS FAVORE FACTVS
     EST SED INTERIM IN PVBLICO REGNI

7   SENATV LECTVS EST ORATOR POPVLI, PRÆTEREA LEGATVS REGIS
     NONNVNQVA[24] FVIT ALIAS ALIBI, POSTREMO

English Works (Rastell 1557): vtcunq´.

Thomæ Mori Omnia Latina (1565): vtcnq;

13. This is the first punctuation break on the tombstone; it helps to emphasize that "IN LITERIS VTCUNQ VERSATUS" forms part of the first sentence; therefore, it refers to Thomas More's entire life.

14. Erasmus, *De præparatione ad mortem* (1534); *English Works* (Rastell 1557); *Vita Thomæ Mori* (1689); and Epistola XII (*Opera Omnia Latina*, 1689): &.

15. *Vita Thomæ Mori* (1689) omits "annos"; it reads: "aliquot juvenis."

16. Erasmus, *De præparatione ad mortem* (1534); *English Works* (Rastell 1557); *Thomæ Mori Omnia Latina* (1565); *Vita Thomæ Mori* (1689); Epistola XII (*Opera Omnia Latina*, 1689); Harpsfield; and *EE* (1941): egisset; Engraving, Chelsea Old Church: ECISSET.

17. Erasmus, *De præparatione ad mortem* (1534); *English Works* (Rastell 1557); *Vita Thomæ Mori* (1689); and Epistola XII (*Opera Omnia Latina*, 1689): &.

18. Erasmus, *De præparatione ad mortem* (1534); *Vita Thomæ Mori* (1689); Epistola XII (*Opera Omnia Latina*, 1689): Shyreno; *English Works* (Rastell 1557): Shyreuo; Harpsfield; and Engraving, Chelsea Old Church: SHIREVO. Shyrevo is used also by Thomas Stapleton, in *Vita Thomæ Mori* (1689), p. 9, col. 2, and can be considered the usual Latin spelling at the time. Even though Thomas More used the letter "y" elsewhere, for instance in "Sydera" (Latin Poem, no. 210, cf. *CW* 3.II), it is likely that he tried to avoid it in the lapidary Latin of the engraving because it is a Greek letter introduced into Latin at a later period.

19. Erasmus, *De præparatione ad mortem* (1534); *English Works* (Rastell 1557); *Vita Thomæ Mori* (1689); Epistola XII (*Opera Omnia Latina*, 1689): ", & in urbe sua pro Shyreno jus dixisset."

20. Erasmus, *De præparatione ad mortem* (1534): invictiss;
English Works (Rastell 1557); *Vita Thomæ Mori*; and Epistola XII (*Opera Omnia Latina*, 1689): imictissimo.

21. Erasmus, *De præparatione ad mortem* (1534); *English Works* (Rastell 1557), and *EE* (1941): "octavo";
Vita Thomæ Mori (1689): "VIII"; Epistola XII (*Opera Omnia Latina*, 1689): "Octavo."

22. *English Works* (Rastell 1557): ommium *Vita Thomæ Mori* and Epistola XII (*Opera Omnia Latina*, 1689): omnium

23. *English Works* (Rastell 1557): vero; *Vita Thomæ Mori* and Epistola XII (*Opera Omnia Latina*, 1689): vere.

24. *English Works*, 1419–21 (Rastell 1557): nonnuncquam; Epistola: nonnunquam.

8   VERO CAMERACI COMES ET COLLEGA IVNCTVS PRINCIPE[25]
      LEGATIONIS. CVTHBERTO TVNSTALLO TVM

9   LONDINENSI MOX DVNELMENSI[26] EPISCOPO, QVO VIRO VIX HABET[27]
      ORBIS HODIE QVICQVAM ERVDITIVS, PRVDENTIVS,

10   MELIVS. IBI INTER SVMMOS ORBIS CHRISTIANI MONARCHAS RVRSVS
      REFECTA FOEDERA, REDDITAMQ; MVNDO

11   DIV DESIDERATAM PACEM ET LÆTISSIMVS VIDIT ET LEGATVS
      INTERFVIT

12   "QVAM SVPERI PACEM FIRMENT FAXINTQ; PERENNEM."[28]

13   IN HOC OFFICIORVM VEL HONORVM CVRSV, QVVM ITA VERSARETVR
      VT NEQ: PRINCEPS OPTIMVS OPERAM

14   EIVS IMPROBARET NEQ: NOBILIBVS ESSET INVISVS. NEC INIVCVNDVS
      POPVLO, FVRIBVS AVTEM ET

15   HOMICIDIS [ ][29] MOLESTVS. PATER EIVS TANDEM IOHANNES MORVS,
      EQVÆS ET IN EVM IVDICVM ORDINEM

16   A PRINCIPE COOPTATVS QVI REGIVS CONFESSVS VOCATVR; HOMO
      CIVILIS, SVAVIS, INNOCENS. MITIS, MISERICORS,

17   ÆQVVS ET INTEGER, ANNIS QVIDEM. GRAVIS, SED CORPORE
      PLVSQVAM PRO ÆTATE VIVIDO. POSTQVAM

25. Erasmus, *De præparatione ad mortem* (1534); *English Works* (Rastell 1557), Epistola: principi.
26. *English Works* (Rastell 1557): Dunelniensi. Epistola: Dunelmensi.
27. *English Works* (Rastell 1557): habes; Epistola: habet.
28. Erasmus, *De præparatione ad mortem* (1534): New line, centered, no inverted commas:

   dit, & legatus interfuit,
                  Quam superi pacem firment faxiuntq perennem
   In hoc officiorum vel honorum cursu, quum it versaretur ut neq

English Works (Rastell 1557): New line, not centred, no inverted commas:
   legatus interfuit.
   Quam superi pacem firment faxiuntq
   perennem.
   In hoc officiorum vel honorum cursu,

Thomæ Mori Omnia Latina (1565, 1566): italics, centered, no inverted commas.
Epistola XII (*Opera Omnia Latina*, 1689): New line, centered, and italics.
Vita Thomæ Mori (1689): New line and centered; not italics.
Harpsfield; Engraving, Chelsea Old Church: Between inverted commas and centered on the
   tombstone.

29. Harpsfield: "In the present Inscription on the Tomb, the state of the marble proves that no
writing ever filled the blank space between HOMICIDES and MOLESTVS." This is the case also in
Engraving, Chelsea Old Church.

18   EO PRODVCTAM SIBI VITAM. VIDIT VT FILIVM VIDERET ANGLIÆ
     CANCELLARIVM, SATIS IN TERRA IAM

19   SE MORATVM RATVS, LIBENS EMIGRAVIT IN CŒLVM. AT FILIVS,
     DEFVNCTO PATRE. CVI QVAMDIV

20   SVPERARAT COMPARATVS ET IVVENIS VOCARI CONSVEVERAT, ET IPSE
     QVOQ: SIBI VIDEBATVR.

21   AMISSVM IAM PATREM REQVIRENS ET ÆDITOS EX SE LIBEROS
     QVATVOR AC NEPOTES VNDECIM

22   RESPICIENS APVD ANIMVM SVVM CÆPIT PERSENESCERE. AVXIT HVNC
     AFFECTVM ANIMI SVBSECVTA

23   STATIM VELVT ADPETENTIS SENI SIGNVM, PECTORIS VALETVDO
     DETERIOR. ITAQ: MORTALIVM

24   HARVM RERVM SATVR, QVAM REM A PVERO PENE SEMPER OPTAVERAT,
     VT VLTIMOS ALIQVOT VITÆ

25   SVÆ ANNOS OBTINERET LIBEROS, QVIBVS HVIVS VITÆ NEGOTIIS
     PAVLATIM SE SEDVCENS FVTVRÆ POSSIT

26   IMMORTALITATEM MEDITARI, EAM REM TANDEM (SI CÆPTIS ANNVAT
     DEVS) INDVLGENTISSIMI PRINCIPIS

27   INCOMPARABILI BENEFICIO, RESIGNATIS HONORIBVS, IMPETRAVIT:
     ATQ: HOC SEPVLCHRVM SIBI, QVOD

28   MORTIS EVM NVNQVAM CESSANTIS ADREPERE QVOTIDIE
     COMMONEFACERET TRANSLATIS HVC PRIORIS

29   VXORIS OSSIBVS EXTRVENDVM CVRAVIT. QVOD NE SVPERSTES
     FRVSTRA SIBI FECERIT NEVE

30   INGRVENTEM TREPIDVS MORTEM HORREAT, SED DESIDERIO CHRISTI
     LIBENS OPPETAT. MORTEMQ;

31   VT SIBI NON OMNINO MORTEM, SED IANVAM VITÆ FÆLICIORIS
     INVENIAT PRECIBVS EVM PIIS

32   LECTOR OPTIME SPIRANTEM PRÆCOR, DEFVNCTVMQ; PROSEQVERE.

Chara Thomæ iacet hic[30] Ioanna[31] Vxorcula Mori
Qui tumulum Aliciciæ[32] hunc destino: quiq: mihi

30. *Epigrammata,* poem 258 (1518, 1520): hoc
Erasmus, *De præparatione ad mortem* (1534); *English Works* (Rastell 1557); *Vita Thomæ Mori*
(1689); Harpsfield; Engraving, Chelsea Old Church: hic.
31. *Epigrammata,* poem 258 (1518, 1520); *Thomæ Mori Omnia Latina* (1565): Iohanna;
Erasmus, *De præparatione ad mortem* (1534); *English Works* (Rastell 1557); Harpsfield; Engraving,
Chelsea Old Church: Ioanna;
Vita Thomæ Mori (1689): Joanna.
32. *Epigrammata,* poem 258 (1518, 1520), *Vita Thomæ Mori* (1689): Aliciæ;

Vna mihi dedit hoc coniuncta virentibvs annis
Me vocet vt puer et trina puella patrem.
Altera priuignis (quæ gloria rara Nouercæ est)
Tam pia quam gnatis vix fuit vlla svis.
Altera sic mecum vixit sic altera viuit
Charior insertum[33] est hæc sit an illa fuit.[34]
O simul, O Iuncti poteramus viuere nos tres
Quam bene, si fatum,[35] religioq: sinant.
At societ tumulus, societ nos, obsecro cœlum
Sic Mors non potuit quod dare vita, dabit.

Conclusions on the Transcription of the Epitaphs

From the previous notes a number of conclusions can be drawn:

1. The text of the engraving as checked in 2008 coincides with that reported in 1932—apart from the date above the epitaph (Harpsfield: "1532."/Engraving, Chelsea Old Church: "ANNO 1532") and the variation in line 2, "ecisset" for Engraving, Chelsea Old Church and "egisset" in Harpsfield: this variation can be clearly identified on the photographs taken and on the notes of June 22, 2008.

2. Looking at the short epitaph and disregarding several errors—*factum* in *English Works* (Rastell 1557) (which the editor would have recognized as an error because he gave the correct English translation: *fortune*) and *Aliciciæ* and *insertum* in Harpsfield and Engraving, Chelsea Old Church —the main variations can be reduced to two groups:

Erasmus, *De præparatione ad mortem* (1534); *English Works* (Rastell 1557): Alicie; Harpsfield; Engraving, Chelsea Old Church: Aliciciæ.

33. *Epigrammata,* poem 258 (1518, 1520); Erasmus, *De præparatione ad mortem* (1534); *English Works* (Rastell 1557); *Thomæ Mori Omnia Latina* (1565): incertum; Harpsfield; Engraving, Chelsea Old Church: insertum.

34. *Epigrammata,* poem 258 (1518, 1520); Erasmus, *De præparatione ad mortem* (1534); *English Works* (Rastell 1557); *Thomæ Mori Omnia Latina* (1565); *Vita Thomæ Mori* (1689): hæc fuerit; Harpsfield; Engraving, Chelsea Old Church: illa fuit.

35. *Epigrammata,* poem 258 (1518, 1520); Erasmus, *De præparatione ad mortem* (1534); *Vita Thomæ Mori* (1689); Harpsfield; Engraving, Chelsea Old Church: fatum; *English Works* (Rastell 1557): factum.

Epigrammata, poem 258 (1518, 1520); *Thomæ Mori Omnia Latina* (1565):	*hoc, Iohanna,* and *Aliciæ*
Erasmus, *De præparatione ad mortem* (1534); *English Works* (Rastell 1557); Harpsfield; and Engraving, Chelsea Old Church:	*hoc, Ioanna,* and *Alicie*
apart from the variation introduced by Harpsfield and Engraving, Chelsea Old Church:	*illa fuit*

3. The variations in the long epitaph are minor apart from what has already been pointed out with regard to Shyrevo, which in the lapidary Latin appears as Shirevo

Translation of the Text on the Tombstone

Thomas More was born in the City of London,[36] **of an honest**[37] **though not famous family, and was always engaged in letters in one way or another.**[38] **After spending several years of his youth pleading in the law courts and administering justice on behalf of the sheriff in his city,**[39] he was admitted to the Court by the Unconquerable King Henry the Eighth, who is the only King to have ever received the unique distinction of meriting the title "Defender of the Faith,"[40] a

36. This extract includes my translation because in some places it differs from that given by Rogers in *SL*, which omits "the City of." I have marked in bold the phrases that differ from Rogers's translation. I include it here because the "City of London" continues to be the usual way to refer to it in English nowadays, but also because throughout the entire epitaph Thomas More is using the Latin terminology of the Roman republic, and the English translation should convey this deliberate intention of the author—for instance, in *urbe, honesta, foro, proquæstor, Princeps, senatu*, etc.

37. *Familia non celebri sed honesta natus.* In classical Latin *honestas* meant both "moral excellence" and "reputation," which in the context of the City of Rome and referring to a family conveyed the "approval of the City." In *The Dialogue against Tribulation*, Thomas More seems to define *celebritas* and *honestitas* as outward goods of fortune (book 3, chapter 7); there he considers good name, honest estimation, and fame. He says that "the three are of their own nature one and the same, but in common speech the three expressions are used to designate different degrees. A good name can be had by anyone, no matter how poor. Honest estimation, in the common use of people, can be had by not just anyone, but by someone with some standing and wealth who is held in some reputation among his neighbors. And when they hear the word fame people think of the renown of individuals in very great and powerful positions who are much and far spoken of by reason of their praiseworthy acts" (book 3, chapter 9; *CW* 12, 211:7–16).

38. Rogers, in *SL*, translated it as, "Thomas More was born in London of respectable, though not distinguished, ancestry; he engaged to some extent in literary matters." As pointed out in the transcription, there is no break into two sentences in the original text: the semicolon added by Roger takes away the emphasis of the original, which is to place More's expertise in letters—*in literis vtcvnq versatvs*—within the first sentence, thus qualifying all of More's life.

39. Rogers, *SL*: "and after spending several years of his youth as a pleader in the law courts and after having held the office of judge as an Under-Sheriff in his native city." Although William Roper already used the word "undersheriff," the suggested more literal translation of the Latin explains the legal nature of the job performed by Thomas More and conveys his style. He was writing also for European humanists, thus the technical English law terms required explanation.

40. This phrase—AB INVICTISSMO REGE HENRICO OCTAVO ... FIDEI DEFENSOR ...

title earned by deeds of sword and pen;[41] he was chosen member of the **Council**,[42] knighted, appointed Under-Treasurer and then Chancellor of Lancaster, and finally Chancellor of England by the special favour of the **Prince**.[43] **Meanwhile, in the public Senate of the realm he was elected Spokesman of the people** [Speaker of the House of Commons];[44] furthermore, he served as the King's ambassador at various times and in various places, last of all at Cambrai, as an associate and colleague of Cuthbert Tunstall,[45] then Bishop of London and shortly after Bishop of Durham, a man whose equal in learning, wisdom, and virtue[46] is seldom seen in the world today. In that place, in the capacity of ambassador, he witnessed to his great joy, the renewal of a peace treaty between the supreme monarchs of Christendom and the restoration of long-desired peace to the world.

"May heaven confirm this peace and make it a lasting one."[47]
He so conducted himself all through this series of high offices or honours that

---

—is similar to the introductory paragraph in the *Responsio ad Lutherum*, which reads, "*inuictissimum ... regem HENRICVM eius nominis octauum, Fide defensorem*"; cf. *CW* 5.I, 1:4–6.

41. Thomas More wrote that "for the faith of Christ he [King Henry] deigned to fight with his pen against the most foolish of heretics"; *Responsio ad Lutherum*, *CW* 5.I, 57:22.

42. Rogers has "King's Council" perhaps to avoid confusion with the city or other councils; I think, however, that there is no danger of confusion, so I prefer not to add to the Latin.

43. Rogers, in *SL*, translates "by the special favour of his Sovereign." The original reads, "miro Principis favour." I have kept "Prince" because—as said previously—Thomas More uses a terminology rooted in the Roman republic.

In fact, Thomas More addressed Henry as "Prince," for instance, in the speech—presumably in English—after being appointed Speaker of the Commons as transcribed by Roper, page 15, lines 5 and 19.

44. Rogers, *SL*, translates correctly "Speaker of the House of Commons"; however, in the letter to Erasmus (*EE*, Ep. 2831, line 58), Thomas More explained his meaning—"*in senatu, quem senatum (vt scis) nos Perleamentum vocamus*"—but kept "*senatu.*" More's phrasing here is extraordinary: "Orator populi"; Cicero, of course, uses "orator" in the title of his most famous books on the philosopher-statesman. More, in writing "Orator populi" instead of Speaker of the Commons, is conceiving that role as that of an "advocate of the people," who indeed are supposed to be represented by the Commons. I have kept "senate" to maintain the Roman link, but nowadays "senate" is used in most countries to designate the upper house; therefore, I have opted for inserting in brackets its meaning: Speaker of the House of Commons. Rastell translated it for "speaker of the parliament."

45. The first of these royal commissions entrusted to More and Tunstall took place from May to October 1515 in the Low Countries and was the occasion for More to write *Utopia*. At the beginning of it he praises Cuthbert Tunstall because of "*virtus eius, ac doctrina*" (cf. *Utopia*, in *CW* 4, 46:17). Tunstall is the only person mentioned in the epitaph apart from More's family and the king. See General Commentary to follow.

46. Thomas More is here giving high praise to Bishop Tunstall: erudition, prudence, and moral goodness or holiness of life—*eruditius, prudentius, melius*—are the three requirements for a bishop, prudence being the key virtue for government, according to Plato and Cicero. Tunstall opposed the royal supremacy of Henry VIII but accepted it in the end. Later developments under Edward VI and Elizabeth made him change his mind, and he was deprived of his bishopric under both.

47. The preceding lines, with their emphasis on peace, indicate More's agreement with Erasmus's and other Renaissance scholars' principal concern for a peaceful Christendom. This line is the only one indented in the main text on his tombstone; on the transcription of the engraving, see in the *English Works* (Rastell 1557); in *Thomæ Mori Opera Latina Omnia* (1565, 1566, and 1689); and accompanying the letter given in Erasmus, *De præparatione ad mortem* (1534) and Epistola XII (*Opera Omnia Latina*, 1689). It is not emphasized in *Antiqua* (1539).

his Excellent **Prince**[48] found no fault with his service,[49] neither did he make himself odious to the nobles nor unpleasant to the populace, but he was **troublesome** to thieves, murderers, [ ].[50] **His father, John More, was a knight and**

48. We find here again the word "Princeps" in Latin. It is used five times in the epitaph, and—apart from what has already been said about the Latin style of the Roman republic—it is worth focusing on this word, which was used to designate the leader during the Roman Empire and was taken up during the European Renaissance.

I. It seems that "*Princeps*" etymologically comes from the substantive "*primum*" and the verb "*capio*," and could be translated as "the first chosen." It meant the first man, first person, chief, most distinguished person, leader, ruler, first in commencing hostilities, etc. In Rome it was first used in the military; it meant the first line of soldiers; later on, these chosen soldiers were positioned in the second line; it was also used to denote the first senator, and this was the use that was taken up to designate the emperor.

II. After the period of the kings, the City of Rome became a republic governed by the senate and the people, the executive being two annually elected consuls. In 49 BC Cæsar took over Rome by military power. He was murdered in 44 BC, and Rome was ruled by a Triumvirate until Octavius Cæsar Augustus (63 BC–AD 14) managed to become sole ruler in 27 BC and, rejecting the title of rex or dictator, choose the title of *Princeps*, as first senator, from 23 BC.

Cicero (106 BC–43 BC) championed a return to the traditional republican government and wrote about the office of the *Princeps* as political leader or ruler: if he was to rule the people properly he himself had to be ruled by virtue. See, for instance, in *De Officiis, Liber I:15*, where Cicero writes that the "*princeps*" must have the virtue of prudence. Thus, in Roman Latin "*princeps*" meant generally the political ruler, leader, or chief; and at some stage the title was given to the emperor as a way to legitimize his autarchy within the constitution of the republic.

III. The Latin Vulgate of St. Jerome (345–420) makes a lot of use of the newer Latin word "*princeps*" as a translation of "arch" or "arcwn"—which meant chief, ruler, captain, leader—as political rulers (Psalm 2:2, *principes convenerunt in unum*), or chief of the priests or chief priests (*principi sacerdotum*, Mk 1:44/*principes sacerdotum*, Mk 11:18), or chief of the devils (*principe dæmoniorum*, Mk 3:22). Though More would try to use the Latin of Cicero rather than that of the Vulgate, this does show continuity in the use of "*princeps*," meaning chief, ruler, leader.

IV. St Augustine (354–430) uses it extensively for instance in the *De civitate Dei*, in which he often mentioned Cicero.

V. In the European Renaissance humanists used once again the word "*princeps*" as a way of linking with Roman culture; see, for instance, *The Prince* (1513) by Machiavelli (1469–1527), and *The Education of a Christian Prince* (1516) by Erasmus, published the same year as *Utopia*.

VI. In Utopia the head of each city is a prince (*Principis magistratus*; cf. *Utopia*, book II, in *CW* 4, 122:19) elected for life, and there is no one head for the whole island (cf. Logan and Adams, *Utopia* (1989), 49n23). Also in book II "*princeps*" is used not only for the person of the leader but also for the capital city (*CW* 4, 112:27). In book I, however, More and Raphæl use both "*princeps*" and "*rex*."

VII. In the epitaph, as said, "*Princeps*" is used five times and "*Rex*" and its cognates are used four, but the emphasis is different. "*Princeps*" is used accompanied by words somehow expressing virtues: special favor of the prince, chosen by the prince, excellent prince, indulgent prince; while the first time that "*Rex*" appears, it is part of the name itself, and the second makes immediate reference to the previous one: "*Rege Henrico octavo (cui uni Regum …)*"; the other two qualify the job or the institution: "*legatus Regis*," "*regius consessus*." Interestingly Thomas More uses "*Rex*" several times in the letter to Erasmus referring to the epitaph, but does not use "*Princeps*" once there; it seems that the Ciceronian and laudatory style of the engraving was dropped in the letter.

In conclusion, Thomas More used both "*Princeps*" and "*Rex*" in the epitaph, and his choice should be reflected in the translation. Rastell's translation kept the distinction between "*Princeps*" and "*Rex*."

49. Wegemer, *Thomas More*, points out that More expanded on this topic in his letter to Erasmus.
50. The space is blank (Engraving, Chelsea Old Church). In former versions it said "*hæreticisque*."

chosen by the Prince as member of that group of judges known as the King's Bench; he was an affable man, charming, irreproachable, gentle, merciful, fair and upright;[51] though venerable in age, he was vigorous for a man of his years; after he had lived to see the day when his son was Chancellor of England, he deemed his sojourn upon earth complete and gladly departed for heaven. The son, all through his father's lifetime, had been compared with him, and was commonly known as the young More, and so he considered himself to be; but now he felt the loss of his father, and as he looked upon the four children he had reared and his eleven grandchildren, he began, in his own mind, to grow old. This feeling was increased by a serious chest ailment, which developed soon after, as an indication of approaching old age. Now sated with the passing things of this life, he resigned office and, through the unparalleled graciousness of a most indulgent **Prince** (may God **look** favourably upon his enterprises), he at length reached the goal which almost since boyhood had been the object of his longing—to have the last years of his life all to himself, so that he could gradually retire from the affairs of this world and contemplate the eternity of the life to come. Then he arranged for the construction of this tomb for himself, to be a constant reminder of the unrelenting advance of death, and had the remains of his first wife transferred to this place. That he may not have erected this tomb in vain while still alive, and that he may not shudder with fear at the thought of encroaching death, but may go to meet it gladly, with longing for Christ, and that he may find death not completely a death for himself but rather the gateway to a happier life, I beg you, kind reader, attend him with your prayers while he still lives and also when he has done with life.

In 1941 the editors of *EE* (cf. Volume X, page 260, note Ep. 2831, line 61) wrote that it was already blank then and stated that "Weever in his Funeral Monuments, 1631, giving the inscription 'now hardly to be read,' includes *hæreticisque*. The word may have been omitted when the monument was restored by Sir John Lawrence in 1644, or in the restoration of 1833." It seems, however, that any blank space kept at a restoration would indicate that the word had been erased before; otherwise, the restoration would have avoided evidence that there was an omission. Probably, therefore, it was omitted soon after the beginning of the Civil War (1642), certainly after 1631, and most likely before 1644.

51. *Civilis, suavis, innocens, mitis, misericors, Æquus et integer*. Rogers, in *SL*, translates *Æquus* for "honest"; Wegemer, *Thomas More*—having discussed previously the meaning of *honestas*/honest (see footnote 50)—suggests that a loose use of honest should be avoided. Cresacre More, translates "*Æquus et integer*" for "just and uncorrupted." "Just and uncorrupted" would be fine if Thomas More were speaking of the qualities of his father as a judge, though indeed "just" is assumed in a judge. More, however, did not use the Latin "*justus*." It seems to me that "just" is too strong to be included within a series of qualities of a person; at times "Æquus" is translated by "impartial or fair," other times "affable or kind"; the meaning—referring to the person, rather than the job—is even-tempered. The phrase "Æquus et integer" is found also in Erasmus's letter to Dorp, [May] 1515, *EE*, 337:572, and translated in *CWE*, 337:600 for "fair and upright."

1   Here lies Jane,[52] the beloved little wife of Thomas More,
2   I intend that this same tomb shall be Alice's and mine, too.
3   One, my wife in my youthful years,
4   has made me father of a son and three daughters;
5   the other has been as devoted to her stepchildren (a rare distinction in a stepmother)
6   as very few mothers are to their own children.
7   The one lived out her life with me, the other still lives with me:
8   I cannot decide whether I did love the one or do love the other more.
9   O, how happily we could have lived all three together
10 if fate and religion had permitted.
11 The grave will unite us however, and I pray that heaven will unite us too.
12 Thus death will give what life could not.[53]

52. John Guy, *A Daughter's Love* (2008, page 10) suggests that "she is often called Jane by modern writers, but in handwritten family documents her name is either 'Joanna' or occasionally 'Joan.'" I have not examined the handwritten documents mentioned by Guy; it is not, however, just more recent writers. Cresacre More, who wrote in English, calls her Jane; this is the name that appears also in the translation of the epitaph published in the *English Works* (Rastell 1557). Her name is not given by the other early English authors—namely, Roper, Harpsfield, and Ro: Ba:. Rogers, in *SL*, and Miller, in *CW* 3.2, call her Jane, and so she is called in the most recent volume of *CWE*, vol. 20 (2020), 86.

53. My translation follows closely that given by Rogers in *SL*, 182–83, and by Clarence H. Miller in *CW* 3.2, poem 258, which are

Elizabeth F. Rogers

My beloved wife, Jane, lies here. I, Thomas More, intend that this same tomb shall be Alice's and mine, too.

One of these ladies, my wife in the days of my youth, has made me father of a son and three daughters;

the other has been as devoted to her stepchildren (a rare attainment in a stepmother) as very few mothers are to their own children.

The one lived out her life with me, and the other still lives with me on such terms that I cannot decide whether I did love the one or do love the other more.

O, how happily we could have lived all three together if fate and morality permitted.

Well, I pray that the grave, that heaven, will bring us together.

Thus death will give what life could not.

Clarence H. Miller

Here lies Jane, the beloved wife of Thomas More, who intend that this same tomb shall be Alice's and mine, too.

One of them, my wife in the years of our vigorous youth, has made me father of a son and three daughters;

the other has been as devoted to her stepchildren (a rare and splendid attainment in a stepmother) as very few mothers are to their own children.

The one lived out her life with me, and the other still lives with me on such terms that I cannot decide whether I did love the one or do love the other more.

O, how happily we could have lived all three together if fate and religion permitted.

But the grave will unite us, and I pray that heaven will unite us too.

Thus death will give what life could not.

General Commentary on the Two Epitaphs

1. Thomas More resigned as lord chancellor on May 16, 1532, the day after Henry VIII pressured the Bishops' Convocation into accepting the king as head of the spiritual order in England, and he decided to write an epitaph to be engraved on his tombstone publicly denying rumors that he had been made to resign by the king. He explained that much in a subsequent letter to Erasmus (*EE*, letter 2831, <June? 1533>):

Some chatterboxes around here began to spread the rumor that I had resigned my office unwillingly and that I had kept that detail a secret. So, after making arrangements for the construction of my tomb, I did not hesitate to make on my Epitaph a public declaration of the actual facts, to allow anyone a chance to refute them, if he could." In the letter he gives a reason for defending himself: "Having written several pamphlets in English in defence of the Faith against some fellow countrymen, who had championed rather perverse doctrines, I considered it my duty to protect the integrity of my reputation.

The content of the epitaph suggests that it is addressed to the king as much as to anybody else. All through the epitaph he praises King Henry as having been a truly Christian prince, and he calls him thus. Thomas More points out how much the king relied on him, specifically by sending him and the then bishop of London as ambassadors to Cambrai for the renewal of the peace treaty among the Christian monarchs. He reminds Henry that—as a Christian prince—he should be willing to "confirm that peace and make it a lasting one." He is telling Henry also that he—More—fought against heretics because this was and continued to be Henry's policy (in the letter to Erasmus, More wrote that the "King appears to be more antagonistic toward heretics than even the bishops are"). And the king had appointed More and Tunstall on the commission to stop the importation of heretical books from the Continent. Henry himself had written in defense of the Faith: this policy, More reminds Henry, merited him the title "Defender of the Faith." That is, in the epitaph, Thomas More continued to advise Henry to keep the Christian values of faith and peace, rather than to succumb to the temptation of lust for power.

More had lost his influence as lord chancellor both to advise Henry against the divorce and against taking over the Church, but Henry continued rejecting heretics and portraying himself as defender of the faith: the epitaph was a last appeal to the king to follow the course of life he professed as a Christian prince.

2. As indicated in the note to his name in the translation, Tunstall is the only person mentioned in the epitaph apart from the king and the members of More's family. Tunstall had received high praise in the opening paragraph of *Utopia*. He worked in the service of the king. In 1515 he went on embassy to the

Low Countries with Thomas More; in 1516 he was made master of the rolls, and in 1522 he became bishop of London (so he was More's local ordinary for some years). While he was bishop of London he was appointed by the king to the anti-heresy commission, together with Thomas More.

Thomas More, John Fisher, and Cuthbert Tunstall were perhaps the three prominent Englishmen most opposed to the divorce. Since the failure of Cardinal Wolsey to obtain the annulment for Henry, the king, advised by Thomas Cromwell, was determined to achieve it by other means, including the repudiation of papal authority over the Church in England in order that his marriage with Catherine be judged in England, rather than in Rome. The two-and-a-half years that Thomas More was lord chancellor, from October 1529 to May 1532, were dominated by the issue. A superficial knowledge of the situation may mistakenly assume that as the chief minister of the king he was most powerful. In fact, this was far from the case. Thomas More was selected as a compromise option between the Duke of Suffolk and Bishop Cuthbert Tunstall: after years of Cardinal Wolsey's chancellorship a layman was preferred, one who had the trust of the king and the expertise of a lawyer. In fact, More had been recommended by Wolsey, but real political power remained in the hands of the two dukes, Suffolk and Norfolk, and later on in those of Thomas Cromwell—who from 1530 was also a member of the Privy Council and gained the confidence of Henry by working for the divorce.

In 1530 Tunstall had become bishop of Durham. When the measures for the Submission of the Clergy were put to the Convocation of York in 1531, he—presiding over the convocation during the archiepiscopal vacancy of York—objected, arguing that the king should not be given the title of supreme head of the English clergy in spiritual matters but only with regard to temporal matters.

Was it wise—we might ask—for Thomas More thus to include in the epitaph one who had opposed the king? Evidently throughout the epitaph More was appealing to the king to reconsider his position and to act as a truly Christian prince, pointing out that he—Henry—had acted honorably by trusting Tunstall and More with the peace treaty of Cambrai. Of course, it was a risky business and one most unlikely to succeed, but was the only resource left to More.

3. Although it is understandable for More to mention his father on the engraving on his tomb out of filial devotion, the first impression is that while listing the offices with which he had been entrusted by the king and the honors he had received from the king, there was no need to dwell extensively on his father. Yet he is not only reminding the king that he had put his trust in him, but he is also placing in front of the king the example of two men—Cuthbert Tunstall and John More—who were erudite, wise, virtuous, affable, charming,

irreproachable, gentle, sympathetic, impartial as judges, and even-tempered, upright in everything.... The time for using biblical or political arguments had gone. Only a change of heart by the attraction of goodness could steer the king back to the right path.

4. Finally, the epitaph mentions his dealing with heretics. His approach is clearly explained in the letter sent to Erasmus with reference to the epitaph. Again, if the purpose of the epitaph, as he says in the letter, was to stop the rumor spread by some, were not Thomas Cromwell, Thomas Crammer, and Edward Foxe, with their leaning toward heresy, the most likely to attack More? Was it not safer to omit any mention of the heretics? On this issue More is proclaiming both to the king and to his possible political enemies that he had followed the king's own policy against heretics—in the letter he writes, as said earlier, that "the King appears to be more antagonistic toward heretics than even the bishops are"—so he boasts that he cannot be blamed; and so far, by <June? 1533>, it seems that he was not attacked on this account, according to what he says in the letter.

5. The epitaph he wrote was a serious attempt to save his life for his own sake and that of his family. More importantly for him, it was a last attempt to change the king's mind and—through *protecting the integrity of his reputation—to defend the Faith* (cf. letter, lines 37–42). But he had to end it on a cheerful note and—as always—in good humor: he added the verses he had written some twenty years earlier after the death of his first wife, Joanna, and his marriage to Alice

> O, how happily we could have lived all three together
> if fate and religion had permitted![54]
> I pray that the grave—that heaven—will bring us together.[55]
> Thus, death will give what life could not.

Even here we can see an advice to Henry to consider matters *sub specie Æternitatis.*

54. Even though written before 1518, when More transcribed this epitaph in the Chelsea Old Church in 1532, he might have had in mind the situation of Henry with regard to Catherine and Anne.

55. St. Augustine, in *The Lord's Sermon on the Mount*, bk 1, ch. 15, says that the Christian would wish his wife to live with him in heaven when they had undergone the angelic change that is promised to the Saints.

Standard Present Sources of the Writings by Thomas More
Early Biographies of Thomas More
A Chronology of Biographical Studies on Thomas More
A Chronology of Studies on the London Charterhouse
General Bibliography

Standard Present Sources of the Writings by Thomas More

Details of available original manuscripts or early sources are given in the "present sources."

Letters

The Correspondence of Sir Thomas More. Edited by Elizabeth Frances Rogers. Princeton, N.J.: Princeton University Press, 1947. This book includes letters in their original language (Latin or English) or gives the reference of 218 letters from or to Thomas More, though only reproduces those not included in the correspondence with Erasmus. Thomas More's correspondence with Erasmus is reproduced in Latin in *Opus Epistolarum Des. Erasmi Roterodami*. Oxford: Oxford University Press, 1906–58). 12 vols. Vols. 1–3, edited by Percy Stafford Allen; vols. 4–8, edited by P. S. Allen and H. M. Allen; and vols. 9–12, edited by H. M. Allen and H. W. Garrod. This work is commonly known as *Erasmi Epistolae*, which is the title that appears on the spine of the twelve volumes, and it is abbreviated as *EE*. The English translation of the correspondence of Thomas More with Erasmus is given in the *Collected Works of Erasmus*, published by Toronto University Press.

St. Thomas More: Selected Letters. Edited by Elizabeth Frances Rogers. New Haven and London: Yale University Press, 1961. It includes, either in modernized English or in English translation, sixty-six letters from Thomas More; all but one are listed in *The Correspondence*. The missing one is letter no. 48 [192*] to John Harris, from Willesden, Sunday <1534>, which comes from a MS immediately after a transcript of More's *Treatise on the Blessed Body*. This letter is referred to in *The Complete Works of St Thomas More*, vol. 13.

A few of the letters from Thomas More mentioned in the *Correspondence* are included in *The Complete Works of St Thomas More*: Letter [4] is included in *CW* 1 (*Life of Pico*) and Letter [5] in *CW* 3.1 (*Translations from Lucian*). The letters that accompanied the publication of *Utopia,* letters [25 and 27] are included in *CW* 4; and the letters to Martin Dorp, letter [15], to the University of Oxford, letter [60], to Edward Lee, letter [75], and to a Monk, letter [83], are included in *CW* 15 under the title "In Defence of Humanism."

A new bundle of letters, which included seven additional letters from Thomas More to Cranevelt, became available in 1989. These were reported by Hubertus Schulte Herbrüggen in "Seven New Letters from Thomas More," *Moreana* no. 103 (1990); he published their full text and translation in "Morus ad Craneveldium: Litterae Balduinianae Novae" [More to Cranevelt: New Baudouin Letters]," *Supplementa Humanistica Lovaniensia XI* (Leuven: Leuven University Press, 1997). Clarence H. Miller published those seven new letters, together with the six letters from More to Cranevelt already included in the *Correspondence*, in "Thomas More's Letters to Frans van Cranevelt Including Seven Recently Discovered Autographs: Latin Text, English Translation, and Facsimiles of the Original," *Moreana*, no. 117 (1994): 3–66.

Hubertus Schulte Herbrüggen published another five letters of More's correspondence in *Moreana*, no. 8 (1965); nos. 15/16 (1967); and nos. 79/80 (1983); and eighteen other letters in *Sir Thomas More: Neue Briefe* (Münster: Aschendorff, 1966).

There are several editions of the last letters of More; a recent and well-known edition is that by Alvaro de Silva, ed., *The Last Letters of Thomas More* (Grand Rapids, Mich.: Eerdmans, 2000). It gives modernized versions of *Correspondence* [194–95, 197–218] with extensive commentary.

The Essential Works of Thomas More. Edited by Gerard B. Wegemer and Stephen W. Smith. New Haven and London: Yale University Press, 2020. This volume includes most of the letters in modern English.

Thomas More's Prayer Book

Thomas More's Prayer Book: *A Facsimile Reproduction of the Annotated Pages*, edited by Louis L Martz and Richard Sylvester. New Haven: Yale University Press, 1969.

All Other Works of Thomas More

All the other works of Thomas More are included in *The Complete Works of St. Thomas More*, 15 vols. New Haven and London: Yale University Press, 1963–97, which contain the original texts in English or Latin, translation from Latin into English, introductions, sources, commentaries, notes, and glossaries; most of them are included in modern English in *The Essential Works of Thomas*

More, ed. Gerard B. Wegemer and Stephen W. Smith. New Haven and London: Yale University Press, 2020.

The Dialogue Concerning Tyndale, reproduced in facsimile and edited with a Modern Version of the Same and an Essay on the Spirit and Doctrine of the Dialogue, by W. E. Campbell. (London, 1927); see the full title of that work in chapter 1 of this book. In addition, the *English Works*, published by William Rastell, 1557, is available, and at least three editions of the same Latin works are also accessible: (1) *Omnia Latina Opera, Lovanni, Apud Ioannem Bogardum sub Biblijs Aureis*, 1565 (BL VOYN 134)—this is the best kept printing of the three; (2) *Lovanni, Apud Petrum Zangrium Tiletanum sub Fonte, Anno 1565* (British Library 3936.i.15); and (3) *Lovanni, 1566* (British Library 632.i.8). There are further editions, such as *Omnia Latina Opera* (Francofuiti, 1689), reproduced in facsimile in 1963.

All the works by Thomas More are available on the website of the Center for Thomas More Studies at the University of Dallas.

Editions of *Utopia*

There are two main types of editions of English translations of *Utopia* in print nowadays: those recently translated from the Latin, and the English translation of 1551 by Ralph Robinson. The English translation by Robinson holds its own value insofar as it has been used in England since the sixteenth century,[56] but undoubtedly for a study of the book written by Thomas More the reader must go to the Latin text or a recent translation from the Latin or, better, to an edition that includes both the Latin and a recent translation. Two of these have prominence among scholars: *Utopia: Latin Text and English Translation*, edited by Edward Surtz, SJ, and J. H. Hexter, in *The Complete Works of St Thomas More*, vol. 4 (New Haven: Yale University Press, 1965); and *Utopia: Latin Text and English Translation*, edited by George M. Logan, Robert Martin Adams, and Clarence H. Miller (Cambridge: Cambridge University Press, 1995). The most recent English translation is *Utopia*, translated, edited, and introduced by Dominic Baker Smith (London: Penguin, 2012). The translation by Paul Turner (1965) departs widely from the original even though—according to Marius in 1994—it was "the only readily accessible English translation of *Utopia* worth reading." Marius's comment in praise of Turner's translation was written

56. Richard Marius's Introduction to the Everyman's edition of *Utopia* (1994) is especially informative because it points out the main change introduced in Robinson's translation: "He converted a solidly republican Utopian commonwealth," writes Marius, "into a monarchy." In fact, however, there is more to it in the so-called English *Utopia*. Produced during the reign of Edward VI, it seems to respond to a genuine concern for the best possible commonwealth under a philosopher-king; it envisaged a government that Jennifer Bishop calls a *monarchical republicanism* and in which citizens take in social reform but always recognize their dependence on the king; Jennifer Bishop, "*Utopia* and Civic Politics in Mid-Sixteenth-Century London," *Historical Journal* 54, no. 4 (2011): 933–53. See also the entry on Ralph Robinson's translation in the index of Guy, *Thomas More* (2000).

in 1994, and in the same place he said that the English version of the Yale edition is rather unsatisfactory; if so, the Cambridge (1995) and Baker-Smith's (2012) translations can be considered improvements.

The edition by J. H. Lupton, *The Utopia of Sir Thomas More* (Clarendon Press, Oxford 1895), is well known, but it is just a printing of the Latin of March 1518 and of the translation of Robinson in 1551, rather than a new translation, and the bibliographical and other data included in his Introduction have been incorporated or superseded in more recent editions.

The Latin and French edition of *Utopia* translated and edited by André Prévost, *L'Utopie de Thomas More* (Paris: Mame, 1978), has scholarly value for students of Thomas More worldwide for its notes and 300-page introduction and because the French translation gives important nuances in understanding the original text by More. This edition includes a facsimile reproduction of the Latin edition of November 1518 and the French translation on opposite pages.

Early Biographies of Thomas More

1558. Roper, William. *The Life of Sir Thomas Moore, Knighte.* Edited by Elsie Vaughan Hitchcock. London: Oxford University Press, London, 1935. Published for the Early English Text Society.

1558. Harpsfield, Nicholas. *The Life and Death of Sr Thomas Moore, Knight.* Edited by Elsie Vaughan Hitchcock. London: Oxford University Press, 1963. Originally published for the Early English Text Society in 1932.

1588. Stapleton, Thomas. *Vita Thomae Mori.* Published in Latin at Douai in 1588, as part of *Tres Thomae, seu de S. Thomae Apostoli rebus gestis, de S. Thoma Archiepiscopo Cantuariensi et Martyre, D. Thomae Mori Angliae quondam Cancellarii Vita, Vita Thomae Mori*; also in the edition of *Francofurti ad Moenum*, 1689. Reprinted in facsimile in 1964.

1588. Stapleton, Thomas. *Histoire de Thomas More.* Translated from the Latin into French by M. Alexandre Martin. Paris, 1849.

1588. Stapleton, Thomas. *The Life and Illustrious Martyrdom of Sir Thomas More.* Translated by Philip E. Hallet. Edited by E. E. Reynolds. London: Burns and Oates, 1966.

1599. Ro: Ba:. *The Life of Sir Thomas More.* Edited by Elsie Vaughan Hitchcock, P. E. Hallett, and A. W. Reed. London: Early English Text Society, 1950.

1627. More, Cresacre. *The Life of Sir Thomas More.* Edited by the Rev. Joseph Hunter. London, 1828.

A Chronology of Biographical Studies on Thomas More

These studies are given in chronological order to help following the progressive understanding of More's life.

1891. Bridgett, T. E. *The Life and Writings of Blessed Thomas More*. London: Burns and Oates.

1892. Bridgett, T. E. *The Wisdom and Wit of Blessed Thomas More*. London: Burns and Oates.

1895. Hutton, W. H. *Sir Thomas More*. London: Methuen.

1904. Brémond, Henri. *The Blessed Thomas More*. London: R. and T. Washbourne, second edition of 1920.

1927. Reed, A. W. "Introduction." In *The Dialogue Concerning Tyndale by Sir Thomas More*, edited by W. E. Campbell, [1]–[10]. London: Eyre and Spottiswoode. Also included in the 1931 edition.

1932. Chambers, R. W. "On the Continuity of English Prose from Alfred to More." Introduction to the *Life and Death of Sir Thomas Moore, Knight, Sometimes Lord High Chancellor of England*, by Nicholas Harpsfield. London: Oxford University Press for the Early English Text Society.

1933. Sargent, Daniel. *Thomas More*. New York: Sheed and Ward, 1933; London: Sheed and Ward, 1938.

1934. Routh, E. M. *Sir Thomas More and His Friends*. 1st ed. Oxford: Blackwell, 1934; 2nd ed. New York: Blackwell, 1963.

1935. Chambers, R. W. *Thomas More*. London: Jonathan Cape, 1976.[57]

---

57. Though Chambers's work was considered the classic modern biography (in 1961, the editor of the *Selected Letters* considered it "the best modern treatment," and McConica, *Thomas More*, places it first in his *Select Bibliography*, calling it, "the classic account"), it seems that its section "The Younger Lawyer: Church or Law?" (Act I, §7) has an unfortunate title: Thomas More always felt that he was very much a member of the Church. For him the Church was never just the concern of priests and those in the religious state. See, for instance, the *Dialogue* (1529), in which, speaking of a particular devotion, he writes, "I surely believe this devotion to be in such a way planted by God's own hand in the hearts of the whole Church—that is to say, not the clergy alone, but the whole congregation of all Christian people—that if the clergy were of the mind to drop it, the laity would yet not allow that."

Chambers also suggests in the same section that "Erasmus [in his letter of 1519] speaks of [More's] early love-affairs, in language which could certainly be understood by his readers to mean that More's youth had not been altogether blameless." The evidence from the letter of 1519 does not suggest so but rather just the opposite. The passage reads, "In his younger days he was not averse from affairs with young women, but always without dishonour, enjoying such things when they came his way without going out to seek them, and attracted by the mingling of minds rather than bodies."

In 1518–19 More wrote a Latin Poem entitled, "He Expresses His Joy at Finding Safe and Sound Her Whom He Had Once Loved as a Mere Boy." Erasmus might have known the poem before or after publication. Perhaps this is the basis for his comment in the letter of 1519, but there is nothing untoward in it; it reads, "You are still alive, Elizabeth, dearer to me in my early years than I was myself.... When I was just a boy, I saw you first.... Sixteen years I had lived—you were about two years younger—when your face inspired me with innocent devotion.... There comes now to my mind that distant day which first revealed you to me as you enjoyed yourself amid a band of dancing maidens.... Once upon a time you innocently stole my heart; now too, and innocently still, you are dear to me. Our love was blameless; if duty could not keep it so, that day itself would be enough to keep love blameless still. Well, I beg the saints above, who, after twenty-five years, have kindly brought us together in good

1953. Reynolds, E. E. *Saint Thomas More*. London: Burns and Oates.

1960. Reynolds, E. E. *Margaret Roper*. London: Burns and Oates.

1962. Vázquez de Prada, Andrés. *Sir Tomás Moro*. Madrid: Rialp.

1963. Marc'hadour, Germain. *L'Univers de Thomas More*. Paris: Librairie Philosophique J. Vrin.

1965. Reynolds, E. E. *Thomas More and Erasmus*. London: Burns and Oates.

1968. Reynolds, E. E. *The Field Is Won: The Life and Death of Saint Thomas More* (1953). New ed. London: Burns and Oates.

1969. Prévost, André. *Thomas More et la Crise de la Pensée Européenne*. Tours: Maison Mame. Spanish translation published by Madrid: Rialp, 1972.

1969–71. Marc'hadour, Germain. *The Bible in the Works of St Thomas More*. 5 vols. Nieuwkoop: De Graaf.

1972. Byron, Brian. *Loyalty in the Spirituality of St Thomas More*. Nieuwkoop: B. De Graaf.

1974. Morales, José. "La formación espiritual e intelectual de Tomás Moro y sus contactos con la doctrina y obras de Santo Tomás de Aquino." *Scripta Theologica* 6, no. 2 (July–December): 439–89.

1974. Willow, Mary Edith. *An Analysis of the English Poems of St. Thomas More*. Nieuwkoop, The Netherlands: B. De Graaf.

1975. Morales, José. "Un Libro Reciente sobre Tomás Moro: Brian Byron, *Loyalty in the Spirituality of St Thomas More*, 1972", Scripta Theologica, Universidad de Navarra, Pamplona, VII-1, January–June 1975, 259–82.

1977. McConica, James. *Thomas More*. London: Her Majesty's Stationery Office, for National Portrait Gallery; 64 pages: A very useful brief synthesis.

1977. Monti, James. *The King's Good Servant*. San Francisco: Ignatius Press.

1977. Trapp, J. B., and H. S. Herbrüggen. *The King's Good Servant: Sir Thomas More*. London: National Portrait Gallery.

1978. Berglar, Peter. *Die Stunde des Thomas Morus*. Olten: Walter-Verlag AG. Spanish edition: *La Hora de Tomás Moro: Solo ante el Poder*. Madrid: Ediciones Palabra, 1993. English edition, slightly abridged: *Thomas More: A Lonely Voice against the Power of the State*. New York: Scepter, 2010.

1979. Marc'hadour, Germain. "The Death Year of Thomas More's Mother." *Moreana* 2, no. 63 (December): 13–16.

1980. Guy, John A. *The Public Career of Sir Thomas More*. New Haven: Yale University Press.

1981. McConica, James. "The Patrimony of Thomas More." In *History and Imagination: Essays in Honour of H. R. Trevor-Roper*, edited by Hugh Lloyd-Jones. London: Duckworth.

---

health, that I may be preserved to see you safe and sound again at the end of twenty-five years more"; *CW* 3, part II: *Latin Poems*, no. 263.

Robert M. Keane objects to the last part of Chambers's phrase "More's youth had not been altogether blameless," and he disagrees with Chambers on this issue. Interestingly, at Lincoln's Inn there are records of the students' behavior at the time, and he points out that Thomas More was not named in any disciplinary action at the Inn; Robert M. Keane, "Thomas More as a Young Lawyer," *Moreana*, no. 160 (December 2004): 41–71.

While dealing with Chambers, it is also necessary to take issue on his suggested date of the birth of Thomas More.

1982. Gogan, Brian. *The Common Corps of Christendom: Ecclesiological Themes in the Writings of Sir Thomas More*. Leiden: Brill.

1990. Martz, L. L. *Thomas More: The Search for the Inner Man*. New Haven: Yale University Press.

1991. Baker-Smith, Dominic. *More's Utopia*. New York: HarperCollins Academic. Repr. Toronto: University of Toronto Press, 2000.

1996. Wegemer, Gerard B. *Thomas More: A Portrait of Courage*. Princeton, N.J.: Scepter Press.

1997. Monti, James. *The Life and Writings of St. Thomas More*. San Francisco: Ignatius Press.

1998. Ackroyd, Peter. *The Life of Thomas More*. London: Chatto and Windus.

2000. Guy, John A. *Reputations: Thomas More*. London: Arnold.

2000. Headley, John M. "John Guy's Thomas More: On the Dimensions of Political Biography." *Moreana*, 143–44: 81–96.

2004. Keane, Robert M. "Thomas More as a Young Lawyer." *Moreana*, no. 160 (December).

2004. Wegemer, Gerard B., and Smith, Stephen W., eds. *A Thomas More Source Book*. Washington, D.C.: The Catholic University of America Press.

2007. Mitjans, Frank. "Non sum Oedipus sed Morus: A Paper on the Portrait of Sir Thomas More and His Family." *Moreana*, nos. 168–70 (December 2006–June 2007).

2007. Mitjans, Frank. "Thomas More on Venerating Images, Devotion to Saints and Going on Pilgrimages." Conference of the Centre of Thomas More Studies, Dallas, www.thomasmorestudies.org/tmstudies/DCH_Mitjans.pdf.

2008. Guy, John A. *A Daughter's Love: Thomas and Margaret More*. London: Fourth Estate.

2010. Marchi, Carlo De. L'affabilitas nei rapporti sociali: Studio comparativo sulla socievolezza e il buonumore. In Tommaso d'Aquino, *Thomas More e Francesco di Sales*. Rome: Edizioni Universita della Sante Croce (EDUSC).

2011. Logan, George M, ed. *The Cambridge Companion to Thomas More*. Cambridge and New York: Cambridge University Press.

2011. Wegemer, Gerard B. *Young Thomas More and the Arts of Liberty*. New York: Cambridge University Press.

2012. Cottret, Bernard. *Thomas More*. Paris: Tallandier.

2012. Curtright, Travis. *The One Thomas More*. Washington, D.C.: The Catholic University of America Press.

2012. Mitjans, Frank. "Reviewing and Correcting the Article on the Date of Birth of Thomas More." *Moreana* 49, nos. 189–90 (December).

2013. Mulliez, Jacques. *Thomas More: Au risqué de la conscience*. Bruyères-le-Châtel, France: Nouvelle Cité.

2014. Betteridge, Thomas. *Writing Faith and Telling Tales: Literature, Politics, and Religion in the Work of Thomas More*. Notre Dame, Ind.: University of Notre Dame Press.

2016. Phélippeau, Marie-Claire. *Thomas More*. Éditions Paris: Gallimard.

2017. Guy, John. *Thomas More: A Very Brief History*. London: Society for Promoting Christian Knowledge.

2017. Paul, Joanne. *Thomas More*. Classic Thinkers. Cambridge: Polity Press.

2019. Mitjans, Frank. "Elizabethan Transformation of the Family Portrait." *Moreana*, no. 212 (December): 141–45.

2020. Dealy, Ross. *Before Utopia: The Making of Thomas More's Mind*. Toronto: University of Toronto Press.

2021. Mitjans, Frank. "*De tristitia tedio pavore et oratione christi ante captionem eius*: The Last Work by St Thomas More," *Annales Theologigi* 35: 11–59.

A Chronology of Studies on the London Charterhouse

There is continuity in the works of William John Duff Roper, Lawrence Hendriks, Margaret Thompson, Dom David Knowles, and Bruno Barber: all base their reference to Thomas More on the account of William Roper. They speak of the prestige and influence of the Charterhouse within the city and of the General Chapter of 1490, which allowed laymen to live in the precinct. They point out that the ten days' time-limit for staying at the guesthouse did not apply.

Unfortunately Gerald Stanley Davies mistakenly writes that "Thomas More …, went, says Erasmus, to live near the Charterhouse for four years" (75–76). It was not Erasmus but Cresacre More who wrote "near." Therefore, when Davies continues saying, "Some writers have recorded this in a different shape, saying that More spent four years as an actual inmate of the monastery" and asserting, "This is highly improbable," he is easily dismissed by Dom David Knowles. In chapter 7 of this book the matter is discussed.

1550. Chauncy, Dom Maurice. *Historia Aliquot Martyrum Anglorum maxime octodecim Cartusianorum*. First Latin edition Mainz, 1550. Latin editions kept at the British Library: Mediolani, 1606 (BL 488.a.7), 1608, and London: Burns et Oates, 1888. English translation: *The History of the Sufferings of the Eighteen Carthusian Martyrs*. London: Burns and Oates, 1890.

1847. Duff Roper, William John. *Chronicles of Charter-House by a Carthusian*. London: G. Bell.

1849. Sutton, Thomas. *Charter-House, Its Foundation and History: With a Brief Memoir of the Founder*. London: M. Sewell.

1889. Hendriks, Dom Lawrence. *The London Charterhouse: Its Monks and Its Martyrs, with a Short Account of the English Carthusians after the Dissolution*. London, 1889.

1921. Davies, Gerald S. *Charterhouse in London: Monastery, Mansion, Hospital, School*. London: J. Murray, 1921.

1930. Thompson, E. Margaret. *The Carthusian Order in England*. London: Church Historical Society.

1954. Knowles, David. *Charterhouse*. London: Longmans.

1961. Knowles, David. *The Religious Orders in England*. Vol. 3, *The Tudor Age*. Cambridge: Cambridge University Press.

1976. Knowles, David. *Bare Ruined Choirs*. Cambridge: Cambridge University Press,

1976. This is an abridged edition, by the author himself, of *The Religious Orders in England*, vol. 3, *The Tudor Age*. Cambridge: Cambridge University Press, 1961.

1969. Cockburn, J. S., H. P. F. King, and K. G. T. McDonnell, eds. "Religious Houses: House of Carthusian Monks." In *A History of the County of* Middlesex, 1:159–69. London: Institute of Historical Research.

2002. Barber, Bruno, and Christopher Thomas. *The London Charterhouse*. London: Museum of London Archaeology Service.

2010. Temple, Philip. *Survey of London: The Charterhouse*. New Haven and London: Yale University Press, for English Heritage.[58]

General Bibliography

Ackroyd, Peter. *Albion: The Origins of the English Imagination*. London: Chatto and Windus, 2002.

Ambrose, St. *De virginibus and De Virginitate*. Patrologiae Latinae 16. Paris: J. P. Migne, 1844–90.

Adams, Robert P. *The Better Part of Valor: More, Erasmus, Colet and Vives on Humanism, War, and Peace, 1496–1535*. Seattle: University of Washington Press, 1962.

Aristotle. *Politics*. In *The Complete Works of Aristotle*, edited by Jonathan Barnes. Princeton: Princeton University Press, 1995.

58. In this 317-page monograph only chapter I (pages 17–38) deals with the pre-Dissolution London Charterhouse; the rest includes the evolution of the site from being in possession of and occupied by Lord North (1545–64), Thomas Howard, fourth Duke of Norfolk (1565–72), and Philip Howard (1572), to being sold to Thomas Sutton (1611). From then on it was used as the Sutton's Hospital, the Charterhouse School, the Merchant Taylors' School, and the Medical College of St Bartholomew's Hospital. Thomas More is not mentioned in the text. The book, however, includes, as Appendix I, a transcript of the North House Inventory, 1565, made for probate purposes on the death of Edward, first Baron North, on December 31, 1564. The original is kept at the Bodleian Library, North MS b. 12, ff. 15–47, and 97–101r. The only books included in the inventory are "certain books of Sir Thomas More's works between him and Frith and Tyndale, and an English translation of the edition of the New Testament by Erasmus" (204–5), "a bible in Latin & a book of St Jerome's epistles, an English bible and two communion books" (223), and "certain psalter books & prayer books, and three English books of parts of the bible" (225). Two of the beneficiaries of the Will of Edward Lord North mentioned in the inventory are particularly interesting: (1) Sir Giles Alington, 1500–1586 (two entries on p. 226, two entries on p. 227, one on p. 244—one of the horses—and on p. 248). He was the husband of Alice, step-daughter of Thomas More; and (2) Mary Scrope, c. 1534–1607 (three entries on p. 207, one on p. 245, two on p. 246, one on p. 247, and one on p. 249). She was the granddaughter of Lord North and the mother of Cresacre More (1572–1649), and thus, Cresacre More had direct knowledge of the Charterhouse and was able to write that Thomas More lived near it.

Among other items, the inventory includes, on p. 231, a picture of King Edward VI, a picture of Queen Mary, one of Christ, one of the Blessed Virgin Mary, and one of Mary Magdalene.

A William John Duff Roper is mentioned in the Introduction (p. 6, note 8). This William John Duff Roper appears as the author of *Chronicles of Charterhouse, by a Carthusian*, 1847 (also attributed to W. J. D. Ryder).

Though the book does not mention Thomas More in the body of the text, the impression gathered from it and from the inventory is that Thomas More's family (Giles Alington and Mary Scrope) knew the Charterhouse during the reign of Mary (1554–58), rather than supporting the thesis that he stayed there.

Armstrong, C. D. C. Article on "Stephen Gardiner." *ODNB*. Published online, September 23, 2004.

Arnold, Jonathan. *Dean John Colet of St Paul's: Humanism and Reform in Early Tudor England*. London and New York: I. B. Tauris, 2007.

———. *The Great Humanists: European Thought on the Eve of the Reformation*. London and New York: Tauris, 2011.

Augustine, St. *The Confessions*. Fathers of the Church 21. Washington, D.C.: The Catholic University of America Press, 1953.

———. *Commentary on the Sermon on the Mountain*. Fathers of the Church 11. Washington, D.C.: The Catholic University of America Press, 1963.

———. *Christian Instruction or On Christian Doctrine (De doctrina Christiana)*. Fathers of the Church 4. Washington, D.C.: The Catholic University of America Press, 1966.

———. *The City of God*. Translated by Philip Levine. Cambridge, Mass.: Loeb Classical Library, Harvard University Press, 1966.

———. *The City of God*. Translated by William Babcock. New York: New City Press, 2012.

———. *De bono conjugali*. Edited by P. G. Walsh. Oxford: Clarendon Press, 2011.

———. *The Good of Marriage*. Fathers of the Church 15. Washington, D.C.: The Catholic University of America Press, 1955.

———. *Homilies on the Gospel of John*. Edited by Philip Schaff. Grand Rapids, Mich.: Wm. B. Eerdmans, 1983.

———. *Opera Omnia*. In J. P. Migne, ed., *Patrologiae Cursus Completus, Patrologiae Latinae* (Paris, 1844–90), vols. 32–47; in particular: vol. 32, *Confessiones, Retractationes*; vol. 34, *De doctrina Christiana, De sermone Domini in Monte*; vol. 35, *In Ioannis Evangelium tractatus*; vol. 40, *De bono conjugali*; vol. 41, *De civitate Dei* (see also Juan Luis Vives, ed.).

———. *The Retractations*. Fathers of the Church 60. Washington, D.C.: The Catholic University of America Press, 1968.

———. *Selected Lessons on the New Testament*. Edited by Philip Schaff. Grand Rapids, Mich.: Wm. B. Eerdmans, repr. 1979.

Backus, Irena, ed. *The Reception of the Church Fathers in the West*. 2 vols. Leiden, New York, and Cologne: E. J. Brill, 1997.

Baker, David. "First Among Equals: The Utopian Princeps." *Moreana*, nos. 115–16 (December 1993): 33–45.

Baker, Sir John. "The Men of Court, 1440 to1550: A Prosopography of the Inns of Court and Chancery and the Courts of Law." *Supplementary Series*. Vol. 18 (II), *J to Y*. London: Selden Society, 2012. It includes entries for John More, Thomas More, and William Roper.

Baker-Smith, Dominic. *More's Utopia*. Toronto: University of Toronto Press, 2000. Originally published by HarperCollins, 1991.

———. "Who Went to Thomas More's Lectures on St Augustine's *De civitate Dei*?" *Church History and Religious Culture* 87, no. 2 (2007): 145–60.

———. "Erasmus and More: A Friendship Revisited." *Recusant History*, no. 30 (2010): 7–25.

Bargen, Darrel W. "The English Manuscripts of Walter Hilton's *Scala perfectionis*: An Assessment of Reception." Ph.D. thesis, University of Alberta, 2017.Barker, Nicolas. *Aldus Manutius and the Development of Greek Script and Type in the Fifteenth Century*. Sandy Hook, Conn.: Chiswick Book Shop, 1985.

Bartsch, Adam. *Le Peintre-Graveur*. Republished as *The Illustrated Bartsch*. Vol. 25, *Early Italian Masters*. Edited by Mark Zucker. New York: Abaris, 1980.

Bateson, Mary, ed. *Catalogue of the Library of Syon Monastery*. Cambridge: Cambridge University Press, 1898. See also under Gillespie, Vincent, and A. I. Doyle, eds.

Baumann, Uwe. "Thomas More and the Classical Tyrant." *Moreana*, no. 86 (July 1985): 108–27.

Benedict XVI. "Catechesis on the Fathers and Doctors of the Church delivered at the General Audiences" (2007–2010); in particular on St John Chrysostom (September 19 and 26, 2007), St Augustine (January 9, 16, and 30, 2008, and February 20, 2008), Boethius (March 12, 2008), Pseudo-Dionysius the Areopagite (May 14, 2008), Peter Lombard (December 30, 2009), and St Bonaventure (March 3, 10, and 17, 2010). Some of these are included in *Christ and His Church*. London: Catholic Truth Society, 2007.

———. *Spe Salvi*. Vatican City: Libreria Editrice Vaticana, 2007.

Berardino, Angelo di, ed. *Nuovo dizionario patristico e di Antichità cristiane*. Genoa: Marietti for Institutum Patristicum Augustinianum, 2006–8.

Bernard, St. "First and Second Sermon for the First Sunday after the Octave of the Epiphany." In *Sermons*. Dublin: Browne and Nolan, 1923.

Boethius. *De Consolatione Philosophiae*. London: Burns and Oates, 1925. This Latin edition includes reference to Thomas More in p. 200 within Appendix IV (De iis qui opus hoc imitati sunt). There are many English translations: for instance, *The Consolation of Philosophy*, translated with an introduction by Victor Watts, rev. ed., London: Penguin Classics, 1999; and *The Consolation of Philosophy*, translated by David R. Slavitt, Cambridge, Mass.: Harvard University Press, 2008, which reads especially well. For an introduction to Boethius, see Henry Chadwick, *Boethius: The Consolations of Music, Logic, Theology, and Philosophy*, Oxford: Clarendon Press, 1981. For the translation by Queen Elizabeth, see Elizabeth I, *Translations, 1592–1598*, edited by Janel Mueller and Joshua Scodel, Chicago: University of Chicago Press, 2009, and *The Consolation of Queen Elizabeth I: The Queen's Translation of Boethius' De Consolatione Philosophiae*, Introduction by Quan Manh, Phoenix: Arizona Center for Medieval and Renaissance Studies, Arizona State University, 2009.

Bonaventure, St. (attributed to him by Thomas More). *The Meditations on the Life of Christ*. Translated and edited by Isa Ragusa. New Jersey: Princeton University Press, 1961; *Meditaciones vitae Christi, olim S. Bonaventuro attributae*. Edited by M. Stallings-Taney, *Corpus Christianorum, Continuatio Mediaevalis* 153. Cambridge, Mass.: Medieval Academy of America, 1997; and *Meditations on the Life of Christ*. Translated and edited by F. X. Taney, Anne Miller, and Mary Stallings-Taney. Asheville, N.C.: Pegasus Press, 2000. For the English abridged and rearranged version, see *The Mirror of the Blessed Life of Jesus Christ*, by Nicholas Love, also known as *St. Bonaventure's Speculum vite Christi*. See also Love, Nicholas.

Brill's Encyclopaedia of the Neo-Latin World: Micropaedia. Edited by Philp Ford, Jan Bloemendal, and Charles Fantazzi. Leiden and Boston: Brill, 2014.

Brockliss, L. W. B., ed. *Magdalen College Oxford: A History.* Oxford: Clarendon Press, 2008.

Bronwen Neil, and Mattew Dal Santo, eds. *A Companion to Gregory the Great.* Leiden and Boston: Brill, 2013.

Burrows, Montagu, ed. *Collectanea.* Oxford: Oxford Historical Society, 1890. It contains *Linacre's Catalogue* (1520) of the books of William Grocyn and the *Will of Grocyn.*

Calero, Francisco, ed. *Tomás Moro.* De Tristitia Christi. Valencia: Ayuntamiento de Valencia, 1984.

Campbell, W. E. *Erasmus, Tyndale and More.* London: Eyre and Spottiswoode, 1949.

Catherine of Siena, St. *The Dialogue of Saint Catherine of Siena.* Translated by Algar Thorold. London: Burns, Oates, and Washbourne, 1925. Reprinted by London: Baronius, 2008.

Catto, Jeremy. "The Triumph of the Hall in Fifteenth-Century Oxford." In *Lordship and Learning: Studies in Memory of Trevor Aston,* edited by Ralph Evans, 209–24. Woodbridge: Boydell Press, 2004.

———. "Oriel in Renaissance Oxford, 1479–1574." In *Oriel College: A History,* edited by Jeremy Catto, 60–93. Oxford University Press, 2013.

Cheney, C. R., ed. *Handbook of Dates for Students of English History.* London: Royal Historical Society, 1945.

Chrysostom, St. John. *Homeliae in Evangelium S. Matthaei,* Latine per Georgium Trapezuntium. British Library Egerton MS 875, c. 1448.

———. Greek MS 23, Corpus Christi College. Homilies on St Matthew, 1–45, transcribed by John Serbopoulos for William Grocyn, completed September 25, 1499; and Greek MS 24, Homilies on St Matthew, 45–90, transcribed by John Serbopoulos, completed May 8, 1500. N. G. Wilson writes that MSS 23 and 24 raise a puzzling question because the last Homily in MS 23 is repeated in MS 24, and only MS 23 has the usual indication of provenance from Claymond. See Wilson, *Catalogue of the Greek Manuscripts of Corpus Christi College.*

———. *Opera omnia.* In *Patrologiae Cursus Completus,* Series Graeca 47–64. Paris: J. P. Migne, 1857–66. In particular, Homilies on Genesis; Homilies on the Gospel of St John; Homilies on the Gospel of St Matthew; De Oratione; and On the Priesthood.

Cicero. *De Officiis / On Duties.* Translated by Harry G. Edinger. Indianapolis: Bobbs-Merrill, 1974.

———. *De Officiis / On Duties.* Translated by John Higginbotham. London: Faber and Faber, 1967.

———. *De Officiis / On Duties.* Translated by M. T. Griffin and E. M. Atkins. Cambridge: Cambridge University Press, 1991.

———. *De Officiis / On Duties.* Translated by P. G. Walsh. Oxford: Oxford University Press, 2000.

———. *De Officiis / On Duties.* Translated by Walter Miller. Cambridge, Mass.: Loeb Classical Library, Harvard University Press, 2005 Originally published in 1913.

———. *De Officiis/On Duties*. Translated by Benjamin Patrick Newton. Ithaca: Cornell University Press, 2016.

Clement of Alexandria. Stromata. PG 8.

Clement of Rome. St. First Letter to the Corinthians. Greek text in *Documenta Catholica Omnia*, www.documentacatholicaomnia.eu. English translation in *The Apostolic Fathers*. Washington, D.C.: The Catholic University of America Press, 1969.

Coates, Alan. *English Medieval Books*: *The Reading Abbey Collection from Foundation to Dispersal*. Oxford: Clarendon Press, 1999.

Comestor, Petrus. *Historia scholastica*. Basel: <Johannes Amerbach>, 1486, after the feast of St Catherine, November 25.

Coogan, Robert. "Petrarch and Thomas More." *Moreana*, no. 21 (February 1969): 19–30.

Coxe, H. O. *Catalogus Codicum MSS. qui in Collegiis Aulisque Oxoniensibus Hodie Adservantur*. Vol. 2 (Pars II), under the section for Corpus Christi College. Oxford, 1852), 5–6.

Cummings, Brian. "Conscience and the Law in Thomas More." *Journal of the Society for Renaissance Studies* 23, no. 4 (September 2009): 463–85.

Curtright, Travis. "Annotations to a Modernized Text of the Pageant of Life." *Web Library of the Thomas More Studies Center*. www.thomasmorestudies.org.

———. Book review, "The Cambridge Companion to Thomas More." *Moreana*, nos. 185–86 (2011): 221–25.

Dawson, Christopher. "The City of God." In *A Monument to Saint Augustine*. London: Sheed and Ward, 1930.

———. *Progress and Religion*: *An Historical Inquiry*. London: Sheed and Ward, 1929; new edition Washington, D.C.: The Catholic University of America Press, 2001.

Dean Perrin, Jac Jr. "Family 13 in Saint John's Gospel." Ph.D. thesis, University of Birmingham, 2012, 70–74.

Dodd, Jon Theodore, trans. *Ordinary and Canon of the Mass according to the use of the Church of Sarum* (1872),

Duffy, Eamon. *Marking the Hours*: *English People and Their Prayers, 1240–1570*. New Haven and London: Yale University Press, 2006.

———. *Fires of Faith*: *Catholic England under Mary Tudor*. New Haven and London: Yale University Press, 2009.

———. *Reformation Divided*. London: Bloomsbury, 2017.

Duffy, Robert A. "Thomas More's Nine Pageants." *Moreana*, no. 50 (June 1976): 15–30.

Dugdale, William. *The History of St Pauls Cathedral, … with Figures of Tombs, and Monuments*. London: T. Warren, 1658.

Emden, A. B. *A Biographical Register of the University of Oxford to A. D. 1500*. Oxford: Clarendon Press, 1958.

Erasmus. *Collected Works of Erasmus*. Toronto: University of Toronto Press. This is a project still in progress. The correspondence of Erasmus from the year 1484 to 1534 has appeared in volumes 1–20, published from 1974 to 2020. Apart from the correspondence, the *Antibarbarians* and the *Enchiridion* are of special importance for this study. The text and the indexes of the *Antibarbarians* are included respectively in *CWE* 23 and 24; the *Enchiridion* in *CWE* 66; and the letter to Colet that preceded the *Enchiridion* (1503) in *CWE* 70.

———. *De praeparatione ad mortem*. 1534. BL 4411.e.16 and 697.b.11.

———. Ioannis Chrysostomi opera. Edited and in part translated by Erasmus. Basel: Froben, 1530.

———. Ioannis Chrysostomi opera. In part translated by Erasmus. Basel: Froben and Herwagen, 1547.

———. *Lucubrationes*. 1516.

———. *Opera Omnia Desiderii Erasmi Roterodami*. Amsterdam, 1969–.

———. *Opus Epistolarum Des. Erasmi Roterodami*. Edited by P. S. Allen, H. M. Allen, and H. W. Garrod. 12 vols. Oxford: Oxford University Press, 1906–58.

Fenlon, Dermot B. "England and Europe: Utopia and Its Aftermath." *Transactions of the Royal Historical Society*, 5th series, 25 (1975).

Ficino, Marsilio. *Commentary on the Symposium*: *De* Amore., Dallas, Tex.: Spring, 1985.

Fisher, Payne. *Tombs, Monuments, &c., Visible in S. Paul's Cathedral Previous to Its Destruction by Fire, A.D. 1666* (1668). Revised and edited by George Blacker Morgan, 1885.

Foister, Susan. *Holbein and England*. New Haven and London: Yale University Press, 2004.

———. *Holbein in England*. Catalogue of the exhibition at Tate Britain. London: Tate, 2007.

Gairdner, James. "Note and Transcription of 'A Letter concerning Bishop Fisher and Sir Thomas More,' from Dane John Bouge to Dame Katheryn Manne." In Notes and Documents, *English Historical Review* VII (October 1892): 712–15.

Gerson, Jean. *Monotessaron*. Cologne: Ludwing van Renchen, not after 1478.

———. *Early Works*. Edited by Brian Patrick McGuire. New York: Paulist Press, 1998.

———. *Josephina*. Edited by G. Matteo Roccati, *Laboratoire de médiévistique occidentale de* Paris (LAMOP). Paris: University of Paris, 2001.

Gillespie, Vincent. "Vernacular Books of Religion." In *Book Production and Publishing in Britain, 1375–1475*, edited by Jeremy Griffiths and Derek Pearsall, 317–44. Cambridge: Cambridge University Press, 1989.

Gillespie, Vincent, and A. I. Doyle, eds. *Corpus of British Medieval Library Catalogues*. Vol. 9, *Syon Abbey and The Libraries of the Carthusians*. London: British Library, 2001.

Gilson, Étienne. *The Philosophy of St. Bonaventure*. London: Sheed and Ward, 1940.

———. Foreword to *The City of God*. Fathers of the Church 8. Washington, D.C.: The Catholic University of America Press, 1950.

Gleason, John B. "The Birth Date of John Colet and Erasmus of Rotterdam: Fresh Documentary Evidence." *Renaissance Quarterly* 32, no. 1 (Spring 1979): 73–76.

———. *John Colet*. Berkeley and Los Angeles: University of California Press, 1989.

Glendon, Mary Ann. *The Forum and the Tower*. New York: Oxford University Press, 2011.

Goldhill, Simon. *Who Needs Greek?* Cambridge: Cambridge University Press, 2002.

González Gullón, José Luís. *La Fecundidad de la Cruz: Una reflexión sobre la exaltación y la atracción de Cristo en los textos joánicos y la literatura cristiana antigua*. Pontificia Universitá della Santa Croce. Rome, 2003.

Gregory the Great. St. *Liber Regulae Pastoralis or Pastoral Rule or Pastoral Care*. Fathers of the Church 11. Washington, D.C: The Catholic University of America Press, 1950.

Hadzsits, G. D. *Lucretius and His Influence.* New York: Cooper Square, 1963.

Haines, Roy Martin. Article on "John Carpenter (c. 1395–1476)." *ODNB.* Published online January 5, 2012.

Harries, G. L. Article on "Humfrey, Duke of Gloucester (1390–1447)." *ODNB.* Published online September 23, 2004.

Harris, Jonathan. *Greek Emigres in the West 1400–1520.* Camberley: Porphyrogenitus, 1995.

Hastings, Margaret. "The Ancestry of Sir Thomas More." *Guildhall Miscellany* 2, no. 2 (July 1961): 47–62.

Haupt, Garry E., ed. *The Tower Works.* New Haven: Yale University Press, 1980.

Haugaard, William P. "Renaissance Patristic Scholarship and Theology in Sixteenth-Century England." *Sixteenth Century Journal* 10, no. 3 (Autumn 1979): 37–60.

Herbrüggen, Hubertus Schulte, ed. "More to Cranevelt." In *Supplementa Humanistica Lovaniensia.* Leuven: Leuven University Press, 1997.

———. "Thomas More's Fortune Verses: A Contribution to the Solution of a Few Problems." Translated by Amos Johannes Hunt. *Moreana,* nos. 185–86 (2011): 121–48.

Herrera Gabler, Jorge Federico. *La Exaltación y Atracción de Cristo en la Cruz: Análisis de la Tradición Exegética y Teológica desde la Patrística hasta Nuestros Días.* Pamplona: Universidad de Navarra, 2010.

———. "Los dichos de 'ser exaltado' en los Padres de la Iglesia." *Scripta Theologica* 45, no. 1, (April 2013): 119–49.

Hervada, Javier. *Tres estudios sobre el uso del término laico.* Pamplona: Ediciones Universidad de Navarra Sociedad Anónima, 1973.

Hibbert, Christopher, and Ben Weinreb, eds. *The London Encyclopaedia.* London: Macmillan, 1987.

Hilton, Walter. *Minor Works (including Mixed Life),* ed. Dorothy Jones. London: Burns, Oates and Co., 1929.

———. *The Ladder of Perfection.* Translated and Introduction by Leo Sherley-Price. London: Penguin Books, 1957.

———. *Mixed Life.* Translated into modern English by Rosemary Dorward. Introduction by John Clark. Oxford: SLG Press, 2001.

Hutton, James. "A Speculation on Two Passages in the Latin Poems of Thomas More." In *Essays on Renaissance Poetry.* Ithaca and London: Cornell University Press, 1980.

Hyma, Albert. *The Youth of Erasmus.* Ann Arbor: University of Michigan Press, 1930. It includes the Latin text of *Antibarbarorum Liber.*

James, Montague Rhodes. "Greek Manuscripts in England before the Renaissance." *Library,* new series, no. 4 (March 1927): 337–53.

Jardine, Lisa. *Erasmus, Man of Letters.* Princeton: Princeton University Press, 1993.

Jedin, Hubert, and John Dolan, eds. *History of the Church.* London: Burns and Oates, 1980.

Jungmann, Joseph A. *The Mass of the Roman Rite: Its Origins and Development.* New York: Benziger Bros., 1955.

Kempis, Thomas à. *The Imitation of Christ, circa 1441.* Translated by Betty I. Knott. Glasgow: Collins, 1963.

Ker, N. R. "The Provision of Books." In *The History of the University of Oxford*, vol. 2, *The Collegiate University*, edited by James McConica. 441–519. Oxford: Clarendon Press, 1984–92.

Knight, Samuel. *The Life of Dr J. Colet, Dean of St Paul's and founder of S. Paul's School.* Oxford: Clarendon Press, 1823.

Leclercq, Jean, OSB. *The Love of Learning and the Desire for God: A Study of Monastic Culture.* New York: Fordham University Press, 1974.

Lewis, Charlton T., and Charles Short. *Latin Dictionary.* Oxford: Oxford University Press, 1962.

Liddell, J. R. "The Library of Corpus Christi College, Oxford, in the Sixteenth Century." *Library*, 4th series, no. 18 (1958): 385–416.

Loewenstein, David. *Treacherous Faith: The Specter of Heresy in Early Modern English Literature and Culture.* Oxford: Oxford University Press, 2013.

Love, Nicholas, trans. *The Mirror of the Blessed Life of Jesus Christ.* Westminster: Caxton, circa 1490. Available at the Lambeth Palace Library.

———. *The Mirror of the Blessed Life of Our Lord and Saviour Jesus Christ.* Written in Latin by the venerable and famous Doctor Saint Bonaventure. Newly set forth in English by Nicholas Love, 1591. Available at the Lambeth Palace Library.

———. *The Mirror of the Blessed Life of Jesus Christ.* Edited by the Monk of Parkminster. London: Burns, Oates, and Washburne, 1926. In modernized spelling.

———. *The Mirror of the Blessed Life of Jesus Christ.* A Revised Critical Edition by Michael G. Sargent based on Cambridge University Library Additional MSS. 6578 and 6686. Exeter: University of Exeter Press, 2004.

Lucian. *Works of Lucian,* 8 vols. Loeb Classical Library, Cambridge, Mass: Harvard University Press, 1913–1967, vols. I-V, translated by A. M. Harmon; vol. VI, by K. Kilburn; vols, VII–VIII, by M. D. Macleod.

———. *Satirical Sketches: Philosophies Going Cheap.* Translated by Paul Turner. New York: Penguin, 1961.

Lucretius. *De Rerum Natura.* Translated by W. H. D. Rouse; edited by Martin Ferguson Smith. Cambridge, Mass.: Loeb Classical Library, Harvard University Press, 1975.

Lupton, J. H. *The Utopia of Sir Thomas More in Latin from the Edition of March 1518 and in English from the First Edition of Ralph Robynson's Translation in 1551, with Additional Translations, Introduction and Notes.* Oxford: Clarendon Press, 1895.

MacIntyre, Alasdair. *God, Philosophy, Universities: A Selective History of the Catholic Philosophical Tradition.* Lanham, Md.: Rowman and Littlefield, 2009.

McConica, James. "The Recusant Reputation of Thomas More." *Canadian Catholic Historical Association.* Report 30 (1963): 47–61.

———. *Erasmus.* Oxford: Oxford University Press, 1991.

McCutcheon, Elizabeth. "'The Apple of My Eye': Thomas More to Antonio Bonvisi, a Reading and a Translation." *Moreana*, nos. 71–72 (November 1981): 37–56.

———. "Homo Viator." *Moreana*, no. 164 (December 2005): 25–28.

———. "Boethius's *De Consolatione Philosophie* and More's *Dialogue against Tribulation* and Other Writings." *Moreana*, nos. 193–94 (December 2013): 160.

McGuire, Brian Patrick. *Jean Gerson and the Last Medieval Reformation*. University Park: Pennsylvania State University Press, 2005.

Manent, Pierre. *Metamorphoses of the City*. Cambridge, Mass.: Harvard University Press, 2013.

Manutius, Aldus. *The Greek Classics*. Edited by N. G. Wilson. Cambridge, Mass.: Harvard University Press, 2016.

Marc'hadour, Germain. "Fathers and Doctors of the Church." Introduction to *A Dialogue Concerning Heresies*, CW 6.

———. *L'Univers de Thomas More*. Paris: Librairie Philosophique J. Vrin, 1963.

Marius, Richard. Introduction to the English Translation of *Utopia*. Translated by Ralph Robinson (1551). London: Everyman Library and J. M. Dent, 1994.

Martin, Christopher J. F. *An Introduction to Medieval Philosophy*. Edinburgh: Edinburgh University Press, 1996.

Newman, J. H. *Discourses to Mixed Congregations*. Discourse 16. London, 1892.

Nichols, Fred J. "More and Martial." *Moreana*, no. 86 (July 1985): 61–70.

Origen. *Homilies on Jeremiah*. PG 16.

Orme, N. "John Holt (d.1504): The Tudor Schoolmaster and Grammarian," *Library* (1996).

———. *Medieval Schools from Roman Britain to Renaissance England*. New Haven and London: Yale University Press, 2006.

Osler, William. *Thomas Linacre*. Cambridge: Cambridge University Press, 1908.

Pardue, Brad C. *Printing, Power, and Piety: Appeals to the Public during the Early Years of the English Reformation*. Leiden: Brill, 2012.

Plato. *De republica sive iusticia*. MS, 1401. At Seville: Colombina Biblioteca.

———. *Complete Works*. Edited by John M Cooper. Indianapolis: Hackett, 1997.

Public Record Office, National Archive of England. *Letters and Papers, Foreign and Domestic, of the Reign of Henry VIII, Addenda*. https://www.nationalarchives.gov.uk.

Ratzinger, Joseph. *The Spirit of the Liturgy*. San Francisco: Ignatius Press, 2000.

Rex, Richard. *The Theology of John Fisher*. Cambridge: Cambridge University Press, 1991.

———. *The Tudors*. Stroud, Gloucestershire: Tempus, 2005. The whole book provides a recent account for the period. But the chapter on Mary Tudor is particularly relevant because it helps to understand the circumstances in which William Roper wrote his *Life of Thomas More*; this is also the case of the aforementioned book by Eamon Duffy, *Fires of Faith: Catholic England under Mary Tudor*. New Haven and London: Yale University Press, 2009.

———. *Henry VIII and the English Reformation*. 2nd ed. Basingstoke: Palgrave Macmillan, 2006.

———. *Henry VIII*. Stroud, Gloucestershire: Amberley, 2009.

———. "Thomas More and the Heretics: Statesman or Fanatic?" In *The Cambridge Companion to Thomas More*, edited by George M. Logan. Cambridge and New York: Cambridge University Press, 2011.

Richards, Emily. "Writing and Silence: Transitions between the Contemplative and the Active Life." In *Pieties in Transition: Religious Practices and Experiences, c. 1400–1640*, edited by Robert Lutton and Elizabeth Salter. Aldershot: Ashgate, 2007.

Rowntree, C. B. Article on "John Batmanson." *ODNB*. Published online September 23, 2004.

Schoeck, R. J. "The Use of St. John Chrysostom in Sixteenth-Century Controversy: Christopher St. German and Sir Thomas More in 1533." *Harvard Theological Review* 54, no. 1 (January 1961): 21–27.

Schüssler, Rudolf. "Jean Gerson, Moral Certainty and the Renaissance of Ancient Scepticism." *Renaissance Studies* 23, no. 4 (September 2009): 445–62.

Sears, Jayne. *John Colet and Marsilio Ficino*. Westport, Conn.: Greenwood, 1980.

Seebohm, Frederic. *The Oxford Reformers: Colet, Erasmus and More* (1867). Edited by Hugh Seebohm. London: Dent and Sons, 1914. Repr. 1929.

Sheils, William. "Polemic as Piety: Thomas Stapleton's *Tres Thomae* and Catholic Controversy in the 1580s." *Journal of Ecclesiastic History* 60, no. 1 (January 2009): 74–94.

Smith, R. D. Article on "William Lily." ODNB. Published online and revised by Hedwig Gwosdek, September 23, 2004.

Stein, Edith. *Ways to Know God: The "Symbolic Theology" of Dionysius the Areopagite and Its Factual Presuppositions*. New York: Edith Stein Guild, 1981.

———. *The Collected Works*. Vol. 1, *Life in a Jewish Family, 1891–1916: An Autobiography*. Washington, D.C.: ICS, 1986.

Stow, John. *Survey of London* (1598). Edited by William J. Thoms. London: Chatto and Windus, 1876.

Summit, Jennifer. *Memory's Library: Medieval Books in Early Modern England*. Chicago and London: University of Chicago Press, 2008.

Swanson, R. N. *Universities, Academics and the Great Schism*. Cambridge: Cambridge University Press, 1979.

Thomas Aquinas, St. *Expositio Continua super Quatuor Evangelistas simul ac Catena Aurea*. Avignon, 1851.

———. *Summa Theologiae*. Edited by Thomas Gilby, OP (1902–75) and T. C. O'Brien, OP. Latin text and English translation, introduction, notes, appendices, and glossaries. 61 vols. London: Eyre and Spottiswoode, 1963–81.

———. *Super Ioannem*. Translated by Fabian R. Larcher. Albany, N.Y.: Magi Books, 1998.

Tilley, Arthur. "Greek Studies in England in the Early Sixteenth Century." *English Historical Review* 53, no. 210 (April 1938): 221–39.

Trapp, J. B. *Erasmus, Colet and More: The Early Tudor Humanists and Their Books*. London: British Library, 1991.

———. "Petrarch's "Triumph of Death in Tapestry." In *Thomas More … and More: Liber Amicorum for Hubertus Schulte Herbrüggen*. edited by Christoph M. Peters and Friedrich-K. Unterweg. Frankfurt on Main: Peter Lang, 2002.

———. *Studies of Petrarch and His Influence*. London: Pindar Press, 2003.

———. "John Colet (1467–1519)." *ODNB*. Published online March 2014.

Trevor-Roper, Hugh. "The Intellectual World of Sir Thomas More." *American Scholar* 48, no. 1 (1978): 19–32.

Vives, Juan Luis. *De civitate Dei*, by St Augustine, with commentaries of Juan Luis Vives. Basel: Johann Froben, 1522.

———. *De civitate Dei* (*The City of God by St Augustine with the Commentaries of Juan Luis Vives*). Translated and edited by Alban Butler. Dublin: J. Christie, 1822.

———. *De civitate Dei* (*Of the City of God, by St Augustine, with a selection of the comments of Ioannes Ludovicus Vives*). Translated and edited by John Healey. It includes a letter of Henry VIII to Vives. The commentaries of Vives are abridged and edited; therefore, this edition does not give an accurate translation of them. London: J. M. Dent and Sons; New York: E. P. Dutton, 1945.

———. *De officio mariti*. 1529; Basel, 1538. Introduction, critical ed., English translation and notes by Charles Fantazzi. Leiden: Brill, 2006.

———. *De Institutione foeminae Christianae*. Bruges, 1523; Antwerp, 1524; English translation as *The Education of a Christian Woman*, by Charles Fantazzi. Chicago: University of Chicago Press, 2000.

———. *Epistolario*. Edited by José Jiménez Delgado. Madrid: Editora Nacional, 1978.

Watts, John, ed. *Renaissance College: Corpus Christi College, Oxford in Context, 1450–1600. History of Universities* 32, no. 1–2 (2019).

Willoughby, James, "The Provision of Books in the English Secular College." In *The Late Medieval English College and Its Context*, edited by Clive Burgess and Martin Heale. Woodbridge: Boydell and Brewer, 2008.

Wilson, N. G. *A Descriptive Catalogue of the Greek Manuscripts of Corpus Christi College, Oxford*. Cambridge: D. S. Brewer, 2011. Wind, E. *Pagan Mysteries in the Renaissance*. Oxford: Oxford University Press, 1980.

Wood, Anthony à. Athenæ Oxonienses. *An exact history of all the writers and bishops who have had their education in the … University of Oxford, from … 1500, to the author's death in November 1695*. London: Printed for B. Knaplock, D. Midwinter and J. Tonson, 1721.

Young, Urban, C.P., ed. *Dominic Barbieri in England: A New Series of Letters*. London: Burns, Oates and Washbourne, 1935.

Zöllner, Frank. *Sandro Botticelli*. Munich and New York: Prestell, 2009.

Esther, Queen, 174
Euripides, 65, 203
Eurydice, 29, 73, 75, 170–71
Eusebius of Caesarea, 37, 87, 93, 94n, 145

Family Portrait, 3, 8n, 14, 72, 282
Fathers of the Church, 20, 26, 27, 49–55,
59–60, 79–80, 82, 87, 91–94, 110, 119, 127,
136, 145, 149, 159–60, 192–93, 207, 211–12,
215, 228, 236, 245, 284–85, 291
Feast of the Purification of the Blessed
Virgin Mary, 16, 132
Ferguson, Wallace K., 44n
Ficino, Marsilio, 65, 89, 103, 288, 292
Finnis, John, 27
Fish, Simon, 93n, 230
Fisher, John, 37, 45, 141, 162, 192, 221, 231,
244n, 246, 251, 272, 288, 291
Fisher, Payne, 34, 288
Fisher, Robert, 45, 55, 82

Foister, Susan, 4, 57–58, 288
Foxe, Edward, 273
Franciscans, 161, 166–67
Fredenburg, Aldene, ix
Froben, Johann, 49, 83n, 170, 186n, 187, 221,
256, 288, 292
Furnival's Inn, 21, 156–57

Gaguin, Robert, 48
Galen, 78, 202
Gardiner, Stephen, 249, 250n, 284
Garrod, H.W., xii, 78, 255, 256n, 275, 288
Gellius, Aulus, 54
Geoffrey of Monmouth, 66
Gerard, Cornelis, 48
Gerson, John, 72, 129, 132, 141–42, 144, 159,
224–25, 288, 291–92; *Monotessaron*, 26,
143, 238, 249
Giggs, Margaret (adopted daughter of
Thomas More and wife of John Clement).
See Margaret Clement.
Giles, Peter, 23–25, 56–58, 71, 169, 194,
196–97, 216, 227n, 237, 254, 283n
Graham, Timothy, ix
Graunger, Thomas (maternal grandfather of
Thomas More), 16
Green, Adam C, ix
Gregory Nazianzen, St., 52, 60, 87, 145
Gregory of Nyssa, St., 60, 110n
Gregory the Great, St., 28, 32n, 37, 51–52, 59,
87–88, 92, 93, 94n, 110n, 136n, 138–40,
145–46, 148, 207, 286, 288
Gregory XII, pope, 142–43
Grocyn, William, xi, 21, 33–46, 55, 60, 65,
72, 77–79, 81–82, 85–92, 100n, 102–4,
126, 129, 130, 143–51, 156, 159n, 161, 167,
169–70, 172, 177–78, 201–2, 226, 286
Guy, John, ix, 3, 4, 8, 9n, 15n, 21n, 78, 107,
108n, 160n, 164–65, 167n, 193n, 199n,
221–22, 244n, 270n, 277n, 280–81

Hairshirt, 173–75, 157n
Hallett, Philip E., xii, 10, 12, 150, 278
Harpsfield, Nicholas, xii, 7–10, 15n, 77, 78n,
149n, 155, 158, 163n, 167, 173–75, 177–79,
221n, 222–70, 278–79
Harris, John (secretary of Thomas More), 8,
9, 123, 146, 222, 232, 247, 275
Hastings, Margaret, 16n, 289
Hausgen, Johann, 93–94
Hegarty, Andrew, ix

Thomas More's Vocation was designed in Garamond and composed
by Kachergis Book Design of Pittsboro, North Carolina.
It was printed on 55-pound Natural Offset and bound by
Maple Press of York, Pennsylvania.